D0942959

DREAM WEST

Dream West. In Fort Apache, *a cavalry officer (John Wayne) recalls the way things once were. Director John Ford split the screen to present the man's romanticized memories in a manner that erases the distinction between past and present, collapsing the West of harsh realities with that of a nostalgic dream. Courtesy RKO Pictures.*

NUMBER FORTY-ONE

Jack and Doris Smothers Series in Texas History, Life, and Culture

DOUGLAS BRODE

DREAM WEST

POLITICS AND RELIGION
IN COWBOY MOVIES

UNIVERSITY OF TEXAS PRESS, AUSTIN

PUBLICATION OF THIS WORK WAS MADE
POSSIBLE IN PART BY SUPPORT FROM
THE J. E. SMOTHERS, SR., MEMORIAL
FOUNDATION AND THE NATIONAL
ENDOWMENT FOR THE HUMANITIES.

Requests for permission to reproduce material from this work should
be sent to:
    Permissions
    University of Texas Press
    P.O. Box 7819
    Austin, TX 78713-7819
    www.utexas.edu/utpress/utexas.edu/index.php/rp-form

∞ The paper used in this book meets the minimum requirements of
ANSI/NISO Z39.48-1992 (R1997) (Permanence of Paper).

Library of Congress Cataloging-in-Publication Data

Brode, Douglas, 1943–
   Dream West : politics and religion in cowboy movies / Douglas
Brode.
      pages   cm. — (Jack and Doris Smothers series in Texas
history, life, and culture ; number 41)
   Includes bibliographical references and index.
   ISBN 978-0-292-70902-7 (hardback) — ISBN 978-0-292-74828-6
(pbk.)
    1. Western films—History and criticism. 2. Politics in motion
pictures. 3. Religion in motion pictures. I. Title.
   PN1995.9.W4B76   2013
   791.43'6278—dc23   2012049808

doi:10.7560/709027

Frontiersmen acutely sensed that they battled wild country not only for personal survival but in the name of nation, and race, and God.

—RODERICK FRAZIER NASH,
WILDERNESS AND THE AMERICAN MIND, 1967

———

FOR MY SON,
SHEA THAXTER BRODE,

whose own youthful enthusiasm for uniquely American ideas rekindled my own long-dormant desire to discover the essence of who we are as a people

CONTENTS

ACKNOWLEDGMENTS

First, with great thanks to Dr. Joseph Agonito, professor and scholar of the West, whose remarkable knowledge of the era and area's history informed my own great love for the frontier's legendary and mythical aspects over the decades during which I had the pleasure to team-teach a course on the subject with this admirable colleague and great friend. Second, to my son Shea Thaxter Brode, whose passion for the project and diligent research—as well as excellent proofreading—brought *Dream West* to fruition.

A particular word of appreciation to all those film companies whose motion pictures are summarized here and specifically for the use of images from their work. As a member of the media focusing on motion pictures and television for the past fifty years, I was provided many of these were provided to use for the purposes of promoting the films at the time of their release and maintaining their profiles in succeeding years. Others are from my personal collection. Each "still" is employed here to augment with visual content the verbal descriptions in order to provide the best academic book possible on the subject matter, to be used for serious study of the Western genre.

DREAM WEST

The flag and the cross. John Ford's mythic vision in My Darling Clementine *posits Tombstone as a representative American community, its people framed by two symbols, one political, the other religious. Courtesy Twentieth Century-Fox.*

"CODE OF THE WEST"

POLITICS, RELIGION, AND POPULAR CULTURE

The era of cowboy politics is over!
—HILLARY CLINTON, NOVEMBER 5, 2008

Famous last words! Ms. Clinton, a diehard Democrat who earlier that year attempted to win her party's nod and run for the presidency, joyously made that statement hours after the ballot boxes closed. The person who won the nomination, Barack Obama, had just been elected forty-fourth U.S. president, the first African American to achieve that office. Republican John McCain, a politician from a Western ("red," in our post-2000 idiom) state, Arizona, along with running mate Sarah Palin, briefly governor of Alaska (far north in geography if red in orientation), had been roundly defeated. The newly elected president previously served as the U.S. senator for an Eastern (blue) state, Illinois, and vice president Joseph Biden as a senator from equally blue Delaware. They, along with many other party-line Democrats as well as liberal independents, believed (albeit briefly) that their victory represented a repudiation by the American people of political attitudes belonging to outgoing president George W. Bush (2001–2009). A Republican conservative like his father, the first president Bush (1989–1993), the man known as "W" had over eight years come to be perceived as the ultimate symbol (for better or worse, depending on one's views) of "cowboy politics."

That term, at least during the past half century, is almost always employed to describe right-leaning Republicans with strong religious ties, particularly to churches of the various Protestant denominations.[1] Although numerous liberals have hailed from Western states—including South Dakota's George McGovern, a Stetson-wearing Democrat who lost the presidential race to Richard Milhous Nixon of California in 1972—the essence of cowboy politics has less to do with geography and more to do with attitudes on small rather than large government, local rather than central problem solving, the issue of lower taxation, and an almost spiritual belief in the benefits of free-market capitalism. After all, the thirty-ninth president, moderately liberal Jimmy Carter, hailed from Georgia, today considered a red state and about a hundred years before that a gray one. His presidency (1977–1981) was in 1980 challenged by conservative Ronald Reagan, born in Illinois (Obama's state, by political orientation if not birth), as blue today as during the Civil War. Reagan had served as governor of a Western (but more often than not blue) state, California. Yet no one described Carter as a cowboy, even if some of the farming jobs he held in his youth might have resembled that form of work.[2] Reagan, who never held any such jobs,[3] wore a Stetson as a Western movie and TV star and vividly looked the part. His defeat of Carter that year was widely seen as an overwhelming victory for cowboy politics.

Yet by 2008, Ms. Clinton and those who like her believed a new, bold era in progressive politics would reign more or less unchallenged for at least four years were in for a major surprise. Immediately, protesters self-identifying as "the tea party" suddenly emerged to oppose, often in loud, angry, even incendiary language, all of those liberal values that Obama, Clinton, and Biden represent.[4] Though all three are, by objective assessments, moderates who lean slightly left of center,[5] they were quickly posited by right-wing radio commentators like Rush Limbaugh as "extremists."[6] Limbaugh proffered a vision of the incoming administration that most tea partiers were eager to accept. Notably, Obama's dream for a universal health-care program would become their key rallying point, decried as symbolic of his supposed desire for ever more intense attacks on the rights of individual Americans as well as on "states' rights." They attack it despite the many Republicans, including both presidents Bush, who admitted the need for such a program. In fact, Obama's plan was modeled on the one Republican Mitt Romney enacted while he was governor of Massachusetts and on which, ironically, he would oppose Obama in the 2012 presidential election campaign.[7]

Those who started the tea-party movement, of course, came up with the name from the Boston Tea Party of 1773. That event took place when a group of colonists dressed as Indians dumped crates of tea sitting unopened on British merchant ships in Boston Harbor into the water rather than purchase and consume it. In large part, the twenty-first-century naming resulted from a misconception of what precipitated that act of civil disobedience some 235 years earlier. Tea partiers of today are outspoken in favoring the lowest taxes possible, with some extremists calling for an end to all taxes. They operate under the impression that angry colonists were moved to open rebellion by high taxes imposed by the British government. In actuality, when taxes on tea, stamps, and other commodities were raised, colonists protested "taxation without representation."[8] However much they disliked higher taxes, there is no evidence whatsoever in any legitimate history of that era that colonists would have resorted to violence over money alone. They were expected to take on full responsibilities of English citizens (paying taxes) without exercising the essential rights of citizens (electing their own politicians to at least argue against such taxes in the British Parliament).[9] As the Obama administration did not attempt to limit the voting rights of Americans in any area of the country, red states included, comparisons to the Boston Tea Party are bogus, however one feels about taxes in our time, high, medium, or low.

The tea-party movement does serve as a venue for people from any state (in the North and East, too, even as there are liberals, Ms. Clinton once among them, in the South and West) who see themselves essentially as traditionalists in politics and religion. From this perch they vent their frustrations at what they perceive as the emergence of an America fundamentally different in nature from what it once was. Or, perhaps, they decry a country so different from the mythic America they believe existed but that on closer examination proves to be the stuff of legend rather than fact. Though he was speaking about the people of Texas specifically, David McComb—a well-regarded historian and professor emeritus at Colorado State University—might also have been considering tea partiers, the red-state mentality wherever it may exist, and adherents of cowboy politics when he asserted: "They have a kind of macho, frontier, independent attitude of 'I can do what I damn well please and nobody else can tell me.'"[10] The point of view Professor McComb describes is, in some ways, more characteristic of the civil-libertarian sensibility than of conventional conservatism of a

The tea party in embryo. Current politics are not all that different from those in America's past. In Duel in the Sun, *Texans, fearful of higher taxes, band together with a "Don't Tread on Me!" attitude toward the railroad. Courtesy The David O. Selznick Studio.*

Republican Party nature. As to the tea-party movement itself, not all who espouse its varied proposals identify as Republicans, though certainly more do than those who express an alliance with Democrats. A great many prefer to call themselves independents.[11]

Yet the presumed tea-party view is conservative in at least one sense: the belief that the best days are gone, that a golden age has come and passed, and that an authentically American way of life can only be redeemed by attempting to bring those glory days back.[12] This is evident in the title of one popular recent book, *Cowboy Values: What America Once Stood For.*[13] To again quote McComb,[14] such people "cling to a mythical past of the cowboy" and choose to believe that such political values, coupled with old-time religion, are the proper means to bring back that faded American hero figure. The yearned-after past the professor describes is imaginary, not actual. It derives not from history books but Hollywood movies and diverse other aspects of popular culture, from such toys for tots as gun and holster sets to the marketing of cigarettes by the Marlboro Man.[15]

There are fairy tales for adults in the form of big, generic films, culminating in *How the West Was Won* (John Ford, Henry Hathaway, and George Marshall, 1962) and bygone TV shows including *Gunsmoke* and *The Life and Legend of Wyatt Earp*. And for children we have the singin' cowboy mini-epics of the 1930s and '40s and TV shows of the 1950s starring Gene Autry and Roy Rogers, as well as *The Lone Ranger* and, with Autry as its executive producer via his Flying A Productions, *Buffalo Bill, Jr.*[16] When scrutinized in terms of true literature marked by historicity, that area generally known as the West, perceived by our mythologists as an American Camelot, has nothing more to do with the actual frontier experience than the vision of King Arthur's court in the Tinseltown musical film *Camelot* (Joshua Logan, 1967) had in common with the primitive mud huts surrounded by a crude wooden wall that served as its inspiration.[17] The ongoing vision of the Round Table and its knights in armor of a type that would not exist for another thousand years conveyed values of an idealized order, communicated as romanticized fantasy. These qualities became ever more enchanting and glorious with each successive retelling. Such a Camelot was the invention of latter-day poets like Thomas Malory and Alfred, Lord Tennyson, eager to create origination myths that would bolster patriotism in times of need.[18] This precisely describes the function of the West in our own iconography and narratives, the key danger being that the most naïve among us may insist this lovely fantasy was once actual and that a Dream West can be reclaimed in our time.

Although printed works, from the highest level through middlebrow fiction to cheap dime novels, have had a significant part in the creation of our myth, nothing can compare to the impact of the movies for what critic Robert Warshow has referred to as "the immediate experience."[19] Seeing is believing, as an old adage contends. So people who "saw" that mythic frontier vividly realized in endless films starring John Wayne and other genre greats believed in it as a tacit reality, no matter how completely manufactured such shared American faux memories of the good old days may have been. "It's *only* a movie," filmmaker Alfred Hitchcock is supposed to have said when people took his films far too literally. Today, true believers trying to bring back what never was, to quote McComb once more, "join a tea-party group and strap on a six-gun and strut around."[20] McComb here specifically refers to the already mentioned movement that came into being shortly after (and to a large degree as a result of) the election of Obama. Thus, many who do not support the tea party perceive it in racist terms, citing nasty caricatures of President Obama as an earlier, less-developed form of primate; the images surfaced at rallies including those held in Chicago on February 19, 2009, and in forty cities nationwide on February 27. Almost all those who claim to speak for the movement deny racist motives, saying the loose national populist movement—rather than "party" in an old-politics sense—sprang from dissatisfaction with mainstream Republican leaders,[21] among them Mitt Romney, and a desire to realign, reorganize, and restructure the Republican Party by seizing control of its grassroots elements to make it truer to an "origination" view of the U.S. Constitution.[22]

For this reason, many tea partiers apparently see themselves less as conservatives, in any old-fashioned sense, than as civil libertarians, with a fierce sense of independence. They often refer to U.S. Representative Ron Paul (R-Texas) as the movement's "Granddaddy";[23] they more or less suggest that America ought to have been fashioned as a confederacy, not a federalist nation. (In fact, of course, it was, though the Articles of Confederation proved to be a disastrous approach.) While most old-time, conventional Republicans had no trouble embracing demands for cutting taxes, other, more radical aspects caused loyalists like Karl Rove to speak in less than glowing terms about movement darling Sarah Palin,[24] among outspoken figures including Governor Rick Perry of Texas. To the delight of tea partiers and the deep consternation of those who oppose them, Perry came to appear extreme, even subversive, when he dared to proclaim that "Texas can leave the union if it wants to!" given enough dissatisfaction with new policies emanating from Washington during the age of Obama.[25]

In interviews with the mainstream press, Perry railed against Obama policies for "redistributing the wealth."[26] He said the beginning of the end of a U.S. golden age came with the 1930s New Deal, which he perceived as transforming a capitalist country into a socialist one: "If Americans want to really go back and historically engage when we really got off track, it started with Franklin Roosevelt and the start of the Great Depression and the maneuvering of Roosevelt (to) create government programs (and) agencies."[27]

For Perry and like-minded Americans, the end of what was best came when rugged individualism that allowed people—and, in time, corporations—to make money in unrestricted ways gave way to a sense of community in addressing demands of the working class to achieve a minimum standard of living by federal intervention on local situations if the problems could not be settled closer to home. No more villainous concept existed than the reality and ideology of unions, which came into their own during Roosevelt's long tenure (1933–1945). This helps to explain Perry's glowing admiration for the right-to-work status of the Lone Star State, where no person can be forced to join a union. Here, then, is cowboy politics, as the concept came down to us, beginning with the failed presidential bid of Barry Goldwater in 1964 and proceeding to the successful ones of Reagan and both Bushes, father and son.

As for working definitions of "red state" and/or "cowboy politics" at this writing, a *Newsweek* piece in April 2010 describes Perry, governor of Texas and then a potential Republican nominee to oppose Obama in the 2012 presidential election, as standing "for less government and more growth, for freedom and against bureaucracy, for Texas and against Washington."[28] Perhaps not coincidentally, the article emphasizes the cowboy qualities of this self-made man: Perry was "raised in a ranch house with no running water in the West Texas town of Paint Creek" and is "ruggedly handsome in a Marlboro Man sort of way."[29] Not all Texans, much less all red-staters, supported Perry or his politics, particularly ideas like secession that struck even some conservatives as too volatile. Others considered Perry's cowboy image as just that, a well-orchestrated ruse on the order of George H. W. Bush, a Harvard graduate, deciding that an "Aw, shucks!" façade would help him overcome his aging-preppy reputation and win the presidency.[30] For some observers, Perry appeared to be "all sizzle and no steak" or, to employ an even choicer bit of Texana, "all hat and no cattle." The image, though, did come across.

Thus Rick Perry of Texas could be posited as the opposite of Jimmy Carter of Georgia. No one could describe the gentle Carter as in any way resembling a cowboy, much less a Marlboro Man who rode the TV West in tobacco ads to the tune of *The Magnificent Seven* movie theme (until, in yet another example of federal intervention in free-trade America, liberal politicians saw to it that TV cigarette ads were banned owing to their ability to hook impressionable audiences on a product dangerous to one's health). Superstar John Wayne provided the template for the Marlboro Man image, right down to the Duke's cancer from smoking. In this he resembled the original Marlboro Man, David McLean, who died from using the product he had made his fortune hawking.[31]

All the same, Wayne had this to say about the election of Carter to the presidency when the star accepted an invitation to Carter's inaugural ceremony: "I'm pleased to be present and accounted for in this capital of freedom to witness history as it happens—to watch a common man accept the uncommon responsibility he won fair and square by stating his case to the American people."[32] By "common," Wayne likely did not mean to imply that Carter was ordinary or average in terms of his abilities. Love or hate Carter and his presidency, he clearly was exceptional, as Wayne well knew and appreciated, regardless of how their political views conflicted. The term "common" also describes Perry, again whether any observer does or does not care for that politician's positions. What Wayne apparently admired in the man from Plains, Georgia, was Carter's actualization of the American Dream. Likewise, presidents Ford, Reagan, and Obama, but not Kennedy or either of the Bushes, exemplified the essential American vision of leaders who hailed from the humblest of origins, beginning with the election of Andrew Jackson in 1828,[33] becoming the top dogs, the foremen of this ranch of a country we call America.

Continuing in that vein, Wayne went on to admit, "I know I'm a member of the loyal opposition—accent on the *loyal*! I'd have it no other way."[34] The trails of conservative cowboy-movie star John Wayne and liberal president Jimmy Carter would cross at least once more on an occasion that defined them both and confounds any simplistic notion of the man known as "Duke." Politics, as the saying goes, makes for strange bedfellows. Few could seem as polar as Wayne and Carter. Yet, a problem all but forgotten today dominated the American political scene between mid-October 1977 and early April 1978, bringing the two together again. This was the heated debate over the Panama Canal. Two treaties called for the canal to be returned to the Panamanian government by 2000.[35] Carter hoped to accomplish this sooner rather than later. Though opposition to his plan was to a degree bipartisan, mainly it hailed from the right, notably from the man who would shortly became the king of cowboy politics, Ronald Reagan, whom Wayne mostly wholeheartedly supported.

To a degree, Reagan's desire to serve as spokesman in this debate arose not only from honest concerns about the plan but also from aspirations for the presidency. He had failed in his challenge to Republican Ford a few years earlier for their party's nomination and was already actively seeking that position for the 1980 contest. Meanwhile, Carter had come to be regarded as weak and, as such, vulnerable in his upcoming reelection bid. Aware of this and eager to win back the White House, Republicans created a "pecking party" order of politics, attacking any Carter position less because they

The reinvention of cowboy politics. In the 1960s, law and order came to be associated with conservative politics. Future president Ronald Reagan intriguingly had appeared in a film with that very title. Courtesy Universal Pictures.

believed it wrong than because each instance in which they could embarrass the sitting Democrat offered another stepping-stone to victory in 1980. They attacked Carter's position on the Panama Canal, although Democratic president Lyndon Johnson and Republicans Richard Nixon and Gerald Ford also had pushed for the swift legal return of the canal to the Panamanian people. Clearly, then, most opposition to Carter on this issue had less to do with political philosophy in any ideological sense than with party politics in the basest form.

From that angle, the opposition was less than loyal, setting America's best interests aside to focus on those of the Republican Party. Reagan did express what appeared a heartfelt concern that many conservatives in the GOP and among Democratic ranks shared: worries that Carter's move would amount to the full "surrender (of) American property" deemed "vital to national security" and further the "American decline" in the nation's worldwide power base. At that moment, Reagan put his old cowboy hat from B Westerns back on, establishing his political image.[36] He would become to American politics what he had once been, on a minor level, in popular culture and what Wayne more than anyone else represented: the Westerner, the "red-stater" long before that term came into existence, or more simply put, "the cowboy." Yet that term has more than one definition. One is the actual, poorly paid, blue-collar worker who rode the range during the nineteenth century and continues to do so today. The other is the hero of American myth, the Lancelot of our Dream West. Reagan might be seen, at least in the Panama Canal context, as standing for the concept of the cowboy as a wild, untamed, often out-of-control fellow who liked to "hoorah" towns, once Dodge City and in this case Washington, D.C.

Wayne, breaking with his friend Reagan, became Carter's white knight, riding to the rescue in the nick of time, saving a Democrat from the Republicans who had him cornered in a symbolic canyon. On October 12, 1977, Wayne sent an official missive to every D.C. politician, Republican or Democrat, about Carter's decision: "I support it based on my belief that America always looks to the *future* and that our people have demonstrated qualities of justice and reason for the *past 200 years*."[37]

Back to the future? Perhaps forward to the past. Either way, those are not the words of a conservative, no matter how often Wayne professed to be one. Rather, it represents the ideology of a progressive traditionalist, that fair and balanced thinking person who, too complex to be boxed into any tight political corner, combines the best of conservatism (closely studying what the founding fathers intended and remaining true to their values) with liberalism (firmly believing the future will emerge as better than the past). Tomorrow can be more a golden age than yesterday if we learn from all that has gone before. Here is the delicate balance at the heart of the American idea.

Wayne continued: "That attitude has made our country a great nation. The new treaty modernizes an outmoded relation with a friendly and hospitable country."[38] He also contacted Carter to let him know that here stood the loyal opposition, supporting a man he had voted against, because Wayne believed him to be correct on this issue. The tactic worked: mostly as a result of the Duke's influence, enough Republicans backed down; the treaty was approved in early April 1978. If Reagan would forever be confused by this single bit of friction between Wayne and him, Carter would never cease to admire the man who arrived on cue like the Seventh Cavalry coming to the rescue of the vulnerable title object in *Stagecoach* (John Ford, 1939), Wayne's first huge hit. Politics and movies, it would seem, are at least in America absolutely inseparable.

No wonder, then, that Carter would say on Wayne's passing two years later: "He was larger than life. In an age of few heroes, he was the genuine article."[39] If Reagan embodied cowboy politics, Wayne symbolized something else: the code of the West, based more than anything else on the notion that a man must listen to his heart and head and then, once he has decided for himself on any issue, do the right thing. It is significant to bear in mind and shocking for some to learn that the phrase "the code of the West" did not yet exist during the nineteenth century, the period in which cowboy stories, movies included, are mostly set. It may have been coined in 1921 by one Mildred Sledge, a screenwriter who in two brief years turned out seven silent Westerns, the final among them titled *The Code of the West* (director unknown). In her films, Sledge—retelling traditional tales from a female point of view—more or less retold Owen Wister's 1901 seminal piece *The Virginian* from the perspective of its heroine, Molly. At about this time Zane Grey (1872–1939)—who seized on the declassé dime novel, transforming it into a middle-of-the-road product published in hard-cover editions for middlebrow target consumers—whipped off the rough draft of a short story with that title. His novel *The Code of the West* would not be published until 1934. That book concerns a stalwart hero who rescues a hapless woman not from the railroad pushing west (railroads and wealthy scoundrels who owned them would be attacked in "serious" fiction like Frank Norris's 1901 novel *The Octopus*) but from an unscrupulous, self-serving man in a suit, the true black-hearted villain of most generic Westerns.[40] In the process of rescuing the American equivalent of a damsel in distress, the hero proved himself an American Hercules, Southwestern El Cid, or Sir Lancelot of the last frontier.

Grey's ideas for the piece were filmed as early as 1925, directed by William K. Howard, then again in 1929 by J. P. McGowan. The final version, based directly on the novel rather than Grey's earlier sketch, would become a Hollywood B movie in 1947, directed by William Berke. At this moment Grey's fiction, both in book and film forms, was about to give way to a more adult order of Western, perhaps best typified by *Shane*, the 1949 novel by Jack Schaefer and the subsequent film (George Stevens, 1953). The greater point is that the code of the West was a twentieth-century invention, an idealized concept imposed on an earlier period much in the manner that

The man who never was. Shane (here played by Alan Ladd) embodies the traditional Western hero as a born gentleman, that is, a fantasy figure created by imaginative writers in the twentieth century. Courtesy Paramount Pictures.

England's Tennyson anachronistically stamped the concept of chivalry on that fifth- or sixth-century ruler who has come down to us as Arthur, though chivalry would not be codified until centuries after that man lived and died, if in fact he ever even existed. *The Code of the West*, then, Grey's book or any of the film versions, expresses an elaborate fantasy of who we were and ought to again become as a people, as Alfred, Lord Tennyson in *Idylls of the King* (1856–1892) and films like *Camelot* and *Excalibur* (John Boorman, 1981) express for the British Isles. Romantic notions of earlier, grander times and people extend deep in time to heroes on the order of Perseus or perhaps Theseus, these even earlier Greek conceptions of the strong, silent hero who arrives to conquer a monstrous Minotaur and save the people of Mycenae, particularly some lovely virgin, from a fate worse than death.

There is not a whit of evidence that such people ever existed, in ancient Greece, in medieval England, or on our own wild frontier. If a coalition of Greeks did follow a king named Agamemnon to Ilium, they did so as pirates eager to sack the city, not noble gentlemen hoping to restore honor to Helen, the supposedly abducted wife of Menelaus who more likely ran off with Paris by choice. Such figures can be wholly created, as in Zane Grey's fiction. Or actual people like Wyatt Berry Earp can be recast, as was done by Stuart N. Lake, a writer claiming to be an objective biographer while swallowing tall tales without any hesitation and relating them verbatim, in the process giving a semblance of history to nostalgic gossip. In time his book *Frontier Marshal* (1939) led to endless films and TV shows. Owing to this reimaging of flawed if fascinating persons, entertainment from Hollywood was believed when seen, despite being only movies; the consummate craftsmanship of the best films, particularly those of Ford, added to the impact with *My Darling Clementine* in 1946. More recent forays into the Western tend to be of a revisionist nature, films like the remake of *3:10 to Yuma* (James Mangold, 2007) denying the very code of the West embodied in the original (Delmer Daves, 1957). The popular HBO TV series *Deadwood* (2004–2006) might be thought of as an outright attack on good ol' *Gunsmoke* and other shows from the golden age of the TV Western, when actors such as

Trail's end. A rough-hewn signpost served as John Ford's signature shot in early epics like My Darling Clementine. *Toward the end of his career he revived it for* The Man Who Shot Liberty Valance, *in which Ford deconstructed the very myths he had earlier helped create. Courtesy Paramount Pictures.*

James Arness brought the John Wayne image as well as the code of the West to the small screen.

All the same, the attitudes of tea partiers and others appear to be based on one absolute idea: that the charming fabrications of the twentieth century in which artists and entertainers of varied creative gifts rewrote the American experience from the nineteenth century in romanticized terms ought to be the source of our daily political and religious lifestyles in the twenty-first. More often than not, such a desire is based on the heretofore unchallenged belief that those bygone Western texts, in print or on celluloid, offered what we would today call a red-state vision, traditionalist and conservative. On closer examination, nothing could be further from the truth.

PART ONE

COWBOY
POLITICS

ROOSEVELT THROUGH REAGAN

Appointment with destiny. The Earps face off with the Clantons in the 1957 Gunfight at the O.K. Corral, *in which politics are barely mentioned. Intriguingly, though, the church is in clear view. Courtesy Paramount Pictures.*

TO DIE IN THE WEST

THE O.K. CORRAL, HISTORY VERSUS FILM

We'll be waitin' fer ya, Marshal, at the O.K. Corral!
—OLD MAN CLANTON IN *MY DARLING CLEMENTINE*, 1946

Truth or dare! Watch any classic Western about the O.K. Corral gunfight, from the first, *Law and Order* (Edward L. Cahn, 1932), through what might be considered the last, *Hour of the Gun* (John Sturges, 1967). Odds are you will come away with the impression that this shoot-out in Tombstone, Arizona, was the culmination of a long-standing feud between the Earps and their adversaries the Clantons or, in those films that play this historical situation on a metaphoric canvas, as an unavoidable conflict between good lawmen and evil outlaws, with (as Superman's creators might put it) truth, justice, and the American way winning out. In such cases the O.K. Corral incident is presented in the simplest of terms, a real-life allegory posited in black and white. But these are literary or cinematic truths. And as such, they are subjective: interpretations by artists, entertainers, or the journeyman storytellers who occupy some middle ground between the two.

Importantly, there is a more objective truth, what we might call the historical one.[1] This did not appear in theatrical movies until the genre we call the Western had seemingly run its course. At last, such rare "oaters," as they were once nicknamed, as *Tombstone* (George Pan Cosmatos, 1993) and *Wyatt Earp* (Lawrence Kasdan, 1994) projected a more modern, in some regards postmodern, sensibility onto that nineteenth-century stage. These films—the former a solid box-office success, the latter something of a disaster—came closer to recapturing rather than reinventing the past. Way back when, in the West that "was" as compared to the Dream West of old movies, any and all pressing social issues were as complex as they are today, defying codification as moral absolutes. The mundane build-up to the O.K. Corral incident had to do with control of the economics in a still emergent community. Such authority would be decided, as always in America, through a political process.[2]

In reality, the situation came down to this: an area newly redistricted, owing to political maneuverings, as Cochise County proved ripe in silver, as such providing financial rewards for whichever faction won the election for sheriff, who traditionally served as the collector of taxes.[3] The bloody gun battle between the Earps and Clantons, so central to Hollywood Westerns, was actually an unexpected offshoot of this considerably larger power play. According to researchers, it also appears in retrospect as an avoidable incident rather than, as movies and TV have it, a fated consequence.

The two men at the center of this long duel were not, as in the most artistic film on the subject, *My Darling Clementine*, Wyatt Earp (Henry Fonda) and Neumann Hayes "Old Man" Clanton (Walter Brennan). Nor did it come down to, as in *Gunfight at the O.K. Corral* (John Sturges, 1957), Earp (Burt Lancaster) versus Neumann's oldest son, Isaac or "Ike" (Lyle Bettger). The primary conflict took place between Earp and John Behan, a man ignored in the former and marginalized as a fictional figure (Cotton Wilson, enacted by Frank Faylen) in the latter. In his position as sitting sheriff, Behan collected the taxes. Here was the key to quick wealth. Now, though, Behan's ability to continue in that role had, beginning in early 1881, grown doubtful. At last he had to face a considerable challenger, newcomer Wyatt Earp, a professional gambler and sometimes deputy to his older brother Virgil, Tombstone's appointed town marshal. However high-falutin' that term sounds, thanks to myth makers including Stuart N. Lake,[4] frontier marshal was a low-paying, less than lofty position consisting mainly of arresting drunken cowboys and other routine chores.[5]

Gunman's walk. Director John Sturges returned to the O.K. Corral in Hour of the Gun *with James Garner as Wyatt and Jason Robards as Doc in a more realistic depiction. The incident has been portrayed as a moment in history that now takes on an aura of national ritual. Courtesy Mirisch/United Artists.*

Every bit as ambitious as Behan, likely driven more by his earnest desire to finally succeed in a capitalist system than by any God-given inspiration to make the West safe for incoming pioneers, Earp intensely wanted to become the sheriff.[6] In an election as vicious, nasty, and low-down as any to take place during the twenty-first century, Earp lost. With that defeat at the polls his dreams turned to dust, a circumstance most early filmed "biographies" fail to mention, much less portray. Yet those movies were basically mythic, set on a Hollywood, not historical, frontier. As to reality, now or then, win the election and rake in profits; lose and you are back to collecting miniscule fines for jailing bums.

This is not the vision of the Old West we discover in pre-1970 films or the paperbacks, comic books, and dime novels or the elaborate stage performances that preceded them.[7] All offered romanticized conceptions of who these people had been and what they hoped to achieve. Even when the incidents were accurately portrayed (this in itself rare), the key motivations of the men who were presented to readers and audiences were idealized fabrications. These visions disappeared following the social, political, and cultural revolution of the late 1960s. A new type of Western emerged that debunked previous legends. Some, like the anti-Custer *Little Big Man* (Arthur Penn, 1970), offered brilliant cinema. Others, including the anti-Earp *Doc* (Frank Perry, 1971), were embarrassing misfires. What they and many others pro-

Politics as usual. History reveals that John Behan (here played by Mark Harmon) and Wyatt Earp waged a long, exhausting, vicious political campaign against one another for the position of sheriff of Cochise County, Arizona. Motion pictures, with their emphasis on action, tend to downplay this history in favor of the brief—less than half a minute—interchange of gunfire between the Earps and the Clantons at the O.K. Corral. Courtesy Warner Brothers.

jected was a nouveau attitude toward the past. Initially, this was taken as far more honest, if only because they offered an alternative or revisionist view.[8] In truth, negativism is not necessarily any truer to life than positive visions. Today, revisionist films seem less realistic than cynical and as simplistic as pre-1970s Westerns.

Still, in the age of political assassinations, the disastrous war in Vietnam, and the Watergate scandal, it is not difficult to understand why a large number of Americans agreed with a statement offered by director Dennis Hopper. His *Easy Rider* (1969) starred Peter Fonda, son of John Ford's Wyatt Earp, as a biker named Wyatt. Their modern motorcycles took the place of old-fashioned mounts. Wyatt was accompanied by a Billy the Kid pal (Hopper's character). *Easy Rider* brought a radical vision to mainstream American movie houses during a turbulent era of sex, drugs, and rock 'n' roll that forever altered the nation. The filmmaker, who earlier had played supporting parts in mythic films starring John Wayne, announced: "I don't believe in heroes any more."[9] It is important to note that a decade later, Hopper did a total about-face. During the 1980 presidential election he supported Reagan over Carter.[10]

In part, Hopper's support for Reagan can be explained as a pendulum swing away from what appeared to many as the failed progressivism of the Carter years. Also, there was the sense that Republican Reagan, much like

The way it was. (a) While the legend of David Crockett recalls him fighting Indians, most of the man's life was spent campaigning (Fess Parker on TV). (b) Likewise, Wyatt Earp, recalled for tracking outlaws, ran a losing campaign for sheriff of Cochise County (Harris Yulin in Doc*). Courtesy Walt Disney Productions; FP Films/United Artists.*

the Democrat Jack Kennedy of some twenty years earlier, radiated movie-star charisma. In Reagan's case, that is what he had earlier been. Reagan was often associated with the Western, hosting the TV series *Death Valley Days* and playing a variation of Wyatt Earp in the 1953 remake of *Law and Order* (Nathan Juran). How fascinating that the film's title would, a quarter century later, provide the anthem for its star's presidential run.

The Reagan campaign relied heavily on what came to be called cowboy politics.[11] The most famous image of Reagan from that time is a shot of him standing proudly in front of the Alamo in San Antonio, Texas. It is intriguing to note, then, that back in 1954 Reagan wanted to play a historical figure who died there, David Crockett, in his friend Walt Disney's TV miniseries. The role went instead to newcomer Fess Parker.[12] Reagan's eventual run for the presidency would be based on an unstated assertion: America, the now-reformed hippie Dennis Hopper included, wanted—perhaps needed—to again believe in heroes. In time, Dennis Hackin's screenplay for *Bronco Billy* (Clint Eastwood, 1980) directly addressed this issue in a film released only months after Reagan assumed the presidency. The film's title character (Clint Eastwood), last of the traveling Western showmen, stages bold episodes for ever-smaller audiences. Eventually he is unmasked as a fraud, an Easterner dedicated to keeping the myth of the Old West alive. The film's primary point is that this masquerade does not matter, that desire qualifies him as a hero.

How convenient for Ronald Reagan, then, that when it comes to choosing the traditional heroes for a uniquely American popular culture, the public has never been mildly intrigued by those remarkable people who won the Revolution or created the Constitution. This period constituted the true birth of the nation.[13] In its place, we instead worship or, conversely, disparage what became a preferred origin myth—the taming of the West. Willie Nelson put it better than anyone: "My heroes have always been cowboys." Willie, it is worth noting, is at this writing a rarity of rarities, the contemporary country-western musical artist who dares stand firm as a liberal. Though we perceive in the twenty-first century a great barrier between red and blue states and their corresponding value systems, that outlaw-artist's worship of the man who rides tall in the saddle makes clear that even this distinction is too simplistic.

The Hollywood cowboy hero, atop some magnificent horse (in comparison to a lowly working man who roamed the range on a wasted nag) became the great American icon. No matter; legends possess a truth of their own. The Western remains an American myth, enshrined by some as the ongoing essence of the country, attacked by others as an outdated, politically incorrect sensibility. If Nelson allows us any insight, though, the West offers a rich, complex vision that cuts across temporal political barriers.

The sickly sweet stench of black powder smoke. While traditional movies turned the O.K. Corral gunfight into an epic duel, more recent ones like Wyatt Earp *reduced such romanticism. Virgil (Michael Madsen) fires from the ground, Wyatt (Kevin Costner) behind him. Courtesy Warner Brothers.*

SHERIFF OF COCHISE

THIRTY SECONDS TO ETERNITY

I don't believe any man's life ought to be summed up by thirty seconds.

—WYATT EARP TO JOHN FORD ON THE

O.K. CORRAL INCIDENT, LOS ANGELES, 1924

This much is fact: at 3:23 in the afternoon of October 26, 1881, four men completed a leisurely stroll along the main street of Tombstone, Arizona, then stepped into an alley adjacent to Fly's Photography Studio. The armed quartet consisted of Marshal Virgil Earp and his deputized younger brothers, Wyatt and Morgan. Also in their company, carrying a sawed-off shotgun, was a gambler and gunman named John "Doc" Holliday, inexplicably a friend to Wyatt much to Virgil's longtime chagrin. Awaiting them were six men, each a member of the town's "cowboy element." Present was Ike Clanton, leader of the group since the death of his father in a shoot-out along the Mexican border. Ike, his brothers Phin (not present this day) and Billy (who was) lived, along with a loose coalition of working hands, horse thieves, and stage robbers, on a ranch outside of town, over by the San Pedro River. Accompanying Ike and Billy was yet another pair of brothers, Frank and Tom McLaury (alternately spelled McLowery or McClowery). Two others, Billy Clairbourne (or Clairborne) and Wes Fuller, briefly joined them, then turned and ran at the first sight of the Earps. Momentarily, the eight remaining men would enter into the West's most famous, or perhaps more correctly, infamous shoot-out.[1]

Why does the gunfight at the O.K. Corral remain so well known, vividly remembered, and endlessly debated? Largely because this incident, despite what we might garner from Hollywood films and TV shows, was among the rare occasions when two men, or two groups of men, actually did approach one other, draw pistols, and bang away. However rampant random shootings were in the West, or for that matter anywhere today, classic "gun duels" were a rarity. A high-noon face-off like the one that opened early episodes of TV's *Gunsmoke* is more a fanciful invention than an actual recurrence.[2] This helps explain why the O.K. Corral has, for more than 130 years, been transformed from a controversial example of police procedure into a wellspring of folklore. What cannot be denied is that the event did in fact happen.

Of the Clanton faction, only Ike survived. Witnesses said he raised his arms high, called out that he wasn't armed, and was allowed to run off. On the Earp side, all were wounded but Wyatt. Virgil took a shot in his right calf, Morgan in the upper back. Doc suffered a nick on the hip. That much is certifiable. Fact, though, has little to do with what we experience in Westerns. In O.K. Corral films, that blink-and-you'll-miss-it gunfight has run up to twelve minutes on screen. This is but the tip of the iceberg, though, as to the mythologizing of an actual event.

Actor Robert Mitchum would narrate a curious prologue to Cosmatos's 1993 rendition in *Tombstone*. Though Mitchum never played Earp per se, he did appear as Marshal Ben Kane, an Earp derivation, in *Young Billy Young* (Burt Kennedy, 1969); the film was adapted from Will Henry's 1956 novel, *Who Rides with Wyatt*.[3] As a result, Mitchum's presence connected this "new" version of the events to past genre renderings. Likewise, his introduction served a distinct purpose for the anticipated viewer. Up until 1970 an audience brought with it to the latest Earp film knowledge of the background. That march to the O.K. Corral had become ingrained via film and television until the experience of watching it turned ritualistic. By the early 1990s, with movie and video Westerns virtually nonexistent, it had become necessary to set the scene.

The violence depicted here, Mitchum informed us, was due to hostilities left over from the Civil War (1861–1865). More intriguing is what simultaneously appeared on screen: flickering images, in faded black and white or golden sepia, of pioneers locked in deadly shootings. To a late twentieth-century audience these appeared to be and were accepted as historical documents. Their age implied authenticity, however illusory. In fact, these were clips from early Western movies, including *The Great Train Robbery* (Edwin S. Porter, 1903). That ten-minute mini-epic had been shot in the wilds of New Jersey by Thomas A. Edison's Black Maria Company.[4] What it offered was not history in the raw, though many turn-of-the-century audiences took it as that, but a (mis)conception of the Old West created by later Easterners unfamiliar with what really took place. Now, those casual viewers who came to see *Tombstone* near the turn of yet another century accepted, after watching the scenes, that the film to follow had firmly been set in a context of American rather than Hollywood history.

Always, the more artistically a film's content is rendered, the easier it is for viewers to assume they have witnessed some past reality or at least a reasonable facsimile thereof. No O.K. Corral film comes close to *My Darling Clementine* in achieving status as a masterpiece. Yet few movies on the subject misrepresent historical fact so blatantly as this 1946 classic. Early in act 2, Wyatt Earp (Henry Fonda) visits the grave of his young brother James (Don Garner), shot down by outlaw cowboys. The engraving on James's stone gives the year as 1882; the O.K. Corral gunfight, with which *Clementine* concludes, occurred one year earlier. James was the oldest Earp, not the youngest; that distinction went to Warren, a half-brother. Nor did James, a bartender, die during the feud, though his fanciful demise would again be a catalyst for the much-awaited showdown in *Gunfight at the O.K. Corral*. In both films, this manufactured incident provided a clean dramatic line based on the idea that the mass audience must always grasp the motivations behind what occurs on screen, regardless of whether a story told in a film happens to be entirely fictional or loosely derived from facts.[5]

The only movie to offer an even more outrageous rewrite of history was *Frontier Marshal* (Allan Dwan, 1939). In it, Wyatt (Randolph Scott) marches to the corral alone. Virgil and Morgan are not in view; it is the death of Doc (called "Halliday" here, played by Caesar Romero) that motivates the climactic duel. This pitched battle is not with Ike Clanton but gunman "Curly" Bill Brocious (Joe Sawyer), a true Clanton comrade who had not been present.[6] In sharp contrast to these old Hollywood representations, *Wyatt Earp*, a would-be epic, flopped commercially. Critics and the few viewers who caught it complained that it played like a docudrama, an educational film

The hero's journey. In Joseph Campbell's writings on myth, one elemental theme is the tireless search for the murderer of a family member. In My Darling Clementine, *Ford reconceived the events in Tombstone to include this recurring pattern. Courtesy Twentieth Century-Fox.*

designed for history classes. For people who wanted a night out at the movies, *Tombstone* had, a half-year earlier, achieved success, in part because, along with a fair amount of historical information, this considerably less ambitious movie delivered the goods. The mass audience may sit still for a helping of "history." But what moviegoers want and demand is myth, not reality; they wanted myth during the golden age of Hollywood and, as *Wyatt Earp*'s financial failure made clear, some twenty years ago as well.

For an example of how this works we might consider *Tombstone*'s opening. Featured here is a genocidal attack by Anglos led by Johnny Ringo (Michael Biehn) on a peaceful Mexican family. The sequence draws from the first raid on a border town in *The Wild Bunch* (Sam Peckinpah, 1969), the initial ultraviolent Western. This film changed all the rules of the genre's game by offering antiheroic figures involved in a ballet of blood. But back to *Tombstone*: no such holocaust took place in Arizona. There were occasional exchanges of gunfire between cowboys and their Mexican counterparts, *vaqueros*, though nothing even approaching the incident portrayed here occurred. It did not exist in Kevin Jarre's screenplay, which if filmed might have turned out much like *Wyatt Earp*. This spectacular massacre was concocted after Jarre, the original director, was replaced after several days of shooting by Cosmatos, best known for *Rambo II* (1985). More incredibly, the incident is never again mentioned in the film, not even by Mayor John Clum (Terry O'Quinn), whose job it would have been to make certain any murder came before local Judge Spicer.

Those who "learn" history from historical fiction such as *Tombstone* are left with the impression that killings were the order of the day way back then, likely because of an abiding racism. If not yet a state, however, Arizona was a U.S. territory.[7] As such, it was policed by federal marshals. A mass murder would have been prosecuted, as the mortal conflicts between the Earps and Clantons were. Racism (which did exist) aside, the perpetrators would have been brought to court, if not necessarily to justice. Also, following the O.K. Corral, Wyatt (Kurt Russell), Doc (Val Kilmer), and several acquaintances ride out to avenge the assassination attempts that leave Morgan (Bill Paxton) dead and Virgil (Sam Elliott) crippled. This vendetta passes for documented history. Wyatt and his posse killed between three and five men before Mayor Clum and other respectable citizens, until then Earp defenders, turned against Wyatt. Clum went so far as to issue a warrant for his arrest.[8] Earp fled the area, a wanted man. In *Tombstone*, Russell's character—who by this point has more in common with The Terminator than with Wyatt Earp— kills thirty men, then departs on his own free will.

The reasoning at the project's studio, Twentieth Century–Fox? Though people no longer turned out for period Westerns, they would respond to a large-scale action film no matter where it is set. Studio executives' thinking was correct about box-office matters, if not as to what academics believe a historically based film ought to achieve.

Tombstone did get some of the history right, such as the escape of Ike Clanton (Stephen Lang) at the end. Even Earp films that purportedly depict the story accurately fail to do so. *Hour of the Gun*, among others, concludes with a shoot-out between Wyatt (James Garner) and Ike (Robert Ryan). Their duel adds dramatic closure but flies in the face of fact, despite a title at the film's beginning that proclaims, "This is the way it was!" That claim, though, must be written off as a minor liberty when one considers *Clementine*. In Ford's film, Doc dies with his boots on. Victor Mature slowly falls out of the frame, his elaborate neckerchief loosely hanging on the corral while lightly blowing in the wind. The moment offers pure movie magic. *Tombstone* lacks any such iconic image. Kilmer's Doc dies as he actually did, lying in bed at a Colorado Springs sanitarium.[9]

Here then is the conundrum that is *Tombstone* and, in truth, most films based on factual subjects and not confined to the Old West. Call it Hollywood versus history. While some details reveal careful research into the costuming, weaponry, and so forth, others acknowledge that ultimately they are only movies. Crowd-pleasing is not a luxury but a necessity in commercial filmmaking, where product proves more prevalent than art. String together a series of factual moments, re-created in precise detail, as a loose narrative, and the result will likely spell financial disaster, the case with *Wyatt Earp*. A similar situation occurred with *The Alamo* (John Lee Hancock, 2004), which offered no dramatic story line to augment its depiction of the Texas revolution.

Despite the commercial success of *Tombstone* and utter failure of *Wyatt Earp*, both managed to get one key detail right. In each, the gunfight is not sparked by the death of a kid brother or Doc "Halliday" but for a less explosive motivation: the Clanton-McLaury bunch rode into town that day wearing guns. As city constables, the Earps had to make a difficult decision, to confront the cowboys and disarm, then arrest them on misdemeanor charges of not checking their weapons according to a town ordinance or to let them ride away, no shots fired, no blood spilled, knowing the cowboys would return, again wearing guns, whenever they chose.[10] Once this ordinance had been challenged and the challenge left answered, its existence on the books would no longer matter. The authority of the Earps, along with that of Clum and other recent arrivals from the East, would be all over.

Here, historically, was an invisible line drawn in the sand. Most likely the Clantons had planned to hang around for a while, then drift off, no guns drawn, much less used. They probably assumed the Earps would back down and things would return to the way they had been in what those in the Clantons' element considered the good old days. It didn't turn out that way. After some consideration, the expensively suited Earps decided to confront the redneck element over what struck some as a minor infraction. Yet to others, the "Don't wear your guns to town" rule represented the most basic aspect of the development of a progressive lifestyle in what had previously been wilderness.[11] The value of that encounter would be debated ad infinitum. Those who believe in rugged individualism side with the Clantons. Others in favor

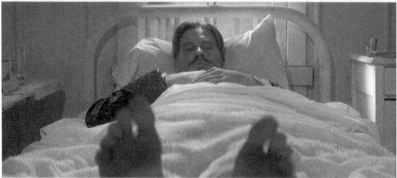

He died with his boots on/off. (a) In the mythic Western My Darling Clementine *Doc Holliday (Victor Mature) goes down fighting. (b) In the more accurate* Tombstone *he (Val Kilmer) expires in a Colorado sanitarium. Courtesy Twentieth Century-Fox; Cinergi Pictures/Buena Vista.*

of community values agree with the Earps. No middle ground exists. Indeed, if there had been any room for a compromise on what in truth came down to the issue of gun control, then or now, the gunfight at the O.K. Corral might have never occurred.

As both early 1990s films portray, here was a reality that must be understood as essentially political in nature. However much we may consider Wyatt Earp the ultimate man of the West, he was born and raised in Illinois, Abe Lincoln country, Barack Obama country. Earp's values, derived from his abolitionist father, Nicholas, were firmly blue state. When the Earps arrived in Tombstone, many longtime residents saw them as Northern or Eastern intruders on what had been a Western and to a degree Southern realm, less a community than a loose confederacy. The cowboys lived in social-libertarian defiance of the type of change these Earps, along with mayor and newspaper editor Clum, crusaded to establish.

At the O.K. Corral the cowboys might well have raised the flag early Texans hoisted in October 1835 as Mexican troops crossed the Rio Grande to disarm them of a Gonzales cannon: "Come and Take It!"[12] Or the earlier flag that tea partiers defiantly waved at their anti-Obama rallies: "Don't Tread on Me!"[13] Though they considered themselves true patriots, tea-party enthusiasts were less likely to fly the American flag, as that quickly came to be seen as a symbol of Obama's federal government. Resistance to change associated in the early twenty-first century with the tea-party movement correlates to the Old West code of the Clantons, not the Earps. We might read the conflict in Tombstone, then, as an attempt to impose blue-state values on an entrenched red-state mentality. The point here is that every film made about the O.K. Corral, with the possible exception of *Doc*, proceeds from an approval of this process. The vision extends beyond the unique subgenre of Earp movies to the body of work we call the Western.

The coonskin congressman. David Crockett (1786–1836), initially a Jackson Democrat, switched to the liberal-progressive Whig Party. Fess Parker plays the crusader for civil rights as he damns the president's Indian-removal bill in the Disney TV version. Courtesy Walt Disney Productions.

RED, WHITE,
AND BLUE STATES

POLITICAL PHILOSOPHY IN
NINETEENTH-CENTURY AMERICA

*If we were the kind of country we're supposed to be, a bill like this
would never have arrived on our desk for consideration.*

—CONGRESSMAN DAVID CROCKETT ON AN "INDIAN REMOVAL
BILL," IN *DAVY CROCKETT, KING OF THE WILD FRONTIER*, 1955

Wyatt Berry Earp (1848–1929) was born into a family of pro-Lincoln, anti-slavery Republicans. During the postbellum period, Earp regularly revealed that, compared with earlier American heroes, he shared more with David Crockett (1786–1836) than with Crockett's contemporary Andrew Jackson (1767–1845). Though both those men began their political careers as Democrats, Crockett switched over to the Whig Party in open defiance of his former commanding officer from the Choctaw Indian War (1813–1815). Jackson had since served as Crockett's political mentor, convincing his fellow Tennessean to run for Congress. The Democratic Party they initially joined first emerged as a great power with Jackson's election to the presidency in 1828.[1] Up until that moment, the political system allowed for a limited sense of democracy in which commoners, or at least those who legally owned land, were allowed to choose which highly educated American aristocrats would serve in the office of the presidency.[2] The candidacy and election of Jackson marked a sea change; one of their own could now not only run but win. Our seventh president actually lived out the fable that would later incorrectly come to be associated with Lincoln, the original Republican president: born in a humble log cabin, destined for the White House.

Jackson's inauguration was viewed by people who aspired to class of a European order as a harbinger of the end of their hope to turn America into an imitation of civilization in the English style. The Jackson inaugural ball was overrun by rednecks who had fought with Old Hickory against the Creeks at Talladega and the British down in New Orleans. According to some scholars, several of these American Nimrods (my biblical reference is entirely intentional) brought with them to the ball Kentucky long rifles and fired at the ceiling. America truly had, for better or worse, at that moment become the country of the common man. As to the subsequent mentoring of Crockett by Jackson and then the latter's left turn, this would be dramatized in the Disney TV shows (1954–1955) and the feature film *Davy Crockett, King of the Wild Frontier* (Norman Foster, 1955).[3] At heart a liberal and absolutely so on the issue of ethnicity, Crockett hoped that Jackson's kingdom of the commoner would extend to people of color, particularly his beloved Indians in general, Cherokee in particular.[4] In fact, Jackson stood for and by the common white man, that dirt farmer posited as the only true American in his era's redneck Democratic sensibility. Though Congressman Crockett did labor at hands-on chores in his lifetime, Crockett's mental construct of the ordinary American extended far beyond white farmers. Jackson's Indian-removal program of the early 1830s resulted in the horrific Trail of Tears,[5] forcing even the Cherokee, mostly farmers and Christians, off the lands that had been guaranteed them by treaties. Crockett bolted the party and joined the Whigs, modeled on the British party of that name.[6]

America's Whigs opposed everything Jacksonian democracy had become: the party of a now-assertive poor white trash. Unable to achieve enough victories at the polls, the Whigs would close up shop in 1856, the same year the new Republicans ran their first candidate for presidency, John Charles Frémont. A former Army officer renowned as "The Pathfinder," he had, with scout Kit Carson, mapped the Far West.[7] His indeed were true cowboy politics if in a notably different context than the phrase signifies today. Four years later, the Republicans won the presidency with Lincoln. Shortly, one after another state in the Democratic-dominated South seceded to form the

The Dodge City peace commission. Sheriff Bat Masterson (Kenneth Tobey), Marshal Wyatt Earp (Burt Lancaster), and Constable Charlie Bassett (Earl Holliman) plan to disarm Texans when they reach town. The heroes in the 1957 Gunfight at the O.K. Corral *are not pistol-toting cowboys but government representatives who impose gun control. Courtesy Paramount Pictures.*

Confederacy, a loose coalition of states dedicated to solving problems and resolving issues on a local level with little if any intervention from the central government.[8] The battle cry of their notion of freedom was "states' rights," including the presumed regional right to own slaves.

Though the Civil War officially ended in 1865, the conflict did not simply fade away. Self-righteous Northerners and embittered Southerners headed off into newly opened territories. Many came to Tombstone. The Clanton family arrived there long before Wyatt Earp.

As deputy marshal in various outposts of civilization, Earp was among the first, and some say he was the first, to hire Native Americans (Mr. Cousins and Mr. Brothers) as deputies. He faced little opposition to such policies in, say, Dodge City, Kansas. We may today perceive—or, rather, misperceive— that town as a symbol of the Wild West, in part because annually cowboys rode the trail there from Texas with their herds.[9] Most townsfolk in Kansas considered themselves to be Northerners; most were, like the Earps, Republicans of a progressive order. This created friction when cattlemen poured into the otherwise sleepy towns in late summer. They arrived to take advantage of the railroads that could transport their beef back East. While there, the visitors would roar out of control. Mostly, drovers felt contempt for the permanent citizens. Lawless moments may be interpreted as miniature attempts to reignite the Civil War.

Though the terms for such polar mentalities were then still "blue" and "gray," they were comparable to today's blue- and red-state dichotomy. Yet mutual dislike was coupled with mutual need. The West and South depended on the North for a market; the North hungered for products, among them cattle. Wyatt Earp, Bat Masterson, James Butler "Wild Bill" Hickok, Charles Bassett, William Tilghman, and other Northerners by birth were hired to enforce the law in "end of the trail" cowtowns mostly in Kansas—Dodge City, Abilene, Elsworth, Wichita—where Texans and fellow Southerners wound up after the long drives. The lawmen's job was to keep the cowboys in line without offending them to such an extreme that angry Texans would search for other markets. A delicate balance had to be achieved. The lawmen enforced this through ordinances that restricted carrying shooting irons in town. However begrudgingly, most cowboys complied.

Not so in Tombstone, deep in the Southwest. Upon arrival, the Earps were perceived by the cowboys as intruders. To succeed in this unfamiliar terrain, Wyatt and his brothers employed the same approach that had worked for them in friendlier climes. As to gun control, here was one more means by which Northern values might be imposed on the South; by which a communal ideology could be forced upon individualistic sensibilities; by which, in retrospect, presently blue states attempted to remake now-red states in their own image through what came to be called "law and order." That term would, within the social and political climate of the late 1960s, become associated with the archly conservative element that eventually rallied around Ronald Reagan. Nearly a hundred years earlier, though, law and order was, ironically from our perspective, a hallmark of liberal progressivism, a position that today describes most members of the Democratic Party. In nineteenth-century America, liberal progressivism had, since Frémont's failed presidential candidacy, meant Republicanism.

This progressivism of Republicans would remain through the Theodore Roosevelt presidency (1901–1909). The nation's first cowboy president, or more correctly an educated Easterner who transformed himself into a Rough Rider via a stay on a Wyoming ranch,[10] claimed to prefer a buckskin jacket and blue jeans to fine-tailored suits. He adored what we call the frontier enough to write the four-volume *The Winning of the West*, which outlined the history of that area from a romanticized point of view. His

The original cowboy politics. America's first "cowboy president" stood for the creation of a national parks system and civil rights for ethnic minorities, also favoring the middle class over big business. Brian Keith plays Teddy Roosevelt, last of the great liberal Republicans, in The Wind and the Lion. *Courtesy Metro-Goldwyn-Mayer.*

domestic policies, however, remained in line with today's sense of liberalism: pro-environment, pro–civil rights, and anti–big business. Unfortunately, no film tells his full story, though Roosevelt is portrayed in *War of the Wildcats* (Albert S. Rogell, 1943), also known as *In Old Oklahoma*. The president is approached by two men, a cowboy former member of Roosevelt's Rough Riders (John Wayne), the other that genre villain the Eastern man in a suit (Albert Dekker). Both are eager to drill on or near Indian-owned land. In the film, Roosevelt openly admits his bias in favor of the onetime sergeant who served with him at San Juan Hill. Yet he makes clear that he will turn over the oil-drilling rights to whichever competitor guarantees him two essential elements: concern for the environment and fairness to the Indians.

During Teddy Roosevelt's turn-of-the-century presidency America entered into a period of cataclysmic change. Along with it arrived a polar alteration involving national political identities. Eight years after his first victory at the polls, outgoing president Roosevelt's viewpoint, so in line with Lincoln's, no longer defined the Republican Party.[11] Teddy Roosevelt would be succeeded by his former secretary of war William H. Taft. Roosevelt became so disenchanted with Taft that four years later he again threw his hat into the ring, running in 1912 on the liberal Bull Moose ticket. Old-time progressive Republicans bolted the party and voted for him. The nouveau conservatives supported Taft, a split that ensured Democrat Woodrow Wilson would win. When Teddy Roosevelt's cousin Franklin Delano Roosevelt sought the presidency some two decades later, he did so as a liberal Democrat. During the first quarter of the twentieth century, what had emerged as the two major American political parties completely reversed their identities.

Back in 1881, that situation constituted the shape of things to come. The cowboy element was at one with Southern Dixiecrats, an arch-conservative wing of the populist Democratic Party.[12] They remained within that party's ranks largely due to inertia and bitterness over Lincoln's election, even as liberalism later manifested through the administrations of Truman, Kennedy, Johnson, and Carter. The confused symbolism about what the term "cowboy politics" meant occurred during the 1964 election, when Texan Lyndon B. Johnson, Democratic president since the death of JFK the previous year, ran against Arizona's Barry Goldwater, a Republican. Both men were known to wear cowboy hats despite the polarity of their politics.

Johnson took the FDR notion of a large federal government further with his Great Society programs, qualifying him as one of the most liberal presidents on domestic issues.[13] But after promising that American boys would not die doing in Vietnam the job that Asian boys ought to be performing, he escalated the war, turning liberals against his "imperialist" foreign policy. These were not far from Teddy Roosevelt's "gunboat diplomacy," if with jets substituted for warships, but in the different context of the 1960s, progressives could no longer ignore such matters.

On the other hand, Barry Goldwater, who favored small government at home, openly admitted that if the U.S. military was going to be in Vietnam, it must be there to achieve an unqualified win.[14] This implied that he might employ nuclear weapons, terrifying at a time when the film *Dr. Strangelove, or How I Learned to Stop Worrying and Love the Bomb* (Stanley Kubrick, 1964) offered an end-of-the-world cautionary fable. It is not for nothing that when in the Terry Southern–authored black comedy a nuclear weapon is dropped on Russia, the character who does it is a man of the West. Major King Kong is played by cowboy character actor Slim Pickens. Major Kong even rides the bomb down, waving his Stetson the entire time. With that iconic image from the movies, the term "cowboy politics" forever ceased to mean liberal progressivism, coming to instead imply a wild 'n' woolly redneck sensibility.

With the failure of Johnson's presidency, many former blue-collar Democrats voted for the supposedly unelectable Richard M. Nixon, a little-liked Republican. Following Nixon's failed presidency and eventual resignation,

Reconfiguring cowboy politics. In the black comedy Dr. Strangelove, Slim Pickens *became a potent symbol beginning in the 1960s as a crazed Texas redneck armed with atomic weaponry in place of old-fashioned pistols. Courtesy Columbia Pictures.*

they then unenthusiastically switched back to Carter. This Marxist dialectic continued: when Carter came to be perceived as a failure, they finally bolted and became Reagan Democrats, voting Republican even if they had not officially changed party affiliation. In time, many would do precisely that. If the stage had been set with Goldwater, Reagan successfully reimagined the term "cowboy politics." In due time, to ensure his eventual election, the first president Bush (George H. W.) studied John Wayne movies, negating his Ivy League wimp image by semisuccessfully posing as a cowboy. His son George W. would identify himself as a Texas rancher. It is not difficult to grasp, then, why from 1970 on the Western movie, which previously appealed to a wide, broad cross-section of the public, came to be considered a red-state art form.

To fully understand the events back in Tombstone of 1881 we must remember that they occurred a full quarter century before party ideologies began to reverse themselves. The chronology leads to confusion about the political situation in Arizona. In *Doc* (Frank Perry, 1971), journalist turned screenwriter Pete Hamill reduced the complexity of the election of a Coch-ise County sheriff in hopes this previously nondramatized incident might comment on a deeply divided contemporary America. In August 1968, the Chicago police force, under orders from Mayor Richard Daley (though a Democratic, a new proponent of law and order), engaged in what would be characterized as a "police riot."[15] Long-haired young people taking to the streets during the Democratic convention were brutally and in many cases unnecessarily assaulted. As the "hippies" hoped to alter the upcoming presidential election, Hamill—who as a journalist reported on that disaster—believed the Tombstone election could be reworked as a metaphor for contemporary politics. In Hamill's reductive version, a newspaperman would represent the modern media that decried the situation in Tombstone. He picked Dan Greenberg, a pithy New York–based comedian, for the part. No wonder, then, that director Perry chose for his Earp not another tall, silent type (Fonda, Scott, Garner, Lancaster, Joel McCrea, Hugh O'Brian) but an actor of less-conventional good looks. Harris Yulin resembled Nixon, the Republican who won the presidency in 1968.

The tradition of reimagining the past to make a statement in the present, which may—if an audience grasps its intended meaning—alter things for the future can be traced back through the films of John Ford to the plays of Shakespeare and, for that matter, the drama of Sophocles. The problem with *Doc* is not its creator's intentions but the ineptness with which they were executed. The historical nineteenth-century liberal Republican Earp was transformed into a twentieth-century conservative Republican. He appears a raw capitalist, interested only in money. Earp attempts to seize control of local law enforcement for no other reason than to intimidate his business competitors. While the actual Earp may not have been the idealized figure of myth moved to wear a badge by deep convictions, neither was he the cold-blooded figure depicted in *Doc*.[16]

The portrayals in *Tombstone* and *Wyatt Earp* come considerably closer to capturing the complexity of a flesh-and-blood man interested in making money, certainly, yet to a degree motivated by a true sense of civic duty, that is, an enlightened capitalist. In *Doc*, Earp appears not only a villain but a self-conscious one, all but tugging at the edges of his moustache while explaining plans to seize power to his friend Holliday (Stacy Keach):

DOC (SURPRISED): We sound like real bad people, Wyatt.
WYATT (CYNICALLY): We *are*, Doc.

Clum, editor of the *Epitaph* (though not in this film also the mayor), serves as Hamill's authorial spokesperson. With elimination of Tombstone's other newspaper, the *Nugget*, which represented John Behan and the cowboy element, the *Epitaph* is falsely portrayed as anti-Earp. As to Behan, Clum here begrudgingly supports him because the man is "dumb but honest." Behan is played by an older actor (Richard McKenzie), turning him into a Gabby Hayes–type, grizzled old-timer. As *Tombstone* and *Wyatt Earp* accurately show, Behan was a young man. He and Earp served as one another's doppelganger, assuming opposing sides in a political and economic conflict. Also, both were enamored with actress Josephine Marcus, who eventually married Earp.[17]

In *Doc*'s O.K. Corral finale the Earps arrive carrying shotguns; historically only Holliday had one. The Clantons are lovable long-hairs, several unarmed. Those Clantons who do carry guns reach for them only after being fired on. One Earp dies on the spot. Showing no emotion for his fallen sibling, Wyatt seizes the opportunity to make a speech about the need for law and order; Holliday is so disgusted that he mounts and rides away. We don't see the legal proceedings the Earps had to submit to, depicted in *Hour of the Gun*. According to *Doc*, presented to a trusting audience as more realistic than any previous Hollywood Earp film, people could walk—or ride—away from a killing. In attempting to diminish the mythic West, *Doc* actually enhanced it.

Man of the West. Few actors have so strikingly embodied the spirit of rugged individualism as Charlton Heston, seen here in Will Penny. *This iconic quality renders him a strange choice for the part of a close ally to gun-control maven Wyatt Earp in* Tombstone. *Courtesy Paramount Pictures.*

"FROM MY COLD, DEAD HANDS"

GUN CONTROL IN THE WEST AND WESTERNS

I'm not saying you can't own guns. I'm not saying you can't carry guns. All I'm saying is that you can't carry guns in town.
—MARSHAL VIRGIL EARP IN *TOMBSTONE*, 1993

In *Tombstone*, one Earp ally, Henry Hooker, is played by Charlton Heston. Hooker's ranch, crossing two counties, was the largest in Arizona at that time. Toward *Tombstone*'s end, Hooker informs a distraught Earp that his men may safely rest on Hooker's property. As with Mitchum, this actor's long association with the Western in nearly a dozen films adds an aura of Hollywood lore to the piece. A fascinating question, though, is why Heston agreed to appear. By gracing *Tombstone* with his presence, this American icon seemingly bestowed his blessing on the project, including the film's values. Yet this onetime president of the National Rifle Association in 2000 held a piece high above his head and claimed that if a federal law were passed that restricted the ownership of weapons, those central government men in black suits—the modern Earps—would have to tear it out of his "cold, dead hands."[1] In *Tombstone* and the history on which it is based, Wyatt and his brothers were willing to do exactly that. Had the Clantons only thought of it, they might have waved "Don't Tread On Me!" banners, the slogan of those New Englanders in Concord, Massachusetts, who opposed their distant government's decision to seize guns and powder, this leading to the opening battle of the Revolutionary War on April 19, 1775.[2]

Simply put, the Clanton-McLaury faction constituted Arizona's predecessor to the tea party. How could Heston, whose positions crystallized the National Rifle Association while setting the stage for the tea party, accept a role in a film that contradicted what he believed? Heston's speech before the National Press Club on September 11, 1997 might well have been delivered by Ike Clanton: "I say that the Second Amendment is, in order of importance, the first amendment . . . America's first freedom, the one that protects all the others . . . It is the first among equals . . . the one right that allows rights to exist."

The greater paradox is that most tea partiers, many of whom wear cowboy hats as a symbol of oneness with the conservative politics of Reagan, Heston, Bush, Wayne, and others, attended and apparently enjoyed *Tombstone*. Many no doubt saw it as an old-fashioned Western of the type that, at least in their minds, embodied the values they embrace. The movie's greatest box-office success came in the West,[3] where the oater is still revered, red states where what is today called "cowboy politics" dominates. Yet judging from *Tombstone* and the vast majority of similarly themed Westerns produced not just recently but over the past century, an irony exists between the perception of what a Western is "about" and the actuality of its message and/or meaning.

Wyatt Earp films are essential to the Western. Yet with the exception only of *Doc*, they come down in favor of the Earps and, by implication, gun control. Case in point: *Wichita* (Jacques Tourneur, 1955). Innocent people are wounded, sometimes killed, during the hoorahing of the title town by visiting Texans. Wyatt (Joel McCrea) has what he considers the perfect solution: arriving cowboys can get drunk, visit whores, hoot and holler, even beat each other to a pulp. But they must check their guns so that bystanders or other cowboys won't die. "If men don't have guns," he tells the town council, "they can't shoot each other." This Western expresses more or less the opposite of a National Rifle Association slogan, "Guns don't kill people; people kill people." According to McCrea's Earp, while that may be partly true, the most effective way to keep people from killing people is to take their guns away, at least when they are around other people in public rather than in the privacy of their own places. A raw capitalist (Walter Coy), fearing that the

Don't bring your guns to town! As depicted in Wyatt Earp, *gun control worked less well in Tombstone, a red-state town in which the Earps were perceived as intruders. Courtesy Warner Brothers.*

Texans might take their herds elsewhere and cost him money, comes around to Earp's way of thinking after his beloved wife is killed by a stray bullet.

Clearly *Wichita*, a representative B+ oater of its era, demands to be read as pro–gun control. Four years later, McCrea would play Earp's protégé Bat Masterson in *Gunfight at Dodge City* (Joseph M. Newman, 1959). When Dodge's town council questions the viability of gun control, McCrea references his earlier role with a wink: "There's a town marshal over in Wichita by the name of Wyatt Earp who gets the job done." Self-referencing, apparently, is nothing new in the movies. Perhaps no Western makes so strong a statement in favor of gun control as this. In the opening, "feeble-minded" (in the phraseology of the era) Billy Thompson (Wright King) reaches in awe for Bat's gun.

BILLY: Can't I just shoot it *once*?
BAT: No! I don't want you to even *touch* it.

Confused, Billy asks why Bat taught him to fire a rifle. Bat replies that such a weapon is used to hunt buffalo. The handgun has a far darker purpose: killing humans. What's it like, Billy asks his experienced mentor, to kill a man? Any romanticism is curtly dismissed:

Well, Billy, I'll tell you. It's not so good. First you stand there, facing him. You want to run and hide. Hide anywhere. But you can't . . . so you watch his eyes, praying to God Almighty he'll back down . . . You try to say something . . . But before you can, it's too late. He's not there anymore. The cuspidor spills and spit rolls all over. People run in and want to buy you a drink. And then you go outside, somewhere where no one will see you. And you vomit.

At film's end, when Bat is forced to face off with a crooked sheriff and shoot him down, most of those words are repeated as a voice-over. With his opponent dead on the ground, we see something that no other generic Western has offered: the hero walks into an alley alone; the townsfolk gather around the fallen body while Bat heads off to puke.

One way to marginalize the impact of such films is to posit Earp and Masterson Westerns as some unique subgenre. Despite the popularity of these movies and the long-running TV shows *The Life and Legend of Wyatt Earp* (1955–1961) and *Bat Masterson* (1958–1961), filmed episodes about one or the other add up to several hundred. The number of Westerns, film and TV, on varied other subjects run into the thousands.[4] Earp cinema, however prominent, constitutes but a miniscule percentage of Westerns. If it was only these films that came out against "the gun," we might argue that they exist as an aberration to the generalized form. That is not the case. The vast majority of Westerns portray guns in an unfavorable light.

This becomes clear in two seminal Westerns starring Gregory Peck, each made during the 1950s. *The Gunfighter* (Henry King, 1950) provided a breakthrough in the creation of that postwar brand of oater known as "the adult Western," playing down action in favor of psychological penetration of a gunman's mind.[5] Predating *High Noon* (1952) and *Shane* (1953), this dark, somber mood piece concerns the Texas *pistolero* Ringo, here called Jimmy, during his final hours.[6] An old man though not yet thirty years of age, in every town he runs into some punk kid eager to build his reputation. In the beginning Jimmy reluctantly kills one such boy (Richard Jaeckel). At the end he is done in by another (Skip Homier), though there's the implication that our anti-hero lets this lad win. In his own youth, Ringo doomed himself the moment he took up the gun. Now, in premature old age, he cannot return to his wife and child, though he dreams of just such domesticity. In the film's finale the cursed kid, virtually Ringo redux, rides out onto the prairie, like Jimmy in the opening, now a Flying Dutchman.

Later that decade, *The Big Country* (William Wyler, 1958) offered one

He who lives by the gun. Ringo (Gregory Peck) must face some punk kid (here, Richard Jaeckel) eager to make his reputation in every two-bit town. Its title aside, The Gunfighter *(1950) was one of the first anti-gun Westerns. Courtesy Twentieth Century-Fox.*

of the gigantic epics that seemed so right for the wide-screen process introduced in late 1954. Peck plays the inverse of his earlier character; here he is James McKay, a refined, educated man from the East who flatly refuses to carry a pistol. Because of an absolute denial to resort to the way of the gun, even when attacked by a man he hates (Chuck Connors), McKay achieves the domesticity Ringo craved and wins in the end, even as Ringo lost. The casting of Peck in polar roles creates a comparison, however unintended, between his two characters and their fates, with gun violence a tragic flaw.

Still, there can be redemption in the Western. This can and does happen, particularly if the gunman senses his mistake early enough. Even Ringo grasped this: "Maybe if I'd only tried sooner . . .." One who does is the greenest member of the title group in *The Magnificent Seven* (John Sturges, 1960). Chico (Horst Bucholz) and two of his *compadres*, Chris (Yul Brynner) and Vin (Steve McQueen), survive the final duel with vicious outlaws. Chico is about to ride off with his companions to new adventures, reconsiders, then heads back down to the village, where he sets his gun aside to engage

An exception to the rule. In Winchester '73, *the hero's (James Stewart) obsessive pursuit of his rifle does not preclude his having it all in the end. Anthony Mann's classic is the most memorable of all pro-gun Westerns. Courtesy Universal Pictures.*

in menial work beside a young woman (Rosenda Monteros) offering him the simple good life. His victory is not lost on the others, who gaze down on the tranquility with open envy.

CHRIS: They win. They always win.
VIN: And us?
CHRIS: We lose. We always lose.

And there are pro-gun Westerns. The title of *Winchester '73* (Anthony Mann, 1950) suggests a pro-gun orientation. Early on, a gunman (James Stewart) enters and wins a Dodge City shooting match judged by law officers Earp (Will Geer) and Masterson (Steve Darrell). The prize is the title rifle, "the gun that won the West." When a villain (Stephen McNally) steals the piece, Stewart pursues him virtually across the entire West. Along the way he meets an eligible young woman (Shelley Winters) but can't consider committing to her until he kills the bad man, though that fellow turns out to be the hero's brother, and reclaims the prize weapon. In the final shot, Stewart has the girl under one arm, the gun clutched in the other. In a Mann movie, one does not have to choose between them.

That memorable film, however, proves the exception to the general rule. This holds true for Hollywood versions of the legend of William H. Bonney, born Henry McCarty and better known as Billy the Kid, the young outlaw who, according to countless old tales, rode free and easy and shot twenty-one men, one for each year of his life.[7] The number was likely six, each shot from ambush rather than encountered in a pure gunfight. Three films will suffice here. In *The Kid from Texas* (Kurt Neumann, 1950), Billy (Audie Murphy) first appears as a gunslick, a punk who shoots first and asks questions later. As in actuality he meets the educated English rancher John Tunstall (here named Roger Jameson, played by Shepperd Strudwick), who at least in movie mythology and New Mexico legend becomes not only the Kid's employer but a kindly foster father. Brought into a fine home for the first time, Billy listens as an elegant young woman (Gale Storm) plays piano. Music hath charms to soothe the savage breast: Billy wants to be a part of that civilized lifestyle. The Englishman makes clear what Billy's first step must be—to hang up his guns. Here we see voluntary rather than forced gun control, acceptable as a rugged individual's choice not demanded by any government. The impact is clear. From the moment they lock away those Colts,

Billy becomes a kinder, gentler version of himself. "You've changed, Billy," his mentor says with a smile, "since we've put those guns away." Sadly, reality intrudes. Members of a rival ranch kill the Englishman. Atavistic, the Kid straps on his pistols, using them even more ruthlessly than before.

The film allows us to comprehend W. H. Bonney's reversion to violence without justifying it. A victim of circumstances, the Kid is doomed from the moment he does "what a man's gotta do"; that is, he degenerates to the machismo of gunplay, mistaking that for true masculinity. "Melancholy" best describes the finale. Billy appears to willingly go to his death at the hands of Pat Garrett (Frank Wilcox), implying a repudiation of the way of the gun.

One element that allows *The Kid from Texas* to stand out among Billy the Kid films is that it is one of the few that ignore the dramatically potent if largely mythical notion of a deep friendship between Bonney and Garrett.[8] Nowhere is that relationship so fully developed as in *The Left-Handed Gun* (Arthur Penn, 1958), derived from a Gore Vidal script and starring Paul Newman as Billy and John Dehner as Garrett. First comes the Kid's admiration for the Englishman, played here by Colin Keith Johnston. His historic name, John Tunstall, is used. Billy discusses him with a cowhand (James Best):

BILLY: He sure doesn't think much of a gun, does he?
TOM: Nah, he's sure a funny one. He thinks the only way to avoid gun trouble is not to wear one.

As in all Billy the Kid films, the Englishman dies unarmed. This time it's best-buddy Garrett who tries to convince the Kid not to seek blood vengeance. Initially it might appear that this and other Billy the Kid movies insist on the need to carry a gun. The pacifist, however well meaning, proves naïve, and his assassins are eliminated only by a smoking pistol. Tunstall's idealistic theory proves sadly inappropriate for the real world. That, however, is not the attitude at work. Yes, guns exist; only a fool would hope or pretend they might simply go away. Yet a distinction is drawn between personal vengeance and law and order. Pat Garrett begs Billy to allow him to legally employ his two guns to bring in the killers, shooting only if they resist. If Billy agrees, he'll achieve the redemption he desires by surrendering the responsibility to the community at large. Instead, he does it his way. The rugged individualist must die by the gun of a man who, owing to the star on his chest, defends social values, an official whose job is to restrain personal freedoms that might also, when considered from a different angle, be described as chaos.

Chisum (Andrew V. McLaglen, 1970) is unique within the Billy Bonney Western subgenre as the first to halt the story before the final showdown. Intact, though, is the key issue of guns and whether it is ever (even after the murder of so fine a man) legitimate to solve problems through violence. That again is how the Kid (Geoffrey Duel) plans to get even with the mob that engineered Tunstall's assassination. As the title makes clear, John Chisum (John Wayne), Tunstall's partner, not only appears but dominates. Here a fictional niece (Pamela McMyler) arrives from the East to fulfill that long-standing genre convention of a civilized woman showing up in the untamed wilderness. She's attracted to both Billy and Pat (Glenn Corbett). At first, former bad-boy Billy appears likely to win her hand. Then the Kid straps on his guns again. Morally disgusted, she turns to Pat, who carries both a star and a gun. What he stands for is not the way of the gun, though he owns, carries, and uses one, but the broader concept of law and order, nineteenth-century fashion.

By 1968, if law and order were still upheld by retro-conservative Democrats like Chicago's Mayor Daley, the idea was well on its way to becoming the hallmark of the Reagan Republicans. Ronald Reagan entirely abandoned film and television for politics, won the governorship of California in 1966, and pushed on toward the presidency. He had been a Democrat and moved over during the early 1960s. Heston made that same change later in the decade.

Shortly before his death, when asked why he went from liberal to conservative, Heston answered: "I didn't. The world shifted around me."[9] That reply helps explain the surprising political subtext of Westerns, even those that, like *My Darling Clementine*, eliminate any actual political contests. John Clum's Law and Order League was pro-church but also pro-education.[10] The first of those concepts is today considered conservative, the latter, liberal. Law and order are not Republican or Democrat. Things change. And as they do, our perceptions must adjust to every topic from history to Hollywood, Westerns included. Such an approach holds true not only for Westerns based on history but those derived from fiction.

The original traditional hero. Owen Wister's The Virginian *fused the nineteenth century's hardworking cowboy with a rare breed, the professional* pistolero, *resulting in an American hero, what Robert Warshow labeled "the Westerner." Gary Cooper, Mary Brian, and Walter Huston star in the 1929 version. Courtesy Paramount Pictures.*

WAY OF THE GUN

VIOLENCE IN AMERICAN LIFE

Ride back, Joey, and tell your mother there are no more guns in the valley.
—SHANE TO THE HOMESTEADERS' SON IN *SHANE*, 1953

So far as the twentieth-century Western novel is concerned, the form begins with Owen Wister's *The Virginian* (1902). Film versions were produced in 1914 (Cecil B. DeMille, director; Dustin Farnum, star), 1923 (Tom Forman; Kenneth Hanlan), 1929 (Victor Fleming; Gary Cooper), 1946 (Stuart Gilmore; Joel McCrea), and 2000 (TV movie, TVM; Bill Pullman; Pullman). A successful NBC series ran from 1962 to 1971. Wister subtitled his book "A Horseman of the Plains" to self-consciously fuse his unnamed cowboy hero with earlier renderings of chivalry. Though we may now connect that term with the British tales of Arthur's knights, "chivalry" originated as a French word from the early Renaissance that posits a man on horseback as the ultimate hero.[1] This vision can be traced back to the Greek classical age. Even humble foot soldiers approaching the walls of Troy carried emblems of a horse as an homage to the goddess Athena. She, in armor, stood for both wisdom and war; importantly, Athena brought the secret of taming horses to their heroes.[2] No wonder the horse was their icon of choice to set outside

Troy while seeming to depart. The continuing preference of a mounted hero over one on foot helps explain the cult of the cavalry over infantry in literature relating to the Indian wars of the Far West. Also, it explains the romanticizing of the cowboy, a man doing a dull job who more often than not did not carry a gun, much less become expert at its use,[3] but not of the mountain man, who walked into the wilderness and regularly fought Indians in Rocky Mountain days that truly were filled with high adventure.[4] While mountain men did own horses, paintings by George Catlin mostly depict them on foot, ruling out the trapper as hero.

Shrouding the past in nostalgia, Americans prefer to see the Old West as the Greeks saw the era of Troy and the English their legends of Arthur: a time of heroes who lived by a strict code, meeting as a community to pledge their allegiance before riding out singly to perform individual valorous deeds. Greek and English conceptions hail not from Herodotus and Holinshed but from Homer and Shakespeare. Derived from epic poetry, they are set in glamorized versions of past periods that more likely were horrible in the daily lives of ordinary citizens. In endless, often ritualized retellings, these literary—and in our time cinematic—landscapes become unrecognizable when compared to the geography of history. Every nation needs its heroes, its origination myth; America picked, in methods both conscious (Theodore Roosevelt's tomes) and unconscious (Buffalo Bill's Great Wild West Show) a Dream West and the heroes who would occupy it. In this vision, eventually perfected during the early twentieth century by Hollywood, the cowboy became the equivalent of the knight, samurai, or, in a subsequent mythic conception, Jedi. The humble cowboy, not the worthier mountain man, achieved iconic status largely because he sat tall in the saddle.

James Fenimore Cooper's tales of Natty Bumppo in the early frontier of upstate New York provided a worthy predecessor to the later variation of what mythologist Joseph Campbell called "the hero with a thousand faces."[5] In the early twentieth century, even as America moved into modernism, Wister rendered the cowboy archetype nameless and set such a fellow high upon a horse in the final frontier of the late nineteenth-century West. From the time of *The Virginian*'s publication for the next half-century—when another writer, Jack Schaefer, would offer an alternative—the American public was in love with generic Westerns. Movies, dime novels, comic books, and in due time TV shows portrayed the image of a cowboy collapsed with that of a gunfighter and a knight without armor. A friend and admirer of Theodore Roosevelt, Owen Wister dedicated his book to the cowboy president. Like Roosevelt, Wister was an educated Easterner who fell in love with, then wrote about a jejune vision of the West. For both men, Western geography implied an ideology, a value system they perceived as descended from ancient traditions yet uniquely American, touching on universal themes while also original and vividly detailed.

The loosely structured set of vignettes focuses on Wister's title character, a mostly silent Southerner who brings the Anglo codes he learned in Old Virginny to a still fresh and isolated corner of the West. During the narrative, Wister's incarnation of the man with no name meets a woman from the East, Molly Wood, shortly after she arrives to become the local schoolmarm. This ploy would regularly be recycled by other writers and by filmmakers, most notably in Ford's variation on the theme in *My Darling Clementine*.

At first, Molly's civilized attitudes cause her to draw back from this virile figure, much as the Brit Cora does from Hawkeye in Cooper's *The Last of the Mohicans* (1826). The Virginian seems to this woman of English values a dark throwback to some earlier form of human existence, the atavistic man-beast so feared by Victorians yet beloved by the Romantics. French philosopher Jean-Jacques Rousseau wrote in 1754, "Natural man is the best man."[6] The Western, from *Last of the Mohicans* through *The Virginian*, is essentially Romantic.[7]

MOLLY: I don't think I like you.
VIRGINIAN: You're going to love me before we get through.

However outraged by his audacity, Molly does in time acquiesce. A major stumbling block to doing so occurs when the Virginian hangs a charming cowpuncher. Steve once rode alongside him as a friend but since turned thief. Here is the code of the West in action. Without effective law established yet in the area or a true sense of community having developed, chaos can only be averted through the most brutal sort of behavior. Steve was warned. He didn't listen. Like the character Jake Spoon in Larry McMurtry's later *Lonesome Dove* (1985) and the 1988 TV miniseries derived from it, Steve accepts his fate. The noose is lowered around his neck not by an angry lynch mob but quietly, by calm friends. These are not the out-of-control rubes we encounter in *The Ox-Bow Incident* (William Wellman, 1943) or *Hang 'Em High* (Ted Post, 1968) stretching the necks of innocent strangers.

The modernist Western. Though Heaven's Gate *draws its subject matter from the Powder River War, which inspired* The Virginian *and* Shane, *this film's approach is decidedly antipastoral, portraying the frontier as filthy and polluted. Courtesy United Artists.*

Rather, they are people with proof, doing so to a friend not out of bloodlust but, in context, necessity. They take no pleasure in the act.

Later the Virginian must shoot it out with Trampas, a smarmy villain who corrupted Steve. Molly begs her now-lover not to go and swears she'll never speak to him again if he steps out onto the street. He does so anyway, wins the gunfight, then returns to find her waiting. The Virginian proves himself "fittest" by surviving and winning her.

Wister (1860–1938) loosely based the book's incidents on the Johnson County War of 1892, in time more realistically and antigenerically realized in *Heaven's Gate* (Michael Cimino, 1980). That deadly conflict between entrenched cowmen and incoming sodbusters would also provide the basis for what many consider Wister's only rival as the great American Western novel, *Shane* (1949), by Jack Schaefer (1907–1991). The book would be filmed in 1953 by George Stevens from a screenplay by A. J. Guthrie Jr., a Pulitzer Prize–winning novelist whose works include *The Big Sky* (1947) and *The Way West* (1949). Each of these would become a film, the former by Howard Hawks (1952) successful, the latter, in 1967 by Andrew McLaglen, not so. There are key similarities other than place and period between *The Virginian* and *Shane*. In each the *pistolero* remains a mystery man addressed only by a nickname. Both authors sensed something special in this type. Wister referred to the Virginian as a "natural aristocrat."[8] Schaefer called Shane a member of a "special breed,"[9] apart from, even above all normal, flawed people. The distinction between these novels is not content but assumed perspective. Wister sides with the ranchers and portrays farmers as petty thieves. Schaefer's book takes the opposite view, idealizing farmers as decent folks. *Shane* might well be thought of as *The Virginian* reimagined from the other end of the gun barrel.

Another notable difference proves more significant for our purposes. Though these fictional tales occur more or less simultaneously in a single area around the Powder River, we ought to note the entirely different eras during which those novelists wrote: Wister immediately after the Western frontier had, according to historian Frederick Jackson Turner, ceased to be,[10] or closed, as the fin de siècle approached; Jack Schaefer at the twentieth century's halfway mark, when values not only regarding the West but American society were in a state of flux. Schaefer's work calls into question everything essential to Wister's earlier vision. Schaefer comes out in favor of community loyalty over rugged individualism. If Wister's work ought to be considered conservative, expressing a red-state vision, then Schaefer's just as clearly

Bang! You're dead. The early oater The Great Train Robbery *concludes as an outlaw turns his gun on the audience in an unconscious act of deconstruction, setting up an ongoing relationship between movies and audiences and eventually serving as the opening logo for the James Bond film franchise. Courtesy Thomas Edison Estate.*

qualifies as liberal or blue state. In the former, the rugged individual emerges as a true hero by living out the American Dream. In the latter, a similar figure rides off alone, begrudgingly accepting that he can never belong to the emergent community owing to past deeds. Perhaps only by reading both back to back or seeing the movies in succession can we grasp the full yin/yang, the wide scope of Westerns for expressing polar political ideas.

Notable too is that *The Virginian* defends the way of the gun. In it the Eastern born and bred woman must adjust her civilized notions. Conversely, *Shane* says that if a man is to truly be a man in a human rather than macho sense, he must give up that way. At *Shane*'s beginning, the title character (Alan Ladd) scares off Morgan Ryker (John Dierkes) and several cowhands as they attempt to intimidate homesteader Joe Starrett (Van Heflin), his wife, Marian (Jean Arthur), and their son, Joey (Brandon De Wilde). The cattlemen wish to bring back open range that Ryker's land-baron brother Rufus (Emile Meyer) insists must remain off limits, with farmers' barbed wire preventing his cattle from grazing there. Shane backs them off, not by using his gun but by revealing its presence as a source of potential strength. And through a show of style identical to Cooper's character in the 1929 version of *The Virginian*, he establishes expertise with the weapon without drawing it. Shane then attempts to do what the Virginian will not consider: setting his gun aside. He becomes a farmhand to appease Marian, a woman of moral conscience and, though none of the characters feels comfortable admitting it, attractiveness. To please her, Shane initially refuses to fight in a rough saloon, even with his fists, against Calloway (Ben Johnson), Ryker's Texas-born top hand.

Midway through the film, however, young Joey persuades Shane to retrieve his six-gun from its hiding place to teach him how to shoot. Significantly, from the film's opening moments Joey is attracted to Shane as a hero figure compared to his grubby-looking farmer father. Earlier, Shane was introduced like a knight, riding into the valley in soft buckskins that apparently had never been dirtied during his journeys. Camera angles for *Shane*'s title sequence were chosen to suggest that what occurs on screen may not be the event as it actually happened. More likely, what takes place is a fond remembrance, visually approximating the novel's point of view. Joey, not the lad's name in the book, is a grown man recalling the story years later. What we witness is a nostalgic dream beginning with Shane's arrival. He appears to be dropped into the valley from up above, in Michael Marsden's words, like

While nobody's watching, Shane, may I touch your gun? Joey (Brandon De Wilde) expresses his hero-worship by sneaking into the barn to fetishistically handle the mysterious stranger's piece. Courtesy Paramount Pictures.

a "savior in the saddle."[11] The piece accordingly concludes with the ascension of Shane. Like politics, religion (to be discussed in detail in this book's second half) is essential to the Western and in truth is inseparable from its implied political content.

On the morning following the gunfighter's arrival by happy accident or some machinery of the gods, Joey slips into the barn where Shane sleeps to consider, then tenuously touch his gun. Here again is a moment of fetishization, implying pre-adolescent Joey's Freudian fascination with that object of male power, modeled ages earlier on the phallus, serving ever since in literature as a fitting symbol for that organ.[12] At the movie's midpoint, Shane takes Joey's breath away by firing at small, white stones. Less favorably impressed is Marian, observing from a distance. She wears her faded wedding gown, drawn from its trunk ostensibly for a July Fourth party, unconsciously on her part to attract this impossibly handsome stranger. Any feelings on Marian's part toward Shane are stalled, if not shut down, by what she witnesses. Marian makes it abundantly clear that she does not intend to have her son grow up to be part of a world in which guns determine outcomes. The two debate in low voices the value of violent action. Finally, the title character sums up his entire attitude: "A gun is a tool, as good or as bad as the man using it." Though the man with no name does not precisely speak these words in *The Virginian*, he might well have.

If we were, while reading or watching *Shane*, to accept our male hero as the author's spokesman (as intended in *The Virginian*), his words offer a justification for continued acceptance of guns in American society. His line has been taken to imply, as Richard Slotkin argues, that "the underlying message of the narrative" is that "'a good man with a gun' is in every sense the best of men."[13] An analysis of the conversation suggests something else entirely. Shane's remark must be considered in context. "Remember that," he—Virginian-like—tells Marian. If in that other work Molly says nothing, defeated in her fast-fading vision of a woman-directed world, Schaefer's Marian refuses to do so. She asserts herself, expressing what might be interpreted as the feminine, even feminist, point of view: "We'd all be better off if there were no more guns in the valley." Here, the man finds himself unable to answer. The look on Ladd's face suggests that Shane has been ideologically defeated. On some level, he grasps that Marian is right. Which means, within the film's dramatic and moral contexts, that he is wrong.

Apparently, Shane tosses this around in his head during the film's second half, if too silent a type to articulate any thoughts or feelings. Shane does bring it up in his brief talk with Joey after the boy's hero has ridden into town alone and killed both Ryker brothers and the hired gun Jack Wilson (Walter Jack Palance). Farmer Starrett and rancher Ryker are presented realistically as two flawed, well-meaning men on opposite sides of the barbed-wire fence. Shane and Wilson emerge as allegorical figures, the latter outfitted in jet black even as Shane appears an Americanized white knight. A kettle drum booms during the prelude to their inevitable duel, the situation elevated from its Western setting to a universal joust between good and evil. Shane's six-shooter may swing by his side in place of the long sword of an English knight or cultivated blade of an Asian samurai. Yet he is one with them. We are no longer revisiting history but whisked away into a land of legend. True to form, Shane lives out his assigned fate as what Slotkin refers to as "an armed redeemer" and "the sole vindicator of the 'liberties of the people,'" as such "the 'indispensable man' in the quest for progress."[14]

The real gunfighter. While The Virginian *and* Shane *transformed the professional* pistolero *into a hero figure, Ford's* The Man Who Shot Liberty Valance *featured a more accurate portrait in Lee Marvin's cold-blooded assassin. Courtesy Paramount Pictures.*

What occurs here reverses all the moral implications in *The Virginian.* There, the hero with a gun, having killed Trampas, reclaims Molly, as she now accepts the wisdom of his ways. Machismo—the way of the gun— wins out as Molly fully submits to male power. The Virginian remains what E. M. Forster might have categorized as a static, or unchanged, character. At the end of *Shane,* Joey begs the gunfighter to come back "home." There are myriad reasons Shane cannot, among them the conflict between Shane and Starrett over beautiful Marian hardly being insignificant. Far more fundamental, though, is the midpoint conversation between Shane and Marian. Eyes misty, he instructs the boy to "tell your mother there are no more guns in the valley" before riding off into a sunrise at once mellow and melancholy. Again, Shane was produced early in the twentieth century's second half, among the first of a revisionist version of the Western that maintained genre aspects only to reverse their implications. As to a pair of previously cited films, which appeared more or less simultaneously at mid-century, we might consider *Winchester '73* the last great film in *The Virginian* mode and *The Gunfighter* an initial foray into the emergent Western redux that would shortly crystallize in *Shane.*

It's a woman's *world! In the early twentieth-century Western* The Virginian, *the female submissively set aside her anti-gun values. In films made after 1950, the woman more likely wins out, as she (Jean Arthur) does in* Shane. *Courtesy Paramount Pictures.*

IT'S A MAN'S WORLD?
GENDER POLITICS ON HOLLYWOOD'S FRONTIER

All you need to make a movie is a guy, a girl, and a gun.
—JEAN-LUC GODDARD, PRESS CONFERENCE FOR *BREATHLESS*, 1960

In George Stevens's 1953 film *Shane*, the title character, not Marian, proves dynamic. She remains constant while he arcs. In so doing, Shane accepts her antigun attitude as the right way, at least for the future, a progressive future, if one that could never have come into being were it not for his final burst of conservative gunplay. Shane's confrontation with three men might be thought of as the last old-time battle, quite necessary for the closure of a way of life from which Shane cannot extricate himself, however much he may want to. And guns, albeit necessary in the past, must, according to this film, have no role in the world Marian will now create. Like the cattlemen he kills, Shane belongs to the nineteenth century; the Starretts presage the twentieth. Dialogue makes this abundantly clear:

SHANE: Your days are over, old man.
RYKER: Yours too, gunfighter.
SHANE: The difference is, I know it.

The Virginian, by allowing the man with no name/man with a gun to win, renders the figure epic. Conversely, *Shane* posits him as tragic, his final victory pyrrhic. Shane assures the community's survival by purging the valley of its links to the past. In so doing, in the only manner open to him, Shane eliminates any chance of finding a home. Like Oedipus of old cleansing Thebes by his cathartic sacrifice, then leaving alone, Shane becomes a self-sacrificial lamb.

If *The Virginian* defined the Western during the twentieth century's first half, *Shane* did so for the next fifty years. Essentially, *Shane* rejects and replaces *The Virginian*, thereby providing a new archetype for an old form. The contemporary Western *Home from the Hill* (Vincente Minnelli, 1960) illustrates the manner in which the "man's man," inebriated in the culture of guns and amoral seduction of women, is criticized rather than celebrated in post-*Shane* Westerns. Robert Mitchum plays the land baron Captain Wade Hunnicutt, who early on is nearly assassinated by a stranger. "I don't know you," Hunnicutt says after the attempt fails. "You know my *wife*," comes the reply. "Stay away!" Shortly Hunnicutt makes clear that his pursuit of (mostly married) women connects with his desire to hunt. The two—sexual conquest, killing—fuse in his psyche: "I take it as my right to cross any man's fences when I'm huntin."

With a double meaning implied for gun as phallus, here is individualism at its least sensitive. "Sensitive," though, is the correct term to describe Hunnicutt's teenage son by marriage, Theron (George Hamilton). In his room, books—presents from his mother, Hannah (Eleanor Parker)—are piled everywhere. Hunnicutt considers them disparagingly, scoffing: "This is a boy's room. Come downstairs and I'll show you how a *man* lives." They visit his den. There, guns, from ancient flintlocks through Wild West Winchesters to state-of-the-art weaponry, line the wall. In between are the stuffed heads of animals he has killed all over the world. Hoping to save Theron from the maternal influence of his artistic mother, Hunnicutt drags his son away from a schoolroom to visit the wilds. "From now on," he mutters, "you're going to learn from *the woods*!"

Notably, Hunnicutt's philosophy is naturalistic, not Romantic. The great outdoors does not constitute some good garden, a concept he would reject as effeminate, but Joseph Conrad's heart of darkness, the jungle. "What a man hunts out there," he explains, "is *himself*." Kill to live; live to kill.

His plan to educate the boy may succeed: the first time Theron fires a

Like father, like son. (a) In Home from the Hill *land baron Wade Hunnicutt (Robert Mitchum) relaxes in his study, its walls lined with guns and big-game trophies, his "bitches" by his side. (b) Rejecting his mother's genteel influence, their son (George Hamilton) gradually assumes his father's macho identity. Courtesy Metro-Goldwyn-Mayer.*

rifle, his eyes light up with orgasmic excitement. Hunnicutt drinks, gambles, and smokes. Spare time is spent with other men and his dogs. He ignores his trophy wife, whom he leaves alone upstairs, unable or unwilling to maintain a complex relationship with the person who exists behind that beautiful façade. His only interest in her is for display or sex, which she has long since come to resent and refuse. The film's authorial voice agrees with her. The designated conscience figure, Dr. Reuben Carson (Ray Teal), upbraids Hunnicutt for his simplistic thinking:

> I want you to know how we Texans get our reputation for violence. It's grown men like you who still play with guns. You never will grow up.

Doc's words to this wealthy cattleman set the stage for another doctor's similar description of two poor cowboys in *Will Penny* (Tom Gries, 1967). The title character (Charlton Heston) helps a wounded pal (Anthony Zerbe) into a small hamlet. As a doctor (William Schallert) treats the bleeding man, he inquires as to what happened. With embarrassment, Penny admits that they entered into an argument with passersby about who fired first at an elk. Dumbfounded, the doctor mutters: "Dangerous children!" A term, "Peter Pan syndrome," would be coined to describe such behavior.[1] In *Home from the Hill*, Doc expresses the same point of view. The seemingly strong father, not the presumed weakling son, rates as an arrested adolescent. Theron is in touch with his feminine side, struggling to resist his dad's brainwashing and become a man in the human rather than macho sense. Like Brandon De Wilde's character with Paul Newman's in *Hud* (Martin Ritt, 1963), Theron has the potential to emerge from under the shadow of traditional masculinity. To do so, though, he must reject the apparent man's man he earlier idolized. The tragedy here is that he proves unable.

Initially Theron is a foil to a rugged ranch hand, Rafe Copley (George Peppard), who recalls his mentor taking him out to hunt. When this youth killed for the first time the older man dipped the boy's fingers in the warm blood and painted a savage sign on his forehead. Not surprisingly, Hunnicutt turns out to have been that mentor and Rafe his out-of-wedlock son. Their relationship serves as a precedent to the similar bond between Newt and Call in Larry McMurtry's *Lonesome Dove* (1985). In a conclusion to *Home from the Hill* that combines Greek tragedy with a biblical sensibility, Hunnicutt's sins from the past bring down his household, himself included. When he is at last shot by that still-angry husband, the fully brainwashed Theron grabs a gun and kills that man rather than allow the court system to handle things. Theron is forced to run, leaving Libby Halstead (Luanna Patten), the girl both boys coveted. It's Abraham, Isaac, and Ishmael all over again, this time with Isaac the one who must go, every man's hand against his, his hand against every man's. Adding to the cautionary fable, the seeming Ishmael figure, Rafe arcs in an opposite direction. Opting for domesticity, he marries the girl impregnated by his own half-brother. In the finale, Rafe appears feminized by her and wants a person-to-person relationship. She instructs him; he rejects the gun culture that he had learned from the now rejected, deceased father.

A predecessor to Hunnicutt as the flawed protagonist of *Home from the Hill* appears in *Tribute to a Bad Man* (Robert Wise, 1956). James Cagney as Jeremy Roddock offers a fully developed portrait of a man of deep emotion whose personal code does not allow him to express his feelings in words. This might make him appear womanly, precisely what he—and all his macho-minded counterparts—most fear. As seen through the eyes of a young drifter, Steve Miller (Don Dubbins), this narrative suggests an explanation for Roddock's behavior but never defends it. He is yet another man who has created an empire with his bare hands. Roddock's common-law wife (Irene Pappas) is Jocasta, adding to the work's self-consciously tragic sensibility. As with the progressive young hero Matthew Garth (Montgomery Clift) in *Red River* (Howard Hawks, 1948), who finds himself locked in a love-hate relationship with an older traditionalist, Tom Dunson (John Wayne), Steve carries principles of the East—liberal, even feminine—onto the prairie.

Steve Miller takes on the role of Roddock's foster son. He grasps Roddock's true, full greatness in the Greek epic-tragic sense of that term. Also, though, he gradually becomes aware of Roddock's deep-seated flaw that might bring this remarkable man down: a harsh, unforgiving attitude toward human weakness. Likely, this prejudice is born of Roddock's own profound if repressed fear that beneath his surface show of unrelenting machismo he himself may actually be the weakest of all men. He resembles Dunson in that character's disdain for "quitters," men who attempt to leave during the cattle drive; Dunson lives in daily denial of having done precisely that fifteen years earlier. Likewise, Roddock wants to lynch cattle thieves. The film hints that he began as just such a thief; what he hopes to hang is that part of himself. Roddock's foster son, again like Matthew Garth, does not so much disagree with the verdict as the process. A trial would also lead to a hanging; the youth never once questions the rightness of legal capital punishment.

To be reborn, able to survive in an emerging world rather than dissolve along with the fast-fading frontier, the traditional male Roddock must learn that "soft" and "gentle" are not one and the same. Yet the ending manages to play as upbeat, Roddock averting his seemingly inevitable fate. About to hang Lars Peterson (Vic Morrow), the son of an old friend, Roddock can't fathom how terribly cold the youth has become.

RODDOCK: I'm sorry you're so hard, boy.
LARS: I learned from you.
RODDOCK: Then I'm sorry for both of us.

With that line, Roddock's arc begins. He spares his captives. Hearing of this, the woman who was about to leave decides to stay. "I love you," Jocasta tells him. Perhaps someday he will be able to return those words. Not yet; he hasn't come that far. But as few actors other than Cagney could manage, he communicates his own like feelings with his eyes. She understands. That's enough, at least for now. Their personal problems are far from solved. But there is a light at the end of their emotional tunnel. As to the boy, who Oedipus-like hoped to win Jocasta away from Roddock, he accepts this. A blue-stater by birth, he—significantly, the audience surrogate—has no problem expressing his feelings in words: "I loved them both," he admits while riding away.

For the red-state male, this isn't so easy, not even the younger incarnations who prove more progressive than their old male mentors. In *Red River*, Dunson as well as Matthew Garth find themselves unable to articulate such emotions. "Anyone can see you two love each other," Tess (Joanne Dru) informs them. They cannot use the word "love" with other men or with women, though that doesn't mean they fail to feel it. Their psyches undergo the emotion; a macho sense of self makes verbal expression impossible.

In *The Searchers* (John Ford, 1956), young Martin Pawley (Jeff Hunter) returns after five years and expects his onetime girlfriend to be patiently waiting. He wrote her only once during the absence. "At least you could have said that you love me," Laurie (Vera Miles) weeps. As if with rocks in his mouth, Marty stumblingly suggests he thought she knew as much without the necessity of words. Men are from Mars, women from Venus. The West only intensifies that truth.

Here is a motif that runs through the genre. In *Duel in the Sun* (King Vidor, 1946), the seemingly cold cattle baron Senator Jackson McCanles (Lionel Barrymore) has not uttered a kind word to his long-suffering wife, Laura Belle (Lillian Gish), for decades. This owes to his fear that she always loved another man, Scott Chavez (Herbert Marshall), an educated, sensitive fellow. After her passing, alone with the corpse and his memories, McCanles sobs: "I loved you, Laura Belle." Likewise he pretends to hate a sensitive son, Jesse (Joseph Cotten), who resembles the wife. At one point, when McCanles hears the boy has been shot, he expresses delight. When fellow old-timer Lem Smoot (Harry Carey) whispers that the son survived, McCanles lowers his head and cries, "Thank God!" Even his seemingly callous bad-boy son, Lewton (Gregory Peck), a nightmare version of the insufferable dad,

Real men don't cry? After decades of maintaining a stoic demeanor, the aging macho (Lionel Barrymore) finally breaks down and tells his doomed wife (Lillian Gish), "I love you!" in Duel in the Sun. *Courtesy The David O. Selznick Studio.*

has a touch of humanity inside him. After abusing Ruby (Jennifer Jones), his half-Indian mistress, throughout, Lewton manages, moments before expiring, to exclaim: "I love ya!" What he could not bring himself to express in words during his brief lifetime becomes, at the all-important moment of this obscure man's impending death, something that he not only does but in fact must say during those brief seconds left to him.

Lewton means it, although Ruby is the one who shot him. This is why audiences find the film's closing so strangely haunting when, moments earlier, like Ruby, we were glad his incalculable cruelty had at last reached an end. If the Western male were as macho as he pretends, utterly without female emotion as he wants (or needs) to believe he is, he would be impossible to empathize with. He redeems himself, if but partially, by revealing some repressed inner sensitivity. Yet his life is spent attempting to live up to a code handed down from previous males or learned through daily survival. Trapped by circumstances, he is tragic rather than villainous. One of the most vivid examples of this occurs in *Red River* when a boy (Harry Carey

Jr.) is killed in a stampede. Dunson wants to tell his sidekick Groot (Walter Brennan) to buy the wife of the deceased a calico dress her husband was supposed to pick up in Abilene. Dunson cannot bring himself to put this into words. The more feminine side of this duo, Groot is comfortable speaking out loud what Dunson cannot for fear of appearing unmanly.

Almost always, a lady from the East offers the chance for such a man's salvation, if only he will take it. In *Texas Lady* (Tim Whelan, 1955) a mature businesswoman, Prudence Webb (Claudette Colbert), takes her winnings from a New Orleans gambling casino and heads for the Lone Star State to reinvent her life. Upon arrival she meets an embittered newspaperman, Clay Ballard (Doug Fowley), who prints whatever the cattle barons want. She buys the enterprise but says, "I intend to change the policy of the *Clarion*." Henceforth, it will represent "the people," the swiftly growing community rather than the last of the rugged individualists. Cass Gower (James Bell), a sympathetic lawyer, warns her: "These men . . . pioneered this area. They fought Indians, outlaws, the weather. Now they run it with an iron hand." But Judge Micah (Ray Collins) believes Texas is poised for change.

As for the cattlemen, their leader states: "This is our country. It's going to stay our country." In time they'll be proven wrong. Before that happens, they scoff at Prudence in what are clearly antifeminist epithets. "A woman running a newspaper?" one laughs. "You ought to be at home, cooking and cleaning for some man." If we never see the railroad, we hear plenty about this harbinger of change. Fearing it will bring progressive ideology with it, the ranchers are dead set against its unwanted intrusion. In contrast, women in Westerns almost always look forward to the coming of the railroad, among them Vienna (Joan Crawford) in *Johnny Guitar* (Nicholas Ray, 1954) and Jill McBain (Claudia Cardinale) in *Once Upon a Time in the West* (Sergio Leone, 1968). Men like the land barons in *Texas Lady* and Senator McCanles in *Duel in the Sun* stand firmly against it. No matter that they along with the farmers and small-scale ranchers would prosper. As arch conservatives, they are blinded by fear and hate. Poking their herds onto cattle cars rather than spending three months going up the trails makes much sense. This renders their approach illogical. Having always done it one way, they can't handle the thought of doing it differently.

Yet all can coexist, thanks to an Eastern voice of feminine reason in *Texas Lady* who makes her philosophy clear with a single phrase: "I believe in progress." She is the liberal; this Western's authorial voice sides with its

The true winning of the West. Despite the notion of men as the pioneers, the process was not complete until the arrival of an Eastern woman with a progressive sensibility. Prudence Webb (Claudette Colbert) brings true civilization in Texas Lady. *Courtesy RKO Pictures.*

title character. Before that will occur there must be (this is, after all, a Western) blood on the streets. More than a gunfight, what we witness is a radical change in the social order. "In a revolution," the editor, now squarely on Prudence's side, explains, "the people take over the town." If this mid-1950s film by implication deals with the contemporary paranoia of a red menace, *Texas Lady* rates as anti-McCarthyist. Its message is that rule by the people is a good thing. This town, America in microcosm, will now become a better place. Capitalism has not been replaced by communism; rather, a delicate balance has been achieved between the two.

"My land!" Most generic Westerns emphasize the spirit of adventure in the American migration. A few, Red River *among them, make clear the essentiality of amassing power and money. Courtesy Monterey Productions/United Artists.*

GO WEST, YOUNG
(BUSINESS)MAN

AMERICAN DREAMERS, POLITICAL SCHEMERS

For many of the ranch owners . . . there was intended but a
temporary connection [with the West] during which there might
be effected the desired improvement in . . . business initiative.

—PHILIP ASHTON ROLLINS, *THE COWBOY*, 1922

Capitalism has been at the heart of the American Dream ever since the publication of Benjamin Franklin's *Poor Richard's Almanack* (1732–1758), with
its rules for making it in the emergent democratic capitalist state.[1] At no
time was this so true as during the early twentieth century, when the Western
film's initial popularity paralleled in the new mass culture a series of dime
novels set in expanding cities. These are referred to as Horatio Alger stories
or, taken together, the Horatio Alger myth. In them, rare poor boys achieve
immense financial success via luck and pluck.[2] A new aristocracy, readers
learned, would be formed by those who gave their private dreams a possibility of realization by adhering to a scrupulous work ethic, then were fortunate
enough to be in the right place at the right time to harvest the rewards.

Such situations did not receive much screen time in the Western, a genre
that favors a romantic dream over the business-oriented reality that defined
expansionism during the nineteenth century. Western filmmakers appear at

times almost embarrassed by the inclusion of everyday issues like money. In Hawks's *Red River* the only time Texas rancher Tom Dunson (John Wayne) mentions cash is when, following the Civil War, he admits, "I'm broke!" Actually, cattle were capital on four hooves.[3] The main motivation for creating businesses like the King Ranch was to establish vast empires, as cash-oriented as any of the financial or banking concerns back East. The term "cash cow" had a literal meaning. A casual viewer would hardly guess a profit motive while observing Wayne in the role of Dunson sounding as if he were primarily committed to a mission for God and country:

> My land! We're here and we're going to stay here. Give me ten years and I'll have [my] brand on the gates of the greatest ranch in Texas . . . I'll have the Red River "D" on more cattle than you've looked at anywhere . . . enough beef to feed the whole country. *Good* beef. Beef to make 'em strong, make 'em grow. But it takes work, it takes sweat, it takes time. Years! Lots of years.

In Martin Ritt's 1963 Western *Hud*, based on the novel *Horseman, Pass By* by Larry McMurtry, Melvyn Douglas as Homer (again a hint of Greek myth) plays an aging version of Wayne's *Red River* character. Homer had no problem with making money, knew he could not survive without a profit, and enjoyed the wealth that came his way. Always, though, there was a sense of mission, now represented by the final Longhorn cattle still grazing. His son, Hud Bannon (Paul Newman), is despicable, not because he makes and likes money but because he thinks of little else other than seducing vulnerable married women, like Hunnicutt in *Home from the Hill*. The focal character in *Hud* is Lon (Brandon De Wilde), who throughout wavers back and forth between the poles of old-fashioned morality and more modern amorality. After the death of his noble grandpa (Lon is the son of Homer's other boy, who was killed by accident during one of Hud's drunk-driving incidents), Lon chooses enlightened rather than raw capitalism. The system survives as the next generation rejects not the idea of capitalism but its worst possible incarnation.

Likewise, movies about the earlier mountain men leave an audience with the impression that the primary reason for heading into the high Rockies was a profound love and deep respect for the region's beauty, coupled with a desire to exist at one with nature. Perhaps some "hivernants" (trappers cocooned in cabins during the winter months) did appreciate the pristine world they discovered. Yet mountain men came primarily to make money.[4] In the process they ravaged the fur-bearing animal population, beginning approximately in 1825 and winding down some twenty years later largely because they had driven beaver, mink, and other breeds into near-extinction. On film, though, trappers and traders have been portrayed as the opposite of all that. In *The Big Sky*, Hawks's 1952 film of Guthrie's novel, the leader of a keelboat expedition upriver to trade with the Blackfoot mentions money at the film's beginning and end. This motive is barely raised during a story that emphasizes adventure—fighting Indians—and romance, as the Kirk Douglas and Dewey Martin characters compete for the Native American beauty played by Elizabeth Threatt. The tendency is even more noticeable in Westerns produced during the mid-1970s. In a confused era, the public turned away from the cowboy as hero, and mountain men temporarily took their place. Often they were portrayed as environmentalists, as in *Jeremiah Johnson* (Sydney Pollack, 1972) and *The Life and Times of Grizzly Adams* (Richard Fridenberg, 1976). The latter, low-budget item from Sun Classics led to an NBC TV series (1977–1978). The title hero (Dan Haggerty) is here fancifully depicted as running a nature refuge. His peaceful menagerie includes a huge bear, if most volumes of mountain-man lore contend that his historical counterpart won his nickname for the number of "griz" he killed or boasted of killing.[5]

Some rare films did address the capitalism issue openly. In *Across the Wide Missouri* (William Wellman, 1951), the narrator (Howard Keel), a descendant of such a child of nature, Flint Mitchell (Clark Gable), states the reason his forebear headed into the wilds: "Lots of beaver meant lots of money!" Fur in the nineteenth century's first half, like cattle in the second, constituted a major industry and delivered huge profits. Men without means might borrow heavily and, after investing in traps and essentials, become fabulously wealthy by selling furs, then buy into businesses such as the American Fur Company or the Rocky Mountain Fur Company. Jedediah Smith (1799–1831) did so.[6] Most contemporaries squandered their earnings on gambling, liquor, and women at the annual spring rendezvous. Others went belly up owing to bad luck. Either way, rugged individualism ruled. One took his chances and could not complain if coincidence or fate did him in. Success called for pluck, but as with the fictional Horatio Alger tales, in the end blind luck prevailed.

This is the theme of the nongeneric Western *East of Eden* (Elia Kazan, 1954) set in the twentieth century. California farmer Adam Trask (Raymond Massey) has a vision that he might elevate his already considerable fortunes by taking advantage of the railroad's ever-greater abilities for speedy delivery, with the concept of employing ice to flash-freeze produce. He carefully works out a daring, expensive plan to ship his crops back East. If the venture succeeds he'll become wealthier. Through no fault of his own, a series of circumstances causes freight cars carrying his goods to be halted en route. As a result, all is lost; he finds himself where he began. Still, there is no bitterness on his part. Someday this will work, he sighs. He has learned by trying that he would not be the chosen one who reaps the rewards. That's the way the system works; he accepts this completely and starts over.

Importantly, the narrative changes in meaning in accordance with the storyteller's point of view. Within the context of the original novel, John Steinbeck set out to express the same liberal values found in *The Grapes of Wrath* and his other works. In the literary version, the patriarch in *East of Eden* rates as a fool, if a noble one. Steinbeck's point is to undermine the American Dream, arguing that most believers in it will, sadly, see their dreams dashed. When Kazan filmed the piece, the director had just admitted to the House Committee on Un-American Activities that he had once been a communist but turned against that political philosophy and now supported the U.S. capitalist system.[7] Though the plot remains the same and even much of the dialogue, the authorial attitude and rearranged context change, reversing the meaning from a critique of capitalism to acceptance of its limitations. A noble acceptance of a terrible situation in the film replaces Steinbeck's rage at its near-universality.

Among the few films to directly address capitalism in a frontier setting was, not surprisingly, one of the rare big-studio Westerns to fail at the box office. *Hudson's Bay* (Irving Pichel, 1940) offered a biography more accurate than most, this time of Pierre-Esprit Radisson (1640?–1710). Founder of a vast Canadian fur-trapping business, Radisson is played by one of the era's most esteemed actors, Paul Muni. In the opening the French-Canadian protagonist and his burly sidekick Gooseberry (Laird Craeger) arrive in Albany to meet moneyed officials and propose a business deal. The Canadians' own government had not been perceptive enough to grasp the potential of fur. Radisson considers business relations more significant than any patriotic loyalties to his land of origin. "You give us the money," he grunts, and he and his men will open up new areas of the Northwest. When these petty bureaucrats also prove blind to the possibilities, an undaunted Radisson heads for London in the company of Englishman Lord Edward Crewe (John Sutton), a character also based on an actual person. While in the film Radisson meets the man in New York State, historically they partnered in Boston. Together they convince King Charles (Vincent Price) to back their project with funds.

Though Radisson's English partner dons buckskins when they approach the title area, he remains Hollywood's man in the suit as to ideology. The two talk constantly about the fortunes they hope to reap. But while Radisson's eyes, like those of his partner, gleam with delight, a dramatic dichotomy appears. A raw capitalist of the type American moviegoing audiences tend to dislike, the Englishman cannot comprehend why Radisson wants to split their profits with local Indians rather than buy them off with beads and booze. Radisson, an enlightened capitalist, at least in this version,[8] wins respect by making certain everyone, race notwithstanding, shares in the wealth.

> CREWE: But you like money just as much as I do.
>
> RADISSON: Yes, I like being rich. But you think that's all I came to Hudson's Bay for?

Again, we perceive that the difference between hero and foil is not whether men wish to make money but the priority they give cash—whether there is room for other facets of a personality capable of fuller, grander visions. An idealized Radisson here speaks about his love for the land and the native people who inhabit it. Presaging Dunson in Hawks's cattle-empire film, Radisson embodies the mythic pioneer, the enlightened rather than raw capitalist who may have high esteem for money but is also wide enough in scope and broad enough in vision to see beyond its limitations. He may have a few historical antecedents. Undeniably, he is the Western movie hero—arriving for a great adventure in this virgin land and putting profits in proper perspective as a true individualist yet equally committed to community values.

Radisson delivers a final patriotic speech about his beloved Canada. This is quite a stretch since, as history notes and the film attests, by establishing the Hudson's Bay Company with British money he set in place those seeds that would eventually lead to English domination of what was then still known as New France.[9] Here we encounter the Hollywood approach

The two faces of capitalism. In Hudson's Bay, *Radisson (Paul Muni) is portrayed as an enlightened capitalist eager to make money, though not at the expense of the environment. His raw-capitalist partner and foil (John Sutton) does not consider anything but profits, their very costuming identifying each man's orientation. Courtesy Twentieth Century-Fox.*

to dealing with capitalism on those rare occasions when mainstream movies openly admit the commercial basis of the West's settling process rather than projecting a glorious dream alternative: the frontiersman hero with insight into the nonfinancial legacy of what he achieves, however grounded the reality may have been in cold cash.

As to raw capitalists, they serve as handy villains in Civil War Westerns. That conflict (1861–1865) has always been a tricky one for Hollywood: make either side out to be the good or bad guys, and you lose half of your potential audience. How much better, then, to posit either the blue or gray as protagonists, the other as decent antagonists, and someone else entirely as the true villain. In *Siege of Red River* (Rudolph Mate, 1954), James Simmons (Van Johnson) is the Southerner who steals a new Gatling gun from Yankees and attempts to transport it to his troops in Texas. Going up against him is the undaunted blue-coat Frank Kelso (Jeff Morrow), who hopes to stop that from happening. On the way, Simmons travels with a loner, Brett Manning

(Richard Boone), who feigns dedication to the Confederate cause. But Manning plans to steal the potent weapon and sell it to the Indians to make war on all whites. By the film's end, Southerner and Northerner put their hostilities aside to keep the villain from completing the deal.

Likewise, in *Rio Lobo* (Howard Hawks, 1970) a Union officer, Colonel Cord McNally (John Wayne), loses a train to a raiding party from the South. Worse still, his favorite young officer dies during the attack, touching McNally's heart as if he had lost his own son. Yet when the war ends and fate throws McNally together with these same Southerners, he expresses no bitterness. They were doing their job even as he did his to the best of his abilities. One soldier admires another, no matter if they once fought on opposite sides. He does request that the former Rebs reveal the name of the traitor in his own ranks who sold them the necessary information to pull off their strategy so that he can now track down this fellow Northerner and execute him for his raw capitalism. As to the rebels, he respects them as men of deep commitment, cleverness, and bravery, admiring their loyalty to a cause.

Nongeneric Westerns, in a conscious avoidance of any expected conventions, project a more realistic portrait. *The Southerner* (Jean Renoir, 1945) focuses on a family of dirt farmers who migrate to Texas in hopes of finding work, which has dried up in their birthplace. Always, they cling to ruggedly individualistic values. Uncle Pete (Paul Burns) advises, "Work for yourself; grow your own crop," though a single storm could ruin everything they've poured into the land. A steady job on a company-owned farm would at least deliver minimal financial rewards despite any variables. A friend of lead character Sam Tucker (Zachary Scott) tries to convince Tucker to take the safe route: "If you're working for a big outfit, you don't get rich but you get your pay." A born and bred red-stater, whether living in the South or the West, Tucker can't take that approach, instead risking everything for the big payoff that never arrives. The question raised by the film is whether Tucker is depicted as a working-class hero or as a dupe seduced by a system that few can lick while fighting for their personal American dreams. Is this a celebration or criticism of the Horatio Alger myth? In the hands of a master like Renoir, the only answer must be a complex fusion of the two. Regarding that little guy with huge hopes, one character states: "If his crops don't pay off, he's got nothing." Sam Tucker must stand by and watch his daughter miss school because she has no coat and might freeze. Yet even for her sake (and he loves her dearly), he will not bring himself to renege on those inherently

American values he believes will someday pay off. If they don't? Then he had the pluck but not the luck and must accept this. Of a factory job he says it "hides your sky and puts out your lights."

There is no happy ending here, only a melancholy vision of a new beginning. When Sam finally grows the perfect cotton crop, it's ruined by rain and wind before the harvesting can begin. As he is about to drop down and give up, the women in his family rally around, forcing him to try again. He rises off his knees to do that. Thankfully, we never do learn for certain if he will ever succeed. That, of course, is not the issue. That he goes on trying, believing, and following his dream is. The guarded optimism with which *The Southerner* ends calls into question all the seeming social criticism that precedes it. Is this, in the final analysis, a tough, cold look at the inequity of America's capitalist system, played out against a backdrop of hard-working individuals who go on believing even when like the Bible's Cain their efforts are not rewarded? This is what the first eighty-five minutes of the ninety-one-minute film suggest. Or must we take into account the last sequence, which suggests that all that has happened up until this closing moment represents a test of Tucker's moral fiber? Thanks particularly to the women, who are able to draw on what novelist Ellen Glasgow once referred to as their "vein of iron" that the strong-willed descendants of earlier pioneers still carry in their blood,[10] they somehow manage to push on. Read in the former light, the film offers a liberal, even radical political statement. Considered as the latter, *The Southerner* proffers a defense of traditional values. Renoir, a French artist here considering America even as de Tocqueville once did, appears complex and sophisticated enough to accept and appreciate both sides or approaches to the story.

Something to sing about. During his years at Republic, Gene Autry's movies were mostly set in a contemporary Depression-ravaged West, his songs echoing the sentiments of the FDR administration. Courtesy Republic Pictures.

REDISTRIBUTING
THE WEALTH

GENE AUTRY, FRANK CAPRA, AND
THE NEW DEAL WESTERN

I think when you spread the wealth around, it's good for everybody.
—PRESIDENTIAL CANDIDATE BARACK OBAMA TO SAMUEL JOSEPH
"JOE THE PLUMBER" WURZELBACHER, OCTOBER 12, 2008

Audiences expected ambitious movies turned out during Hollywood's
golden age to offer complex visions of the state of the world. Yet precious
few top Westerns were produced during the 1930s.[1] A temporary disappear-
ance of the form derived in part from the box-office disaster of *The Big Trail*
(Raoul Walsh, 1930), a film that might have proven popular only a few years
earlier. Then similarly themed Manifest Destiny movies like *The Covered
Wagon* (James Cruze, 1923) and *The Iron Horse* (John Ford, 1924) reaped
large profits. In the 1920s, visions of a pioneer era when anything seemed
possible reflected a generalized sense of optimism. The stock market roared,
making American Dreams come true. In this context, an earlier era of unbridled optimism served as a fitting metaphor for the prosperity of the present. But an upbeat tone left Dust Bowl audiences cold. Notable exceptions
that became successful Westerns during the 1930s include *Jesse James* (Henry
King, 1939), which portrayed the post–Civil War outlaw as an earlier variation on the era's own John Dillinger–type bank robber, officially a criminal

though a folk hero to the public. *The Plainsman* (Cecil B. DeMille, 1936) scored with viewers by emphasizing the years during which "Wild Bill" Hickok was a wanted man and ignoring his long career as a lawman.[2] The big Western would be revived by *Stagecoach* (John Ford, 1939), focusing also on a likable young outlaw, the Ringo Kid (John Wayne). Following this film's surprising box-office success, the big studio Western returned.

During the Depression, however, low-priced oaters, aimed at rural areas and juveniles everywhere, flourished. Noteworthy is that in such apparently unrealistic examples of the genre as singing-cowboy films, values that defined each period made themselves felt. Nowhere was this so obvious as in the hourlong pictures released by Republic, the era's dominant force in B Westerns, many featuring Gene Autry, who starred in them under his own name. Typical was *Gold Mine in the Sky* (Joe Kane, 1938). Its self-consciously contemporary narrative concerns a young woman (Carol Hughes) who returns West after a sojourn in New York and Chicago. Sadly she admits, "The stock markets cleaned me out." Gene and sidekick Frog Milhouse (Smiley Burnette) nod, consoling her by singing Horace Heidt's title ballad. Here is a Woody Guthrie/Pete Seeger–inspired ditty in which a cowboy mournfully addresses his mount. Also touched on by implication is a universal need during financially troubled times to find alternative treasures in the mind and clouds, a "pie in the sky" of liberal protest performers.

Few Autry musicals, however, so openly embraced the politics of President Franklin Delano Roosevelt as *The Old Barn Dance* (Joseph Kane, 1938). Gene arrives in Grangeville to sell horses to the farmers as he's done for years. Now his clients are considering new-fangled tractors. This would not only eliminate the need for animals but put farmhands out of work. Simultaneously, a new strain of raw capitalism exerts a corruptive influence on the local communications media. The owner of the company selling these mechanized contraptions pushes for a radio station to nab Gene, sign him for a show, then pay him to sing (literally) their praises. If not, the tractor company will pull all advertising. Gene refuses. Sally Dawson (Joan Valerie), a go-getter of the Lois Lane variety (*Superman* likewise a pop-culture fantasy projection of the 1930s), slips into the title festivity to record and air his performances, interspersed with commercials. Listening, locals assume that trusted Gene has offered an endorsement. Farmers who hesitated to embrace change now hurry to purchase tractors. While there's nothing wrong with these devices per se, manufacturers are in league with the finance office. If a payment should arrive late, small print in contracts allows this conglomerate to seize the tractors and the farmers' land. Distraught citizens turn on Gene, now a predecessor to Gary Cooper's protagonist in *Meet John Doe* (Frank Capra, 1940). Like that character, Gene refuses to be destroyed and organizes the populace into a union. A force to be reckoned with, they turn to politics.

Autry also embodies the FDR populism in *Mountain Rhythm* (Reeves Eason, 1939). This contemporary tale opens as Gene and Frog, driving a humble wagon, pick up Depression-era hobos Rocky (Jack Pennick) and the Judge (Ferris Taylor). A bus headed for an upscale resort recklessly passes, forcing them aside. The man in the suit, here called Cavanaugh (Walter Fenner), plans to invest capital and turn the area into an exclusive resort. But the nouveau-poor ranchers refuse to sell out, so Cavanaugh decides to seize their lands by devious means. Outside his property holdings, a hobo camp has been constructed. Rocky and the Judge live there; Gene and Frog feel comfortable here. Gene learns that a public auction will sell off open grazing land that ranchers have long relied on. Cavanaugh plans to buy it, restrict it, then run them all out of business.

The natural leader, a tough ranch woman called Ma Hutchins (Maude Eburne), grasps that if they continue with their traditional ruggedly individ-ualistic ways of handling problems they will all hang separately. Gene comes up with a solution: "Pool your money!" Operate communally; form a true collective that can buy the grazing land, then allow all the neighbors, now fellow travelers, to socialistically share.

Their microcosmic New Deal approach forces the big-money types out, unable to stand up to the little people when they embrace solidarity. The businessman is not their only enemy. A banker every bit as evil as Henry F. Potter (Lionel Barrymore) in Frank Capra's *It's a Wonderful Life* (1946) joins forces with the raw capitalist. They send outlaws to rob the pooled money, then blame the crime on innocent hobos. The next big-business scheme is to stage a fake gold strike. Cowboys desert ranches to try to get rich quick, allowing men in suits to seize the lands. But the villains didn't count on Gene. Like a Cooper or James Stewart character in a Capra film, he explains that while everyone was off on a wild goose chase, the much-maligned hobos completed their roundup with no hope of reward. These are not lazy bums but comrades. Now realizing their mistake, ranchers embrace hobos, and they drive away their common enemy. Blue-collar people work together once they discover the wisdom of redistributing the wealth.

Liberalism spills over into full radicalism in *Rovin' Tumbleweeds* (George Sherman, 1939). After a flood devastates a farming community, Gene is interviewed on the radio as a leader of those who halted the raging waters by turning out and communally piling sand bags high. The young reporter, Mary Ford (Mary Carlisle), assumes Gene will offer a humble tribute to his friends' courage. Instead, he seizes the mic, attacking a do-nothing government, particularly their representative:

> GENE: I just want to tell you people we wouldn't have suffered this loss of life and property if that cheap politician Congressman Fuller had put through the flood-control bill.
> MARY: (*flabbergasted*) Uh . . . this is no time to talk politics.

Actually, that's precisely what it's time for. Gene's friends move into a tent town as the Randville Development Corporation seizes their lands. The much-hated politician (Gordon Hart) fails his constituency not from

One more face in the crowd. With the advent of modern media Autry was depicted as a radio performer who was hired to sing mindless ditties and seized the "live" situation to instead deliver radical messages. Here, Gene does the honors in Stardust on the Sage. *Courtesy Republic Pictures.*

incompetence or laziness but purposefully. He wants contributions from raw capitalists toward his reelection fund. They need a flood that will force commoners off their lands. The conglomerate will then buy up the area at low prices. Here is another Autry vehicle that predates *Meet John Doe*. The corporation at once withdraws sponsorship from the young woman's radio show after Gene's comments. She's then sent by her boss to locate him. The idea is to put Gene on the air as the voice of the common man. They presage the Barbara Stanwyck and Cooper characters in Capra's forthcoming classic. Yet in no way does Gene become Lonesome Rhodes (Andy Griffith) in *A Face in the Crowd* (Elia Kazan, 1957). Like John Doe, Autry is the real deal. Gene goes on the air, tossing away commercial tunes intended to lull listeners into a sweet sleepwalking state. Instead, he performs protest songs railing against those who hired him, much like Woody Guthrie in life and as played by David Carradine in *Bound for Glory* (Hal Ashby, 1976).

When not performing, Gene leads a caravan of outdated trucks worthy of John Ford's forthcoming film version of *The Grapes of Wrath* (1940), guiding poor farmers to where they might find work. Frightened locals want to run the newcomers out, fearful they will be undercut by workers settling for slave wages. When Gene and Frog stand up to their resistance, the locals are thrown into a stir. Guthrie-like, Gene sings:

> *They beat us for nothin'*
> *And throw us in jails.*
> *Better than ridin' the rails.*
> *Everything's rosy,*
> *We're comfy and cozy.*
> *What this country needs is more jails!*

As to the radio offer, Gene agrees only if all in his traveling commune are bailed out of jail. Soon Autry is, in his words, "a one-man relief agency on behalf of all migratory workers." His songs help convince locals they were wrong; these are their brothers and sisters in poverty and pain. A Mr. Smith who goes to Washington, Gene runs for Congress. His radio profits are divided equally among those out of work. Gene explains the need to redistribute the wealth nearly seventy years before Barack Obama's presidency. During his celluloid campaign, Autry also insists on the absolute importance of raising taxes:

Some of you were against the flood-control bill because Congressman Fuller said it would raise your taxes. And after all his ballyhoo, I don't blame you. But did any of you find out just how much it would raise them? Well, I can tell you. About one-quarter of one percent. With that amount, homeless ranchers could return to Green Valley and relieve the labor situation here.

The reporter, like Ann Mitchell, Stanwyck's character in *Meet John Doe*, begins the piece as a smart, slick, shallow, self-interested, modern girl. She becomes a true believer in Autry and his liberal politics, particularly the tax-raising concept. In office, Gene refuses to make political appointments and instead awards jobs to the most qualified. Even he can't get the flood-relief bill passed. Old politicians stall, relying on business as usual and deriding this young idealist. The only old-timer to lend Gene an ear is Senator Nolan (William Farnum), who admires the younger man's grit and dislikes lobbyists. When the older congressman passes away, the progressive bill dies with him. Another flood occurs. Gene convinces the out-of-work farmers to help fight the tide alongside those who tried to keep them out of the valley. He argues that these folks shouldn't be held responsible; they'd been brainwashed by the worst of raw capitalists and dishonest pols. Working-class people, now in solidarity, turn back the flood tide. The limitations of local self-interest are set aside. Next up is passage of that relief bill. If the ending seems more idealistic than true, a similar complaint can be leveled against any Frank Capra film.

Communal values would continue to dominate Autry's vehicles during the next decade. *Under Fiesta Stars* (Frank McDonald, 1941) pairs Gene with a by-now obligatory young woman from the East, here Babs Erwin (Carol Hughes). They jointly inherit a mine and a ranch. Initially she, a New Yorker with an eye toward making a fast buck, plans to sell both for profit. Despite her legal right to do so, Gene stands firm: "This mine is *not* going to be sold. It's going to be worked for the benefit of every ranchero [working] on it." Despite co-ownership, Gene forsakes rugged individuality by representing group values. His soft, sweet songs convert her. When they, now soul partners, realize the mine can't be developed without new equipment, Gene suggests they create a unique (and FDR-like) delicate balance between capitalism and communism by pooling local financial resources. Once this is accomplished, the commune divides all profits equally. He

The moral breaking of a law. As with many protesters to follow, Gene's unrelenting crusade caused him and sidekick Smiley Burnette to land in jail. Here they sing their troubles away in Sunset in Wyoming. *Courtesy Republic Pictures.*

and she, despite owner status, willingly accept the same amount as previous employees, now also in a sense partners. No one rakes in huge profits; everybody makes good money. Capitalism does survive the Great Depression via redistribution of wealth.

By the early 1940s the big, ambitious, studio Western was back in development. This allowed for serious themes to be expressed in movies that reached wider audiences. A communal ideal is further forwarded in *Brigham Young, Frontiersman* (Henry Hathaway, 1940). Early on, while the Mormons still live in Illinois, leader Joseph Smith (Vincent Price) speaks of a "brotherhood plan."[3] No man can pile up more riches than his neighbors, "like that anthill, over there," he explains, offering an example from nature to the title character (Dean Jagger). After learning from Indians while traveling west, Young tells fellow Mormons, "No man may buy or sell land." A fictional villain, Angus Duncan (Brian Donlevy), opposes this edict and is interested only in personal profit; he is a throwback to 1930s raw capitalists. Smith and Young are here communistic.

When women run the West. (a) Joan Crawford plays a fair-minded, left-leaning boss in Johnny Guitar, *sharing the profits equally with workers. (b) Barbara Stanwyck embodies the opposite in* Forty Guns, *ruling by intimidation. Courtesy Republic Pictures; Twentieth Century-Fox.*

In the postwar years, leftist thinking would be closely scrutinized by the House Committee on Un-American Activities (HUAC) and the Senate Permanent Investigations Subcommittee chaired by Joseph McCarthy. During the McCarthy era, the scrutiny led to the infamous blacklist of supposed communists in the movie industry, though in truth anyone with a liberal-leaning background immediately became suspect.[4] Yet even during those dark days, wily filmmakers slipped themes surrounding the redistribution of wealth past censors. In *Johnny Guitar* (Nicholas Ray, 1954), Vienna (Joan Crawford) plans to share profits from her saloon with the staff. Crawford is costumed in red during much of this color noir. Not that a strong female character necessarily implies leftist thinking. Ray's view would shortly be countered by that of right-wing director Sam Fuller in his politically opposite *Forty Guns* (1957). Here Jessica Drummond (Barbara Stanwyck) is the woman with the whip, uncaring for employees, thinking only about how much wealth she might acquire. Nowhere does the film's authorial voice criticize her approach. Westerns once again managed to convey contradictory themes according to their creators' views.

Last of the giants. The old-time conservative cattlemen are often portrayed as anachronisms attempting to halt the coming of the twentieth century. Lionel Barrymore embodies the type in Duel in the Sun. *Courtesy The David O. Selznick Studio.*

DON'T FENCE ME IN

RUGGED INDIVIDUALISM AND OPEN RANGE

We have money. We want to have more *money.*

—CATTLE BARON LORD PETER IN *JOHNSON COUNTY WAR*, 2002

"There go the last of the giants," Prudence's lover, Chris Mooney (Barry Sullivan), sighs as the old-timers, heads unbowed, ride off into the sunset at the end of *Texas Lady*. Earlier, when she first articulates her progressive plan, a bystander informs Prudence that the area's biggest cattlemen "have run this country for so long it's become sacrilegious to stand up against them." These kings of cattle have taken on godlike aspects, if those of false gods, that give them mythic status. In time, the townspeople tell the big ranchers, "You'll have to accept that the old days are gone." At the finale, they do. A deal is reached between individualistic cattlemen and the growing collective of townspeople, small-scale ranchers, and dirt farmers. The town serves as their bastion even as the range was for cattlemen, all this achieved by a woman.

In a Western, the worst men are those who take up guns to violently oppose change, particularly change imposed from a federal level. In *Sea of Grass* (Elia Kazan, 1947), adapted from a novel by Conrad Richter, Bryce Chamberlain (Melvyn Douglas) is an Eastern-born, highly educated lawyer living on America's final and fast-fading wild frontier, the once wide-open spaces inhabited only by a few cattlemen and their cowboys now in the process of settlement by dirt farmers and townspeople. Chamberlain takes on a job as an agent for the national government at the request of the new settlers, community-oriented types who sense that they must all hang together or be hanged, possibly literally, by the unfriendly old-timers. The potential nemesis of these farm families is the rawest of raw capitalists, the cattle baron Colonel James Brewton (Spencer Tracy), a vivid representation of the rugged individualist. For a man of Brewton's conservative-libertarian politics, all the problems that arise on this range ought to be settled locally. This increases Brewton's hostility toward Chamberlain (already intense, as Brewton despises educated people, particularly from the East) owing to Chamberlain's emergent ties with the federal government, as a once-regional dispute will now be settled by the national legal system. When Brewton, furious, suggests that secession from the union ought not to be ruled out, this fictional character from a sixty-five-year-old film presages a position expressed by Texas Governor Rick Perry during the first decade of the twenty-first century. The federal government won't waver; if Brewton and his ilk refuse to bow to progress, the military will be brought in to disarm the cowboys and cattlemen, precisely what they most fear. Similarly in *Duel in the Sun*, Senator McCanles learns that his worst nightmare has come true: the railroad, which will bring in "nesters," is headed for his town. In defiance, this cattle baron rounds up his men, planning to kill the unarmed Asians laying down track. The confrontation serves as the film's centerpiece, thematically and visually. Here, too, a lawyer named Langford (Otto Kruger) and a doctor, Lem Smoot (Harry Carey), argue that the law is on their side. Cattle baron McCanles hisses, "There's *my* law, right there!" as he points to mounted cowboys with rifles ready.

Or, as Gene Autry joyfully sang in his theme song:

> *Where you sleep out every night,*
> *And the only law is right!*
> *Back in the saddle again.*[1]

Yet Ford, the greatest of all Western directors, saw things differently. At a political rally near the end of *The Man Who Shot Liberty Valance* (1962), crusading reporter Dutton Peabody (Edmond O'Brien) attempts to make some sense of the entire history of the West. Peabody's speech summarizes not only

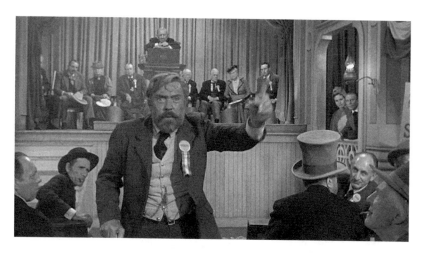

The march of time. In Ford's penultimate Western, The Man Who Shot Liberty Valance, *Dutton Peabody (Edmond O'Brien taking over for the deceased Thomas Mitchell) directly addresses the film's audience, summing up frontier history from the progressive point of view. Courtesy Paramount Pictures.*

Western history but also the vision we receive of it while watching Western movies, particularly those of a liberal, progressive order. Having listened to a pompous orator (John Carradine) speak on behalf of cattlemen who are sitting on the right side of the screen from a viewer's perspective, Peabody addresses the issue of statehood from viewpoints of the farmers, townspeople, and small-scale ranchers, Tom Doniphon (John Wayne) included:

> While under the spell of his eloquence, I could almost see once again the vast herds of buffalo, and the savage redskin, wandering with no law but the law of survival: the tomahawk and bow and arrow. And then with the westward march of our nation came the pioneers . . . and the boldest of them were the cattlemen, who regarded the wide-open range their own domain. Their law was the law of the hired gun. Now, today, has come the railroad and the people. Hardworking citizens, the homesteader, the shopkeeper. The builder of cities. We need roads to lead to those cities. We need statehood to protect the rights of every man and woman, however humble.

They need, the filmmaker's spokesman continues, for the federal government to impose order on local chaos. Ford's authorial voice sides with liberals who believe that change is good, not conservatives in favor of maintaining the status quo; the farmers who wave signs proclaiming "Progress with State-hood" rather than cowboys shouting "Keep the range open!"; with law and order, not anarchy; with progress, not traditionalism; with community values over and above rugged individualism. In later years, John Ford proudly considered himself a Republican.[2] Thus he has often been misinterpreted as a conservative. The problem in understanding his work, so often progressive in nature, comes in assuming he was a twentieth-century Republican. Ford's personal hero, as *Young Mr. Lincoln* (1939) with Henry Fonda in the title role makes clear, was Honest Abe, the bygone liberal Republican.

Antilibertarian thinking exists not only in big Westerns but B features as well. *Tornado Range* (Ray Taylor, 1948) opens with this statement: "Pioneers discovered the land they had come for was in the hands of a small group of ranchers who meant to keep [the range open] for their cattle." The hero (Eddie Dean) arrives to impose national values on the local area. Under the Homestead Act of 1862,[3] he asks armed militiamen who try to block his way, "Are you men prepared to defy the United States Congress and the highest court in the land?" Though some consider doing so, most back off. Despite its identity as a rootin', tootin', shootin' oater, *Tornado Range* defends the imposition of blue-state values on red ones. The winning of the West, to borrow from Teddy Roosevelt, could not occur without this necessary civilizing process, as cowboy movies mostly reveal.

The ultimate dramatic slight to the cattleman was to move him beyond tragic figure through outright villain to object of ridicule. That would occur in *Liberty Valance*, derived from a short story by Dorothy Johnson, a writer with a protofeminist sensibility. The hero, Ransom Stoddard (James Stewart), yet another populist, progressive lawyer from the East, kills (or thinks he does) the ruthless Valance (Lee Marvin). Like Jack Wilson in *Shane*, Valance does the cattle barons' dirty work such as running off stock and terrorizing farmers. Stoddard is then nominated for political office as a liberal Republican. His opponent, a conservative Democrat favoring open range, appears as a caricature of all cinematic barons who preceded him. Running on a law-and-order ticket, Stoddard wins. Meanwhile, Doniphon (Wayne), the man who actually killed Liberty Valance, fades away, Shane-like. Though he was on the right side, he had used the gun.

Wayne would in time play his share of cattle barons, if relatively enlightened ones, in such films as director Andrew McLaglen's *McLintock* (1963)

"Only a man who carries a gun needs a gun!" Harry Carey speaks that line at the end of Angel and the Badman *after Quirt Evans (John Wayne) decides words are mightier than the sword—or pistol. Courtesy John Wayne Productions/Republic Pictures.*

and *Chisum* (1970). Earlier, the man known as Mr. Conservative enacted the voice of the common man, not only in Ford films but in others that the Duke devised for himself under the banner of his own company, Batjac Productions. In *Angel and the Badman* (James Edward Grant, 1947), wounded loner gunman Quirt Evans is cared for by a group of gentle farmers. As he recuperates, water stops running through the land. When he learns that nearby rancher Fred Carson (Paul Hurst) dammed the source, Quirt rides over to convince the unpleasant fellow that whatever his legal right as an individual, damming the water "ain't neighborly." Quirt informs Carson that a man ought to take into consideration the well-being of his fellow man, the community at large. The only angle from which this might be considered conservative is that the problem is resolved on a local level, without a need for federal intervention.

Wayne's Quirt is that most admirable of movie heroes, the mediator who manages to resolve long-standing arguments. In actuality, such problem solvers were few and far between. "The cowboy and the farmer should be friends," a hopeful chorus sings in *Oklahoma* (Fred Zinnemann, 1955). "Should be" seldom turns into "will be" in Westerns. In *Guns and Guitars* (Joseph Kane, 1936), cattle fever spreads across Texas. The plot deals with the need to move beyond a local approach to the problem to regional and in time national solutions. In a similar vein, the importance of enacting federal laws that limit localized freedoms is basic to *Home on the Prairie* (Jack Townley, 1939). Gene Autry and sidekick Frog run a government inspection post. Their task is to ensure that no sick "dogies" pass over into the national market. One rugged individualist, Belknap (Walter Miller), attempts to rush his herd through. Given the potential for hoof-and-mouth disease, Gene and Frog will not allow this to happen. The worst of the raw capitalists, H. R. Shelby (Gordon Hart), takes a self-serving position: "Move 'em out and then let somebody *else* worry." He lacks any sense of community, local or national.

The raw-capitalist rancher is often shown as a villain, his only interest the acquisition of ever more land, power, and money. Among the most vicious to appear on screen are the characters played by Edward G. Robinson in *The Violent Men* (Rudolph Mate, 1955), Donald Crisp in *The Man From Laramie* (Anthony Mann, 1955), Louis Jean Heydt in *The Badge of Marshal Brennan* (A. C. Gannaway, 1957), Leslie Nielsen in *The Sheepman* (George Marshall, 1958), Lee J. Cobb in *Lawman* (Michael Winner, 1971), Jon Cypher in *Valdez Is Coming* (Edward Sherin, 1971), Gene Hackman in *The Hunting Party* (Don Medford, 1971), Robert Duvall in *Joe Kidd* (John Sturges, 1972), George Hamilton in *The Man Who Loved Cat Dancing* (Richard C. Safarian, 1973), Clifton James in *Rancho Deluxe* (Frank Perry, 1975), John McLiam in *The Missouri Breaks* (Arthur Penn, 1976), Jason Robards in *Comes a Horseman* (Alan J. Pakula, 1978), Sam Waterston in *Heaven's Gate* (Michael Cimino, 1980), John Russell in *Pale Rider* (Clint Eastwood, 1984), Ray Baker in *Silverado* (Lawrence Kasdan, 1985), Richard Bradford in *The Milagro Beanfield War* (Robert Redford, 1988), Pat Hingle in *Gunsmoke: To the Last Man* (TVM, Jerry Jameson, 1992), and David Carradine in *Miracle at Sage Creek* (James Intveld, 2005).

Often the rancher's nefariousness is heightened by making him British; an aura of "class" adds to an American audience's immediate sense of dislike. Alan Rickman in *Quigley Down Under* (Simon Wincer, 1990), David Fox in *Promise the Moon* (TVM, Ken Jubenvill, 1997), Christopher Cazenove in *Johnson County War* (TVM, David Cass Sr., 2002), and Jeremy Irons in *Appaloosa* (Ed Harris, 2008) all come to mind.

He can, in some cases, be an Eastern capitalist hoping to bring a big-city approach to family-farm country. *Cattle Town* (Noel M. Smith, 1952) takes place after the Civil War when the governor of Texas (Charles Meredith) sells large sections of government-owned open land to a syndicate head, Judd Hastings (Ray Teal), to save the state from bankruptcy. Initially Hastings appears enlightened, requesting that the governor send special agent Mike McGann (Dennis Morgan) to make sure the small-scale ranchers whose herds graze there move off. We expect the leader of the little people, Ben Curran (Philip Carey), to fight. He does not; he organizes his friends for an exodus. Now, though, the capitalist shows his true (and raw) colors. He orders his men to slow down the evacuation for as long as possible. If the cattle are not removed from his land by a certain date, they will become his property. Upon arrival in the disputed area, McGann is shocked to realize that any resistance to moving the herds will not come from their current owners but from a baron hoping to acquire vast wealth.

The antipopulist villain cuts across race and gender boundaries. The character manifests as beautiful if ruthless women, played by Veronica Lake in *Ramrod* (Andre de Toth, 1947), Alexis Smith in *Montana* (Ray Enright, 1950), Jeanne Craine in *Man without a Star* (King Vidor, 1955), and Barbara Stanwyck in *The Violent Men* (Rudolph Mate, 1955) and *Forty Guns* (Sam Fuller, 1957). The villain takes the form of Latinos in the characters portrayed by Pedro Armendáriz in *The Wonderful Country* (Robert Parrish, 1959) and John Saxon in *The Appaloosa* (Sidney J. Furie, 1966). He can be fictional or factual. New Mexico's famed rancher John Chisum is lionized in John Wayne's depiction of him in *Chisum* (Andrew McLaglen, 1970) and vilified in *Pat Garrett and Billy the Kid* (Sam Peckinpah, 1973) and *Young Guns II* (Geoff Murphy, 1990) as played by Barry Sullivan and James Coburn, respectively. Likewise, budget knows no restraints; actor Roy Barcroft played a ruthless cattle baron in more than two dozen singing-cowboy mini-epic films. In nongeneric Westerns, this role may be portrayed in a more sympathetic light, Lear-like, a great man who does bad things. Such a deeply troubled figure appears in *The Big Country* (William Wyler, 1958). Charles Bickford's cattle baron, Major Henry Terrill, appears polite, even civilized, and open to a modernized West. He approves of his daughter (Carol Baker) marrying an Easterner (Gregory Peck) and is quick to speak against violence, which he professes to abhor. Yet he demands that guns be employed when dealing with a white-trash family that encroaches on his land.

Some of the most complex cattle barons are portrayed by Hollywood's greatest actor, Spencer Tracy, who assumed the role for the first time in *Sea of Grass* as Colonel James Brewton. Going up against Brewton is Eastern lawyer Bryce Chamberlain. On the very day Lutie (Kathryn Hepburn) arrives by train to marry Brewton, Chamberlain explains to the wide-eyed young woman, "We're making history in Salt Fork today. I hope it will be the right kind." By that he means limiting the power of the cattlemen, particularly Lutie's intended. The barrister hopes to win a conviction against the colonel for having his cowboys run a farmer off his own land. Everyone knows Brewton is guilty; many are fearful to return a fair verdict. "A lot of land for one man," the farmers mutter. What they want are rights to the water Brewton controls. The colonel sets forth his defense:

> I have sympathy for the early pioneer who came out here and risked his life and his family among the Indians. And I have little charity for the nester who waited until the country was safe and peaceable before he filed his homestead on the range of someone else who had fought for it.

His words echo the social Darwinism of Herbert Spencer.[4] His viewpoint is self-serving. Homesteaders file on government land that is legally offered to them. The colonel, believing he has the market cornered, cannot know that in time the federal government, in the manner of Roosevelt Republicans, would operate as a trust-buster. His words would be echoed often, notably by Ryker in *Shane* when Starrett says the farmers are on the right side of history:

> *You* in the right? Listen, Starrett, when I came to this country you weren't much older than your boy there. We had rough times. Me and other men that are mostly dead now . . . We *made* this country. Found it and made it [on] hard work and empty bellies. Cattle we brought was [run] off by Indians and outlaws. They don't bother you much because *we* handled 'em. Made a safe range out of (all) this . . . then people move in who never had to rawhide it through the old days. Fence off my range, fence my cattle off from water . . . an' you say we have no *right*? The men that did the work, run the risks? *No right*?

Ryker is not some motiveless malignancy but a flawed person whose entire design for living has been challenged. Starrett can only counter by taking his

Social Darwinism in action. The mightiest of the old-timers, Matt Devereaux (Spencer Tracy) grows paranoid as newly arrived Easterners change the face of the West in Broken Lance. *Courtesy Twentieth Century-Fox.*

blue-state approach of relying on federal rather than local authority that so antagonizes Ryker and other individualists: "The *government* doesn't see it that way." If Schaefer and Stevens clearly make Ryker an antagonist rather than a villain, it is also obvious that this Western's loyalties are with the progressives.

In *Duel in the Sun* it is his money that Senator McCanles cares most about when opposing incoming people: "New immigrants will put in *taxes!*" Schools and the like—fire departments, police, and so forth—will cost him. In opposing him, a kinder, gentler man of the West, Lem Smoot, is accompanied by a suited, Eastern lawyer, Langford (Otto Kruger). Enlightened men can see what the hard-core conservative cannot: there are worse things than higher taxes. More often than not, the female lead speaks for this liberal point of view. That principle is in *Sea of Grass* embodied by Lutie, at once old-fashioned feminine and forward-looking feminist; Chamberlain, the lawyer, tells her that "it'll be a woman's country" once schools and churches are established.

The true villain. In many Westerns the villain is less likely to wear black garb than a suit, identifying him as a raw capitalist rather than an adherent to the code of the West. Few actors ever filled the role so effectively as Raymond Burr in Count Three and Pray. *Courtesy Copa/Columbia Pictures.*

A shift in values. During the twentieth century's second half, the stigma of the suit would be questioned in movies that revised attitudes in earlier oaters. In The Man Who Shot Liberty Valance, *the unarmed Easterner (James Stewart) gradually replaces the armed and ready cowboy (John Wayne) as top dog in town, even winning away the woman they both love. Courtesy Paramount Pictures.*

Without a strong, at times even defiant woman to stand up to him, a cattle baron finds himself without the conscience that he probably does not know he desperately needs, as in the case of Wayne's Dunson in *Red River*. In *Broken Lance* (Edward Dmytryk, 1954), Tracy's Matt Devereaux appears even more tragic than his Brewton in *Sea of Grass*, as here his Latina wife (Katy Jurado) feels too intimidated to oppose his often absurd, ego-driven choices. Devereaux unwisely divides his kingdom among scheming sons (played by Richard Widmark, Hugh O'Brian, and Earl Holliman) and the sole loyal one (Robert Wagner), who becomes a male Cordelia. Devereaux's conflict puts him in a more sympathetic light here than in *Sea of Grass* since his enemies aren't humble farmers but a huge mining company. Owned by an Eastern conglomerate, this operation pours waste from copper excavations into the rivers that both big-time ranchers and poor squatters depend on. What eventually brings this cattle baron down is a conservative's insistence on dealing with the problem through direct action rather than the slow-moving legal system. It is his reactionary methods, not his sincere if admittedly self-interested concern for the environment, that creates the film's tense dramatic situation and his fall from grace.

With axes and saws, the loggers of the Wentworth Lumber Company marched into the forests of Mt. Warner and bared the land.

But Nature rebelled — and every inch of rain that fell on the thirstless hills became a threat of death — a tumult of destruction that swept the valleys below.

A cry in the wilderness. The need for state and/or federal government to intrude and save nature from man's careless commercial exploitation becomes clear in a series of didactic cards that openly declare the liberal message of Sunset in Wyoming. *Courtesy Republic Pictures.*

SILENT SPRINGS, VANISHING PRAIRIES

ENVIRONMENTALISM AND THE WESTERN

Drilling isn't environmentally destructive.
—SARAH PALIN, SEPTEMBER 8, 2008, ON OPENING THE
ARCTIC NATIONAL WILDLIFE REFUGE TO OIL DRILLING

Broken Lance is but one of many Westerns in which raw capitalism takes on a far darker dimension when it threatens the natural environment. In *Back in the Saddle* (Lew Landers, 1941), copper miners move into cattle country and use a local river as a dumping spot. Herds that drink from the water die. Cattlemen want the miners out and will do almost anything to precipitate that, even resorting to violence. In what serves as a paradigm for future Westerns, Gene Autry—assuming the moderate negotiator role—talks them into remaining calm. As a voice of common sense and reason, he suggests a compromise: "There must be some way you can build drainage pits so that everybody is happy." Yes, but that would cost money—if not a great amount, enough to diminish huge profits. The raw capitalists refuse, forcing a range war with environmentalist red-staters.

Here the Western appears at odds with the values of those who, in the twenty-first century, consider themselves conservatives. The New Right, as Chris Matthews of NBC and many other progressive journalists have defined it, proudly voices an antagonism to all environmental concerns.[1] During her vice-presidential run in 2008, one the New Right's most outspoken heroes, Sarah Palin, attacked "extreme green" types, eliciting applause for doing so, most often in what are considered red states.[2] In mid-June 2011 moderate Republican and candidate for the 2012 Republican presidential nomination Mitt Romney dared admit he believed in global warming and that human-kind by wasteful energy habits partly contributed to the dangerously esca-lating situation. He was shouted down by the Far Right's chief watchdog, Rush Limbaugh, on his radio show.[3] As to Palin, if this self-styled "maverick" (not insignificantly, a Western term) imagined herself as speaking for the nineteenth-century West, or even our dream of it, she was dead wrong.

Like Hastings (Ray Teal) in *Cattle Town*, the anti-environmentalist figure in Westerns would likely be some smarmy type representing huge Eastern corporations that are derided in films that enjoyed their greatest box-office success in what we today call red states. This man in the suit moved from the sidelines to center stage in films produced during the post–World War II period, when the sense of cynical self-interest encountered in the era's *noirs* likewise made itself felt within the context of this rural genre. Kirk Douglas's character Fallon in *The Big Trees* (Felix E. Feist, 1952) embodies this type, his cold, capitalistic approach scrutinized in an era when conservationists came out of the closet, many inspired by the writings of marine biologist and environmental activist Rachel Carson (1907–1964).[4] Carson wrote dur-ing the 1940s and 1950s, her work culminating in 1962 with *Silent Spring*. Its popularity forced mainstream America to consider and adapt pro-nature attitudes. At the movies, Walt Disney contributed to the growing concern, with documentaries like James Algar's films *The Living Desert* (1953) and *The Vanishing Prairie* (1954), entertainment that educated audiences about the need to protect natural resources. The Western proved a natural cinematic canvas for these principles, today codified as liberal-progressive in orienta-tion, if earlier embraced by many conservatives.

A handy villain for environmental Westerns was long provided by oil. In *Git along Little Dogies* (Joseph Kane, 1937), "black gold" threatens to con-taminate streams in rich Texas farmland. Autry initially stands against such drilling. "This has always been cattle land and it always will be," he proclaims. This sentiment suggests the film will emerge as an early example of the pro-environmental Western. If produced decades later that might have happened. Instead, the piece reflects the Great Depression, when the need to get businesses rolling again subsumed conservationism. Gene opposes drilling not as a naturalist but as a narrow-minded reactionary who fears change. Then he, an FDR-inspired economist who places financial recovery first, learns that oil wells will bring in the railroad, ending the annual long drives that diminish the weight and therefore the value of the livestock. Gene reverses position and convinces his fellow range riders to do the same. Clean water is never again mentioned, though the problem has hardly gone away.

Here Gene is a progressive only in a 1930s business-driven sense. This film was one of the first to shift away from an image of the banker as a villain, invariably the case in the early 1930s. The local banker (William Farnum) does support oil drilling and advances rig owners money to get started. Yet he does so believing this will result in good prospects for the entire community. When oil wells are about to shut down because of lack of capital, he becomes depressed that he may have done more harm than good and shoots himself in the head. Gene covers for him, in part owing to the banker's altruistic motives and because Gene is now a true believer in oil. The bad guy (Weldon Heyburn), though a worker for the oil company, hopes to sabotage the enterprise. This would allow him to seize control, buy up land cheap, then reopen the wells for his own benefit. Gene foils this capitalist-individualist, speaking as a good New Dealer: *Everyone* will be rich!" He even sings the FDR theme song, "Happy Days Are Here Again." Conservation is momentarily forgotten.

Not that the issue would remain entirely absent from the era's Autry vehicles. *Springtime in the Rockies* (Joseph Kane, 1937) introduced the need for an enlightened approach to farming via the time-tested formula of cowboys opposing sheepherders on open range. For once, the reason for their antagonism is articulated rather than appearing as only blind prejudice: sheep eat not only the top of the grass but the roots, resulting in barren prairies the next year. Here is another film in which Autry moves beyond his agreeable early drugstore-cowboy image to become a voice of moderation. The cowboys want to lynch sheepherders; Gene will have none of the violence. Initially his solution is to send them back where they came from: "I'm as much against sheep as you are. I'm against murder *more*." Serendipitously they are visited by a young woman (Polly Rowles) who has been studying animal husbandry in college and now is heading west to apply "modern scientific methods." The conservative traditionalist in Gene causes him to try and talk her out of raising sheep. Gene's liberal side allows him to gradually agree with her.

Even as World War II closed the book on the Depression, so did America enter an age when environmental issues replaced poverty as a key cause. As Carson later put it, "Only within the present century has one species—man—acquired significant power to alter the natural world" for better or worse.[5] Autry Westerns responded. *Sierra Sue* (William Morgan, 1941), released the same year that Carson's writings first exerted impact, concerns poisonous weeds threatening the grazing cattle. Ranchers decide to deal with this in the old-fashioned way, by burning the entire prairie to destroy a dangerous growth. Another reimagined good banker (Frank M. Thomas) insists he will not call in their notes so long as this natural threat exists. Later he goes further still, purchasing seed out of pocket. Meanwhile, the Department of Agriculture, a federal agency, sends in Gene, an expert on weed control, to solve things through science. This is presented as a good thing, though Ms. Carson might reserve the harshest criticism for such modern approaches! Autry's adversary, the banker Bromfield (Robert Homas), heads the cattlemen's organization. An old-timer, Bromfield insists that the only way to fight the problem is a traditional approach; he orders his land burned. Scientifically educated Gene (long before the Right demonized science along with environmentalism) explains that burning will spread rather than solve the weed problem. The ranchers turn to chemical spraying, seemingly an enlightened approach at the time, though environmentalists have long opposed spraying synthetic concoctions on the good earth.

Again, the issue of violence as a last resort in an attempt to maintain individualism is addressed. At one point Bromfield takes up arms to stop Gene and his crew from spraying his fields. In the film, despite its largely red-state target audience, Bromfield represents the hopeless crackpot conservative element. Today, viewers may perceive him in more complex ways, perhaps as a righteous antigovernment individual standing up to an advancement that creates problems all its own. The film does not address the consequences of spraying, largely because they were not yet fully recognized. In this case, Bromfield might be seen as a civil libertarian rather than a conservative. If environmental issues appear at best clouded here, the political point of view is clear. Contrary to popular opinion, particularly in today's red states, of the Western as an entertainment form that validates a conservative viewpoint, *Sierra Sue* shows that individualism in local areas must be curtailed by the federal government.

The same year, stripping mountains for wood by big timber companies

Seeking out the enlightened rich. Gene brings his ballads to the wealthy, some of whom are won over to his environmental cause. Sunset in Wyoming *does not attack the institution of capitalism, only businesspeople who refuse to take into account the natural world. Courtesy Republic Pictures.*

became the central issue in Gene's *Sunset in Wyoming* (William Morgan, 1941). Cutting down tall trees on Mount Warner devastates farmers and cowboys below. "Nature rebelled," we are informed, as "every drop of rain that fell" on the barren incline "became a torrent" that wiped out buildings, crops, cattle, and people. "Strip that mountain of every tree that grows," an overzealous timberman instructs his crew. He represents yet one more million-dollar corporation that cares nothing for natural habitat. The commune down below only asks the company to "from now on plant something for everything [it] cut down." Though this sounds like a logical solution, the timber company's administrators toss the problem to state and federal officials: "Deforestation is a government matter." Yet when the cattlemen decide to lynch those responsible, Gene insists that law and order be obeyed. One of the ranchers asks, "Whose side are you on, Autry?" As always, the side of meditation and mediation.

Gene goes to visit the absentee owner of the lumber concern far off in a huge city. "Sometimes, a company gets so big that the men on the top don't know what's going on at the bottom," he muses. Gramps (George Cleveland), a decent enough sort, is at heart an environmentalist. Unfortunately, control has been seized by a mid-level employee, Larry (Robert Kent), who represents the emergent corporate mentality that considers profits and nothing but. The problem is not the concept of capitalism, only its raw extreme when there is no oversight by the federal government. In a perfect world, that would not be necessary. We do not live in a perfect world. This suited villain is opposed by Gramps, a more enlightened entrepreneur who advises, "Making money is fine, but some ways of making it are not." This is the Hollywood paradigm, and not only for Westerns: criticize capitalism at its worst while defending basic principles of the economic system. Gene's solution is to turn the area into a park for wildlife with "every single beast in his natural habitat, Nature's wonderland!" Gramps agrees.

A closet populist, Autry circulates a petition among locals requesting that the land be seized by the state. When this happens, Gene explains, "all our problems are over. They'll start planting things instead of cutting them down." Locals agree. They not only accept but are eager for government takeover. When Gene forces money-mad Larry out and restores Gramps to his rightful position, the corporation supports rather than opposes the refuge plan. The conclusion is an early on-screen precursor to a major company changing its tune and going green in the popular progressive twenty-first-century sense.

Exploitation of the land by miners who cut deep into and across the earth, stripping away quality soil that might be needed later, did seem a likely cause for another environmental Western. Surprisingly, though, *Stardust on the Sage* (William Morgan, 1942) set up the premise only to conclude with a dishonest resolution. The head of Rawhide Mining Company (Emmett Vogan) is the worst sort of Westerner, a man in a suit who aligns himself with Eastern money interests. Together they sell stock in the venture to naïve local cattlemen who assume this activity will help them navigate into a progressive future. Gene is set up as a traditionalist: "Me being a cattleman, I'd like a cattle community like Rawhide [to] stay that way." However much that sounds like the opening of a pro-nature piece, with conservatism and conservation linked, Gene turns out to be a conservative in the most reactionary sense. He refuses to consider new ideas, good or bad, and objects to mining not out of any great love for the land but from a deep-seated fear of change.

A nice local boy (William Henry), sucked into the plan, dons a suit and invests the cowboys' pooled money in the mine. This proves disastrous. An early example of modern media manipulation is on hand as an ambitious blond (Edith Fellows) interviews Gene on the radio, asking what he thinks of the quality of local cattle. Autry replies: "Great!" The show is taped rather than live. As Autry leaves, she edits the piece so his answer appears to be in response to the question "What do you think of the mine?" As Gene is a hero of the locals, they hurry to invest. "Radio certainly reaches the masses!" the woman notes. The result leaves Gene furious. Radio-station managers use their power to turn everyone against Gene, and he becomes a Frank Capra–style Everyman, unfairly cast as an enemy of the people. At this point the film compromises its opportunity for a pro-environmental statement. The mine isn't so bad, Autry concludes, so long as the Eastern cartel is out and it's now owned, regulated, and run by Westerners. A concern for conservation is dropped as *Stardust* abandons environmentalism for staunch regionalism.

Even in films that did not directly address issues related to the environment, this new sensibility made itself felt through other avenues. These include the selection of songs and the manner in which they were performed. In *Trail to San Antone* (John English, 1947) Gene plays a returning World War II veteran who now considers the landscape in a new way. "That's my home," he sings, sitting inside a cabin gazing out at the wide-open spaces with new appreciation. As Gene sings of the mountains, cutaways allow us to see them in their natural glory. The same holds true for the rivers and prairies until his window transforms into a virtual screen on which natural beauty is projected as sight and sound charmingly merge.

Gene Autry's competitor to become the top hand at Republic studios got his start as a sideline singer with the Sons of the Pioneers who often was billed as Dick Weston.[6] Roy Rogers won his first speaking role as a bad guy put in his place by Gene in *The Old Corral* (Joseph Kane, 1938). Rogers's charisma led to leading roles, initially in period-piece pictures playing the title characters in *Young Buffalo Bill* (Kane, 1940), *Young Bill Hickok* (Kane, 1940), and *Jesse James at Bay* (Kane, 1941). In the postwar era Rogers did make contemporary environmental oaters, most prominent among them *Susannah Pass* (William Witney, 1949). This Tru-Color film reprised the wildlife-refuge theme, here wed to a fish hatchery, both relatively new concepts. The opening sets up a value system that dares question hunting:

in pastoral blue-greens a deer and her newborn graze. Men enter; the tone turns grim. Not unlike the classic death scene for the title animal's mother in Walt Disney's *Bambi* (1942), shots ring out. In *Susannah Pass* it's the baby that's killed.

The film focuses on two brothers, the good Russel Masters (Lucien Littlefield), who wants to keep the lake clean so locals can raise trout as a communal endeavor, and the bad Martin (Robert Emmett Keane), who hopes to buy up the property and search for oil. Costuming fits this theme, the good one decked out in a leather jacket, signifying closeness to nature. Such symbolism works less well today, as some animal's life had to be sacrificed. The bad brother most often appears in the genre villain's guise of big-city suits and ties. Dale Evans plays a marine biologist who joins Westerner Roy, a rough-hewn conservationist, to stop the exploitation. The film turns overtly didactic, rare for Republic, as Roy directly addresses the camera to deliver an environmentalist speech about ensuring that our children's children "will have the same possibilities as our forefathers had" back when conservatism and conservation were not perceived as conflicting interests.

By the early 1950s, "environmentalism" had entered the popular lexicon. *Hills of Utah* (John English, 1951) returned to the ploy of big-business copper mines in conflict with cattle companies. In the time of Rachel Carson, environmental issues are developed. Unconcerned about the condition of local land, miners pollute water the cowboys depend on for grazing areas. Cattle that drink from the streams die, as in *Back in the Saddle* ten years earlier. This time, Autry openly addresses the pollution issue. Still, we are dealing not with a message movie but entertainment, the product of a Hollywood that was nothing if not capitalistic. So the final result is a compromise, more ideal than real. Miners, willing to meet old-timers halfway thanks to Gene, request a right of way. This allows toxins to run off to a place where herds don't graze. Slow-to-change cattlemen won't consider this; they believe the environment should be protected. From our perspective, ostensible hero Autry, adept at solving problems, comes across as an unworthy compromiser. By insisting the cowboys go along with this plan, Gene ensures that the pollution problem gets altered but not solved.

Closer to a modern (liberal) sensibility is *Blue Canadian Rockies* (George Archainbaud, 1952). A rancher's daughter (Gail Davis) decides to turn a high timber area into a dude ranch. Her father (Don Beddoe), angered, sends Gene to halt her project. Initially, Gene agrees with the old-timer, though eventually he's won over to the dude-ranch idea. What he doesn't realize is that besides bringing folks in to visit, she plans to create a wildlife refuge. There will be no cutting of timber, which infuriates a big company operating nearby. Her progressive views also lead to a requirement that people employed at the ranch all be Native American. Hallmarks of their rich culture are placed on view for educational as well as entertainment purposes. Won over, Gene proclaims, "That's a great idea, protecting our wildlife!" while honoring the Indians. She and Gene agree that hunting will not be tolerated, and everyone will be free to explore nature and peacefully learn about it. Gene and sidekick Pat Buttrum balk at that idea but give in and come to believe she's right about this too. When they do, they have, knowingly or not, subscribed to the concept of gun control. Nothing could be more progressive than that.

From "my" to "our." (a) Red River *depicts a rugged individualist's sense of personal ownership. (b)* Bend of the River *provides an alternative as farmer Jeremy Baile (Jay C. Flippin) insists to colleagues (Chubby Johnson, Stepin Fetchit) that all profits must be shared equally. Courtesy United Artists; Universal Pictures.*

RED STATES, RED MENACE

OF COWBOYS AND COMMUNISM

I didn't truckle for gold. I told them the truth. It mattered
little to me whether they liked it or not. I did my job!
—FRANK NORRIS, *MCTEAGUE*, 1899

Nongeneric films set in the West can relate realistic human dramas with-out clichés or conventions. Eric von Stroheim's much-mangled *Greed* (1925), adapted from Frank Norris's 1899 novel *McTeague*, is such a piece. The film, not surprisingly a box-office dud, conveys its anticapitalist theme without pulled punches. Two friends in California overcome any arguments, even when McTeague (Gibson Goland) wins away the fiancée (ZaSu Pitts) of Marcus (Jean Hersholt). Then a lottery ticket, purchased for the girl by her since-jilted suitor, pays off, and Marcus seethes. For the once-destitute cou-ple, the sum ought to allow them to live out the American Dream. But for Norris, those who win big in the system become the greatest losers. To sug-gest this is to attack not only the system's inequities but the system itself. The wife, now obsessed with the idea of money, hoards the coins until they can-not afford the basic necessities. Eventually, her husband, crazed with hunger, strangles her to death. Marcus, unable to forget or forgive, tracks McTeague into America's hell on earth, Death Valley. There the two carelessly spill their all-important water while wrestling over gold. In the film's final long shot, the winner, McTeague, sits waiting to die, refusing to crawl away, as that would mean leaving his fortune. The ideology: capitalism kills. The implication: communism is an answer.

Norris's story achieved some popularity in book form because a small intellectual elite following proved large enough to qualify the cheaply printed tome as a success. The MGM film failed, as a naturalistic vision of the West as cruel jungle rather than romantic garden was not the sort of thing that drew in a mass audience. This does not mean Hollywood could not criticize the unpleasant realities of capitalism. *Bend of the River* (Anthony Mann, 1952), from the 1950 novel *Bend of the Snake* by William Gulick, concerns the scout Glyn McLyntock (James Stewart) and his rogue companion Emerson Cole (Arthur Kennedy) competing for the hand of a beauty, Laura Baile (Julia Adams), as they guide a wagon train into the far reaches of Oregon. There's gunplay aplenty, essential to the package that ticket buyers of the 1950s expected. The screenplay was written by Borden Chase, often associated with films starring John Wayne and in particular the classic *Red River*, causing Chase to be perceived as right-wing. Yet in *Bend of the River* he tells a similar story from the opposite point of view.

Once again there is the man with a dream. A farmer named Jeremy Baile (Jay C. Flippin) plans to seed the Northwest. Chase allows him a speech like that of Dunson, Wayne's character in *Red River*, in which Dunson uses the pronoun "I" in stating his ambitions for the ranch. At a similar point in this film, Jeremy Baile spells out his vision; however, "I" is replaced by "we," in

> a new country where we can make things grow. We'll find a valley where the earth is rich. We'll use the trees that nature has given us, cut a clearing in the wilderness. We'll put in roads. We'll build our homes, build 'em strong to stand against the winter snow. We'll have a meeting house. We'll have a school. Then we'll put down seed. They'll be apples. Pears. In a few years, we'll bring fruit to the world.

All is communal in a situation identical to some group undertaking in examples of Soviet cinema like *Old and New* (Sergei Eisenstein, 1929). Yet this film does not, like *McTeague*, attack capitalism per se. The farmers hope to make money. So do the townspeople in Portland who sell them supplies. They party together after the caravan's arrival in a scene that resembles *Red*

River's end-of-trail sequence. We meet what appears the equivalent of the enlightened businessman in that film. In this film his name is Hendricks (Howard Petrie). Plans are made to send more supplies up to settlers by riverboat for the coming winter. Eventually, McLyntock and Jeremy Baile head back to Portland to find out why the supply boats did not arrive. The town is now a cesspool. Formerly friendly Hendricks has turned nasty. Why? Gold has been discovered in the mountains. He can sell the settlement's goods to miners for ten times what he asked from settlers.

This approach—openly criticizing the worst aspects of capitalism without challenging the system itself—continues a tradition that dates back to the birth of the big Western with *The Covered Wagon*. Based on Edward Emerson Hough's 1922 novel, James Cruze's 1923 film brings that author's Manifest Destiny theme to the screen: God wanted the West settled, so going there was not only an American right but a Christian duty. As the heroes of *The Covered Wagon* are farmers, this isn't a hard sell; they dream of becoming the Poor Richards of the West, getting rich slowly. The villains are those who desert the dream for the lust for gold. Halfway through this 1848 journey to Oregon the pioneers learn the precious metal has been discovered in California. Half the people in the train throw their plows away and head in that direction. Hero Jess Wingate (Charles Ogle) sticks to his original plan. In a symbolic shot, the caravan splits in half. The raw capitalists head out to make it or break it in the chaos in California. Enlightened capitalists continue on to the rich northern farmlands. There is no question as to which set of characters wins full approval from the authorial voice.

The emblematic scene conveys the paradigm of the Hollywood Western and, in truth, American commercial film: uphold the essential principles of capitalism and the need for a moral conscience. While this seemed fair enough when the principle was applied to farmers, the vision would prove trickier when dealing with the railroads. Most progressives decried the underhanded means by which tycoons calculatedly seized land and power to produce the highest profits. On August 19, 1882, a political cartoon appeared in the *Wasp*, a nineteenth-century West Coast magazine with leftist leanings, in which the Southern Pacific was depicted as an immense octopus, each of its tentacles strangling some form of human life: cities, bridges, ships at sea, factories, and groups of people as well as individuals. Searching for a follow-up to *McTeague*, Norris seized on illustrator G. Frederick Keller's concept, fully fleshing it out for his next novel.

"I been workin' on the railroad." As in John Ford's silent The Iron Horse, Sergio Leone in Once Upon a Time in the West *lionized not the entrepreneurs but blue-collar types who performed the grunt work of building a railroad. Courtesy Paramount Pictures.*

In *The Octopus: A Tale of California* (1901) Norris tells the tale of the 1880 Mussel Slough tragedy.[1] The railroad seized, by legal if immoral means, land belonging to farmers and ranchers in the San Joaquin Valley. Despite earlier range wars between those two groups, in this setting they are depicted as a single entity, united communes of hardworking people standing up against the rugged individualists. The political novel preached to the converted, those academics who read liberal political tracts. Hollywood wanted no part of it. *Greed's* box-office disaster would teach studio heads a lesson: the public wished to be mesmerized with glorious myths of national greatness. Railroads would be treated no differently than the farmers in creaky Conestoga wagons.

If *The Covered Wagon* rates as Hollywood's first attempt at an epic Western, *The Iron Horse* (John Ford, 1924) stands as the initial example of that form to reach great artistic heights. Ford's innate genius, hinted at in earlier, smaller oaters, exploded on the screen with this immense cinematic retelling of the against-all-odds task of completing the first transcontinental railroad. Nowhere is there a hint of the grim realism of France's Emile Zola that had inspired Norris's vision. As in his later masterworks, Ford revealed himself to be the Shakespeare of the cinema. Pageantry and sweep, intimate sentiment and broad humor, and unbridled patriotism to inspire all who saw it characterize Ford's approach. Like the Bard playing to groundlings, Ford chose to focus not on entrepreneurs but the common men who did the hard work of laying track. His hero (George O'Brien) is a scout, Fenimore Cooper's Hawkeye on horseback. Following him comes an integrated group of blue-collar types: Irish and Italian immigrants, former Yanks and Rebs cooperating in the rebirth of a nation, Anglo and Asian workers side by side.

Intriguingly, the tycoon (Will Walling) is kept in the background, though he appears an honest capitalist inspired by Lincoln himself (Charles Edward Bull) to push ahead not only for possible profits but also "impelled westward on the strong urge of progress." Marauding Indians aren't the villains, either, but rather naïve souls hoping to hang onto their land. A raw capitalist (Cyril Chadwick) works for the tycoon yet hopes to sabotage the grand scheme for individual profits. A decade and a half later, Hollywood's spectacular showman Cecil B. DeMille would tell essentially the same story in *Union Pacific* (1939). Once more, a scout (Joel McCrea) is the central character. Again, Indians—if antagonists—are not evil. That distinction goes to a banker (Henry Kolker), the designated heavy of Depression-era films as well as in Ford's *Stagecoach*. In the DeMille film, the self-serving banker, hoping to profit by manipulating the railroad's failure, hires cut-throats to block its completion. The railroad tycoons are kept in the background here, with the false suggestion that they are benign. We do get to meet General Grenville Dodge (Francis McDonald), another entirely sympathetic character who builds the town at end of track.

That year, 1939, when the studios finally returned to the big Western, *Dodge City* (Michael Curtiz) told the same story from another perspective. Dodge (Henry O'Neil) is the first character we meet, riding west on the original train into the city that will bear his name,[2] in the company of two suited railroad tycoons. Played as enlightened capitalists, they are interested in doing good for the country. In an indelible image, a stagecoach tries to race the train but can't keep up with it. Dodge peers out at the coach's driver, sensing with sweet-spirited sadness that, in a Spenserian sense, the stagecoach was a good idea whose time has passed. Dodge says of the mechanized steel contraption, "Gentlemen, that's the symbol of America's future. Progress! Iron men in iron horses. You can't beat 'em."

Owners of the stage lines are transformed from tragic victims to hissable villains in *A Ticket to Tomahawk* (Richard Sale, 1950), in which such a person (Mauritz Hugo) tries to blow up the railroad so it won't cut into his profits. The setting now relocated to Colorado, a fictional railroad tycoon (Paul Harvey) says to Kit Dodge:

There's a lot at stake in this railroad, [and] I'm not talking about any personal advantages to me. I'm talking about [the] country! They [the stage-
line owners] are only thinking about themselves . . . and not the country!

For a mass audience that likes things structured, the poles were outlined
during the film's first ten minutes. The country is a federation, not a con-
federacy, and national interests must take precedence over local concerns.
This paradigm, once set in place, would carry through virtually all railroad
Westerns to appear in the postwar era: *Dakota* (Joseph Kane, 1945), *Tycoon*
(Richard Wallace, 1947), *Rock Island Trail* (Kane, 1949), *Canadian Pacific*
(Edwin L. Marin, 1949), *Santa Fe* (Irving Pichel, 1951), *The Denver and the
Rio Grande* (Byron Haskin, 1952), *Kansas Pacific* (Ray Nazarro, 1953), *Over-
land Pacific* (Fred F. Sears, 1954), and *Night Passage* (James Neilson, 1957).
A resurgence of big business in America after more than a decade and a half
of weak economic times led to a renaissance for Western movies that pro-
vided false odes to industrial imperialism. Even in that era's most left-leaning
Westerns, motivations of railroaders went unchallenged. Despite communal

End of an era. The opening scene of Dodge City *visually formalizes the passing of a way (the
stagecoach) as a wave of the future (the railroad) appears. No matter how hard humans and
beasts try, the race will be won by the machine. Courtesy Warner Brothers.*

"The Octopus" revisited. With misshapen fingers resembling cruel tentacles, a raw-capitalist railroad owner crushes a humanlike doll in Once Upon a Time in the West. *Courtesy Paramount Pictures.*

characters gathered around saloon keeper Vienna (Joan Crawford) in her socialistic enterprise, *Johnny Guitar* presents the railroad man (Rhys Williams) in a favorable light. He wants to be fair with this strong-willed woman and pay Vienna well for a right-of-way across her land.

With a new decade, though, came an altered outlook. The 1960s overturned all that had been accepted in the past. The shift was obvious even in conventional oaters. In the final third of *How the West Was Won* (George Marshall, 1962) we do not see tycoons but their representative, a line boss (Richard Widmark) who is openly vicious and insensitive, caring naught for Anglos or Indians whose lands the tracks must pass through. In the hands of a self-professed Marxist moviemaker, the results would prove considerably more merciless. *Once Upon a Time in the West* (Sergio Leone, 1968) is, in its narrative, homage to and reworking of *Johnny Guitar*. Here, the woman waiting patiently for the railroad's arrival is Jill (Claudia Cardinale). But if Vienna's enemies are covetous townspeople, in Leone's vision they fade into the background. When cold-blooded killer Frank (Henry Fonda) rapes and attempts to murder Jill, we learn he works for railroad tycoon Morton (Gabrielle Ferzetti). The lovable outlaw Cheyenne (Jason Robards) describes Frank and his railroad tracks: "You leave a slime behind you, like a snail." At last, something of the vision of Norris's *Octopus* arrived on screen, if in a European-lensed epic.

Once Upon a Time employs its fairytale motif for the most ironic purposes, as at last viewers encounter an honest vision of the iron horse. Leone's film was co-written by Bernardo Bertolucci, whose radical politics are obvious in his own films including *Before the Revolution* (1964), *The Conformist* (1970), and *1900* (1976). Then again, it must be noted that while the film reaped huge box-office returns in France and Italy, it bombed in the United States, where its radical vision proved too much for mainstream audiences. Also a box-office failure was *Blood Red* (Peter Masterson, 1989), which came closer still to the heart and soul of Norris's novel. This film lionizes the leader, Marco Collogero (Eric Roberts), of Sicilian farmers who attempt to hang onto their grape orchards as railroads rip through the area. There's an irony in the nasty raw capitalist being played by Dennis Hopper, a 1960s leftist who in the 1980s announced he had joined the Far Right only to satirize a king of capital in this film. When Collogero, aware the local politicians are bought off, questions justice in America, he is told, "Justice wears a blindfold. Here, she's deaf and dumb. And she's owned by the railroad."

The new breed of intellectual filmmakers who emerged early in twenty-first-century Hollywood proved able to make films that defy genre and project a more truly anticapitalist vision. Somehow they have managed to win respectable profits along with critical kudos. The most significant piece is *There Will Be Blood* (Paul Thomas Anderson, 2007), adapted from the 1927 novel *Oil* by Upton Sinclair (1878–1968). The California story conveys without consideration of audience expectations the vision of that exposé writer whose 1906 book *The Jungle*, a tirade against working conditions in Chicago's meat-packing industry, is the only rival to Norris's *Octopus* as the period's greatest muckraking work. In *There Will Be Blood* Daniel Day-Lewis plays Plainview, a charismatic individual who shows up in a pleasant community requesting to drill for oil. At first he appears the most decent of capitalists, promising to raise the standard of living for all and use part of the profits to build schools. No sooner is he allowed to begin his project than he despoils the environment and, octopus-like, strangles with invisible tentacles all the residents. Anderson's vision is identical to Sinclair's: this is not another of the Old Hollywood defenses that capitalism does work when practiced by enlightened rather than raw tycoons. The very business of capitalism turns anyone who succeeds at it from enlightened to raw. Finally, the commercial motion picture, including what may be termed a Western, can fully embrace radicalism.

Another country, another revolution. Westerns dealing with Mexico's revolutions regularly place American mercenaries in this boiling pot. Here Rico (Lee Marvin) considers his confused loyalties in The Professionals. *Courtesy Columbia Pictures.*

ONCE UPON A TIME IN A REVOLUTION

RADICAL POLITICS AND THE WESTERN FILM

There is but one legitimate form of war and that is The Revolution!
—VLADIMIR ILYICH LENIN IN *POTEMKIN*, SERGEI EISENSTEIN, 1925

"All power to the people!" That phrase became a popular rallying cry during the late 1960s, when radicalism swept across America, however temporarily. Always reflecting the times during which they are produced, films from this era crystallized such left-of-center values.[1] Among the first was *The Professionals* (Richard Brooks, 1966), in which a seemingly benign American, Joe Grant (Ralph Bellamy), hires four mercenaries for what appears a noble purpose: to rescue his wife from the supposedly ruthless bandit Raza (Jack Palance) who kidnapped her. Two of the professionals, Bill (Burt Lancaster) and Rico (Lee Marvin), previously fought for Pancho Villa in the Mexican Revolution but left when they grew disenchanted after idealism quickly became tainted by the poison of absolute power.

BILL: You want us to go back to Mexico?
RICO: This time, strictly for cash!

The leader, Bill, and dynamite expert Rico are accompanied by bow-and-arrow master Jake Sharpe (Woody Strode), marking one of the first film roles for an African American, however belatedly, as a full and equal character in a community of male professionals. Also along is Hans (Robert Ryan), a skilled wrangler, to handle the horses. The four men complete their journey to Mexico only to realize they've been had. The American's wife, María, a working-class Mexican who married the capitalist only to escape her humble origins, now realizes that decision was a mistake. She was not kidnapped; she chose to run away with the outlaw, her former and current lover. He's less a thief than he is a true revolutionary. In the process of returning María to her husband, the professionals transform from individuals into a tight team. No sooner do they fulfill their mission than they liberate María from the real oppressor, her husband, and send her back home with Raza.

Midway through the film, while watching a brutal attack by Mexican rebels on a *federales* train, this exchange takes place:

> HANS: What are Americans doing in a Mexican revolution anyway?
> BILL: Maybe there's only one revolution. From the beginning. The good
> guys against the bad guys. The question is, who are the good guys?

Their brief exchange, however mild from a twenty-first-century perspective, seemed incendiary in a Hollywood film of that time. So was the notion of a female revolutionary, Chiquita (Maria Gomez). The first mainstream publication to usher in the era of modern feminism, *The Feminine Mystique* by Betty Friedan, appeared in 1963. Popular culture in due time spread to the mainstream the concerns of those more intellectual types who read serious works for pleasure. Though voluptuous, certainly, Chiquita does not remain in camp cooking and washing. She rides with the men, is an expert shot, and lives as an equal to her fellow revolutionaries, as does the black man among Anglos in the opposing group. When Chiquita and Bill, her former lover, find themselves in a duel, she knows he will not take her gender into consideration. They fight to the death (hers). For those who comprehend the women's movement at its most essential, with equal rights go equal responsibilities, even in this extraordinary Hollywood scene.

If Hollywood was not yet ready to tackle a movie with such a woman as the lead, European filmmakers were already on that cutting edge. Louis Malle (1932–1995) would become famous for leftish political films documenting

Girls with guns. Feminist Westerns portray women as revolutionary leaders. In Viva Maria! *two French beauties (Brigitte Bardot, Jeanne Moreau) strike a blow for the greater cause. Courtesy United Artists.*

the deadly monotony the working class endured on France's assembly lines in *Humain, Trop Humain* (1975) or analyzing in fiction form the plight of ethnic workers in *Alamo Bay* (1985). One aspect of his talent was to couch radical political statements within the context of agreeable crowd-pleasers. In *Viva Maria!* (1965) Malle offered two female lead characters named Maria: one (Jeanne Moreau) who has participated in the Irish Republican Army and escapes to Mexico, though that country is never named, and another (Brigitte Bardot) who runs a traveling circus. Together they break all boundaries, cultivating the art of striptease while going against the establishment: the monarchists, the military, the aristocratic class with its capitalism, and ultimately the Church as an agent of the status quo.

Few films so majestically employ the Mexican Revolution as an objective correlative for the modern international one as *Duck, You Sucker* (Sergio Leone, 1971). Co-written by Sergio Donati, it involves John M. (James Coburn), a fugitive from the Irish Republican Army's fight for independence who flees his beloved Emerald Isle when British police close in, and Juan M. (Rod Steiger), a bandit John meets while motorcycling around Mexico. Within the context of the sort of large-screen action and broadly played comedy that characterize Leone's signature style,[2] step by step John guides Juan away from his low-level raw capitalism (stealing for himself and family) to dedication to a cause (robbing the rich to give to the poor). When the self-serving Juan is cheered by the masses, his friend laughs:

JOHN: You're a hero of the revolution!
JUAN: I don't want to be a hero. I just want the money!

By film's end, Juan cares nothing about dollars, only the cause, though it takes the death of John to make him fully grasp this. By cross-cutting between the current revolution and John's earlier role in the Irish struggle, Leone suggests without needing to state openly an overriding vision of revolutionaries everywhere: there is but one revolution; all local examples are variations on this greater universal theme. Perhaps more intriguing even than the leads is the third significant character, Dr. Villega (Ronolo Valli). Modeled on Russia's Leon Trotsky (1879–1940), who, like his fictionalized screen counterpart, did indeed meet his death in Mexico,[3] if at a later date and under entirely different circumstances. Villega is the movement's intellectual leader, more opposed to monarchists than emotionally involved with the proletariat; this is his great failing. Leone's values become clear when, to save his life Villega names names, leading to execution of numerous labor heroes, yet believes in an entirely logical way that he can go on supporting the cause. Forced to recognize the falsity of the compromise, Villega dooms himself by refusing to leap from a locomotive that's about to crash into an enemy train; he is aware now of the contradictions in his way.

By employing Mexico's revolution to comment on the universal concept of a people's revolt, Leone drew on a tradition from previous films including the unfinished masterpiece of Soviet director Sergei M. Eisenstein (1898–1948), *¡Que Viva Mexico!* (1932).[4] Having completed several films about the Russian Revolution, among them *Potemkin* (1925) and *October: Ten Days that Shook the World* (1927), the champion of montage was eager to emerge on the international scene as a communist propagandist. Initially he traveled to the United States hoping to make a film for producer Jesse Lasky of Paramount based on *An American Tragedy* (1925), the novel Theodore Dreiser built around the true story of a poor boy who became a murderer to rise in class by accumulating wealth. Eisenstein also spoke with writer Jack London about collaborating on *Sutter's Gold*, which was to have depicted the discovery of that precious metal in California as the downfall to all those glorious dreams of a pure farming community. Finally, Eisenstein elicited funding for a film about the Mexican Revolution from an American communist, Upton Sinclair. Heading south, he shot more than 200,000 feet of film for the project with Sinclair. The symbolic story focused on a peasant (Martin Hernandez) whose life is ruined when he attempts to stop an aristocrat from raping an innocent village girl. A slowdown in shooting and arguments with Sinclair led to the work's seizure by its U.S. producers, who edited it and released the piece as *Thunder over Mexico* in 1933. Even in an incomplete state, the film—filled with images of brutality to humble laborers—does suggest a worldwide continuum of oppression leading to inevitable rebellion everywhere.

In the Hollywood studios, many of their Mexican Revolution Westerns were biographies of colorful leaders Benito Juárez, Pancho Villa, and Emiliano Zapata, further described in the next chapter. There were fictional pieces as well that conveyed at least a hint of the moral outrage Eisenstein intended for his epic. These films flourished during the 1950s, even as the Western entered a period of transition that linked old-fashioned oaters with the coming darker visions. No film so perfectly captures the moment as *Vera Cruz* (Robert Aldrich, 1954). An aging Gary Cooper embodies previous stalwart heroes from *The Virginian* through *High Noon* as a dignified Southern colonel, Ben Trane. He rides south after the Civil War to make a new life. The colonel is joined en route by Joe Erin (Burt Lancaster), an animalistic killer presaging spaghetti-Western characters yet to come, particularly Eli Wallach's role in *The Good, the Bad, and the Ugly* (Sergio Leone, 1966).

Once upon a time in Mexico. Following the American Civil War, an embittered veteran (Gary Cooper) joins a soldier of fortune (Burt Lancaster) south of the border, the two serving in Vera Cruz *as foils for America's polar values. Courtesy Hecht-Hill-Lancaster/United Artists.*

In *Vera Cruz*, the two men form an uneasy pair; each approaches the Mexican Revolution as a rugged individualist, out strictly for himself. Initially Trane asks one of Emperor Maximilian's officers, Henri de Labordere (Cesar Romero), about joining their forces, indicating his mercenary approach: "How profitable?" Then a Juarista (Morris Ankrum) sighs: "The peasants have no way to pay you." Later this revolutionary explains, "We offer you more than money: a cause!" In time Trane moves over to the peasants' side. Erin laughs at this as absurd and continues to seek cold cash. Both initially believe themselves to be realists, yet Trane reveals himself a closet idealist still, even as Erin degenerates into nihilism. Importantly, it is Trane who survives and succeeds.

Another character who, like Trane in *Vera Cruz*, finds himself on the wrong side of history and fails to arc is Ethan Edwards, John Wayne's antihero in *The Searchers* (John Ford, 1956). Two years after the Civil War he finally returns to Texas, and the medal Ethan bestows on his niece (Lana Wood) is not from the Confederacy but French, suggesting he fought for the monarchist side after heading into Mexico. No wonder, then, that he will finish Ford's film as a crushed, lonely, tragic figure. More than a decade later, in *The Undefeated* (Andrew McLaglen, 1969), Wayne played Colonel John Henry Thomas, a former Union officer herding cattle over the Big River to deliver them to Maximilian's troops for money. But in the company of a former Confederate, Colonel James Langdon (Rock Hudson), who, like Ethan Edwards (at first), plans to sell his gun to the *federales*, Thomas crosses not only the Rio Grande but through conflicting sides, as both of this film's Anglo cowboy heroes reject mercenary interests for the greater moral cause of the people.

Two films from the mid-1950s, both co-starring Gilbert Roland in almost identical roles, offer variations on the theme of an initially cynical American anti-hero who sets aside mercenary capitalist leanings to become infected with commitment to a cause. In both films, the gun for hire is from the beginning working for the good guys if for the wrong reason. In *The Treasure of Pancho Villa* (George Sherman, 1955) and *Bandido* (Richard Fleischer, 1956), Tom Bryan (Rory Calhoun) and Wilson (Robert Mitchum), respectively, sell their gun hands to a dedicated revolutionary (Roland). The revolutionary speaks nearly identical words at this point in both films: "You don't understand us. To you, the revolution is a chance to make money." The moral tug of war for the lead character, then, is not between the *fascisti* and democrats but an inner conflict. At *Treasure's* end, Bryan could grab the money intended for Villa and hurry back stateside but instead delivers it to the off-screen title character. Mitchum's anti-hero in *Bandido*, at first out to make a buck, admits, "I'm in this for the profit." In each case our cowboy hero is won over by the goodness of the cause that touches some long-repressed sense of decency deep within him, the best aspect of his "American" personality (altruism) as compared to the raw capitalism that initially motivated him.

In 1969, the same year McLaglen's highly traditionalist *The Undefeated* appeared, one of the new Westerns tackled the Mexican Revolution from a more timely, 1960s perspective. In *100 Rifles* (Tom Gries, 1969) a wicked American capitalist (Dan O'Herlihy) is identified as a railroad man in league with the local fascist dictator (Fernando Lamas) since that will allow U.S. interests to make money, although they are hampered by chaos from revolutionaries. The cowboy hero (Jim Brown) who gradually moves over to the right side (the left, that is) is black. The emergent civil rights movement allowed African American actors like Brown and Strode (in *The Professionals*) to at last take center stage. More significant still, perhaps, is that the character in *100 Rifles* as written is not necessarily African American. Having a black actor portraying a racially nonspecific character forwarded the civil rights theme further even than *The Professionals*, which was written to feature a black character. In *100 Rifles* we encounter colorblind casting,

One great, worldwide revolution. John (James Coburn), seen from the point of view of Juan (Rod Steiger, off screen), originally appears to be the bandit's chance for capitalist gain in Duck, You Sucker. *Under John's mentoring, Juan instead becomes a true revolutionary. Courtesy United Artists.*

resulting in an on-screen person who moves beyond racial limitations. Compared to the situation in *The Professionals*, the issue of race is never raised and is relegated to a non-issue.

Reflecting the rising tide of feminism as well, the leader of the revolutionaries is a woman (Raquel Welch). Again in *Two Mules for Sister Sara* (Don Siegel, 1970), it is a woman (Shirley MacLaine) who not only inspires the cowboy (Clint Eastwood) to arc but clearly points the way. "The French are torturing the people," this faux nun on a mission tells him, "forcing them to become one of their colonies. I hate that!" Considering the year *Sister Sara* was made, this might be read as the actress speaking about Vietnam as much as the character addressing a historic situation in Mexico. As to his previous commitment in the Civil War, the man in the serape says, "Everyone's got to be a sucker once." By film's end, he is fully converted.

The relationship of politics to religion in the Western genre is implied if not fully developed in *The Wrath of God* (Ralph Nelson, 1972). This film opens with the executions of several peons by Mexican troops. A priest (Robert Mitchum) arrives to give absolution but turns out to be a former IRA member who wields a machine gun. "That's one hell of a mass, Father," an onlooker comments after the priest shoots down the would-be executioners. He appears a false priest even as MacLaine is a pretend nun in *Two Mules for Sister Sara*. In truth, here is religion in the finest sense, not as some arm of and voice for the status quo but a champion of the people and a Christlike inspiration to the poorest of the poor. Such a vision is expressed in *A Town Called Hell* (Robert Parrish, 1971), with Robert Shaw in the role of a priest. The opening features an attack by peasant revolutionaries on a church that caters to high-born aristocracy. The rebels kill all of the worshipers along with the pretentious priests attending to them, with full authorial permission. Shaw's maverick priest, however, they come to adore.

It is important to restate that the Western is a broad enough genre to include multiple points of view. An alternative to most prorevolutionary films, *Cannon for Cordoba* (Paul Wendkoes, 1970) features an alternative vision. The title bandit (Raf Vallone) steals six cannons that General John J. Pershing (John Russell) sent to the Texas border to restore order. As it's illegal for the American military to pursue adversaries across the Rio Grande, Pershing sends a mercenary, Captain Rod Douglas (George Peppard), accompanied by a *Dirty Dozen* team of misfits to retrieve the cannon. Anyone expecting Douglas to be won over was in for a shock. The bandit turns out to be a low-life killer and rapist as well as torturer who uses the cause as a means to fill his own pockets. By implication, *Cannon for Cordoba* suggests that Villa, Zapata, and all their ilk were essentially like this fictional representative. "The revolution was made for people without direction," a character explains. "Now, they have several," all moving toward chaos. Once again, then, no single statement is promoted in the genre. The form can be employed for reactionary or revolutionary purposes. Yet there are far more examples of the latter than the former, defining the Western in practice if not essence.

A more modern and in some ways postmodern variation appears in *The Old Gringo* (Luis Puenzo, 1989). A fictional American woman (Jane Fonda) with no political allegiances heads to Mexico to reinvent her life as a governess. Upon arrival she's thrust into the company of a self-styled rebel general (Jimmy Smits) and the cynical American writer Ambrose Bierce (Gregory Peck). Here at last is a film that dares articulate the true meaning behind all that talk about "the land" and peasants' love and need for it in so many previous works. An American reporter (Jim Metzler) states outright the goal of the revolution: "Private property [will be] abolished in Mexico." This subgenre of the Western, like the historical event on which it is based, is about a desire less for democracy than for communism. Owing to the verbal primacy of the piece, which emphasizes lengthy conversations and stream-of-consciousness narration from the female lead, it is easy to grasp why *The Old*

Gringo proved more successful as a novel by Carlos Fuentes than as a motion picture. All the same, we encounter the least simplistic vision ever of the events, the good, bad, and ugly of revolution: the randomness of death and absurdity of violence, both accompanied by the laughter of abject madness. The film also conveys the inevitability of change, the natural evolution of political ideology, the downtrodden's decision to determine their own destiny, and the necessity of standing on the right side of history even when it obviously fosters much that is clearly wrong.

History versus Hollywood. (a) Wallace Beery, MGM's top character lead, played Villa in the same over-the-top manner as he did his other lovable buffoons. (b) A generation later, Yul Brynner portrayed Pancho as a sophisticated military strategist in Villa Rides! *Courtesy Metro-Goldwyn-Mayer; Paramount Pictures.*

13

VIVA JUÁREZ! VIVA VILLA! VIVA ZAPATA!

THE BIOGRAPHICAL WESTERN AS POLITICAL ALLEGORY

This land is your land; this land is my land . . .
This land was made for you and me.
—WOODY GUTHRIE, 1933

At the end of *The Old Gringo*, the film's fictitious revolutionary leader (Smits) faces charges that he shot an innocent American (Peck) while in a rage brought on by alcohol mixed with sudden power. His fate will be decided by commanding officer Villa, who considers the man calmly. "You know I love you like a son," Villa states, "but you have disobeyed orders." There is no hint of emotion in Pancho's voice, though we note sadness in his eyes as he sentences his *compadre* to death. The condemned calls out "Viva Villa!" one final time. Villa is here played by Pedro Armendáriz Jr., a shrewd choice; his father, the great Pedro Armendáriz (1912–1963), embodied that fabled bandit in many Mexican-produced films and TV series. He was not, however, the first to play the part. That honor went to Pancho Villa himself, in a Hollywood-financed movie that combined footage of actual events with staged scenes for what would eventually be released as *The Life of General Villa* (Raoul Walsh, 1914). Hollywood Marxists hurried down to Mexico, inspired by the success not only of the Russian Revolution but the manner in which Eisenstein realistically captured its surface while employing montage for subliminal manipulation. There they hoped to use their own craftsmanship to lionize Villa as a social bandit.

Villa actually put off attacking his enemies at Ojinaga until a Mutual Films crew arrived to film the event.[1] While Villa played himself (with Walsh subbing as the young Villa), all other roles in this lost movie were handled by professionals. And so the Mexican Revolution provided a venue in which Westerns could express radical views. Any threat of social upheaval was downplayed by locating the action in a Third World country. The premise was that seeing is believing! However naïvely, people trusted the photographic image. "The camera can't lie" soon emerged as the essence of twentieth-century modernism. Of course, it can and in fact does, always, restructuring reality rather than objectively representing it. When such a realization dawned, the era of postmodernism began.[2]

But these were nothing if not modern times. During the Depression, intellectuals and artists openly questioned the seemingly failed capitalistic system. The success of the Russian Revolution a decade earlier caused many to consider what had occurred overseas as a possible remedy here at home. Though Hollywood would not dare to suggest a violent overthrow of the U.S. government, glorifying doing that in other lands provided the perfect means to suggest a need for serious change. *Viva Villa!* (Jack Conway, Howard Hawks, William A. Wellman, 1934) offered a tribute to a "Mexican hero." The villain is President Porfírio Díaz, a spokesman for Spain's "arrogant aristocracy." In Ben Hecht's fanciful screenplay, Pancho Villa's father (Frank Puglia) dies at the hands of a firing squad. Sand flows through the doomed man's fingers as he calls out: "Land!" Here is the peasants' revolt in Russia transferred to a North American state—closer if, wisely, not too close to home for comfort.

As incarnated by Wallace Beery, Villa is a broadly played ignoramus with a heart of gold, a vision that has nothing to do with the historical figure but well served the star's popular persona.[3] The audience's point of view is determined by a U.S. reporter (Stu Erwin) who initially abhors the bloodshed but comes to believe (and informs his readers back home, even as this film informs its audience) that however terrible the violence may be, it is necessary to achieve a greater good. Francisco Madero (Henry B. Walthall), a gentle inspiration to Villa, is played as a combination of Jesus and Vladimir Lenin, a savior who transforms mindless bandits into idealistic revolutionaries. A fictional figure

(Joseph Schildkraut) who turns against Madera is Trotsky by way of Judas. There can be little doubt *Viva Villa!* is as much about the Russian Revolution as Mexico's. "Out of years of battle," the film's closing credits inform us, "arose a new Mexico devoted to liberty and justice." That stated message can be generalized to read, to borrow from English author James Barry, that all this has happened before, and all this will happen again.

Over at Warner Brothers, co-screenwriter John Huston reached back further in Mexican history for *Juarez* (William Dieterle, 1939), dramatizing the 1863 revolt by the Mexican people against French Emperor Louis Napoleon III (Claude Raines). Produced five years after *Viva Villa!*, this film's social consciousness appears less influenced by any positive views of the bygone Russian Revolution than by a desire to express a more up-to-date warning against Hitler. Louis Napoleon, the film shows us, had hoped to "restore to our *race*—and the world—prestige" (emphasis mine). Connecting the historical leader (though American loyalties were in 1939 shifting from Germany to the French) with the Third Reich, the filmmakers created a cautionary fable condemning all racially motivated imperialism. Napoleon sets Austria's Emperor Maximilian von Habsburg (Brian Aherne) on the Mexican throne, believing conservative Spanish aristocrats will appreciate a man of class. The common people of the land refuse to accept him for exactly those reasons.

Despite vivid south-of-the-border settings, *Juarez* played as a nongenre film. Or if it did belong to a genre, then it was a biographical film rather than a Western. Always, though, the mass audience much preferred movies that concerned the men who battled on the front lines, Villa emerging as the most appealing. Partly as a reaction against what the Mexican people viewed as Beery's offensive caricature, coupled with a desire to recognize or perhaps manufacture a people's hero for their country, Latino filmmakers seized control of their own Robin Hood. The John Wayne of Mexican movies, Pedro Armendáriz Sr. proved perfect to embody the renowned yet unpretentious image. The first film, a modest venture called *Vuelva Pancho Villa* (Miguel Contreras Torres, 1950), failed to fully realize this vision. The focus remains on an initially apolitical peon (Rudolfo Acosta). After *federales* invade and Villa liberates the village, the young man joins up, realizing that the revolution is more important even than his love for his woman. Villa remains remote throughout, a simplistic savior figure.

One of those who saw this movie was Ismael Rodríguez (Ruelas, 1917–2004). A filmmaker too, he was inspired to lure Pedro back to the part while

Dumb like a fox. In several films shot in Mexico, Pedro Armendáriz Sr. portrayed a more rounded and complex Pancho Villa, pretending to be naïve in order to seize the upper hand. Courtesy Películas Rodríguez.

providing the actor with a more fully realized vision. The approach was clear in the first of a trilogy, *Así era Pancho Villa* (1957). The writer-director employed three introductory devices. There is an image of a shrine Pancho created in his lifetime to house his eventual corpse and a plea to the people to relocate his long-buried bones here. This is spoken by Pedro, embodying Villa's undying spirit. Next there is homage to *Citizen Kane* (Orson Welles, 1941). Borrowing its classic final shot, Rodríguez's camera pushes downward through myriad objects, invaluable art mixed with worthless junk, until finally it arrives at this movie's Rosebud: the head of Villa in a bottle, pickled by his enemies. Just as Welles unlocked the mystery of a great but flawed man, so does this aspiring auteur. Finally, there are Rodríguez's own words, describing his aesthetic: included here are vignettes told and retold until no one could verify the degree to which any one was factual or fabrication. "I have wanted to believe them," Rodríguez admits, explaining: "I will tell them as if they were true" and "in my own voice." It is necessary for us to recognize the uniqueness of the telling as well as the universality of the tale.

As John Ford himself would in time venture, when the legend becomes fact, print the legend.

Rather than ignore Beery's buffoonish approach (many of the indigenous Villa tales include this element), Rodríguez introduces it to expand from that point. In this incarnation Villa embodies a variation on the ancient wise fool figure, pretending to be dumb, even crazy, to—like the fox—trick enemies and win. The first film contains stories already presented in *Viva Villa!* In one, a man loses control, tries to rape a woman, then shoots her farmer husband when he hurried to her rescue. Villa surprises everyone when he seemingly forgives his soldier despite a promise that all transgressors will be executed. With a broad grin, Pancho insists this man marry the newly widowed woman, much to her horror. No sooner has the wedding taken place than Villa orders the man's execution. Instead of being left penniless, the now twice-widowed woman will receive full compensation due the survivor of any member of Villa's army. This Solomon-like wisdom is emphasized by a sequence in which Pancho studies a book about that Hebraic king's approach.

The most telling episode is a tale that involves Villa and a good priest loyal to the cause. When a dying soldier whispers during his swift confession the location of hidden ammunition, Pancho insists that the priest break his vows and reveal the whereabouts. The priest refuses, certain Villa will honor his commitment to Catholicism. With regret, Pancho orders him shot. Loyalty to Pancho Villa must not take second place to anything. The revolution is not only a new politics but also a new religion, the two inseparable.

The second installment, *Pancho Villa y la Valentina* (1960), opens with several of Villa's men pouring kerosene over a bound youth, planning to set him on fire. When Pancho asks what crime he's been found guilty of, he's told the man named his dog after the general. On the one hand, a dog can be considered a lowly cur, and this one is particularly ugly. In such a case, the naming would be an insult. On the other hand, a dog may be thought of as man's best friend, its ugliness endearing. The naming could be considered a warm salute. Without cross-examining the accused Pancho assumes the best, setting this man free. If the fellow is not already a Villa supporter, he'll be a convert from this moment on.

Openly admitted are Villa's sudden extremes that made him as unpredictable as the Old Testament Yahweh. In the Little General we witness his notably brutal slaying with a machete of a revolutionary he believes to be a traitor.

Immediately afterward, Pancho cares for a child, constantly risking his own life to save the orphan and weeping aloud when the little one expires. But even a larger-than-life figure must have a weakness. In Pancho's case it is, Ulysses-like, the face (and figure) of some beautiful woman. He grows tongue-tied at the sight of the other title character (Elsa Aguire), a dominatrix who seduces the general but may be the mistress of the army officer (Arturo Martinez) pursuing him. No matter; Pancho can forgive her anything. At heart, he's a romantic. The film's audience loves him all the more for it.

The third, *Cuando ¡Viva Villa! es la muerte* (1960), reveals in its anecdotes that the complaints of Villa's grotesque cruelty were all grounded in truth. Rodríguez nonetheless argues in favor of forgiving Pancho. Though he steals the woman of a close friend, Pancho graciously returns her when "done." If he must execute a former ally, he takes the responsibility of doing so himself rather than leaving the task to a firing squad. Perhaps most telling is the tale of the purportedly poisoned coffee. Aware that some close ally is a traitor, Villa insists he knows the man's identity. He has a peasant woman serve all his officers coffee, insisting only the guilty man's cup contains poison. At gunpoint, he forces them to drink. One tries to run away and is shot. The others are concerned: What if Villa had been mistaken and poisoned one of the loyal company? He laughs, drinking the guilty party's cup. There was no poison. He used the ruse to make the betrayer reveal himself. When Villa is finally assassinated, Rodríguez leaves us with the impression that a truly radical innocent has been murdered by lesser men and must be thought of as a sacrificial lamb, dying in the name of a specific sort of freedom: common people retrieving their land, communal values defeating capitalist tyranny.

During the post–World War II era of McCarthy's witch hunting, it became necessary to couch any such statements so the artist-entertainers would not be blacklisted. In *Viva Zapata!* (Elia Kazan, 1952) Marlon Brando stars as "the Villa of the South." Though the script was written by John Steinbeck, in this fearful era it was necessary to insist the revolution was democratic, not communistic. So when Zapata complains that Díaz is a false president owing to fixed elections, a *compadre* explains that to the north, America is a "true democracy" as compared to their false one. Developed here is a liberal-progressive theme suggested in *Viva Villa!*—the need for universal education as a means to achieve power for the people. In the film's most touching sequence, Zapata forges consummation with his beautiful wife (Jean Peters) on their wedding night. Instead, she teaches him to read.

On the importance of literacy. Liberal-minded writer John Steinbeck and director Elia Kazan employed Emiliano Zapata to express their progressive values. The hero in Viva Zapata! *(Marlon Brando) asks his bride (Jean Peters) to teach him to read. Courtesy Twentieth Century-Fox.*

Villa would also be the subject of a 1950s Hollywood film, if one of the B movie order, *Villa!* (James B. Clark, 1958). Pancho was played by Mexican actor Rudolfo Hoyes Jr. rather than a Hollywood star in makeup. He appears dignified rather than clownish. In one of scriptwriter Louis Vittes's innovations, the tale is told over the shoulder of an American cowboy hero (Brian Keith) who, like his counterparts in many fiction films, crosses over from mercenary to true believer. This device would be further developed in *Villa Rides!* (Buzz Kulik, 1967), with Robert Mitchum playing the fictional rugged individualist who by film's end has come to see the light. Intriguingly, the screenplay by Robert Towne and Sam Peckinpah (the latter originally set to direct) distances its title hero (Yul Brynner) from Beery's buffoon. More than clever, this Villa comes across as calculated. He and his men make ready to ride to the aid of a town besieged by Colorados, the virtual S.S. of the Mexican army. Even as innocent people including friends of Pancho are hanged, the social bandit refuses to allow his cavalry to ride in and save them. Only after the atrocities have been completed do they attack. Villa's

Of politics and religion. A meaningful statement can, in a movie, be conveyed in purely visual terms. Hated federales *fire on peasants from behind crosses, implicating the Catholic Church in the fascistic regime in* Viva Zapata! *Courtesy Twentieth Century-Fox.*

reasoning: to win over the villagers from being apolitical types to becoming fervent followers who hate the Colorados as he does, it's necessary that they suffer terribly. A dark view from post–Korean War years is superimposed on a cinematic canvas of the past.

Likewise, a sense of cynicism suffuses *Pancho Villa* (Eugenio/Gene Martín, 1972), which begins long after the hero's golden age has faded. The year is 1916; a past-his-prime Pancho (Telly Savalas) and his onetime *compañeros* drink in a makeshift movie house, watching black-and-white films about the good old days. Pancho grows angry with American businessmen who rip him off for guns that are never delivered. Fearful he's no longer perceived as a hero to his countrymen, Pancho decides to cross the border and bring the revolution to the United States. The incident involving an attack on Columbus, New Mexico, is based in fact. Yet the film's style is anything but realistic, combining elements of previous non-Westerns like *The Mouse That Roared* (1959), *Dr. Strangelove, or How I Learned to Stop Worrying and Love the Bomb* (1964), and *The Russians Are Coming, The Russians Are Coming*

(1966). The American West the aging revolutionaries invade has more ice cream parlors than saloons, which, surprisingly, was the case in reality.[4] The military commander (Chuck Connors) is a martinet who combines aspects of George C. Scott's crazed general in *Strangelove* with that actor's Oscar-winning turn in *Patton* (1970). The obligatory cowboy (Clint Walker) turns out to be a henpecked husband intimidated by his wife (Anne Francis). A small-town sheriff wants to ticket Pancho for driving his car too fast (25 mph) down Main Street. Believing himself about to die of a heart attack, Pancho becomes a pathetic crybaby. He cares less about accomplishing anything of value than in posing for photo opps. The final image of Pancho's train crashing head-on into another carrying U.S. troops plays as both apocalyptic and nihilistic, a fitting Villa Western for the period that would see the release of *Taxi Driver* (1976).

Every bit as appropriate for the early twenty-first century was *And Starring Pancho Villa as Himself* (Bruce Beresford, 2004), which brings us full circle. Larry Gelbart's script focuses on the Hollywood film crew that arrived to capture events of the Mexican Revolution on celluloid. While the original *Life of General Villa* set into motion the assumed realism of the camera age, helping to create modernity, nearly a century later here is its postmodern bookend: a film that deconstructs the film that started it all. It's a movie about movies—making movies, watching movies, and the extreme danger of believing movies. As ever, this film draws issues from its own era and presents them in a historical setting. The reason for a possible invasion of Mexico by the American military is a need for its oil reserves, threatened by the revolt. While earlier films attempted to determine whether Villa (Antonio Banderas) was a social hero or cold-blooded killer, this one says we can never know. He is both and neither. He was a man, as Hamlet would say: take him all in all, we will not see his like again. The masses draw their idea of Villa from movies, more true to the surface of life than any preceding art form yet equally (perhaps more) dishonest about the essence. Films of the twentieth century wove their magic spell by manipulating the public with the then-new notion that seeing is believing. This idea failed to take into account that what we see and believe is an artistic construct, as far from the reality that inspired it as a painting, novel, or piece of music. Films of the twenty-first century attempt to shake us into postmodernist awareness: Open your eyes; grasp that we can never know anything for certain.[5] Take in all; trust nothing.

Particularly anything we've ever seen in the movies!

The emergence of an American myth. During the first half of Red River, *Wayne played his young cowboy for the final time; in the movie's second movement he emerges as the cattle baron. Courtesy United Artists.*

ALL THE RIGHT STUFF
THE WORLD ACCORDING TO JOHN WAYNE

Funny, but I never thought of myself as a cowboy.
—JOHN WAYNE, PRESS CONFERENCE
FOR *BRANNIGAN*, LONDON, 1975

Any discussion of the Western and its tendency to lean left must pause for
a long, hard look at the films of John Wayne, particularly those beginning
in 1960. Hollywood's compleat, canonical superstar then found himself in
a position to determine the political undercurrents of what appeared to
be nothing more than big, entertaining oaters. In *North to Alaska* (Henry
Hathaway, 1960), when federal troops arrive in Skagway to resolve a feud
between Sam McCord (Wayne) and some unpleasant neighbors, he makes
clear that their intervention is not welcome. Stay the hell out, he snarls; let
the two camps decide locally who wins this mine by Spencer's social Darwinism. Survival of the fittest, winner take all. In his most personal project,
The Alamo (Wayne, 1960), speeches of a patriotic nature abound. Here is
Wayne the "America, how I love her!" flag-waver. Amid all the sound and
fury, though, one statement stands out. Wayne became so fond of the words,
penned by James Edward Grant, he insisted they be included on the album:

Republic! I like the sound of the word. Means that people can live free, talk free, go or come, buy or sell, be drunk or sober, however they choose. Some words give you a feeling. Republic is one of those words.

These are not the sentiments of the historical Crockett, here employed as a template on which Wayne imposes his own views in the present on a situation from the past. Wayne had reason to squirm while watching *The Last Command* (Frank Lloyd, 1955), an earlier Alamo film.[1] In it, Tennesseans who follow Crockett to Texas wear identical buckskin jackets and coonskin caps to those of their leader (Arthur Hunnicutt). The idea, if we accept image as ideology in the primarily visual art of film, is left-leaning. This shouldn't come as a surprise from a director whose previous work includes *Mutiny on the Bounty* (1935), championing a workers' revolution against those in command. Wayne felt the need to project an oppositional vision; his Tennesseans each wear some clearly distinguishable costume, caps made from animals as diverse as possum and skunk. These are individualists, aligned in a loose confederacy.

"I'm not thinkin'," Wayne's Crockett declares toward the end of *The Alamo*. "I'm rememberin'." From that moment on, his work would grow ever more melancholic. Wayne, always the film's voice if not its writer or director, reflects on his life and values, offering emotional and ideological autobiography presented in the guise of a generic Western. The fictional George Washington McLintock in *McLintock* (Andrew McLaglen, 1963) and basically factual, though more casually so than his Crockett, John Chisum in *Chisum* (McLaglen, 1970) serve as the authors' mouthpieces, even if these films were officially written by Grant and Andrew J. Fenady, respectively. Wayne's role as the aging but still dominating patriarch is clear from *McLintock*'s opening shot. Like cattlemen in earlier films, McLintock must deal with the reality of settlers moving onto open range. In this role, Wayne surprises us with his less than conventionally conservative stance. Other ranchers, like land barons in old movies, talk about running off the sodbusters. McLintock accepts change and attempts to convince others to go along with "progress," long since established in oaters as a feminine or liberal value. His main concern is not the ranch he owns but those newcomers he believes will likely try and fail. "Even the *government* should know you can't farm 6,000 feet above sea level," he scoffs. He is talking, of course, about federal, not local, politicians.

The problem, as he sees it, is not with farmers. He admires them from a

King of the cowboys. In McLintock, *one of John Wayne's most personal projects, the Duke played a progressive cattleman who stoically accepts the coming of the future and, to a degree, even embraces it. Courtesy Batjac Productions/United Artists.*

distance as yet another aspect of the American Dream he embodies. Politicians in Washington may mean well, but such distant meddlers have no appreciation for regional problems. All the same, he argues in favor of statehood, which his longtime neighbors, true reactionaries, resist. Things change, the progressive McLintock grasps; attempting to stem the tide must fail. Go with the flow, the liberal in Wayne whispers; go slow, his conservative instinct insists.

McLintock owns the water rights so necessary for lumber mills. Yet he will not withhold from others this key to success in the Southwest. All the same, they'd better not dump waste into the rivers that would poison his cattle. Here is an environmentalist of a practical nature. If he is savvy at business, McLintock despises a certain sort of colleague. Wayne is the enlightened capitalist; the raw variation, Matt Douglas (Gordon Jones), is as proud of his citified clothes as McLintock is of range wear. Douglas perceives everyone—cattlemen, lumbermen, incoming farmers, townspeople—as potential prey for exploitation. Money, for McLintock or the sodbusters, is but one aim, while it is Douglas's only interest. Clearly, Douglas embodies the dark side of capitalism.

"There's no such thing as free land," McLintock tells a recent arrival. "You make a go of it and you've earned it." With that phrase he echoes Dunson in *Red River*, following a continuum. We encounter here John Wayne's code boiled down to its essence: no handouts, no free rides. Hard work is the only way. "I don't give jobs," he tells hopefuls. "I hire men" who earn their pay. And in his enlightened form of capitalism, they are paid well, never exploited as they would be by Matt Douglas.

Douglas claims to be from Boston, though he's a faux blueblood. He's accompanied by his obnoxious son, Junior (Jerry Van Dyke), just returned from an Ivy League education in the East. Wayne's McLintock sneers at Junior's self-important ways and affected manners; he is especially disdainful of his degree. It would be wrong, though, to read this as some redneck's knee-jerk view of education. McLintock is impressed to learn that a young Native American, Davy Elk (Perry Lopez), attended an unpretentious college. He studied hard, earned A's, and is now a brilliant young businessman employing his acumen to win a partnership in the top local store. This is owned by Jewish businessman Birnbaum (Jack Kruschen), fair and generous to a fault, close friends with Black Irishman McLintock. Both well-intentioned capitalists employ their hard-earned successes to allow other ethnics a fair chance to likewise reach the top of the heap in the colorblind society they are in the process of creating.

Neither a party-line conservative nor an arch liberal, McLintock is, like Wayne, a progressive traditionalist: in favor of hanging onto what's best about the past while accepting that change is inevitable and, mostly, benign. Practicality is not everything. McLintock appreciates that Davy also studied philosophy to become a well-rounded man. It's important to him, too, that the young cowpoke (Patrick Wayne) who hopes to marry his daughter (Stefanie Powers) has attended engineering school. There the young man learned new scientific approaches; he'll be able to reap from the land without despoiling it. To Wayne's brand of conservatism, so obviously different from much of today's, science is to be lauded, not disparaged. This helps establish the fellow as a fitting fiancé, though McLintock rejects Junior flat out. What he despises is, then, not education per se but that Junior learned nothing—nothing practical and no philosophy—while at what appears to have been Harvard or Yale. He was enrolled only because of his father's influence. While there, Junior slipped through with minimum effort, receiving gentleman's C's. With that criticism of Junior in mind, it's a shame Wayne wasn't around to comment on the second President Bush's Junior-like qualifications for office.

In *McLintock* Wayne appears to endorse some views that might be termed liberal. McLintock wants to bring all the people together and thus is anything but a throwback to the days of rugged individualism. He sees that in the future, communal activity will be necessary. McLintock brings cattlemen

John Wayne's America. More ideal than real, Wayne's Dream West in McLintock *is a place where ethnicity doesn't matter. He and his Jewish businessman friend (Jack Kruschen) mentor a Native American (Perry Lopez) to also become an enlightened capitalist. Courtesy Batjac Productions/United Artists.*

and farmers into friendly contact for the first time at a lavish party on his ranch. There they understand that the narrowness of attitude that kept them at odds in the past ought to be put aside. McLintock brilliantly aligns rugged individualism with the communal values of a cowboy-inspired president, Teddy Roosevelt, as to the environment; deciding that his daughter and son-in-law will do best if they start from scratch, McLintock wills his landholdings to the national parks system. At one point, Junior calls McLintock a reactionary, "my generation's term for your generation." Certainly, Wayne was in the 1960s labeled such by numerous college students, more often Ivy League types than those at humbler, state schools. McLintock lets the slight go by unanswered.

Wayne's character in another film, *Chisum*, would express a view about the changing West in a dialogue between Chisum and his foreman, Mr. Pepper (Ben Johnson):

PEPPER: People crawling around, moving in. Too many changes!
CHISUM: Well, things usually change for the better.

Of these two characters, Chisum assumes the liberal view.

Not all men in suits are necessarily bad. John Tunstull (Patric Knowles) wears one in *Chisum* until his untimely death. But he's a gentleman in a literal sense, a man whose genuine gentleness causes him to be killed early on

A Manichean choice. In Angel and the Badman, *Wayne's gunslinger has to choose between his pistol and the Good Book, redeeming himself by picking the latter. Here, gunslick Billy the Kid (Geoffrey Duel) in* Chisum *must make that decision, dooming himself by sticking with the pistol. Courtesy Batjac Productions/Warner Brothers.*

by rugged individualists, rednecks who use gun violence to resist change and progress. Even as Wayne's Chisum mourns the death of his partner, our hero does not approve of fighting fire with fire. When Billy the Kid Bonney (Geoff Duel) straps on his pistols to shoot down the killers, Chisum does not approve. Cowhand Pat Garrett (Glenn Corbett) takes a vow as a local lawman, then heads out to bring in the assassins as well as his former friends, including Billy, who illegally pursue them. Of this Chisum approves. "Billy wants revenge," says Garrett, Chisum's protégé. "Mr. Chisum wants justice. There's a big difference." There is: justice is the way of the progressive; revenge, the wild, chaotic West that must give way to law and order. To borrow an expression from Sergio Leone, once upon a time in the real West the law was considered liberal, even anticonservative.

At one point Chisum speaks nostalgically about the cattle baron he once was: "There was land here for the taking . . . keeping, if you were willing to fight rustlers, disease, the land itself, Indians." That was then; this, now. We might think of *Chisum* as a sequel to Hawks's masterpiece, if hardly achieving anything close to that earlier film's artistic level. Wayne's on-screen persona listened to what the woman (Joanne Dru) said about his immaturity at *Red River*'s end. As a result, he grew, learned, and altered for the better.

At one point, Pepper calls for the survival of the fittest in civilization as in nature as the only solution to the feud between Chisum and Murphy (Forrest Tucker):

My opinion is all this speechifying, storekeeping, and prayer meeting don't amount to a spit in the river. There's only one thing that's gonna make [people] know who's the bull of the woods. Just [Chisum] and Murphy, head to head, horn to horn, and one hell of a fight. One of you's got to lose, so the other one walks away with the herd and the whole shebang.

That's it in a nutshell: not the way it should be to a well-intentioned though ineffectual liberal like the late Mr. Tunstull, but as Chisum knew, things would turn out. When they fight, Murphy is literally impaled upon a bull's horn. Chisum does not celebrate this violence but decries it. He was not contemptuous of Tunstull's liberal humanism. As a realist, Chisum knows that in the end physical action will succeed where words fail. A key line of dialogue occurs when Billy decides to take off on his own. Chisum tries to tell him that Tunstull would have frowned on this. "It's what *you* would've done twenty-five years ago!" the boy replies. For once, Chisum has no answer. The Kid's right about that. But the vengeance-crazy boy of *The Big Trail*, *Stagecoach*, and *Red River* was no more. John Wayne—person and persona—mellowed. In his place we encounter a mature man who sincerely hopes the Tunstull way—a way without guns—might eventually work. Garrett appears to be talking about the film's star as well as its leading character when he explains:

Mr. Chisum's changed with the times. He doesn't like to let on, but he *cares*: about the people here, and the town, the territory, the Indians. Oh, he's independent [and] likes to do things his own way. But he cares.

Perhaps this is what the second president Bush meant when he spoke early in his first term of "conservatism with compassion."[2] However rugged an individual he may be, Wayne embodies the enlightened rather than raw form of capitalism. Wayne, Tom Dunson, John Chisum, George Washington McLintock, the Duke—whatever we call him—rejects any easy extremes of liberal or conservative thinking. As such, he offers an ideal paradigm for the libertarian approach. Perhaps this helps explain why Wayne would at about this time turn down a role in a film designed with him in mind by conservative writer John Milius, *Dirty Harry* (Donald Siegel, 1971), which came out in favor of the very sort of vigilante mentality that Wayne, in *Chisum*, rejects. It's worth noting again that Wayne turned down an offer by

The last sunset. Wayne's later cattleman heroes, all alter-egos for the star, do not fit into the simple conservative stereotype that fans worship and critics despise. He is the best of the "old men," and when there is no country left for such, so much the worse for us all. Courtesy Batjac Productions/Warner Brothers.

Eastwood, who did play Harry Callahan, to appear together in a movie Eastwood would have directed. John Wayne was a constitutional conservative, not a moralistic one. The Bill of Rights was the Bill of Rights, and that was that. When in the early 1970s many Christian conservatives banded together to try and censor new Hollywood films, Wayne—the supposed reactionary—assumed what some considered a liberal stance, though anti-censorship is more correctly identified as libertarian. Not that he approved of some films. He would have no truck with them, including Clint Eastwood's. That was beside the point. Let the free market—the people, through individual capitalist choices—determine whether the stuff would survive or go away. That, to John Wayne, was not liberalism or conservatism but Americanism.

Essentially, Wayne wanted no part of government interference as to what moviemakers might choose to offer. As to the new Hollywood, which he openly despised, Wayne's attitude more or less came down to this: I disagree with everything you are doing, but I would go down fighting, if necessary Alamo-like, to protect your right, according to the Constitution, to do it. His succinct code was then not left or right but freedom of choice—Don't tread on me! On the issue of gun control, that would have qualified him, like Charlton Heston, as a conservative. On the issue of censorship, that would cause him to be seen, again like Heston, as a liberal. Neither of those terms sufficiently describes either Wayne or Heston. Both were libertarians of a civil order, against anyone who would dare to try and tread on them—from the left or from the right.

"So that's what we been fightin' fer!" The American flag contains ideological implications; fittingly, the religious, political, and military leaders of a frontier community accept it in Drums along the Mohawk. *Courtesy Twentieth Century-Fox.*

FLAG-WAVING ON
THE WILD FRONTIER
STARS AND STRIPES AS POLITICAL IDEOLOGY

Well, I reckon we better be gettin' back to work.

—GIL TO LANA, FINAL LINE IN *DRUMS ALONG THE MOHAWK*, 1939

John Ford's vision of America is perhaps nowhere so clearly depicted as in *Drums along the Mohawk* (1939). Here is a film about one of America's first frontiers, upstate New York during the Revolutionary War where colonials form a makeshift militia for protection against the British and their Indian allies. Male settlers wander in from far-flung farms to Fort Stanwix, there practicing marching and marksmanship even as in peaceful times they occasionally come together for barn-raisings and holiday parties. Other than for those rare communal gatherings, all remain isolated, working the land, succeeding or failing in this unsparingly rugged country, patiently waiting to discover which of those extremes will prove true for any among them. While every pioneer attempts to make a go of it within the capitalistic system, survival of the fittest is balanced with group loyalty. Here is not just one particular polis but America in embryo. When, for instance, a sweet pair of newlyweds, Lana and Gil Martin (Claudette Colbert, Henry Fonda), arrives, all the locals join together to help get them started. Yet when their home is burned down during an Indian raid, the couple receives no charity or handouts. Nor do they expect, wish, or request any. That's not the American way; at least, not in the mythopoetic vision of our cinematic Shakespeare.

What they do ask for and receive are grunt-level jobs. These pay menial wages, earning them bed, board, and a few coins, which they stash away for a fresh start. What they plan for and are allowed to pursue is a second chance, at some indeterminate date, to make it in a land that's in the process of becoming the United States of America. Perhaps next time, pluck will be accompanied by luck. No one can know that for certain. What is clear is that all those living in this microcosm of a new nation begin with equal opportunity. Whether anyone's work is rewarded, like that of Abel, or comes to naught, as with Cain, must be accepted as the will of some higher power: destiny, God, coincidence, fate, or whatever one might choose to call it. The American Dream within a democratic capitalist system is that anything is possible while nothing is guaranteed. Whatever will be will be. One can only wait to find out.

John Ford, a twentieth-century Republican, was conservative on issues of national defense and unquestioning patriotism. All the same, in many social areas he appears far closer to Republicans of the nineteenth century, including his revered heroes Abraham Lincoln and Wyatt Earp, both represented by one of his favorite actors, Henry Fonda. Fonda identified as a Democrat in the twentieth-century liberal sense of that term. Importantly if somewhat confusingly, the politics of the director and his star had much in common and few differences. Ford, as progressive in some ways as he was traditionalist in others, made his earliest films even as the identities of the two predominant political parties reversed. Perhaps the term "liberal Republican" or "progressive Republican" best describes him; that party continued to have such a wing (referred to as Rockefeller Republicans, after Nelson A. Rockefeller of New York) until after Ford's passing. Many view the failure of Rockefeller to win the presidential nomination away from Goldwater for the 1964 election as the beginning of a stampede within the party to the purer or more extreme conservatism of today.

At the end of *Drums along the Mohawk*, an integrated group of settlers (Anglos, Indians, African Americans) composed of equally brave women, who helped to fight, and men have held the fort until a force from George Washington's army can arrive to relieve them. With the war now over, the first true American flag is waved high in the sky. Each individual, Anglo or other ethnicity, female or male, smiles and salutes it, momentarily captured in a tight image. Ford then returns his viewer to the collective in a group shot. The focal figures, Colbert's and Fonda's characters, stand in the center. Now, the husband shrugs; the threat is over. It's time to abandon the group, at least until some new situation, pleasant or ugly, demands that it be reformed. Let's go home, he whispers, and get back to work—their individual work, the community having temporarily come together as a social unit to achieve what only a group could accomplish. Husband and wife stroll out the stockade doors, nodding goodbye, with their child. One after another the other families will shortly follow suit. They will again become far-flung individualists until necessity, that mother of invention, demands that they all come together again.

"Thirteen stripes for the colonies," a frontiersman (Ward Bond) notes. "And thirteen stars in a circle for the union." Thirteen distinct stripes signify the singularity of each colony; thirteen stars in a pattern symbolize solidarity or, as members of the Continental Congress put it on June 14, 1777, a "constellation." After toying with many possible presentations, flag designer and Declaration of Independence signer Francis Hopkinson turned over to Betsy Ross (possibly) or Rebecca Young (more likely) the pattern suggested to him by fellow patriots, and these women wove it into full realization. Here was, in visual, symbolic form, the delicate, uneven balance that is America.[1]

The flag's vision has, from inception through all the necessary adjustments during America's expansionist era, depicted the philosophic as well as political heart of the nation: seemingly oppositional ideas coming together for not only a New World but a New World Order. The American idea was set in cementlike material that proposed a tenuous and unique coming together of opposites: self-reliance and dependence on others. As we watch the flag wave in Ford's film, we must note what these old-timers might have called "the fly in the buttermilk." One early conception for the banner would have had stars and stripes in equal size, suggesting equal weight in the American ideology it represents. Instead, Hopkinson was instructed to create an intended imbalance.[2] The concept of a constellation community in white and blue takes up one-quarter of its surface; the red and white representation of self-reliance, rugged individualism, and the separation of the states as distinct stripes, three-quarters. If we read the political information that the flag's creators intended and symbolically projected, we must realize that in their America, community values and rugged individualism were not created equal.

Like it or not, the latter prevails. In our century, for a contemporary conservative Republican or an adherent to the tea party, here is America as it was conceived and ought to remain. For a modern liberal Democrat, this has implied an awkward situation that ought to be rectified in a nation that necessarily evolves with changing times. Nowhere in our popular culture is this imbalance more vividly dramatized than in Western movies. In *The Big Trail*, Wayne as Breck Coleman, archetypal all-American rugged individualist, guides a wagon train—the American community in miniature—westward. As the pioneers are on the verge of reaching their destination, Breck Coleman learns the two villains he's vowed to kill are nearby. They are murderers; he, less motivated by social responsibility to the good people he travels with than by personal vengeance, is out for blood. The outlaws made the mistake of bushwhacking his friend. Killing them will perform a great public service.

For our uniquely American hero who believes that individual stripes should constitute three-quarters of what he does, the stars in their courses relegated to one-quarter, that's all well and good, an acceptable by-product of his primary responsibility to self. Now, though, he faces a difficult decision. The wagon master begs Coleman not to abandon them to winter elements. Simple pilgrims, they are unprepared to handle the crisis. They need him; to go off now would, the older man from the East insists to this red-stater, be wrong. The Westerner's reply: "Maybe so, the way *you* look at it." East is East and West, West, geographically but also in core values that form an often at-odds-with-itself American ideology that leads to friction in the ranks of the citizenry.

As noted earlier in this book, the meaning of any film derives less from what the hero says than from what he does. A man's actions, particularly in a Western, are what define him. And what Coleman does next contradicts his retort. He sets aside the coming confrontation with the bad guys to get the pioneers across, blazing the way through a blizzard. Once the farmers are safe and any duty to community is realized, Coleman returns to individualism. Zeke (Tully Marshall), the hero's mentor, offers to go along. Coleman will have none of it, though he does request that Zeke help him guide the caravan. With those folks settled, Zeke ought to stay and ensure they remain well. Coleman heads out—alone—to get his own job done now that his chore for humanity at large, or at least his fellow Americans, has been completed.

A man's gotta do . . . but as this film suggests, not necessarily as his first

"A man's gotta do . . ." Few films present the American dichotomy of rugged individualism versus community loyalty as effectively as The Big Trail. *Breck Coleman (John Wayne) must balance the satisfaction of his personal quest with a concern for the American community. Courtesy Fox Film Corporation.*

priority. There are private and public demands. Despite what the flag's iconography may tell us, that red-state values should take precedence, Westerns more often project a blue-state philosophy. This explains why the cowboy hero here sets rugged individualism aside in times of crisis to acquiesce to community needs.

There are exceptions to the rule, certainly. Perhaps the most notable is in *Hondo* (John Farrow, 1953), inspired by a Louis L'Amour short story (in which the main character's name is not Hondo) and after the film's release novelized by that noted Western author. The *Hondo* script by James Edward Grant was written specifically for Wayne. This began a trend, discussed in the previous chapter, in which Wayne's motion pictures project his politics, not those of other filmmakers who hired him as the centerpiece of their visions. Indian scout and gunfighter Hondo Lane is a loner. Sam, the dog that accompanies him, is not Hondo's but exists as a fellow loner traveling in the same direction. In the conflict in Arizona, Hondo chooses not to take

A man alone. Hondo, *produced by Wayne under his Batjac banner, allowed the Duke to present his own vision of the West. Here the most rugged of all individualists confronts an abandoned mother (Geraldine Page) and son (Tommy Rettig) on the prairie. Courtesy Wayne-Fellows/Warner Brothers.*

sides, instead dealing with Anglos and Apaches as an outsider in each camp. As a result he is partly welcome in each (Hondo is a "half-breed," presumably) and prefers to avoid friction if he can.

When a child (Tommy Rettig) tries to pet Sam, Hondo warns the boy that to do so is not wise. When the kid continues anyway, Hondo stands back and allows Sam to bite him. The boy's liberal-progressive mother (Geraldine Page), standing for female principles of what would be considered political correctness today, is outraged. She also cringes when Hondo teaches the boy to swim in sink-or-swim style, throwing him into the water and waiting to see if the boy drowns or not.

Here is individualism at its most rugged. When Apaches take to the warpath, Hondo helps the cavalry and pioneers, less out of loyalty to them than because he realizes this is the best way to get himself, the woman, and the child out of harm's way. When the Apaches are defeated, he bears them no grudge. Indeed, he admires them, muttering, "End of a way of life. Good way! Too bad." A liberal would want to try and do something to at least help these vanishing Americans. Wayne's Hondo perceives the situation in terms of survival of the fittest, not morality. As to this noble race, their time has come and gone. Nothing can be done about it. This is not to disparage these people. A good way! Too bad. Herbert Spencer was right, at least in the world according to John Wayne.

Hondo is a "pure" Wayne film. The Duke is not working for one of those true artists—Ford, Hawks, Huston, and their peers—with visions of their own. His director is a competent craftsman, John Farrow, and many later pictures would be directed by a (sad to say) considerably less competent journeyman, Andrew McLaglen. What we see and experience in them is not a director's vision but John Wayne distilled.

His films for other auteurs prove far more complex, politically speaking. One striking example is *Rio Bravo* (Hawks, 1959), produced because director and star shared a mutual dislike for *High Noon* (Fred Zinnemann, 1953). So far as Hawks and Wayne were concerned, that film, written by the liberal Carl Foreman—who would shortly be blacklisted—and produced by liberal-message moviemaker Stanley Kramer, set out to attack everything Wayne and Hawks believed in. *High Noon* was intended as a thinly disguised metaphor for the McCarthy years, when people in Hollywood, like those in the fictional Hadleyville, allow old friends to be destroyed rather than getting involved and standing by them. More so, *High Noon* could be read as an attack on capitalism. When townsfolk finally refuse to help Will Kane (Gary Cooper), they do so less because they are afraid for their lives than because they're worried about the profit margin. "Folks up North are thinking about this town," the mayor (Thomas Mitchell) explains. "Thinking about sending *money* down here. But what will they do if they read about shooting in the streets?" Think twice, likely cancel. *High Noon*, often considered the greatest Western ever made, is less a genre film than Henrik Ibsen's *An Enemy of the People* (1882) reconfigured as an American version of that social drama and cautionary fable about the dangers of raw capitalism.

But to again borrow from the Bard, here's the rub! Some twenty-five years after *High Noon*'s initial release and its general acceptance, for better or worse, as the seminal example of the liberal Western, William F. Buckley Jr.'s conservative news magazine the *National Review* printed a list of the 100 greatest conservative movies of all time and counted *High Noon* among them. A different context caused what might appear to be a fixed piece to seem the

An enemy of the people. High Noon, *often thought of as a liberal Western, can alternatively be read as archly conservative. The community members, represented by political (Thomas Mitchell) and religious (Morgan Farley) leaders, scorn the true hero (Gary Cooper). Courtesy Stanley Kramer Productions/United Artists.*

opposite of what everyone had, happily or begrudgingly, once agreed that it purported to say. Cooper's Will Kane begins the film as a liberal, believing in the good of his community and that right can only be achieved by group action. When they let him down, he steps out and, to his own surprise, gets the job done with help only from his wife, Amy (Grace Kelly), proving that rugged individualism combined with family values works best. When Kane throws his badge down into the dust before leaving town a changed man, the gesture may, at least in retrospect, be read not as Wayne interpreted it at the height of the Cold War, the badge as a symbol of America and therefore qualifying this as an anti-American movie,[3] but a rejection of community in favor of individual effort, that is, conservatism.

High Noon, at least by implication, comes out in favor of guns. Kane's wife takes the feminine anti-gun position throughout most of the film but reverses herself in action when she instinctively seizes a gun and shoots one of the bad men. In the back, no less! Clearly, she is the one who arcs here.

In no way does she later regret the violence she has done. If anything, it has liberated her from those constricting liberalisms she once believed in.

High Noon is, by implication, a pro–capital punishment film, certainly a conservative viewpoint. Kane sends the killer off to be executed, but some apparent liberals—up North!—decide instead to rehabilitate him, then turn the man loose. He goes back to his horrible old ways. If only they'd hanged him all would have been right. Yet that was not how Wayne and Hawks read the implications. They conceived of *Rio Bravo* as *High Noon's* antithesis. In *Rio Bravo*, townspeople offer to help Sheriff John Chance (Wayne) when he's threatened by a villain (John Russell). The hero refuses their help, insisting that as a professional he can do it alone. That's all well and good until we examine the implications of Hawks's ending. When Chance tries to handle things by himself, he cannot. He then accepts help from those very types—the town drunk (Dean Martin), an old, lame man (Walter Brennan), and a young kid (Ricky Nelson)—Kane rejects. If in retrospect the supposedly liberal film *High Noon* may strike us as surprisingly conservative, so does the more apparently conservative *Rio Bravo* now play as a liberal tribute to community values. The point is, politics in Western movies, as in the American society they reflect, are less simple and defined than we might wish to believe.

In addition to Wayne, other actors have reached for auteurism, even in films they did not happen to direct. The superstar who most fully represented a political point of view that stood in direct opposition to Wayne's was Paul Newman. In two of his best-known Westerns, Newman embodied characters who appear every bit as ruggedly individualistic as Wayne. In *Hud* his character, like Wayne's in *Hondo*, never alters from that position. Where Wayne makes an epic hero of such a man, Newman and like-minded director Martin Ritt present the figure as tragic if not villainous. Early on in *Hombre* (Ritt, 1967), Newman plays much the same role. In a telling scene, a pleasant U.S. Army sergeant (Larry Ward) tries to help John Russell (Newman) out of a jam when a vicious gunman (Richard Boone) attempts to take away his stagecoach ticket. But when the outlaw then turns his wrath on the soldier, Russell makes no effort to come to his aid. He is, clearly, a rugged individualist. By the conclusion, though, our *hombre* has navigated a 180-degree turn. Though he doesn't like the community of people he's been thrown together with, when they are menaced by the gunman and his men, Russell resists as long as he can an inner urge to go out and sacrifice himself so they might

Period Westerns as a reflection of contemporary society. The election of John F. Kennedy as president coincided with films that shared his emphasis on communal activity over the rugged individualism of the Eisenhower era. One of the first—and best—was The Magnificent Seven. *Courtesy Mirisch/United Artists.*

survive. In the end, though, he does that. The final shot transforms him into a Christlike savior, as also happens when Newman's almost identical hero in the non-Western *Cool Hand Luke* (Stuart Rosenberg, 1967) goes the same route.

Politics merge with religion as to each film's ideology. In truth, the two have always interconnected in Hollywood movies, Westerns in particular. Whether any one viewer perceives *High Noon* as liberal or conservative, it is significant that when townspeople meet to discuss the political issue of whether to stand behind their menaced lawman, they do so in church, with the minister and the mayor together deciding Will Kane's fate.

If *High Noon* represented the individualistic Republican political agenda of the 1950s, *The Magnificent Seven* (John Sturges, 1960) might be thought of as that film's complement. As John F. Kennedy ascended to the presidency, this new sort of Western portrayed community values that would be expressed during the early, optimistic days of his New Frontier. Here was a cinematic reflection of the time: a number of gunmen who have for some time been trying to survive as loners come together and form a community that puts mercenary values aside in order to do the right thing. Each man is redeemed by his dedication to a decent cause (saving a community of Latino farmers from outlaws) with the exception only of one (Brad Dexter) who cannot make the transition. He and he alone dies believing that the entire venture had a mercenary basis. While that may have been true of a film made during the previous decade, here was a new sort of Western for the New Frontier audience.

PART TWO
GOD'S COUNTRY

RELIGION IN THE WESTERN FILM

Manifest Destiny—the movie! The theory that a wilderness awaited conquest by civilized Christian Anglos was immortalized by nineteenth-century painters. In the early twentieth century this visualization would be carried over to films such as The Big Trail. *Courtesy Fox Film Corporation/ Twentieth Century-Fox.*

ODES TO AMERICAN IMPERIALISM

MANIFEST DESTINY IN WESTERN MOVIES

One nation, under God . . .

—PLEDGE OF ALLEGIANCE, REWRITTEN IN THE EARLY 1950S

If *The Alamo* had been John Wayne's most politically motivated movie up until 1960, it also contained the Duke's first overt statement on religion. The character he plays, the historical David Crockett, heads down Texas way to reboot his devastated political fortunes and failed capitalistic endeavors, the case with the actual Crockett,[1] but also because he suffers from a malaise more modern (true to 1959, when the film was finally finished) than one Crockett was likely to face in 1835-1836. Wayne's Davy experiences mid-twentieth-century existential angst. His followers note this, complaining that when the colonel looks at women, he no longer appears to be "starvin.'" In time, the parson (Hank Worden) quietly confronts Davy on this:

PARSON: Davy, don't you ever pray?
CROCKETT: I never had the time!

Wayne's Crockett grouses these words and wanders off alone. The incident occurs one-third of the way through the director's cut. That full version retains eleven minutes of scenes edited from the readily available road-show print.[2] The parson is later wounded and dies in Crockett's arms with the Tennesseans gathered around. Before expiring, he explains that though he never left a small area back in Tennessee, he metaphorically experienced the world through Davy's eyes. Now it's Crockett's turn to speak. He rises, gazes heavenward, and directly addresses his Lord. Any internal doubts that were driving him toward nihilism are clearly gone. Though the term was yet to be popularized, he is born again. Wayne's Crockett confers with a higher power he now knows in his heart to be there and proclaims that the parson did not die in vain.

That man's passing hardly ends the concept of faith in the film; rather, it provides a sacrificial lamb necessary for its rebirth. Finally, Crockett fights for his God as well as country. Within the film's context, they become inseparable.

This holds true for his men. In this interpretation of what the Alamo ought to mean for people of Wayne's own era, out of the ashes will grow spiritual rebirth, indicated in the final shot when survivors leave the fort while in Dimitri Tiomkin's score celestial music plays:

> *And the small band of soldiers,*
> *Lies asleep in the arms of the Lord!*

Even *The Alamo*'s advertising logo hinted that this was a right-wing message movie: "The mission that became a fortress, the fortress that became a shrine."[3] Before the last battle, Crockett's men spend their final hours huddled together on the wall. One claims that when they die, that will be the be-all and end-all. Parallel to Crockett's own earlier words, he speaks not as a typical frontiersman but as a citizen of a Cold War world that appeared about to blow itself up with nuclear weapons. How could even the most earnest go on believing?

Screenwriter Grant structured what occurs next as a full Socratic dialogue; arguments forwarded are presented less for the sake of drama than as propaganda, religious as well as political. If Americans' will to defend the nation—its principles and its geography—were to be restored to the glorious level of what General Eisenhower called the "crusade in Europe," then the combination in the rewritten pledge to the flag—one nation, under God—

The turning point. Early in The Alamo, *the Davy Crockett of John Wayne's imagination expresses his lack of interest in religion to the parson (Hank Worden), whose death allows the hero to regain his faith, allying it with his political convictions. Courtesy Batjac Productions/ United Artists.*

must be accepted. If the true essence of the red menace was godlessness, the faith-based origins of capitalist democracy had to provide a corrective.

One by one, others shout this doubter down. "I believe!" each calls out in turn. Crockett says not a word; he observes. His melancholy smile makes clear that he approves. If the impact might be labeled simplistic, Wayne intended it to be just so. No wonder he chose to set, atop his version of the Alamo's shrine, a cross that had been dislodged and now tilts to one side. How appropriate for his purposes that Wayne doesn't have Crockett set it aright. To do that would suggest that when audiences left the theaters, they had no responsibility because John Wayne had once more fixed everything; the job was therefore accomplished, freeing viewers to go home happy. Instead, the final image that we see is the cross still in need of righting. The meaning and purpose of Wayne's Alamo movie is that viewers must take on the responsibility of doing the job themselves. As we leave the theater, we do not experience a sense of closure and completion but have been indoctrinated with the notion that the mission—once Crockett's, now ours— has only begun.

A question regarding *The Alamo* has always been why this film lost money. One argument might be that the project, originally to have been completed three years earlier,[4] suffered from bad timing. *The Alamo*, properly understood, is less about the famed battle in any docudrama sense than an objective correlative for the time it was created, the 1950s, when the Russians launched Sputnik before America could get an object into space and, for many citizens, a sense of defeatism replaced old-fashioned U.S. optimism. Wayne's film about an old frontier was calculated to kick-start the will to head off to new ones, outer space included. But even as the film appeared in fall 1960, John Kennedy won the election on his own New Frontier ticket. To the chagrin of Wayne, the liberal Democrats had seized the banner of optimism and were waving it, inadvertently blunting the purpose of *The Alamo*. What was supposed to have been the final film of the 1950s instead became one of the first of the 1960s, competing with liberal Democrat Kirk Douglas's *Spartacus* (Stanley Kubrick, 1960), an ode to communal endeavor that would more closely express the Kennedy years in costume-film form. More than anything else, Wayne's work of personal expression was doomed by poor timing.

Wayne would support Barry Goldwater in his bid for the presidency in 1963–1964. Though the Arizona senator was widely perceived as an arch conservative (even as Wayne was misperceived), Goldwater like Wayne assumed a civil-libertarian stance, as his voting record reveals. During the late 1960s and early 1970s, the first period during which Hollywood genre films were taken seriously by critics of culture—high-, low-, and middlebrow—Philip French offered a means of comprehending the wide spectrum of styles and substances possible within the Western's broad canvas. French structured the genre into polar opposites: Kennedy Westerns opposed to Goldwater Westerns.[5] Liberal or conservative, *High Noon* or *Rio Bravo*. Everyone, make your choice! These terms perhaps simplified nuance, but they did reveal that even the humblest examples of the oater suggested statements, whether the filmmakers were aware of them or not. As to more ambitious Westerns, they were often planned by people on the left or right who consciously knew exactly what they were doing and why.

Today, when many intellectuals and academics consider themselves poststructural,[6] any easy dichotomy appears suspicious. We see everything, pop culture included, as existing in shades of gray. Still, the Western does say different things when shaped by different hands. *The Alamo*, properly understood, appeared out of step with the emergence of *Playboy* and soon the Peppermint Twist and Peace Corps. Many if not all prior examples of the genre share a point of view Wayne conveyed: the fusion of politics and religion in the single genre that most clearly reflects American ideologies. Among these was Manifest Destiny, providing an intellectual justification for an in-progress physical act of going west during the age of settlement. In some form or another, Manifest Destiny had been in effect long before John L. O'Sullivan employed that term circa 1840 for a news story in which he defended the controversial Mexican-American War.[7] Ernest Lee Tuverson has described Manifest Destiny as "a vast complex of ideas, policies, and actions" that did not seem to originate as parts of a single, ongoing sensibility until O'Sullivan pointed out that they had more in common than was previously noticed; once their commonality was seen, the truthfulness of the ideology appeared obvious.[8]

A forerunner of expansionism justified by religion might be seen in those Spanish conquerors of the New World holding crosses as high as their swords. They later would be dismissed as "impure Christians" by English Protestant arrivals because they were Catholics and of Mediterranean heritage.[9] Certainly, the idea existed in embryonic form when the 1620 Plymouth Rock landing began the winning of the West by Anglo pilgrims whose compact reinvented English ideas of democracy combined with the extreme morality of their sect: Puritanism.[10] John Wayne's signature term, "pilgrim," refers to a man on a religious or political journey as an inward trek to enlightenment as well as a geographical one toward some set destination. Those who later pushed farther west refused to leave that term in New England. Expansionism could unseat Indians from their lands by removal or genocide based on a belief, as yet unquestioned, of American excellence, a sense of Anglo racial superiority by which white Protestants seized lands not only from native peoples but also from Spanish Catholics who had arrived in the Southwest first.[11]

Theirs was the justification employed for an illegal war in the mid-1840s under Democratic president Polk's watch. He and other post-Jacksonians embraced Manifest Destiny, while Crockett and his liberal-progressive Whigs, Henry Clay and Daniel Webster among them, and Lincoln and the liberal Republicans to follow in their path denounced it. If our European cousins failed to create John Winthrop's "city upon a hill" (1630), here was humankind's second chance to get it right. Or, for those who damned such claims of Anglo religious and racial superiority, to get it all wrong.

In many ways, idea and action merged when President Thomas Jefferson completed the Louisiana Purchase in 1803 and soon sent Lewis and Clark

Imperialism, Anglo-style. Classic Hollywood films depicted the westward movement without questioning its moral base. In The Far Horizons, *Lewis (Fred MacMurray) and Clark (Charlton Heston) inform Native Americans that their homelands now belong to the United States. Courtesy Pine-Thomas/Paramount Pictures.*

out to map the young nation's new resources. A Hollywood version of the expedition, *The Far Horizons* (Rudolph Mate, 1955), made clear that the idea of Manifest Destiny had not disappeared even by the middle of the twentieth century. It showed, too, that a modern film about this historic movement could continue to project a belief, since questioned, that Americans possessed a divine right and responsibility to push ever farther westward. In their quest, God's best—themselves and their eventual descendants—are depicted pushing onward into an amoral wilderness that God ordained them to cultivate into a good garden.[12]

Before the trek begins, Lewis (Fred MacMurray) confers with the president (Herbert Heyes). Jefferson informs the explorer that he and Clark should travel from sea to shining sea:

MORTIMER LEWIS: Beyond the limits of the [Louisiana] Purchase? But we
don't own [those lands].
JEFFERSON (SHRUGGING): Neither does anyone else.

That, of course, was far from true. People of native, Spanish, Russian, French, and other origins lived across the continent. Anglo Protestants, though, were considered within the context of the expedition, historically and cinematically, to be the only real Americans. Jefferson reminds Lewis:

> We are surrounded by foreign powers who would love to see us fail. The dream on which this nation was built will never be secure till the U.S. stretches from the Atlantic to the Pacific.

Might would make right as God, or so they believed, stood firmly on their side.

This helps explain why an accurate patina of flowery religiosity exists in much of the dialogue we hear in movies about the settling process. "Go forth into the wilderness to make a new home," a preacher all but commands the newlyweds in *Drums along the Mohawk* as they take leave of Albany and head toward central New York, which then constituted "the West," as this term indicated more an inner idea than any geographical place. Most historians note the religious impetus for the physical trek: "The discovery of a New World," Roderick Nash notes, "rekindled the traditional European notion than an earthly paradise lay somewhere to the west."[13] Any hardships experienced in the forest were part of the spiritual process: "The original settlers," David Ross Williams writes, "brought with them the desire to suffer in the wilderness in order to be ravished by the love of God."[14] While that may not have been the case with the Catholic conquistadors who entered the southernmost areas of the Americas, here was a viewpoint that existed deep within the Protestant vision of and for America.

Twentieth-century mass entertainment has, in part, entailed presenting drama that implies a justification of American history and the mindset that allowed for what in retrospect appears less than admirable courses of action. An early example is Edward Emerson Hough's *The Covered Wagon* in print (first in the all-American *Saturday Evening Post*, later in book form), then in the large-scale 1923 film derived from it. There is never any doubt in these works that the settlers truly are pilgrims: they pray before leaving civilization in Missouri and again when they reach their destination in Oregon, as well as each morning and evening along the way. The silent film's title cards remind us that these pioneers are spurred on less by capitalism, though that is never denied, than by a desire to fulfill some vague but important mission. A belief that they are doing God's work permeates the film, adding seriousness to broad romantic melodrama.

The first sound-era Western epic, *The Big Trail*, begins with the following

That which does not kill us makes us strong. In Ford's Drums along the Mohawk, *a frontier couple (Henry Fonda, Claudette Colbert) live out Manifest Destiny by moving west and, in spite of many hardships, eventually achieving the American Dream of financial success through luck and pluck. Courtesy Twentieth Century-Fox.*

dedication: "To the men and women who *planted* civilization in the wilderness" during "the *conquest* of the West" (emphasis mine). The tribute is at least free of sexism, as it admits the important role females played. Included, though, is a sticky term for people of a politically correct leaning: "conquest"! What had once been accepted as a neutral word, even a positive one, now sticks in the craw of many as pejorative. At the end, when the pioneers find themselves trapped in a blizzard that seems likely to keep them from reaching their biblical promised land, the scout (John Wayne) is reminiscent of Shakespeare's Henry V on the eve of a seemingly insurmountable battle (for what today is considered morally dubious, the conquest of France):

> We can't turn back. We're blazing a trail that started in England . . . not even the storms of the sea could stop those first efforts . . . they blazed it on through the wilderness of Kentucky. Not hunger nor massacres could stop them. Now, we've picked up the trail again. Nothing can stop us.

We're building a nation, but we've got to suffer. No great trail was ever blazed without hardship.

No pain, no gain. So they continue on, and in time they conquer. In part, they succeed owing to a sense of continuum that, in his rough eloquence, this early guise of the Duke perceives as essential to the American character: a national purpose. These pioneers must dedicate themselves to something bigger and greater than themselves. They have to accept their identity as representatives of an abiding Anglo imperialism that—in the seventeenth, eighteenth, and nineteenth centuries and still in effect certainly during the first half of the twentieth—remained in the process of being justified. "By right of exploration," Lewis says later in *The Far Horizons* while shoving a pole bearing an American flag down into virgin soil, "I claim all the lands we have traveled for the United States." That, as they say, is that.

At least for the time being, 1805 or 1955. Yet the thrust of twenty-first-century revisionism, in venues as far flung as historical studies and modernist moviemaking, questions everything once simply and easily accepted, most notably the relationship of politics to religion in America.

The town tamer. During the postwar years, Ford's vision of the world as reflected in his Westerns appears to have brightened. (a) In My Darling Clementine *the town of Tombstone is initially perceived in the noirish darkness of night. (b) When the hero (Henry Fonda) leaves, it has been transformed into civilization at its most tolerant and benign. Courtesy Twentieth Century-Fox.*

THE TOWN AND THE CITY

SPACE AS THEME, PLACE AS CHARACTER

To me, it's land as God made it. And wants it to stay. And I
got a hunch he wants me to help him keep it that way!
—BREWTON TO LUTIE, *SEA OF GRASS*, 1947

In any Hollywood Western, as in American history, the first thing pilgrims do upon arriving at their destinations is to attempt to re-create what they left behind by setting to work constructing not only their farms or ranches but towns. This unit will prove as essential to a national idea of community as homesteads are to the equally important concept of individualism by ownership. A subgenre of Westerns is composed of films that, like *The Covered Wagon*, *The Big Trail*, and *The Way West* (Andrew McLaglen, 1967), are about the experience of expansion. Another is made of films like *Arizona* (Wesley Ruggles, 1940) and *Appaloosa* (Ed Harris, 2008) that focus on the development of some raw outpost of civilization that will in time become a town and if all goes well will transform into a city. The all-time biggest if not the best epic, *How the West Was Won*, focused first on the former subgenre, then the latter.

The ever-changing image of frontier towns in the work of any major film-maker reveals his or her own altering and possibly maturing attitudes, the different conceptions of society that the places signify in genre pieces produced in subsequent periods, or a complex combination of the two. John Ford's ideas were evident in his pre–*Iron Horse* silent shorts, many of them lost today. In *Straight Shooting* (1917), for example, Cheyenne (Harry Carey) is a good bad man reformed by protecting new arrivals in a God-forsaken stretch of prairie. *Rustlers* (1919) has Hoot Gibson's character doing much the same as a dedicated government man who rids a new settlement of a ferocious gang preying on the people. In each, the citizens themselves are dear hearts, albeit sheeplike in their willingness to accept their fates until the savior figure arrives. The films establish a theme that will be developed by later genre practitioners including Clint Eastwood. Ford's attitude during the 1930s toward towns and people who inhabit them cannot be analyzed because, with the Depression-era decline of the big oater, he drifted away from his favorite genre.

After a ten-year hiatus, Ford returned to the Western with his seminal *Stagecoach* (1939). Though this intimate epic unfolds mostly on the Arizona desert and within the tight confines of the title object, the narrative opens in one town and ends in another. These serve as bookends, providing a meaningful contrast that underlines the film and Ford's personal vision of the West, which, in his work, represents America itself. The first town, Tonto, is glimpsed by daylight. Civilization has been established, as evidenced by details like the absence of gunfights in the streets. But there now exists a moralistic intolerance its practitioners mistake for a true moral conscience. In the historical West as in Western movies, the terrible irony is that an anti-Christian treatment of Jesus's lame and poor soon follows the coming of Christianity as an institution.[1] Sympathetic characters—drunkard Doc Boone (Thomas Mitchell), working prostitute Dallas (Claire Trevor)—are told that they are persona non grata, then escorted to the outgoing stagecoach by an unpleasant group of respectable women with pinched faces and wearing drab clothing. Descendants of Anglos who landed at Plymouth, they are hardly portrayed in a likable light. However flawed Doc and Dallas may be, Ford finds these Black Irish Catholics morally superior to their tormentors. These dregs of society will reveal their true colors under pressure. It is they who save the life and baby of a pregnant Anglo woman (Louise Platt) who initially disdains them. The film follows her arc as Mrs. Mallory comes to realize these lower-class types reveal true grit.

Encouraged to leave ASAP, too, is Hatfield (John Carradine), a professional gunfighter modeled on fallen aristocrat Doc Holliday.[2] Status as a high-born Southerner does not win him a reprieve from solid middle Americans determined to complete the civilization process. All are on board the stagecoach when, after a battle with Geronimo's Apaches, it at last pulls into Lordsburg. Other travelers include a whiskey drummer (Donald Meek), a corrupt banker (Berton Churchill), a driver (Andy Devine) who bears more than passing resemblance to a Shakespearean clown, and a young outlaw, the Ringo Kid (John Wayne). Despite that colorful nickname, the Kid is not based on the historical John Ringo. His given name turns out to be Henry; he has more in common with New Mexico's William Bonney, Billy the Kid, whose birth name was likely Henry. By referencing several real-life outlaws, Ford and screenwriter Dudley Nichols avoid becoming entangled in history of any narrow, limiting sort, thus freeing themselves to work instead within mythic realms set against a historical backdrop.

Though an agent of the law is on hand to greet the survivors of the trip and arrest Gatewood, the banker, who absconded with Tonto residents' cash, we see little if any law and order here. Cowboys drink on the streets and fire pistols into the air. Ringo will shoot it out with Luke Plummer (Tom Tyler) and his brothers without interference. Dallas spots a wide assortment of whorehouses in which to work; all now are closed back in Tonto. Clearly, Lordsburg signifies the chaos in some wide-open towns even as Tonto does its opposite. What makes *Stagecoach* so thematically significant is Ford's tacit avoidance of any expected moral contrast, that is, the daylight Tonto good, the nightlife Lordsburg bad. The towns appear equally awful to the viewer although in totally different ways. For Ford, like Shakespeare, all and any extremes prove equally offensive. Necessary is a healthy balance, though that does not yet appear to exist: a place where a drunken doctor, perhaps even a prostitute, can be tolerated so long as they do not disrupt daily activity.

In 1939 Ford apparently did not believe that ideal could be achieved. In his microcosmic portrait of America, there are only these two repellent places with the arid desert between them. Decent lawman Curly (George Bancroft) frees Ringo to run away with Dallas despite the lad's supposed crimes, and these two head across the border to Mexico. There, perhaps, still exists some unspoiled frontier where those who tried but failed to make it in America—a nation founded on the idea of second chances—will receive another try. To visualize that dream would be to destroy a vague ideal by rendering it too realistic and as such, unbelievable. Mexico remains disembodied, in the words of social critic Slotkin, as "a recovered Garden of Eden for an Adam and Eve" to live in, perhaps happily ever after.[3] A sense of positivism surrounds Ringo and Dallas's exit onto the horizon; Doc Boone is being ironic but not pessimistic when he says, "That'll save 'em from the blessings of civilization."

Perhaps owing to his specific growth as a person and an artist or as a result of the Depression and the impact it had on American society, Ford here is less simple and sentimental than in the silent-film era. He might even appear something of a radical, not hesitating to bitterly damn the ruined dream of a Utopian America, Eden rediscovered once mankind, forced to abandon paradise and move east of that garden so long ago, travels west. Apparently the American second chance to get it right—one's own house upon a hill or a city placed there—had failed. Only a year or so later, Ford's patriotism would be revived by the U.S. entry into World War II. But the sense of exultation that briefly flowered at the last good war's successful conclusion would be swiftly followed by letdowns, economic and spiritual. These would cause that revitalized sense of group mission from the early 1940s to be replaced by something called "the lonely crowd" beginning in 1946.[4]

Ford's first postwar Western, *My Darling Clementine*, offers a bizarre combination of darkness and light, thereby reflecting the director's ever more complex authorial voice. When Wyatt Earp (Henry Fonda) and his brothers Virgil (Tim Holt) and Morgan (Ward Bond) first see the town, they—and we—perceive Lordsburg under another name, Tombstone. In the night, shootings occur on the streets and prostitutes stroll everywhere. One in particular, Chihuahua (Linda Darnell), a younger version of Dallas without the experience that bolstered her character, appears to be the town's unofficial hostess. *Stagecoach*'s drunken Doc and fallen aristocrat are here collapsed into one character, Doc Holliday (Victor Mature). Yet Ford perceives a possible halfway point between anarchy and fascism, a true, workable, American moral code as compared to a moralistic one that in its simplicity resembles New England's Puritanism.

Earp initially takes on the job of city marshal only to avenge the death of his youngest brother, James. Halfway through, Wyatt transforms.

DOC: Maybe you're planning on cleanin' up this town?
WYATT: Hadn't thought about it that way, but now that you mention it, that's not a bad idea!

As the four days during which the film's narrative takes place (historically, Earp and his brothers remained in Tombstone for roughly two years), the town transforms under their influence. Semiotic images of civilization appear: a new barber's chair, the arrival of hardworking farm folk, the intrusion of high culture in the guise of a semicompetent Shakespearean actor, establishing of law and order through gun control, the promise of the area's first schoolmarm, and, most significant in our context, the building of the town's first church. All point *Clementine*'s cinematic Tombstone in the direction of *Stagecoach*'s Tonto. Several undesirables are forced out, including one Native American, owing less to his race than to his tendency toward drunken violence; other Indians who do not disturb the peace are welcome to remain. A gambler who arrives on the stagecoach is told to leave at once because of his reputation as dishonest. Yet prostitutes are as plentiful at film's end as at the beginning. The town madam (Jane Darwell) is treated respectfully by Earp. Nor does he try to shut down the gambling operation owned by Holliday and even enjoys it and the free flow of liquor in the saloon so long as everything is up front and honest. Guns, though, are forbidden within the town limits.

Again, Ford proves himself a master rather than mere journeyman by transcending obvious right/wrong dichotomies. Anything that does not physically endanger another person's body is allowed, if circumscribed by group rules. Each person's soul remains his or her own moral business, in civil-libertarian style, so long as people do not bother their neighbors. The result is a vision of American society's potential for salvation through tolerance: allow sinning, if that's what it is, to continue and only contain it as the real Earp did by establishing a red-light district. Now, the equally abhorrent extremes of Puritanism and anarchy—of Tonto and Lordsburg—are avoided to the betterment of all. For Slotkin, "Ford in *Stagecoach* sees no hope within American 'sivilization'"; he notes, however, that in *Clementine*, "democracy, equality, responsibility, and solidarity are achieved."[5] If *Stagecoach* presented extremes, each serving a cautionary purpose for the viewer, *Clementine* allows us a more realistic paradigm in which a delicate balance is successfully created.

When we do see conventional Christians practicing their faith, it's a far cry from the self-righteousness on view in Tonto. Here, the women all smile rather than crankily look down WASPish noses at people in any way different. Perhaps in due time they will evolve into *Stagecoach*'s biddies.

Semiotics and the Western. For followers of Peter Wollen's system of discovering meaning in motion pictures by seeking out a continuum of visual signs and symbols that unlock the true meaning, My Darling Clementine *offers a metaphor for the installment of the finest sort of civilization in any American community: (a) law and order in which the town police do not carry*

guns; (b) the arrival of culture, via a Shakespearean actor; (c) decent, middle-class people joining the diverse mix without any small-minded prejudice toward nonviolent riff-raff; (d) modern technological conveniences such as the Bon Ton Tonsorial Parlor; (e) the first schoolmarm; and (f) the first, if unsuccessful, medical operation. Courtesy Twentieth Century-Fox.

We can hope that won't happen. Clementine (Cathy Downs), as respectable an Eastern woman as anyone could hope to meet, expresses a gay attitude about life, coaxing reluctant Wyatt to join her in a dance. She's even tolerant of Chihuahua, never condemning the girl, unlike *Stagecoach*'s Lucy Mallory, who had to learn tolerance of difference, be it race, class, or whatever. At the end, Wyatt temporarily leaves. He will return to marry Clementine, the new schoolmarm. Together they will keep this town a liberal bastion of civilization rather than allow it to sink back into chaos like Lordsburg or become the kind of narrow-minded Tonto that Ford clearly detests.

Shortly after helping Wayne direct *The Alamo* on a noncredit basis, Ford began the new decade with one of his darkest films. In *Two Rode Together* (1961) he returns us to the Wyatt Earp character, now played by James Stewart. Earp is given the fictional name Marshal McCabe, but his introductory scene makes clear this is *Clementine*'s marshal revisited—and revised. With feet sprawled far apart as he sits on his porch, Stewart's McCabe appears all but indistinguishable from Fonda's Earp in one of that earlier film's most memorable moments. The stagecoach drops off a gambler, and McCabe delivers the same speech to him Earp did to the man's counterpart. Once the reference is clear, we notice in contrast how different the two Earps, similar in appearance, are in attitude. The vivid contrast allows us to see how much Ford's vision has altered over fifteen years. If the marshal of the early postwar era was dedicated first to individualism in the best sense and later to the communal good, this one is a self-serving individualist. He's on the take; he frequents brothels, drinks too much, lies to his cavalry-officer best friend (Richard Widmark), and is out for whatever he can get. All the same, Ford does not condemn him as a villain but rather accepts the man as anti-hero.

McCabe, when all is said, gets the job done. He maintains in town that balance between respectability and low-lifes that did not exist in *Stagecoach*, although this marshal does so realistically rather than with the idealism of Fonda's Earp. Wearing the same costume he wore as McCabe, Stewart embodies Earp by name in *Cheyenne Autumn* (1964), though in this, Ford's final Western, the delicate balance comes undone. In Dodge City, when locals of all possible classes hear about a get-rich-quick scheme, they rush out like so many circus clowns to grab what they can for themselves and kill Indians along the way. The somber tone and serious style of Ford's body of work gives way to the broadest form of burlesque.

Those films were shot for wide screen and in color. Ford reverted to his old standby black and white for *The Man Who Shot Liberty Valance*, perhaps to suggest that he was less interested in making a Western than in offering a perhaps belated corrective to the mythology present in all his earlier Westerns. It is not for nothing that *Liberty Valance* was not shot in Monument Valley. We see the drab city that, at the turn of the twentieth century, a once-wild town called Shinbone has become. It is peaceful, stable, and quietly modern in all respects. A flashback returns us to the days when this place combined the chaos of early Tombstone and of Lordsburg. The tale concerns the process of change, enacted less by the craven lawman (Andy Devine) than by Stewart's character, Ranse Stoddard, a lawyer and a teacher.

Essentially, he becomes a male schoolmarm, the role taken on by women playing the lead female characters in so many Westerns. Stoddard even wears an apron and waits tables to make ends meet. A West where men were men and women were women, Ford reveals in this early example of revisionism by the artist who had perfected those myths, never did exist. Perhaps it is only coincidental that we don't see or even hear about a church during the flashback, though one does exist in the framing device. This film's focus is, after all, politics. Yet other films like Ford's *Clementine* convey that to understand the process by which the West was won we must regularly return to a town's spiritual center, its church.

The politics of nostalgia. In the early twentieth century, a state senator (James Stewart) returns to the now civilized, once wide-open town he helped tame. He stands before the dusty stage that first brought him here in The Man Who Shot Liberty Valance. *Courtesy Paramount Pictures.*

18

GLORY IN THE
(WILD)FLOWER
ROMANTICISM ON THE OPEN RANGE

With the flowering of Romanticism in the eighteenth and early
nineteenth centuries, wild country lost much of its repulsiveness.

—RODERICK FRAZIER NASH, *WILDERNESS*
AND THE AMERICAN MIND, 1967

Shortly after the release of *Avatar* (James Cameron, 2009), conceived and executed over a ten-year period at an estimated budget of $350 million to $500 million, a backlash from the political religious right set in. Early reviews in trade publications and the mainstream press, appearing during *Avatar's* mid-December holiday release, had mostly been of a positive nature. Critics expressed praise for Cameron's technical achievements at blending live-action 3-D with computer animation, some claiming he had reinvented the art of filmmaking. In a thematic vein, reviewers noted that Avatar's narrative, imagery, and ideology drew heavily from a large backlog of liberal-progressive popular culture. The second wave of criticism, mostly adverse, began before the year's end. In the neoconservative *Weekly Standard*, reviewer John Podhoretz attacked *Avatar* for the very element that, in addition to craftsmanship, many liberal critics supported: transforming left-leaning ideas—

anticorporate, anti-imperialist, and pro-environmental—into entertainment aimed at the mass audience. Though not a disparaging word challenged earlier assessments of the film's technical accomplishments, Podhoretz called *Avatar* "an undigested mess of clichés . . . taken directly from the revisionist Westerns of the 1960s."[1] Such films began with *Little Big Man* (Arthur Penn, 1970) and continued on to *Dances with Wolves* (Kevin Costner, 1990). Essentially, conservatives and liberals saw the very same elements in *Avatar* but not surprisingly reacted to them in oppositional ways.

Considering the film's wide popularity, Ann Marlowe notes in *Forbes* that "right-wing attacks on *Avatar* show a . . . tone-deafness to what most Americans find inspiring."[2] If, as Podhoretz claimed, *Avatar* projected an extreme, even subversive vision, why did the mainstream public so adore it? Critic Mike Taibbi pointed out on MSNBC-TV that "in the red states it's doing just as well as in blue states."[3] Observers agreed that, properly understood, *Avatar* had less in common with the science fiction and epic fantasy genres its futuristic setting would suggest than with the Western. *Avatar's* out-of-control military commander (Stephen Lang) represents a variation on General George Custer but not the complex, fascinating, questionable character that history reveals him to have been;[4] rather, *Avatar* presents the commander as so many revisionist films (*Sitting Bull*, Sidney Salkow, 1954; *Tonka*, Lewis R. Foster, 1958; *The Great Sioux Massacre*, Salkow, 1965) have posited Custer: a racist extremist representing Anglo-Christian society eager to wipe out a primitive race of people of color considered inferior to those hailing from civilization because their spirituality is drawn from the woods in which they live, particularly their trees.

With politics already part of the equation, religion entered the controversy even as *Avatar* edged upward toward status as the most popular movie of all time. Podhoretz's dismissal of the film, "with its mindless worship of a nature-loving tribe and the tribe's adorable pagan rituals,"[5] apparently resonated in Rome. Days before *Avatar's* scheduled opening in Italy, Vatican spokesman Federico Lombardi condemned what he called its obvious intent to "promote the worship of nature" in a Vatican radio broadcast. *L'Osservatore Romano*, the Vatican print news outlet, contended that *Avatar* "gets bogged down by a spiritualism linked to the worship of nature"; Lombardi drew from sitting Pope Benedict XVI's warnings about the "dangers of turning nature into a new divinity."[6] Whether one agrees or disagrees that such a thing is dangerous, Lombardi's use of the word "new" rings false.

Prelude to Avatar. *In Westerns of a romantic leaning, the male hero, often a military veteran, learns to love nature by embracing a woman who lives within its grandeur. In* Broken Arrow *James Stewart's character surrenders to the beauty of both (the love interest played by Debra Paget). Courtesy Twentieth Century-Fox.*

Neopaganism, if that is indeed what *Avatar* promotes, by its very name speaks of bygone ways, standards, laws, and most of all ancient nature gods. In Western culture neopagan thinking emerged as a dialectic swing away from the Puritanism that gripped much of Europe during the seventeenth century.[7] Romanticism's roots are generally acknowledged to be grounded in Germany's Sturm und Drang movement, which dared to challenge the prevalent attitudes about enlightenment through reason and favored a return to emotions as the source of salvation.[8] Soon a pastoral tradition sprang up in the arts in which simple farmers were idealized over more civilized people owing to their closeness with the earth, for example, the Celtic notion of a female Mother Nature as compared to a later Judeo-Christian concept of a male sky god.[9] The Romantic movement, which gradually grew out of artistic *divertissements*, fully blossomed in France at the time of the French Revolution (1789–1799), in part inspired by America's break from monarchical Britain. The French commoners were aided by American patriots like philosopher-pamphleteer Thomas Paine. A total overthrow of a long-empowered aristocracy by the working class did not end with political reform; as always, social change affected the popular culture that reflected the period during which it came into being. All at once, folk art, long considered inferior to high or sophisticated culture, was revered as a more honest art form.[10] Classical music gave way to Romantic symphonies composed across Europe by Haydn and Beethoven foremost among many others as this new political, artistic, philosophical strain spread.[11]

If the birth of Romanticism in politics, philosophy, and the popular arts was joyously welcomed in the newly liberated France, it was frowned on in England. During the transition from the eighteenth century to the nineteenth, the Lake School poets attempted to introduce Romantic ideas to that classicist country, which maintained a king by divine right despite advances in democracy. In time, poets like George Gordon, known as Lord Byron, and Percy Bysshe Shelley were pressured into leaving the British Isles and wandered throughout Europe. They became men without a country, other than, that is, their mental realm of Romanticism, which evolved for them a political as well as a philosophical or religious vision.

The Romantic neopagans openly rejected Christianity, with its insistence on a dichotomy in which God and nature existed in a constant state of war. In that rejected paradigm, the devil served as an emblem of evil more often than not encountered in the seductively dangerous realm of nature. The conflict occurred not only in the world but for humans internally; their Christian duty was to leave nature behind and rise up to a level with the angels. For its adherents, Romanticism was supposed to replace the dichotomy with acceptance of a pre–Judeo-Christian belief: God and nature are one and the same, existing not in opposition but in symbiosis, with nature serving as God's manifest presence on earth.[12] In the Romantic worldview, to worship nature, whether the earthly wilderness and its creatures or human emotion and sexuality, was to worship God. These ideas made their way across the ocean to America, where they immediately conflicted with earlier imposed, now firmly entrenched Puritan conservative Christian values.

To the extent American politics have been torn between competing concepts of rugged individualism and communal loyalty, religion in America likewise reveals a moral tug of war between the Puritan separation of soul and body and a Romantic insistence that physicality ought to be reveled in as an expression of that very spirituality. The Romantic approach presented precepts that would later be codified as pantheism, in which a oneness with nature does not create a barrier between humans and God but allows people to transcend the here and now.[13] American authors who swiftly embraced Romanticism, or a slightly altered form known as transcendentalism, included Edgar Allan Poe and Nathaniel Hawthorne. Poe's stories take place in some strange neverland, while Hawthorne's are for the most part set in his own New England environment.

Typical of Hawthorne's approach and outlook, his "Young Goodman Brown" (1835) concerns a Puritan crippled with guilt because he would like to slip out of town and off to the Indian village whenever he hears their nightly tom-toms. Afraid to admit this to fellow citizens, he at last gives in, only to discover all of the townspeople are already there dancing naked about a totem pole. For better or worse, this is the way of all flesh. An all but identical image, though with an Anglo individualist rather than a full community, appears in *Dances with Wolves* (Kevin Costner, 1990). And no matter how severe its shortcomings, and they are numerous, Roland Joffe's 1995 film of *The Scarlet Letter*, Hawthorne's historical novel of 1850, did effectively present Hester Prynne (Demi Moore), the lone female who dares to surrender to sensuality in nature—going so far in her situational context as to embrace the Indians—as the single sympathetic character on view in her Puritan village. The primary purpose of the first great and uniquely American literature, which came into being during the nineteenth century, was to reject in an emergent national artistic sensibility the social, religious, and cultural code that was established during the sixteenth century and solidified in the eighteenth.[14]

Quickly it became obvious that the West was the proper place for a national Romantic vision to be enacted in a new form of fiction that would qualify as indigenously American in both style and substance: a yet developing literature for an embryonic country that was gradually forming political and religious systems all its own. If we search for an origination point of American Romanticism in the Western, likely it is to be found in the work of James Fenimore Cooper and set on the first frontier of upstate New York. In *The Pioneers* (1823), first to be written in his quintet of tales about frontiersman Natty Bumppo (or Bumpo), we meet the hero as an older man attempting to live in the confines of a civilized town in an area where he blazed the trail and cleared the wilderness. Appreciation is not in evidence here; citizens have short memories. They are outraged that anyone, Natty included,

"The man who knows Indians." James Fenimore Cooper's early incarnation of the Western, as filmed in 1992 by Michael Mann, posits Hawkeye (Daniel Day-Lewis) as Rousseau's "natural man." Though born Nathaniel, this romantic figure feels far more comfortable with his Native American blood brothers (Russell Means, Eric Schweig) than in the company of other Anglos. Courtesy Twentieth Century-Fox.

would dare disturb a Sunday's solemnity with liquor, shouting, and other "natural behavior." Puritans shove the buckskinned drunkard into the stocks, humiliating a true pioneer and the greater, larger, partly historical and partly mythical pioneer spirit he embodies. Natty's beloved blood brother John Mohican, also called Sagamore or Chingachgook, squats and wails by his friend's side. What they need is someone to save them from "the blessings of civilization."

In subsequent installments of the saga, Cooper would flash back and forth in time. Always, Natty is the best (Anglo) man because he is Romantic philosopher Jean-Jacques Rousseau's "natural man."[15] Slotkin might call him "The Man Who Knows Indians,"[16] one who has learned their ways while, in a Romantic sense, rejected the seemingly civilized Christian but more often than not inhumane ways of Anglo society. Cooper's books about Bumppo include *The Deerslayer* (1841), *The Pathfinder* (1840), and *The Last of the Mohicans* (1826), presented here in the order in which the stories occur. He would lionize Bumppo in *The Prairie* (1827), in which we discover Nat (at this point, he has actually become the first Man with No Name character) alone, his longtime Native sidekick having passed. Always, though, it has been *The Last of the Mohicans* that most completely captured the public imagination, first in book form and then in its various motion-picture incarnations.

A still-young Bumppo, temporarily nicknamed Hawkeye, and Chingach-gook along with his son Uncas, who does not survive the story, come face to face with Cora Munro, daughter of a British officer serving in the French and Indian wars. At first glimpse of the pair, the fresh-from-England lady is shocked, even repelled by what appears to be a combination of man and beast from the woods. She wants to hurry away to her aristocratic father or her officer fiancé, Duncan Hayward. But as the narrative unfolds, Cora and her younger sister are abducted by hostile Hurons, and her notion of Bumppo alters. This natural man is in fact a natural aristocrat, not by birth, like the older English order, but by actions. He does so even as the twentieth-century Horatio Alger hero becomes a king of capital owing to his luck and pluck; he too earns it.

If there is a flaw to Michael Mann's mostly excellent 1992 film version, it is that screenwriter Chris Columbus was allowed to kill fiancé Duncan off along the way, while in Cooper's novel he remains very much alive. How much more effective to have finished the film with Cora's self-conscious choice between the two men. As in Edgar Rice Burroughs's similarly struc-tured novel *Tarzan of the Apes* (1912), featuring the same romantic triangle reset in Africa, and the legendary MGM film version, *Tarzan, the Ape Man* (W. S. Van Dyke, 1932), Cora (Madeleine Stowe) should, like Jane, decide for herself whether to return to England with a yet-living fiancé or remain in the forest with her natural man (Daniel Day-Lewis). In so doing, Jane and Cora reject the Victorian world for the natural green one, Christianity for paganism, classicism for Romanticism.

In *Avatar* the gender roles are reversed, but the message remains the same. Ross Douthat noted in the *New York Times* that *Avatar* represented "an apo-logia for pantheism."[17] "Pantheism," the scientific term for neopaganism in both philosophy and the arts, represents an attempt to reach out to God or the gods by navigating to rather than avoiding nature. Equally essential is embracing as holy the natural self, the flesh, rather than perceiving it as a holdover from animal origins. In our context, it is worth noting that in the early twentieth century, the poet-philosopher D. H. Lawrence (1885–1930) left the British Isles—strongly urged to do so—and traveled to the American Southwest. Lawrence hoped to there learn from, rather than like previous Christian missionaries teach, the Native people he encountered.

Previous Anglos saw the Indians as children in need of education, moral and otherwise; D. H. Lawrence followed the William Wordsworth adage

"It's the Good Book, Nesby. Hold it close. It'll make ya feel good!" A Texas Ranger captain (Ward Bond) does double duty during an Indian raid, simultaneously serving as a religious leader in The Searchers. Courtesy Warner Brothers.

that "the child is father to the man,"[18] reversing the long-standing imperialist aspect of coming to America. Lawrence's novel *The Plumed Serpent* (1926), written in Taos, New Mexico, offers a female Anglo Christian who, as a tourist in Old Mexico, falls under the spell of ancient pagan god Quetzalcoatl and joins a cult planning to bring back pagan worship. A classicist would have portrayed the young woman as delusional and in need of rescue; Lawrence applauds her surrender to the realm of senses.

Earlier authors like Cooper and Longfellow, notably in his *Hiawatha*, made the mistake of attempting to capture the glorious, rich wilderness in the high-poetic language of Scotland's Sir Walter Scott, whose 1819 novel *Ivanhoe* served as a template for Cooper's *Last of the Mohicans*: two young women abducted by villains and in need of rescue by a man of civilization (Ivanhoe) and a green man from the woods (Locksley, A.K.A. Robin Hood). In addition to resetting the tale in the New World, Cooper shifted the heroic status from the old order of knights to the new one, the natural man, the best man. This led to an awkward fit between form and content. Gradually, others learned from these writers' mistakes. Mark Twain and Walt Whitman relaxed literary technique to present the prose and poetry of a people's republic in the people's own language, a remarkable innovation.

Now, nature and art were completely collapsed: the first word of the title of *Leaves of Grass* (1855) refers to the paper on which Walt Whitman's philosophic poetry was presented as well as a reference to the trees that in ancient times led to the cult of Druidism, a term roughly translating in our own language to "those with knowledge of the Oak."[19]

Pagan knowledge, which Wordsworth would call "primal sympathy,"[20] once came naturally to us. For modern man this knowledge had to gradually be reclaimed. "We learn by imitation,"[21] Wordsworth sadly noted, referring to the process by which young people are propagandized by society. His hope was for people to "unlearn" all that cultural baggage by recovering an ability to listen to the basic, beautiful voice of the wind, not for him the devil's call but God's own whisper, to retrieve a lost vision of the good.

This had been the thrust of Wordsworth's most quoted poem, "Ode: Intimations on Immortality" (1802–1804), with the line "Now is the hour of splendor in the grass, of glory in the flower." This open invitation to embrace the wilderness incurred the wrath of Puritans who believed his phrase to be obscene and anti-Christian. From a right-wing point of view, it was and is. What Wordsworth meant, of course, was the human need to find spiritual splendor in the grass by rediscovering heaven in the earth, not somewhere high above. No wonder so many European Romantics looked to America as their greatest inspiration. They considered the Indians higher rather than lower beings. In *Avatar* the people of the forest are blue, not red. The white hero must be the man who comes to know them, Indians or whatever we call these people possessing primal wisdom. Today, such visions are located by artists in a futuristic fantasy. Up until the oater fell out of fashion with audiences, the literary genre that most perfectly expressed these encounters was the Western.

Nature girl. The Romantic sensibility that flowered in the nineteenth century reached back beyond Judeo-Christian religions to the pagan idealization of pre-Eve earth goddesses. Audrey Hepburn incarnated the concept in Green Mansions. *Courtesy Metro-Goldwyn-Mayer.*

19

HEARTS OF DARKNESS, SOULS OF LIGHT

VISIONS OF NATURE IN
AMERICAN FILM AND FICTION

Wordsworth wrote in "Lines" (1789) of his spiritual betterment after leaving the putrid city to wander free and liberated in the woods, sensing his own conversion:[1]

Though changed, no doubt, from what I was when
first I came among these hills

An almost identical line appears in *Valley of the Giants* (William Keighley, 1938), a Western based on a novel by the now forgotten, onetime best-selling author Peter B. Kyne. The title refers to California's redwoods, among the oldest trees on earth. Wayne Morris plays Bill Cardigan, a young man born and raised here. He has grown up as pure and innocent as the forest, apparently never attending a formal church service yet experiencing divine glory in the wildflower, discovering a spiritual splendor in the grass. He's visited now by Lee Roberts (Claire Trevor), a woman from civilization in the worst sense of that term. Despite her inherent goodness, she's been corrupted by the ways of the world; she has become a hypocrite for whom lying comes as easily as telling the truth does to him. She is a raw capitalist of a self-serving order, amoral enough to do anything for money.

Shortly, though, Lee senses herself shifting in relationship to her new surroundings. "It changes you," Bill whispers, "living in the woods." By film's end, the woman has arced; she comes to love the forest that she initially found foreboding while also, in a parallel and synergistic pattern, falling in love with Bill. As in all romantic narratives, they are one and the same: geography is character; place is person.

This philosophical or theological approach can be traced back in developing American popular culture not only to the birth of motion pictures but to the preceding print forms from upper-middlebrow literature like Longfellow's *Hiawatha* (1855) to declassé pulp fiction on the order of *Deadwood Dick* dime novels to quaint operettas, *Rose Marie* most famous among them. Place as a character appears in some of the greatest literature America has produced. Whitman in his revolutionary prose poetry of the mid-nineteenth century and soon Mark Twain in *The Adventures of Huckleberry Finn* (1884–1885) pioneered this literary approach. Twain's boy hero runs away from his home in fictional St. Petersburg, Missouri. Huck is sickened by the superficiality and hypocrisy that make up everyday life. Only on the Big River can he listen to the wind, discover his individual identity and embrace it, and enjoy a warm relationship with the finest person he knows, the escaped slave Jim. Let Tom Sawyer remain behind, hopelessly trying to hold onto the primal sympathy these boys once shared while every day becoming what, in the grandeur of his youth, Tom professed to hate. Huck will have none of that. As for his friendship with Jim, that would be verboten back in the conventionally religious town, where a church serves as the epicenter of all that residents believe is right with their antebellum South. But Twain, the sympathetic reader, and eventually Huck himself sense the established order to be all wrong.

Here is a Southern version of the relationship that Fenimore Cooper developed between a good, honest, natural man of color and that rare white hero who desires to become his blood brother. Natty and the Sagamore soon grasp that this is possible only if they "light out for the territories" (in Huck's words) beyond the reach of conventional politics and religion, those two elements inseparable in more conservative Christian cities. The Hawkeye-Chingachgook relationship would in time be recycled as the Lone Ranger and Tonto, reaching the level of ritual when extended to radio, television, movies, and even comic books during the 1940s and 1950s. On television another pair was most effectively conveyed on an NBC series, *Daniel Boone* (1964–1970), with Fess Parker as a highly fanciful version of the pioneer

"Glory in the flower." The tradition of a civilized male rediscovering paradise with a woman who possesses "knowledge of the Oak" is reflected in A. E. Hudson's Green Mansions, *starring Audrey Hepburn and Anthony Perkins. Courtesy Metro-Goldwyn-Mayer.*

and Ed Ames as his Native American equal and friend Mingo. A similar duo would rest at the heart of Ken Kesey's 1962 novel *One Flew over the Cuckoo's Nest*, in which McMurphy aligns with the Chief. That book's Western aura would be all but eliminated for the 1975 film in which Kesey's cowboy hero, self-consciously modeled by the author on Kirk Douglas's Western roles, became a contemporary street person in the guise of Jack Nicholson.[2]

Endless variations on this theme could include, as in Kyne's novel *Valley of the Giants*, romance in a double sense of the term whenever a man-woman love evolves. In W. H. Hudson's novel *Green Mansions* (1904) and Hollywood's surprisingly belated film of it (Mel Ferrer, 1959), a civilized man (Anthony Perkins) slips into a South American rainforest where he becomes enamored of Rina "the Bird Girl" (Audrey Hepburn). She, like Neytiril (Zoe Saldana) in *Avatar*, makes her home in a tree. Embracing Rina, the youth symbolically wraps his arms around nature, God's kingdom on earth, leaving wicked society behind. Before encountering Rina, the hero was blinded by the brainwashing civilization process. Now, without a word spoken between them (they communicate mentally, emotionally, spiritually), he sees deeper, knowing he has been reborn for the better in nature—the nature around him, the nature inside him.

One of the best expressions of American romanticism appeared in Conrad Richter's novel *The Light in the Forest* (1950) and the Walt Disney film version (Herschel Daugherty, 1958). Here a young Anglo (James MacArthur) has spent most of his life among the Native people of colonial

Pennsylvania after being abducted as a child. When a treaty decrees that he must be returned to white society, the boy soon discovers he hates everything that he encounters there in that tight circle of cabins cut into the woods and organized around a whitewashed church. Though the frontier scout (Fess Parker) who accompanies True Son home is a fine fellow, that's because he's another variation on the man who knows Indians, preferring life in the wilds to civilization. That good-natured, righteous man's moral opposite in the town (Wendell Corey) is a racist bully who represents the moral ignorance in civilization. As for a possible light symbolizing wisdom, God, or both, True Son sees that liberation can only be achieved by returning to the forest.

It is what the hero of a thousand faces learns in some variation on the essential Romantic theme, be he called Tarzan, Mowgli, or Hawkeye and whether his adventure in self-discovery and the meaning of the world takes place in Africa, India, or upstate New York. This tradition continued into the back-to-nature craze that roughly ran between 1965 and 1985. Then mainstream Americans turned away from their habit of staying in motels during weekend escapes to instead go camping. The trend would be reflected by the absorption of such modern yet retro attitudes into Hollywood films.

When Thomas Berger's Western burlesque novel *Little Big Man* first appeared in 1964, the critically acclaimed work was thought too "edgy" for mainstream Americans. It did become a cult favorite among many intellectuals who approved of its then-radical vision of society as corrupt and hypocritical and wilderness the place where moral redemption was possible. The hero is another white abducted by Indians only to discover that he prefers their lifestyle. The onset of "future shock" and "information overload," described by Alvin Toffler,[3] turned many middle-of-the-roaders toward radicalism during the late 1960s. When Berger's book, originally considered too subversive for Hollywood, was produced as a film (Arthur Penn, 1970), it became a box-office hit. The lead was played by a new youth star from *The Graduate* (Mike Nichols, 1967), Dustin Hoffman. His presence in *Little Big Man* as Jack Crabbe suggests that the tale was set in the past but intended as commentary on the present—the Far West Indian wars employed as an on-screen allegory for the controversial U.S. presence in Vietnam—as the offbeat, thoroughly modern hero bears witness to atrocities whites commit against native people.

A decade after the release of *Little Big Man*, these stories in mainstream movies were no longer groundbreaking but expected. In *Legend of the Lone Ranger* (William A. Fraker, 1981), when the orphan boy who will in time become the title character is adopted by a Native tribe, balladeer Merle Haggard informs us:

> *He learned the wisdom of the forest.*
> *He learned the way of the wind.*

Some books and films served as cautionary fables, though, warning against the romanticizing trend by dramatizing an opposing conclusion. In James Dickey's novel *Deliverance* (1970) and John Boorman's film version (1972), four pseudo-sophisticated Georgia suburbanite males choose not to play golf over the weekend but instead to become Iron Johns,[4] taking off into the wilds to experience whitewater on the Cahulawassee River only to get far more than they bargained for. Initially the piece seems to be shaping up as a Wordsworthian idyll of a more rugged order. When they reach the backwoods, one of the group (Ronny Cox) finds himself drawn into a banjo duo with a half-wild boy. In performing together the man hears for the first time a stir of ancient echoes, likely to lead him back to a primal sympathy that can set him free from the constraints of stale suburban life. In truth, the child is not innocent but mentally retarded; to join his way of seeing isn't enlightening but atavistic, for the sensibility of the piece is not Romantic but naturalistic.

When the four men push ever deeper into this local pocket of a final frontier, the people they meet—hillbilly rednecks, far removed from church, state, the female principle, and everything else that might have gentled them—turn out to be not pure and good but savage and cruel. They plan, with animal-like cunning, to first rape, then kill these normals. In this fervently antiromantic vision, the only way to survive and perhaps return home is to fight fire with fire. The central character, Ed Gentry (Jon Voigt), previously the most thoughtful among the group, sets all civility aside to brutally end the threat. He manages the difficult climb up a mountain to kill the intended killers. In the process, he experiences a spiritual alteration that in context, however necessary, appears less than enlightening. Surrendering to what are indeed dark gods, he does get back in touch not with some gentle primal sympathy but a basic bloodlust. If his consciousness is altered, the context hardly allows us to perceive that transformation to a less civilized, raw state as something we ought to emulate.

When the three survivors crawl back to civilization, they silently share, from that moment on, a terrible secret. What they have experienced out

Dancing with Native Americans. Liberal-romantic works like Dances with Wolves, *directed by and starring Kevin Costner, portray a return to nature and native people as a source of liberation from questionable societal codes. Courtesy United Artists.*

there could hardly be considered a light in the forest, unless one refers to the light of the moon and to them as its werewolf-like minions. It is unlikely they will ever again venture off the golf course in their spare time.

A counterweight to *Deliverance* that would appear in 1990 was *Dances with Wolves.* "I've always wanted to see the frontier," John Dunbar (Kevin Costner) explains, "before it was gone." In this, perhaps the most pastoral of romantic Westerns, Dunbar abandons a wartorn civilization to disappear into a peaceful second Eden. Here he finds a fairytale world where the Cheyenne are not the fierce warrior nation history tells us about;[5] they are a sweet, peaceful people born out of the joint imagination of Costner and writer Michael Blake. At mid-movie Dunbar whirls around a bonfire with Natives he's come to love and accept, Hawthorne's young Goodman Brown reimagined as a cavalryman. Experiencing total transcendence, he becomes one with them. Wordsworth-like, Dunbar reconnects with a benign natural refuge capable of restoring his world-weary soul.

John Dunbar relearns, in the film's Romantic context, a desirable form of childlike wisdom that for him and all civilized men has long been buried under the awful baggage acquired by attending society's schools, churches, and other institutions. Shedding this burden along with his tight military outfit, he emerges half-naked as a finer person. Dunbar can finally rediscover splendor in the grass and glory in the flower in a spiritual as well as sensual sense. For the pantheistic sensibility, the two are one and the same. From a classicist, condemning point of view, *Dances with Wolves* precedes *Avatar* as a radical undermining of Judeo-Christian values by idealizing nature. From that perspective, what Dunbar achieves—while so appealing to the romantic—displays humankind in a state of devolution. One of the soldiers who discovers Dunbar wearing animal skins venomously exclaims that he has "gone back!"

Kurtz, Marlon Brando's character in Francis Ford Coppola's *Apocalypse Now* (1979), could be considered a philosophical alternative to Dunbar in *Dances with Wolves*. For in Coppola as in Joseph Conrad's *Heart of Darkness*, we observe a paragon of society reduced to base savagery by the primitive wilderness rather than, as in romantically inclined works, enlightened by close contact with nature. Costner's outlook is anticlassicist. The natural world—woodland, prairie, rainforest, deserted isle—appears not as some untamed jungle but as God's good garden. For neopagan, pantheist, or romantic, a hero like Dunbar hears the primal sympathy that during a person's civilization process becomes ever softer. The romantic hero—Hawkeye, Tarzan, Dunbar, or John Morgan (Richard Harris) in *A Man Called Horse* (Elliot Silverstein, 1970)—is that rarest civilized being who follows the now dim but never mute ancient voice.

If the Western is by its very nature predisposed to a romantic outlook, not all Westerns assume one. Again, this genre is large and broad enough to include varying, even oppositional points of view. In Delmer Daves's *Broken Arrow* (1950), the Anglo hero (James Stewart), derived from a real-life man named Tom Jeffords, allows himself to fall under the spell of the Apache nation, even marrying an Apache woman (Debra Paget). As a result he becomes a better person, qualifying the film as romantic. *Arrowhead* (Charles Marquis Warren, 1953) features Charlton Heston as scout Ed Bannon, modeled on the historical Al Seiber. He too has lived with Indians and is a man who knows them. Instead of spreading the word about their goodness, he warns naïve whites that Apaches are cold-blooded "red devils" not to be trusted. Well-meaning Anglos who refuse to listen are butchered by their supposed friends. Though he has a Native American mistress (Katy Jurado), their strictly sexual liaison is of a highly sadomasochistic nature. When she

A study in contrasts. (a) Broken Arrow *presents an Army scout (James Stewart) in a loving marriage with a Native American woman (Debra Paget). (b) In comparison,* Arrowhead *depicts disrepect between a similar figure (Charlton Heston) and a Native American woman (Katy Jurado). Courtesy Twentieth Century-Fox; Paramount Pictures.*

"The captivity myth." From Fenimore Cooper's "Eastern" novel The Last of the Mohicans *to John Ford's* The Searchers *(seen here), the Anglo woman's fate worse than death was being taken by a dark race. Walt Disney's* The Light in the Forest *is one of the few films to depict the perspective of women who actually preferred their Indian husbands. Courtesy Warner Brothers.*

can finally stand no more and commits suicide, Bannon shows no remorse. The film appears to have been designed as a classicist answer to what Warren considered *Broken Arrow*'s naïve attitudes. A single situation, then, can be dramatized to effectively depict a romantic or classicist outlook.

More recent films tend toward political correctness and therefore a romantic view. But not all. In *Streets of Laredo* (TVM, Joseph Sargent, 1995), adapted from the 1993 novel by Larry McMurtry, young Joey Garza (Alexis Cruz) kills indiscriminately. A nihilist, he is so amoral it can't be claimed that he takes pleasure in murdering people, animals, whatever has the misfortune of appearing in his line of vision. Garza is incapable of joy or any other emotion; he operates out of a mind the pursuing Anglo lawman Woodrow Call (James Garner) initially can't comprehend. Garza's grotesque actions appear even less likely after the hero meets the youth's Hispanic family, a decent, devout Catholic mother (Sonia Braga) and gentle younger brother and sister. With such a biological and social background, how could Joey have turned out so terribly violent? "He was a nice kid," a townsman recalls, until he was taken by the Apaches and lived with them for three years. In McMurtry's Westerns, nurture supersedes nature, qualifying *Streets of Laredo* and its authorial voice as classicist and even antiromantic.

A half-finished church. The most potent symbol in My Darling Clementine *appears when the first service takes place in front of the half-built structure. Marshal Earp has then completed half his job of bringing a Christian set of values to this remote outpost of civilization. Courtesy Twentieth Century-Fox.*

A CHAPEL IN THE CANYON

RELIGIOSITY, AMERICAN-STYLE

Huh! Church bells in Tombstone.

—MORGAN EARP IN *MY DARLING CLEMENTINE*, 1946

Religion in America, like its politics, came into existence as a conservative code carried over from England that in time learned to coexist and, despite seemingly oppositional qualities, meld with a rough romantic point of view. The resulting dialectic at least in part derived from anti-Anglican continental attitudes though also forged out of actual experiences with the wilderness. This paradigm is nowhere so strikingly explored on screen as in Ford's *My Darling Clementine.* At mid-movie Wyatt (Henry Fonda), Morgan (Ward Bond), and Virgil (Tim Holt) Earp stand before the marshal's office watching in surprise as a long line of orderly wagons pour into the settlement. Up until now, the brothers have witnessed only wild and woolly locals. The settlers' unofficial leader (Russell Simpson) pulls his buckboard to a halt so as to invite the Earp brothers to a Sunday morning gathering. When Virgil asks if this is to be a camp meeting, the old-timer takes good-natured offense: "No sech dad-blasted thing! *Regular* church!"

Shortly these fine folk congregate on the edge of town, where the wooden frame of a building in progress stretches toward a pristine sky. A bell sounds from its half-finished tower. Pioneers form a community and sing, with seriousness, "Yes, we will gather by the river," a Christian hymn that, drawing on the tale of John the Baptist, emphasizes (even as the Lake School poets of nineteenth century England did) nature in general and water in particular as a source of godliness on earth. As Wyatt escorts Easterner Clementine Carter (Cathy Downs) into their company, the old-timer joyously announces:

> I hereby dedicate the first church of Tombstone, which ain't got no name yet, and no preacher. Now, I don't claim to be a preacher, but I've read the Good Book from cover to cover an' back ag'in. An' I ain't never read a word ag'in dancin'. So we'll commence by havin' us a dad-blasted good *dance!*

Taking time out from the film's vengeance narrative to offer a defense of dancing, even on the Sabbath, may strike a casual viewer as curious. To the student of Ford, here the auteur makes his own identity as an Irishman and the social history of his people an integrated aspect of this Hollywood entertainment, in the process converting a public product into personal art. Ford was descended from the Feeney clan that began its emigration to America during the nineteenth century's second half.[1] He remained aware always of the Tudor conquest of his own land during the sixteenth century, the manner in which Henry VIII imposed not only English politics but also the Anglican Church (the two of course inseparable) on Gaelic people.[2] In addition to forcing an ostensibly civilized system of politics and religion on the still-pagan citizenry, these conquerors also strictly insisted on stamping out the indigenous folk culture so as to (or so the Brits believed) raise the Irish up to a higher level.[3] This process of cultural imperialism entailed an attempt to stamp out all customs deriving from Druidism, every aspect of that lifestyle from the primitive (that term employed here in a nonpejorative sense) language to the love of dancing.

Puritanism as a term may have officially indicated the most extreme incarnation of English Protestant sects.[4] But a Puritan strain ran deep in the Anglican outlook; in fact, it represented that point of view taken to its logical extreme. The famous phrase "The devil is in the fiddle" first emerged at this point in time. To dance was to celebrate as the pagans did; dancing was perceived as atavistic in the British politicoreligious system.[5] Dancing at court was barely tolerated and only if it were of the most formal manner, with

Terpsichore as characterization. (a) In Clementine *Fonda's character begins by dancing stiffly but swiftly loosens. (b) The actor's notably different character in* Fort Apache *cannot rid himself of his deep social and religious anxieties, attempting to remain ramrod-straight throughout. Courtesy Twentieth Century-Fox; Argosy/RKO Pictures.*

absolutely no abandonment to the senses. As a result, dancing was outlawed in Ireland for well into the seventeenth century, since the locals insisted on joyously flailing their arms and legs. Some scholars of dance argue that the tendency in Irish jigs to keep the upper part of one's body relatively still while moving the legs came into being here. An Irish man or woman could dance in the privacy of his or her house with no fear that a Redcoat walking by on patrol and taking a casual peek through the window would notice; thus dancing from the waist down evolved as a form of secret defiance.[6]

Ford's films demonstrate an awareness of his own history, not only in the movies set in Ireland such as *The Informer* (1935), *The Plough and the Stars* (1936), and *The Quiet Man* (1952) but in his American-set Westerns as well. *Fort Apache* (1948) offers the most accurate depiction on film of an American army post in the Southwest, but its subtextual meaning implies a metaphor for the Anglo invasion of Ford's Ireland. The isolated title fort is inhabited almost entirely by Irish. Their charmingly crude *demi-monde* remains unchallenged as genial and jolly until the arrival of a new commanding officer (Henry Fonda). Owen Thursday is aristocratic English. Immediately he demands rigid adherence to a Puritanical code. While Thursday does not outlaw dancing per se, not having the authority to do so, he clearly does not approve of it.

At the noncommissioned officers' ball, Thursday looks down his nose at the festivities and suffers silently. Then the wife of a sergeant requests the honor of a dance. Begrudgingly, Thursday agrees, though obviously this discomforts him, both the dancing and her perceived (on his part) lack of class. While they dance, Thursday attempts to keep his eyes coldly trained on the ceiling while her own big, warm orbs work at trying to break his concentration. They make an odd couple, to be sure, as we watch the sweet sensuousness of her movements compared to his tense, measured steps. Toward the end of their dance, though, we notice that he appears to be surrendering, if ever so slightly, to the joys of Terpsichore. A certain hint of freedom (he would call it chaos) appears to be forcing itself loose in the movements of his legs, much to his dance partner's delight and that of other Irish observers.

Could there be even a touch of primal sympathy still existent, if deep and dormant, within his tight, tall frame? Always, there's the hope on the part of the citizens of this Western polis, and the audience observing, that he will arc. Toward the end, Thursday proves incapable of doing so, or at least until it is too late to do anyone any good. When Thursday is finally killed by Apaches in a Custer-like massacre he brings on himself and the outpost, the command passes on to an Irish junior officer (John Wayne). We sense at once that the Little Ireland of Fort Apache, this American-set microcosm for the Emerald Isle, will now function fully again owing to a sense of home rule. All the same, Kirby York does adapt some traditional elements from his predecessor into his own emergent style. If York does not become, like Thursday, a martinet, he will insist on a somewhat more formal code of conduct than what once existed here. For Ford as for Shakespeare, all extremes are offensive. Fort Apache is, when we last see it, as near to perfect as possible, for a delicate balance now exists.

In *My Darling Clementine* the dance, which continues for quite a while through this idyllic interlude, is not solemn like the self-appointed parson's mercifully brief sermon but spirited and ongoing, the sort of celebratory gayness that East Coast Puritans would not approve of. We aren't told these settlers' specific denomination, but we can pretty much assume they are not ultraconservative Baptists who condemn dancing as a return to pagan sensuality.[7] The enthusiasm with which these decent women and men perform in the shadow of the huge rock formations surrounding them makes clear that they do not hold that the devil is in the fiddle. Ford's best Christians have tempered any existing methods of practicing their faith in the light of everyday realities. Dancing for them is, however terrible a throwback it might appear to conventional Puritans, a way to celebrate their love of God. There could be no more vivid natural setting for this uniquely American experience than Monument Valley. In *Clementine*, when our hero and his "lady fair" join the social fun, the viewer senses this is the way things ought to be in America. The work ethic presses down on them all week long. Thank God it's Friday (or Sunday, in this instance), and it's time to enjoy rather than repress their natural side and do so, appropriately enough, in the natural world.

Historically speaking, there were few if any homesteaders in Arizona at the time of the O.K. Corral gunfight.[8] The lines of Conestoga wagons, a significant visual detail in Ford's film, are anachronistic if one approaches the piece with a tunnel vision that every film drawn from historical occurrences must be fashioned as a docudrama. The Western, properly understood, exists in the territory of America's Homer, not Herodotus. Ford works not as a literal historian but in the tradition of a literary one, as did Shakespeare, although Ford's pages are composed of celluloid rather than paper, his pen

The pleasures of a Sunday social. The emergent hybrid American religion could allow for serious-minded sermons to be balanced with the spirit of fun so elemental to the national character in Clementine. *In* Angel and the Badman *John Wayne takes his turn (a) churning frozen custard and (b) even babysitting! Courtesy John Wayne Productions/Republic Pictures.*

the camera. Ford's art, hailing from an approach that was already old when the Bible was first set down in permanent form, draws on the tradition of recalling events from an ancient past to convey an interpretation of their potent meaning for people of the artist's time.

The result is an elemental American legend, actual moments transformed into pop-culture allegory. To view *My Darling Clementine* as Ford's version of what really did occur in Arizona in 1881 would be to misread the movie, just as watching a production of *Henry V* with the belief that Shakespeare offered an unvarnished depiction of British royalty would be misreading the play. Old Will's history plays and Ford's films are drawn from facts, but they are hardly bound by them. Wyatt, like Lincoln, comes to represent unique American royalty, an aristocracy based not on genetics but great words and deeds, not on bloodlines but on accomplishments in a brave new world worthy of the Bard's tempest-tested island, that hath such amazing people in it. What *My Darling Clementine* depicts in symbolic form is the creation of a specifically American religion.

A vision of the frontier's unique reconfiguration of religion is furthered in *Angel and the Badman* (James Edward Grant, 1947). John Wayne's good badman character joins a religious sect for a communion in a canyon, no church yet existing. Previously this character, Quirt Evans, the ultimate American individualist, avoided organized religion. The gunman anti-hero was turned off by the verbal hysteria that imposes a strictly moralistic value system on jus' plain folks who live their daily lives close to the earth. All that changes when Quirt comes in contact with a progressive group that has managed to hang onto the best in Judeo-Christian tradition yet adapting its basic rules to the immediate setting. These people are interested only in an admirable morality derived from the Ten Commandments. They do not, like East Coast Puritans, moralistically punish people for laughing on the Sabbath. If anything, they encourage it, with a great picnic after a brief service not unlike the one depicted in Ford's *Clementine* one year earlier. For Quirt, this is an entirely different concept of religion, one he can admire. Quickly he is converted to such a footloose form in which courting pretty girls is not frowned upon but encouraged.

As Quirt helps these good farming folk make frozen custard for their dessert, the individualist joining in a group effort for perhaps the first time in his life, his obvious enthusiasm reveals he's been converted, not by that old-time religion in the British Puritan sense but good-time religiosity of an

American order. The only restriction he needs to learn from them is "Thou shalt not kill." *Angel and the Badman* rates as a precursor to Batjac productions, the first of those films Wayne designed for himself during the postwar period when indie production gradually eased out the old studio system in Hollywood.[9] Unlearning the way of the gun makes a fellow more, not less, of a man. As in *Shane*, which followed, this can only be accomplished when the tough guy allows himself to fall under the shadow of a good woman who conveys the female principle, Jean Arthur in that George Stevens film, Gail Russell here.

Such a woman is an earthly rather than ethereal angel. When his pals go up against a gang, at Quirt's command they use clubs to knock enemies off horses rather than shoot them. At the end, this Billy the Kid type does what's necessary to survive in an ever more civilized America. He faces his worst enemy (Bruce Cabot), an unredeemed gunfighter, with no pistol even though the bad man is armed. Instead it is the Pat Garrett figure (Harry Carey Sr.) who shoots the enemy down, legitimized as this lawman wears an official badge and does so only to save an unarmed potential victim. Here's the Billy Bonney ritualistic tale rewritten with a happy ending, and the reason for that is simple: this Kid chooses not to take his guns to town. As a result, he gets the girl and a new way of life. From this day forth he will be a Christian farmer, if clearly not in any Puritanical sense of the term.

The notion of a rustic altar is as much Southern as Western, transplanted to the frontier from the Ozarks.[10] This helps in understanding why upper-class Anglos in oaters are likely to scoff at unpretentious hill people, many of whom hail from less exalted backgrounds in the British Isles (Scotland and Ireland) and find no contest between natural and sacred. *The Last Bandit* (Joseph Kane, 1949) begins as Lorna Gray (Adrian Booth) prepares to marry outlaw Jim Plummer (Forrest Tucker) in a woodland glade. Ideas presented in relatively ambitious films trickled down to B singin' cowboy features as well. *The Old West* (George Archainbaud, 1952) opens with hero Gene Autry conducting a church service in the wide-open spaces. The music combines rhythms of Western ballads with rhymes from country gospel:[11]

> *Who put the moon in the starry sky?*
> *Somebody bigger than you or I!*

This film is actually about the need for the cowboys on view, as well as

Marion Morrison, better known as John Wayne. The Duke's character accepts the Good Book from gentle Quakers; from that moment he refuses to use his pistol, even in self-defense. Courtesy John Wayne Productions/Republic Pictures.

audiences watching it, to embrace a faith-based value code while still surrendering to the joys of nature. The piece implies that no conflict exists between the two, despite any insistence of those early Puritans to beware the natural side of oneself. "Doin' what comes naturally!" That ideology would be celebrated in song by Irving Berlin, the most typically American of all Tin Pan Alley composers, in the musical Western *Annie Get Your Gun*, first on Broadway in 1946, then as a major movie in 1950 (George Sidney). As in the romantic tradition, it is Annie, straight from the backwoods, who must teach the civilized people she meets, many hypocritical, how to be honest by reaching back and embracing their own primal sympathy. Similarly, in the earlier musical Western *The Old West*, Gene tells an antisocial kid (Dick Jones), modeled on one of those juvenile delinquents even then beginning to appear in postwar movies owing to their sudden prominence in society,[12] "We're trying to make this a civilized town." That remains a formidable problem even the good-hearted leader Gene can't solve. When a parson (House Peters Jr.) arrives and reads from the Bible, things swiftly change. Peters convinces people that their well-intended desire to clean up the area can't work so long as the approach remains secular. He insists on "the miracle of belief."

In its period setting, *The Old West* offers a reaction against the Godless communism perceived as a potential nemesis at the time this film was made.[13] That is, this Autry vehicle is driven by the same postwar sense that politics had to be backed up by religiosity as the only possible reaction against the Soviet state. In retrospect this singin' cowboy film can be seen as directly related to the controversial decision that the phrase "under God" should be added to the pledge to the flag recited daily by grade-school students in a ritual act of indoctrination not only to politics but to religion as well. Here was the beginning of the end, then, of the wall that Jefferson and others had early on erected between the two in America,[14] a land that, according to its Constitution, was to offer freedom not only of religion but also from it.

Toward a uniquely American religion. In such films as The Big Trees, *a paganlike worship in the heart of nature, providing light, not darkness, is fused on the frontier with Judeo-Christian traditions. Courtesy Warner Brothers.*

MULTICULTURALISM, MORMONISM, AND MOVIES
HOLLYWOOD'S HISTORY AND
CULTURAL APPROPRIATION

What Harlem has come to mean in the short span of twenty-five years . . .
can be compared only with the pushing back of the Western frontier.
—ALAIN LOCKE, *THE NEW NEGRO*, 1925

In *The Old West*, the parson talks Gene out of taking off after two varmints
who ambushed him: "Vengeance is mine, sayeth the Lord." At mid-movie,
yet another prayer meeting takes place on the prairie. This time, more people
attend. Everything good on view is achieved through an American practicality; Gene draws the final hold-outs in with a free horse show. In this version
of the paradigm, though, there is, compared to Ford's adult Western, a patina
of Puritanism. At the end, all prostitutes and gamblers have been driven out,
the town purified.

Such a process was criticized in works like Bret Harte's seminal short
story "The Outcasts of Poker Flat" (1869) and in time its various film versions, by Ford (1919), Christy Cabanne (1937), Joseph M. Newman (1952),
and Paul Stanley (TVM, 1958), as well as the retitled *Four of the Apocalypse*
(Lucio Fulci, 1975). In all versions strong and weak we encounter a truly progressive Western in ascendance, Harte's literary anecdote the creative effort
of a true man of the West. Townspeople in "Outcasts," insistent on creating

a Christian civilization, assume an extremist position. They drive all undesirables away from civilization, like Ford's overly moralistic townsfolk in *Stagecoach*, not his enlightened ones in *My Darling Clementine*, who force only the violent ones out. The outcasts, however lowly (gambler, prostitute, drunkard), must face a raging blizzard in which they will slowly freeze to death. Yet the author reveals to his audience that each is in fact a worthy if flawed human being who ought to have been treated in a truly Christian rather than narrowly Puritanical manner. Harte's story sets the pace for Ford's *Stagecoach*, with its similar gambler, whore, and drunkard, and for numerous other, more forgiving works by an authorial voice that always takes a moral stance while consistently avoiding any simplistic moralistic one.[1]

The creation of a uniquely American form of religion would be the subject of *Count Three and Pray* (George Sherman, 1955). Our central character here, Luke Fargo (Van Heflin), is a self-styled preacher who returns to his hometown following the Civil War to serve as a local minister, only to discover that the church has burned down. Rebuilding this parsonage becomes his dream. Meanwhile, he decides to hold makeshift services on the plains. Though menfolk do not see any great problem, the women, more conventionally Christian and recalling the biddies in *Stagecoach*, do. "Meeting *outside* the church?" a WASPish matron (Nancy Kulp), asks. "It just ain't fittin'. It's *heathen*." Fargo begs them to celebrate religion not in the retro European sense of a carefully constructed retreat but deep within the natural world. The situation boils down to realism as opposed to idealism. They have no choice; they meet here or they don't meet. In an anti-Puritanical turn of events, the disrespectable women of the prostitute class support the pastor. One even uses her earnings—apparently from husbands of those conventional ladies—to buy the minister his suit!

A similar story was set in the Pacific Northwest in *The Big Trees* (Felix Feist, 1952). Religious people live far from town, deep among the ancient redwoods. Though they build log cabins to inhabit, they choose not to construct a church but pray in an open-air chapel surrounded by the trees. These they perceive not in a strict Puritanical sense—as elements of Wicca, the dreaded "woode"—but much as Joyce Kilmer would in his most famous poem. If only God can make a tree, there is the element of religion within it, not only in the much-feared pagan sects but in Judeo-Christian ones as well. Their prayers, though spoken in a pagan setting, are Christian, resulting in a uniquely American hybrid religious experience. Trees are, for them, not the horrific monster vegetation from which that serpent slipped down to tempt Eve but an imprint of the Creator's work.

Alicia Chadwick (Eve Miller), an Amish woman, attempts to explain their code to the uncertain outsider Jim Fallon (Kirk Douglas):

CHADWICK (DREAMILY): This is our church.
FALLON (CYNICALLY): A tree's a tree.

When he, one more evil raw capitalist, threatens to cut the redwoods down for profit, she invokes religion at its purest as the means by which her people will defeat the big-business mentality that foreshadowed contemporary corporate America: "With the help of the Lord, we'll stop you." When their nonviolent protests fail to halt the timbermen, they seize clubs and guns and head out to kill the capitalist intruders if necessary to save God's country. At that moment, old-time religion and radical political action join forces.

In *Wagon Master* (John Ford, 1950) members of the Church of Jesus Christ of Latter-Day Saints are presented as one more group of good Christian pilgrims headed west. Barely mentioning that the Mormons trekked to Utah owing to heated and at times openly violent opposition toward their sect in the East, Ford depicts them here as an Amish-like group, subscribing to a few curious habits that qualify them as unique, in the film's context nothing more than charming aspects of a nonevangelical sect. The sense of abiding tolerance that in Ford's work represents the essence of America at its most admirable is present.

Ford's Mormons, though highly religious people, worship in the very heart of nature. More significantly, they behave as good Christians do in the world according to "Pappy," as members of Ford's stock company referred to their patriarch: accepting lost rejects from more conventional Christian society into their midst. A run-down medicine show performed by a drunken Shakespearean actor (Alan Mowbray, reviving his *Clementine* role) and a sassy madam (Joanne Dru as a variation on Claire Trevor in *Stagecoach* as well as her own admirable prostitute in Hawks's *Red River*), scorned elsewhere, is welcomed with open arms. The dramatic situation is presented through the eyes of typical cowboys Travis and Sandy (Ben Johnson and Harry Carey Jr. reprising their characters from Ford's *Rio Grande* the same year). Again, the boys serve as audience surrogates, normals coming in

Realigning a public perception. One way of making Mormons appear more acceptable to the mainstream was portraying them favorably from the point of view of an agent of the norm. A lovable cowboy (Harry Carey Jr.) admires an elder (Ward Bond) in Wagon Master. *Courtesy Argosy/RKO Pictures.*

contact with people whose ways are a bit different but, in Ford's presentation, no less worthy.

In the two cowboys' eyes the Mormons prove as likable as nonreligious outcasts. The horse trader Travis may join the church and marry the madam, a possibility presented as feasible. The Indians pose no major problem,[2] as one unique culture already living on the frontier opens its arms to another in the spirit of what we would today term multiculturalism. To induce an audience to accept such diversity, Ford cast Native American athlete-celebrity Jim Thorpe as the young chief. Only the lowest white trash, the Clegg family gang, a fictionalized equivalent of the Clantons from *Clementine*, stands in the way of a homogeneous American community or, more correctly, coexisting communities, each tolerating the other if not necessarily integrating with it. The Cleggs are unacceptable because they are violent and dishonest; race and class status have nothing to do with it. As in the Earp movie, this trash factor must be stomped out like bugs menacing a landscape that in its abundance proves rich enough to support different good nations of people.

A decade earlier, *Brigham Young, Frontiersman* (Henry Hathaway, 1940) was released by Twentieth Century-Fox. An odd hodgepodge of quasi-historical materials and fictional contrivances, the final result was not what studio boss Darryl F. Zanuck (1902–1979) originally hoped to produce. Zanuck intended a straight bio-pic of Young (1801–1877), to star the great character actor Walter Huston. When that actor chose not to participate, Zanuck cast a fine if less-known performer, Dean Jagger, added that third word to the title to entice audiences to take the film as a traditional Western, then beefed up a conventional love story between the young Mormon Jonathan Kent (Tyrone Power) and his "Gentile" (Christian but non-Mormon) fiancée Zina Webb (Linda Darnell). Those box-office stars received top billing.

D. F. Zanuck had no particular commitment to the Church of Latter-Day Saints. As producer, and like his friend Ford ultraconservative as to patriotism though a social liberal, Zanuck consistently tried to employ his movies as means by which the public might be deprogrammed from prejudices. Future projects would address issues facing Jews (*Gentleman's Agreement*, Elia Kazan, 1947) and African Americans (*Pinky*, Kazan and Ford, 1949). Other studio chiefs were inspired by Zanuck to do the same; his legacy places him among the first, with *Brigham Young, Frontiersman* an early, imperfect effort in this direction.

The movie begins in Illinois during the mid-1840s when Mormon leader Joseph Smith (Vincent Price) is jailed in Carthage on various charges and killed by a mob. The Mormons rally under Young and hurry across the river during the dead of winter while locals fire at them. In addition to intolerance for quirks such as multiple wives, residents are furious that the Mormons do not vote with them on key issues; the conflict is cast as political as well as religious. In its simplified form, Zanuck's film, however watered down, did present Mormons favorably. Darnell's fiancée convert acts as audience surrogate, an agent of the norm.

In actuality, locals did not pursue the Mormons with firearms when they calmly, quietly left some two years after Smith's assassination. Important, too, is that historically Smith was jailed not solely on trumped-up charges, as in the film, but for a violent crime against a Gentile newspaper that printed what he construed as anti-Mormon views.[3] While that hardly legitimizes the man's lynching, any fair overview must note that Smith was not the innocent pariah that the Zanuck-Fox film presents to the mass audience. However prejudicial the people of Illinois may have been, their decision to create an

Mr. Zanuck on civil rights. Legendary director Darryl F. Zanuck set out to achieve for Mormons what he had for other minority groups in his socially oriented films—breaking down stereotypes by portraying marginal groups as ordinary people. In Brigham Young, Frontiersman *Dean Jagger plays the title character, with John Carradine as his frontier scout. Courtesy Twentieth Century-Fox.*

anti-Mormon armed militia was necessitated by an abiding fear of the Mormon militia, already armed and ready for conflict.

The legitimacy of their fears would in time be rendered clear by the 1857 Mountain Meadows massacre, covered in the following chapter. Also eliminated from Zanuck's film was the Mormon attitude toward African Americans as inferior.[4] This position was offensive to many in Illinois who, like Lincoln, were fervently antislavery and perceived this racist view as legitimizing the deplorable situation in the South. The conditions in Nauvoo, Illinois, were complicated, not simple. A corrupt white superintendent of Indian affairs, the film's man in a suit, tries to talk the Native people into pushing Mormons off their land, but a bond is struck by the two minority groups, both portrayed as benign. Frontier scout Jim Bridger (Arthur Aylesworth) shyly inquires as to Young's wives; that problem is treated as a genial gag, as this mountain man has two wives of his own, Indian sisters. Mary Astor plays Young's first wife. A young girl (Jean Rogers), rarely seen, is presented falsely as a kind of adopted daughter rather than an underage bride. Young's ten other wives, mentioned in one throw-away line, are never displayed.

Throughout, the film plays down multiple marriages by focusing on a one-on-one marriage between Jonathan and Zina. The authorial approach was to play this possible if rare arrangement as if it were typical of the entire community. This rewriting of history may be perceived sympathetically as a desire to remain nonexploitive about an issue that all too often is made more primary to Mormonism than it actually is. However, it can be viewed as a failure of courage on the part of the filmmakers to fully present the truth or, worse still, a kind of cover-up.

The film, arriving on theater screens at a time when Mormonism had for some fifteen years found itself under extreme attack in printed popular culture and benign neglect in movies, was appreciated by church members. Despite minor grumbles about inaccuracies, the abiding Mormon view was expressed by Heber J. Grant, president of the church from 1918 to 1945. "Wonderful!" Grant stated in summary.[5] He added, in terms more fascinating today than then, that "we cannot expect the people [non-Mormons in Los Angeles] to tell the story as we would tell it," that is, from the inside. Grant saw this not as a flaw but a boon, Mormons receiving a much-appreciated pass from mainstream media to their audiences. "It is of course a (motion) *picture*" (emphasis mine), Grant continued. By this he meant, with no hint of criticism, a Hollywood product, as such a film made to entertain vast audiences and in the process make money, "and we could not [thus] hope that they would make a picture at their expense, running into a couple of million dollars, to be just as we would like it." *Brigham Young, Frontiersman*, Grant argued, was at the time the best that Mormons, or any minority to be presented by Hollywood, could hope for. If the Gentiles who made it didn't truly understand their ways, those filmmakers had at least made every attempt that an outsider could to offer a considerate picture, which had not been the case in the past.

That was then; this is now. In the age of political correctness the term "cultural appropriation" has entered our academic and intellectual discourse.[6] Beginning in the late twentieth century and reaching full crescendo during the opening decade of the twenty-first, the concept came into more widespread and in some cases mainstream use as well. A working definition describes cultural appropriation as "the taking over of creative or artistic forms, themes, or practices by one cultural group from another."[7] Mostly

Mormons and ethnic minorities. Brigham Young, Frontiersman *portrays the peaceful coexistence of Mormons and Native Americans but leaves out the Mormons' decision to draw their "red brothers" into the Mountain Meadows massacre. Courtesy Twentieth Century-Fox.*

the term was held in reserve for "Western appropriation of non-Western or non-white" forms of art and communication, often "carrying connotations of (racial/ethnic) exploitation and (cultural) dominance."[8] Among the infamous examples would be the black-face tradition in which white singers wearing highly exaggerated makeup performed what are now considered extreme caricatures of African American musical performers. Likewise attacked have been the Uncle Remus tales, indigenous to the antebellum slave communities, as written down by Joel Chandler Harris. His intent was to preserve what he loved in a folk culture that might otherwise have been lost, since it was illegal for slaves to learn to read or write. Early on, Harris was lauded by liberals white and black for so doing but in time attacked for cultural appropriation.[9]

Not every African American critic agreed, however, that appropriation was a harmful thing. Alain Locke (1886–1954) argued that in addition to him and other members of the Harlem Renaissance self-consciously forging a uniquely African American cultural identity, there must be a give and take between Afro- and Anglo-Americans, a two-way street described by Locke as "cultural pluralism."[10] A modern equivalent to Locke's term would be "postmodern hybridity," or the natural, even unavoidable coming together of varied cultures in a nation, and beyond that, between American and other cultures in an age of constant international contact. In a postmodern world, any presentation of a minority culture within a mainstream movie ought to be accepted positively or negatively based on the merits or deficiencies of the individual work, in terms of the intentions and impact of its content, at least according to such a theory.

This concept of postmodern hybridity, important for our study, can be and here is also applied to the depiction of any minority group, even those considered white, by the larger white majority, ranging from alternative life-styles as varied as gays and, for this volume, Mormons. Would a person in Grant's position, for instance, today still approve of a producer like Zanuck, a well-meaning outsider to the Mormon way, although sympathetic, dis-seminating images of Mormons in the film *Brigham Young, Frontiersman*? Would Grant's forgiving tone for liberties taken or mistakes made in the service of this portrayal be replaced by anger, even outrage at the thought that Mormons themselves were deprived of an opportunity to present their own image? Or can it be counter-argued that this sort of limitation would lead to a narrowness in which only members of any one group can ever offer portraits of themselves in art and commerce? It is a tricky question that is rendered moot with the 2006 release of an entirely different film, one that deals with a dark truth most Mormons would understandably prefer to have tucked away in some secret corner of their history.

The man and the massacre. While many Mormons contend that Brigham Young remained unaware of his militia's intentions, September Dawn *(starring Terence Stamp) suggests otherwise. Courtesy* September Dawn/Voice Pictures/Black Diamond.

END OF THE TRAIL

THE DARK SIDE OF FAITH

Your damned religion! Jane, I fear its invisible
hand will turn its hidden work to your ruin.

—JIM LASSITER TO JANE WITHERSPOON IN ZANE
GREY'S NOVEL *RIDERS OF THE PURPLE SAGE*, 1912

Mainstream moviegoers were confronted with an almost entirely disparaging portrait of Mormons in *September Dawn* (Christopher Cain, 2006), a fictionalized rendering of a historical occurrence. The screenplay by Cain and Carole Whang Schutter sets a conventional star-crossed romance between a Mormon youth, Jonathan Samuelson (Trent Ford), and a Gentile, Emily Hudson (Tamara Hope), against the backdrop of the Mountain Meadows massacre. This incident occurred on September 11, 1857, near Cedar City, Utah, home to what was at the time a notably zealous and cultlike community. Historically speaking, William H. Dame commanded a local Mormon militia known to be fully armed, highly trained, and deeply resentful of any Gentiles who happened upon what they considered their promised land.[1] Dame learned that a non-Mormon wagon train, passing by on its way from Arkansas to places west, had camped nearby. Concerned about President James Buchanan's recent dispatch of more than 2,000 federal troops into the territory upon the threat of a separatist uprising on the part of Mormons and their Indian allies, local Mormons were further alarmed by a highly debatable belief that Arkansas residents had years earlier been responsible for the death of Joseph Smith, though that man's assassination took place in Illinois. Under Dame's command the Mormon militia surrounded the camp and launched an attack that would have catastrophic results, both immediately and for generations thereafter. In the film, Dame becomes Bishop Jacob Samuelson, played by Jon Voigt.

The Mormons may have sincerely believed the settlers were government spies, or they may have been motivated by a desire for revenge for past occurrences. Desiring to conceal their identity, the militiamen initially planned to disguise themselves as local Paiutes so the holocaust, when eventually discovered, would be blamed on their friendly neighbors. Accompanied by members of that tribe, the Paiutes convinced by Mormons that those quietly camping nearby posed an immediate threat to their own Native way of life, Paiutes and militia members followed Dame in a blood-thirsty attack. When the caravan agreed to surrender after promises there would be no more violence, they were slaughtered, men, women, and children. Some seventeen boys and girls under the age of eight were spared and adopted by Mormons. The bodies of others were left to rot or be picked apart by wolves and vultures rather than allowed burials. This decision was made by the Mormon hierarchy so that if and when the government investigated, the massacre would be blamed on the Indians, not the Mormons.

With the start of the Civil War and its all-encompassing impact on the federal government, charges were not brought for almost two decades. One man was eventually tried, found guilty, and executed. An ongoing controversy remains as to whether Mormon leader Brigham Young (Terence Stamp in the film), who claimed total ignorance of the massacre, knew or approved of what occurred and set to work on a massive cover-up. Mormon historians insist Young had been entirely unaware of what a small coterie of Mormons was doing and so ought to be considered free of guilt. Most non-Mormon historians conclude that if not a direct participant, Young nonetheless should be held responsible for the slaughter owing to his heightened rhetoric in the days preceding the incident.

The latter is the approach assumed by Cain in *September Dawn*. In the screenplay, words known to have been spoken by Young within previous sermons are taken out of context and placed in his mouth immediately before

The quick and the dead. In September Dawn, *(a) a Mormon militiaman cold-bloodedly murders a helpless mother; and (b) a child is killed by bow and arrow so Mormons can lay blame on their Indian allies. Courtesy September Dawn/Voice Pictures/Black Diamond.*

the massacre. This liberty with his words is the basis for the film's controversy. Though it cannot be denied that Young made such statements, suggesting an element of complicity or outright guilt, there is no evidence he said them to directly incite the killings. This allows for a Mormon claim that the film unfairly twists the truth by altering context. However, there is no argument that what has been twisted here—or, in a less subjective term, dramatized—is the truth. Young said what he said.

Some Mormons objected not only to Cain's approach but to the very notion that anyone today would choose to make a movie about that long-ago incident. The thrust of this argument is that, on other occasions, the hospitality and goodwill of Mormons can be documented. So, to proceed from such a position, the massacre cannot or at least should not be considered typical of the way Mormons generally operated with strangers. Rather it was a one-time aberration brought on by a darkly perfect storm of awful circumstances.

Again, then, the concept of political correctness is raised. Even if an incident is portrayed in an authentic manner, does a screen representation, simply by its existence as a film, misrepresent a more general truth? Did filmmakers imply to the public that a small, independent group calling itself Mormons can, does, or should represent all Mormons, then and now? From a politically correct point of view, a slurring of the religion and its lifestyle has occurred, even though the film contains no major inaccuracies as to what took place according to numerous historical records.

Fundamental to this in the history of Westerns is the understanding that mass audiences will learn about any aspect of the past only from some Hollywood film on the subject rather than choosing to read history. Yet often only in a written text, allowing for multiple interpretations of an event, can most people grasp the broader truth that is not possible to communicate in a commercial film, however lofty its ambitions. By its very nature, the Hollywood narrative must proceed from a single dramatic perspective, that of the auteur or primary artist, whether the writer, director, or producer.

"History written in lightning," President Woodrow Wilson said about *The Birth of a Nation* in 1915, the first film to seriously raise tricky issues of historical veracity.[2] As with D. W. Griffith's version of the postbellum South in which the Ku Klux Klan were portrayed as Arthurian knights, or that silent film about Pancho Villa discussed earlier, the fascinating problem has to do with film's origination in the photograph, created to allow for a precise documentation of reality. Early Realist theorists, Siegfried Kracauer among them, argued that a movie shot on location essentially conveys reality in the raw.[3] Yet later film aesthetician Rudolf Arnheim would assert that the uniqueness of this art form derives from its greatest single danger: a seemingly objective, unmanipulated vision of the world can be rendered every bit as subjective, and therefore manipulative, as any other art form in the editing and camera angles.[4]

An earlier work, *Riders of the Purple Sage*, widely read and seen in its many film versions, is one some observers credit as creating a long-standing prejudice against Mormons. The 1912 novel by Zane Grey stands apart from his run-of-the-mill romances set on a make-believe frontier. Though *Riders* does suffer from melodramatic indulgences, Grey attempts to offer considerable substance and meaning in this mass-market potboiler marbled with a social message of an anti-Mormon bent. For Grey, the Mormons were not the much-oppressed minority hoping only to live in peaceful harmony if granted religious freedom. Grey perceived Mormons as unsparing and oppressive to anyone who did not acquiesce to their beliefs. Like early Puritans, supposedly in search of religious freedom yet denying it to anyone who didn't accept their way, Grey depicted Mormons living in Utah as intolerant, particularly of rare wavering females in their community, growing absolutely wrathful when an independently minded woman defied the patriarchal lifestyle.

Though it is unlikely Grey would have thought of himself as a proto-feminist, there is an aspect of feminism in this book in the protagonist Jane Witherspoon. Before his death, Jane's father encourages her to marry a prominent Mormon church member in the Cottonwoods, the sect's headquarters. Jane's father represents Mormon patriarchy in the household like that of church leaders among Utah's Mormon pioneers. Jane's intended, Elder Tull, is a purposefully unflattering caricature of Brigham Young, a mature man who craves Jane partly for her beauty but also for the lands she will inherit. Despite being brainwashed by her father and the church (here called LDS, Latter-Day Saints), Jane hesitates because she listens to her own primal sympathy, which whispers to that element within her that has not yet been silenced that she does not love this man.

Still, conditioned by her society, she would have gone through with the marriage for her father's sake. Once he has passed, however, her hesitation increases. Partly this is due to a friendship with the Gentile Bern Venters, a mentor figure who tries to persuade Jane that she alone ought to decide her future. With her father gone, does Jane believe the Mormon faith to be right for her, or should she consider a mainstream lifestyle? So far as the Mormon community is concerned, the suggestion that a woman could and should choose a life for herself marks Venters as a target. Again, what we today consider to be feminist issues are raised. Jane would be a secondary wife to patriarch Tull, as he is already married. Jane's inner self craves equality.

A woman's courage. Jane Witherspoon (Mary Howard) stands up to male bullies, the man in black (George Montgomery) aiding her against a political elite that has no religious affiliation in this 1941 B-movie version of Riders of the Purple Sage. *Courtesy Twentieth Century-Fox.*

As a strong, independent woman, she can only happily live in a relationship of equals. On the other hand, she experiences guilt in that no-man's (or -woman's) land of what Freud would in time identify as her superego: those values absorbed since birth that she has not been entirely able to divest herself of plague her ego even as her id insists that she must live free. The Mormons put pressure on her to relent, threatening to drive Jane off her ranch and apply unfair but unfortunately legal business practices to force her into bankruptcy. A weak woman might capitulate; Jane becomes the proverbial worm that turns, furious that such threats would be voiced. Coming to her aid is one of those lone riders of Western myth, Lassiter. As expected, the two fall in love. But he has a secret agenda. Grey's story takes place in 1871; fourteen years earlier Lassiter's niece was abducted by Mormons after an incident not so very different from the real-life Mountain Meadows massacre. Lassiter's agenda, besides saving Jane's body and soul, entails finding his now deceased sister's only child, whom he fears to be under their power.

Not surprisingly, Mormons heatedly rejected Grey's vision as simplistic.

At the time, most mainstream readers believed Grey was essentially correct despite some notable mistakes as to details of Mormon lifestyle, among them a less than accurate usage of the term "elder." There can be no question that a huge prejudice against Mormons was, if not initiated by Grey, surely solidified in his scathing portrayal, one that still exists among many other Christian sects. As often happens, the powers that be in Hollywood turned to this bestseller for film material while timidly excising the very element that had given the book its wide range of interest. The hope had been to have the first *Riders* film released in 1915 to capitalize on the novel's great popularity; however, a movie did not appear until 1918. The delay occurred because of "the Mormon issue" and how it ought to be presented, if at all. In what did emerge on screen, the issue was not presented. Writer-director Frank Lloyd closely kept to the original plot, with William Farnum and Mary Mersch playing Lassiter and Jane. Kathryn Adams enacted the mysterious (and, again, strong) female character of the Masked Rider, a black-clad lady outlaw who turns out to be a beautiful girl, possibly the missing niece for whom Lassiter still searches. In the film the villains attempting to force Jane into a marriage or drive her off the land have become conventional people in power from countless genre pieces, merely men in suits. The effect is to reduce the work's importance by eliminating its controversy.

The reason for Hollywood's decision can be viewed, depending on an observer's temperament, as courageous or cowardly. The producers understood that, as the world had learned from Griffith's much-damned and -praised masterwork and a president's all-too-accurate statement about it, movies reach wider audiences than novels. Often a movie that does not prove to be a box-office hit is seen by more people than will ever read the latest bestseller. Likewise, commercial movies invariably have reduced complex ideas to comparatively simple images, particularly so during the silent era, when the lack of spoken dialogue made complex characters impossible to achieve. The resultant films are more powerful perhaps than their antecedents in text yet lack the richness of texture even a journeyman writer on the order of Grey can present in book form.

Essentially the first feature-length film based on a book was *The Birth of a Nation*. But the producers of *Riders of the Purple Sage* were inclined to glance back on the impact of Griffith's work three years earlier and calculate the effect their own movie might have once the book's version of history appeared in film form, rewritten in lightning. No one in Hollywood or for that matter America had forgotten the violent riots, including pitched battles between blacks and whites and in many cases African Americans accompanied by enlightened whites versus those of a more traditionalist order, outside the nation's theaters in 1915–1916.[5]

This was the conundrum for the committee members at Fox Film Corporation, forerunner of Twentieth Century-Fox: could they possibly reveal in the relative simplicity of a silent film that a single, isolated group of Mormons had become corrupt and ruthless? Or would easily impressionable viewers leave theaters fired up by a belief that they had been informed this was the more general Mormon way, with perhaps the most irresponsible elements believing they had been instructed to go out and beat, perhaps kill, Mormons on sight? Would the film, by accurately admitting to and depicting a single and, for most Mormons, detested transgression by a small minority within their own minority be received as a blanket condemnation of an entire group, that body of people at the time of this film's release harmless enough, and perhaps an incitement to brutal anti-Mormon activity? Interpreting their decision to cut out any and all references to

Good guys wear black! As film historian William K. Everson has noted, heroes are as likely to dress in dark garb as white. Star Tom Mix, with wonder horse Tony, proved a perfect choice for Lassiter *in the silent version of Grey's tale. Courtesy Tom Mix Family/Estate.*

Mormonism and to go so far as to suggest that the wicked businessmen were anything but Mormons, can lead to the conclusion that the film must be considered a betrayal of Zane Grey's personal vision. In a sense, it is. From a contemporary and more politically correct point of view, however, favoring not the rights of any individual artist so much as a responsibility to those people—particularly minorities—portrayed, the decision could be lauded as ahead of its time in terms of sensitivity to an oft-maligned subculture.

Whether the decision was right or wrong or, to avoid moral categorizing, wise or foolish, it did set the pace for all future theatrical versions. In the next film (Lynn Reynolds, 1925) the story became an epic adventure for one of the most popular of all silent-era cowboy stars, Tom Mix, notable for its gorgeous location cinematography. This was followed in 1931 by Hamilton MacFadden's version, which rates as the grimmest and most realistic in approach, with George O'Brien offering a notably low-key portrayal of the gunman Lassiter compared to Mix's over-the-top drugstore-cowboy outlandishness. The final theatrical feature, called *The Riders of the Purple Sage* (James Tinling, 1941), reduced the piece to an enjoyable if economical B Western from Fox. A decision to shoot in color was not justified by the set design, which proved skimpy and unconvincing. Here George Montgomery, shortly to emerge as a leading star of B oaters, enacted Lassiter.

The most faithful version was a made-for-TV movie (TVM, Charles Haig, 1996) that co-starred Ed Harris and Amy Madigan as the heroic couple. Finally, Jane's oppressors were played as members of a religious cult, though the filmmakers chose to imply that they were Mormon rather than actually stating so outright. This resulted in an attempt to have it both ways, condemning the atrocities of religious extremists in general while refusing to stir up any dormant hostile feelings that might cause problems for contemporary Mormons. With a potentially bigger audience even than movies, TV producers believed more than the filmmakers at Fox some eighty-eight years earlier that they had to assume responsibility for how such material might affect less sophisticated viewers. For one thing, the political career of Mitt Romney, a Republican and a Mormon, might be at stake if the film were to refer to Mormons as Mormons.

The result mixed a certain amount of artistic courage with a sense of social caution, revealing the complexity involved in the Western genre and, for that matter, all supposed commercial entertainment. It also confirmed, for anyone who did not know so already, that what may seem like nothing more than a time-killer always conveys a way of seeing the world to its receiver, for better or worse.

Ride beyond vengeance. In The Searchers, *macho Texans consider killing all Comanches to make up for the abduction of two white women. A religious Ranger captain (Ward Bond) insists that as Christians they must extend the quality of mercy as outlined in the Good Book that guides him. Courtesy Warner Brothers.*

RIDE OUT
FOR VENGEANCE
REVISING A WESTERN PARADIGM

Man's gotta do what a man's gotta do, right?
—MADAME LOUISE IN *SERAPHIM FALLS*, 2006

With *Riders of the Purple Sage*, Zane Grey created a genre classic so seminal that its title is known to people who have never read the book. Beyond that, and whether he consciously intended this or not, Grey re-created the figure of the cowboy hero, whom critic Robert Warshow would eventually identify as "the Westerner."[1] Grey retained key elements Wister had introduced at the turn of the twentieth century and added others to this yet embryonic American hero who would not be reconsidered until the publication of *Shane*. What remains unchanged, however, is a potent aura of mystery that surrounds this created dream figure for our American mythos. Our own unique American variation of what Joseph Campbell would call "the hero with a thousand faces" either has no name (the Virginian), one (Shane), or two (Jim Lassiter), though somehow his given name slips into obscurity until he is identified only as Lassiter. He may, like his predecessor in Wister's novel, be anchored in one place, or he might be some Flying Dutchman, serendipitously arriving in a remote valley precisely when most needed, as in Jack Schaefer's and Grey's variations on that theme. The Virginian appears as a live-and-let-live type who kills villainous Trampas only because that nasty, ill-spoken oaf will not leave our hero alone. Shane sides with farmers in their stand against ranchers mainly owing to an incarnation of the female principle. Lassiter, though, brings an entirely different agenda to the genre. He is out for vengeance. Nothing short of that will allow him to ease down or back off. Lassiter is, simply, a man on a mission. And, while he might not perceive it as such, the term "mission" suggests a religiosity to his search.

In the first significant study of Western movies, William K. Everson noted that Grey's narrative addition, though in fact introduced in several dime novels from the late nineteenth century, would completely alter the genre paradigm.[2] The first wave of sound Westerns, running from an ambitious A project like *The Big Trail* directed by Walsh to scores of B budget items starring Bob Steele and Johnny Mack Brown, were concerned with a vengeance-driven hero. Often the death of a father or father figure would, Hamlet-like, provide the protagonist's motivation for violent revenge. Sometimes the hero's beloved brother would fall prey to killers, an idea that would worm its way into fictionalized accounts of the Earp-Clanton conflict; and, while less than factual as to events leading up to the O.K. Corral gunfight, they are historically accurate in terms of what happened afterward.[3] Even when the number of Westerns being produced in America began to diminish, from *Nevada Smith* (Henry Hathaway, 1966) to *Seraphim Falls* (David Van Ancker, 2006), the theme of vengeance would continue to be essential to manner and meaning in the genre.

At its highest level of accomplishment—*Red River, High Noon, Shane, Johnny Guitar, The Man from Laramie* (Anthony Mann, 1955), *The Searchers, Ride Lonesome* (Budd Boetticher, 1959), *Unforgiven* (Clint Eastwood, 1993), *Open Range* (Kevin Costner, 2003)—the Western approximates for America the level of Shakespearean tragedy: *Julius Caesar, Macbeth, King Lear*, and, most overpowering, *Hamlet*. As with each play, the element of vengeance in each of these films is essential to theme and narrative. Likewise, the B Western of the order churned out by lesser studios like Lone Star and PRC during the 1930s and '40s and spaghetti and paella Westerns by their continental counterparts in the 1960s offered the equivalent of many less prestigious Elizabethan-era works such as Thomas Kydd's *The Spanish Tragedy* (1587) and John Webster's *The Duchess of Malfi* (1614).

The plots of these minor movies and theater pieces were also motored by a desire for revenge on the part of villain, hero, or both. This had been the case with Shakespeare's own first—and fitful—attempt to create a full tragedy, *Titus Andronicus* (1588), a rather obvious and shallow imitation of the Roman vengeance plays of Seneca the Younger from the era of Nero that had proven popular when revived for the London stage.[4] All the above, like gangster and noir pieces from Hollywood, contained the essence of a vengeance-driven drama from its origin in ancient times: a stoic hero kills in what he believes to be righteousness and does so in ways that lead to a theater of cruelty underlined by a bizarre sense of the blackest sort of comedy.

Though John Wayne never precisely said "a man's gotta do what a man's gotta do" in a film, more often than not his character was motivated by the same sort of thinking. In thematically ambitious movies like *The Big Trail*, an inner conflict renders this rationale far more interesting, the character more human. In these movies, the vengeance theme is not presented at face value but rather in a paradigm of consciousness and conscience, forcing the audience, like the protagonist, to at least consider the value of personal revenge in terms of societal obligations, that is, as rugged individualism set against communal responsibility. In so doing, the Western becomes thoughtful, even morally questioning the vengeance theme at its very center.

Later films would take this hesitation further, offering a challenge to the concept of vengeance, more often than not in a religious context. One approach was to place a hardened outlaw in the midst of a Christian wagon train, then gradually reveal the impact these pilgrims have on his morality. A typical example of this subgenre appeared in *Bad Bascomb* (S. Sylvan Simon, 1946), one of those films broad to the edge of burlesque that MGM turned out with the beloved macho buffoon Wallace Beery. His title character, trying to escape the law, joins up with a Mormon caravan and pretends to be one of them while planning to use them for his own ends. Finally, though, he sacrifices himself so they can live, painfully leaving the innocent child (Margaret O'Brien) he has come to deeply love.

A more fully developed variation on this theme appears in *The Last Wagon* (Delmer Daves, 1956). A similar train is intimidated not by the outlaw (Richard Widmark) who joins them but by a vicious lawman (George Matthews). This marshal upbraids the religious pilgrims for showing the fugitive some human kindness. "You *Christers!*" he hisses and spits. In time it is not the corrupt lawman (now deceased) but the outlaw who saves the train's survivors from marauding Indians. After performing a courageous act, a self-consciously Christian authority figure, the historical Bible-reading

General Howard (Basil Deardon, returning to a role essayed earlier in the same director's *Broken Arrow,* 1950), pardons Widmark's character, Comanche Todd, a fictional creation derived in part from an outlaw known as the Apache Kid.[5] "I rely on the Good Book for guidance," Howard, who reads but does not thump the Bible, proclaims with a gentle smile.

The film is not limited in its spirituality by Judeo-Christian values. During the trek, a boy (Tommy Rettig) who idolizes the gunman asks Todd, "Do you think you'll go to heaven?" The youth hopes to meet him there so they can hunt and fish. Having been raised by Comanches, Todd explains the Native American vision of the afterlife and why he prefers it to the Christian vision. All who listen appear to have been made stronger and fuller human beings after accepting this alternative. We also learn during Todd's heart-to-heart talk with a beautiful pioneer woman (Felicia Farr) that his own white father had been a deeply religious man who hoped to carry "the word of his Lord to the whole west."

PIONEER WOMAN: His God. Not yours?

COMANCHE TODD: Nope. Not since Paw got hurt bad.

His father's death, we learn, caused Todd to live in existential doubt typical of contemporary cinematic heroes of the mid-1950s also anachronistically placed on the frontier in Westerns from that period. He did convert to the Comanche vision of God in nature, becoming a pantheist, though a notably violent one. Todd became embittered when his Comanche wife and child were killed by Anglos who professed to be good Christians. By film's end, Todd again embraces Christianity without giving up Comanche views. He and Farr's character, now a committed couple, are seen riding off, side by side, not to some town but out of one, into nature. There, we must assume, they'll attempt to balance the best of each one's religious views, thanks to one more uniquely American collapsing of what previously seemed unresolvable opposites.

Few films offer as broad or profound an arc for the man of vengeance as *The Bravados* (Henry King, 1958). Gregory Peck plays Jim Douglas (perhaps it is coincidental that he shares a first name with Grey's Lassiter), a rancher who believes four outlaws murdered his wife. In the opening, this latest lone rider visits a town where the captured men await execution. The local religious leader (Andrew Duggan) watches the stoic figure arrive, somehow

A feminine touch and the religious influence. A woman (Joan Collins) who resembles the Virgin Mary statue and a kind-hearted, merciful-minded religious leader (Andrew Duggan) hope to save an avenger's soul in The Bravados. *Courtesy Twentieth Century-Fox.*

sensing he's on a mission, one that this dark-clad clerical figure believes in his heart to be from God. The rider, however, perceives himself differently. He has come only to watch the villains hang. "The law's going to do the job for me," Douglas explains, willing to let vengeance take a public course. As such he references the man-with-a-gun theme from this book's first half.

Yet he tells his old friend and former lover Josefa Velarde (Joan Collins), "I don't go to church any more." Owing to what has happened, he lost his faith. How could there be a God, he, like Banquo after the destruction of his family by Macbeth, questions, if such an atrocity can occur? If a benign, all-powerful force exists, why did it not intervene? The woman, a devout Catholic, points to the church: "There's a woman inside you might do well to talk to." When Douglas does accompany her inside, he stares hard and long at the statue of the Virgin, which appears to have been modeled on actress Collins. Her character, Josefa, in context represents the statue come to life, offering him salvation if only he can see it.

Likewise, the preacher is not some fire-and-brimstone type but a true believer in forgiveness. He tells the congregation on the eve of the hanging, "At Golgotha, Christ took time to pardon a common thief." He does not ask for mercy for the outlaws' lives, believing they are getting what they deserve. This is, after all, not some lynching on the part of a mob but the result of a fair jury trial. On the other hand, he does request that all present pray for the condemned men's souls. Keenly listening to him are locals who come

"Vengeance is mine." Jim Douglas (Gregory Peck) sells his soul to the devil when he succumbs to a dark instinct to personally judge and execute an outlaw (Lee Van Cleef) in The Bravados. *Courtesy Twentieth Century-Fox.*

together in harmony: Anglo Protestants, Latino Catholics, and even the town's one Jewish family. However unlikely this may have been on the historical frontier, the drama mirrors a post–World War II climate of emergent Judeo-Christian unity.[6]

In contrast to Douglas, a good man who has been sorely tested, the imprisoned killers and rapists are nihilists. Zachary (Stephen Boyd), the leader, openly jokes about religion, purposefully insulting the devout Latino deputy Primo (Ken Scott).

ZACHARY (SARCASTICALLY): Primo, would you pray for us?
PRIMO: What should I pray for?
ZACHARY: That we'll go to heaven.
PRIMO: I can't do that. But I will pray for God to forgive you.
ZACHARY: (*sardonically*) We'll settle for that.

When the outlaws escape and a posse proves unable to ride them down, Douglas goes on a vengeance trail, now an avenging angel worthy of the Old Testament. One by one, he tracks three of the men (Boyd, Lee Van Cleef, Albert Salmi) and executes each in cold blood. Where the community at large failed, this rugged individualist appears to succeed. A certain goodness remaining within him will not allow Douglas to take pleasure in these acts, though it's clear that he does derive satisfaction—and a frightful kind of release—from each ritualistic killing. Finally, he follows the youngest, Lujan (Henry Silva), over the border into Mexico. There Douglas finds himself disarmed by the youth's wife. Waking, he learns that while the outlaws were truly despicable, it was not the Bravados gang but his seemingly harmless neighbor (Gene Evans) who murdered Douglas's wife, then blamed it on the bunch that happened to be in the area at the time. However much these men deserved to die, Douglas had no moral right to act as their judge, jury, and executioner.

There can be but one reaction from a man who grasps his own tragic mistake yet still suffers existential doubts while not entirely going over to nihilism: "Oh, *God*!" Returning to town, Douglas heads directly to church. There he is joined by Josefa and his daughter. The man who has wrongly put Old Testament vengeance into action now seeks New Testament redemption for his own sins. Rejecting an eye for an eye, he has learned the hard way that vengeance is the Lord's. "I was wrong," he cries out openly. The townsfolk know nothing of this, aware only that he has rid them of a biblical scourge. Douglas's only hope for personal redemption will come by embracing family values in marrying Josefa and together raising his innocent child with love. At the movie's end, Jim and Josefa are in a buckboard with his daughter, leaving town together to re-create their lives—and a family unit—back at his ranch. To the townspeople, the man who believes himself to have sinned, perhaps beyond forgiveness, is a true hero. As Douglas prepares to leave, they gather before him on the street like a chorus in a Greek tragedy, a dramatic structure Christianized by having the priest in front:

MARSHAL: (*admiringly*) You will be in our thoughts, always.
DOUGLAS: (*quivering with guilt*) And in your *prayers*. Please!

No single Western so well combines a rejection of vengeance-motivated violence with pro-Christian attitudes. Any Protestant notion of a perfect "elect" living in the American microcosm has given way to an artistic geography in which redemption remains possible for the worst sinners, like Jim Douglas, those who desperately want forgiveness but don't necessarily believe they deserve its mercy. It matters little that the confused, decent townsfolk (America itself, in miniature) believe that Douglas rescued them from an amoral force of evil. That in a sense is true, though he has done so at the possible cost of his soul. If he is indeed a knight, he hardly deserves

Just say "no" to vengeance. In Nevada Smith, *the title character (Steve McQueen) dedicates his life to wreaking vengeance on the man who murdered his parents. When the opportunity arises he instead walks away, owing to the influence of a wise priest. Courtesy Paramount Pictures.*

the white mantle of purity. The old-fashioned hero is gone; in his place we discover the anti-hero of modern literature and cinema.

At mid-century, then, the Western rejected vengeance of a personal order that had more or less been accepted at face value during the last days of Victorian-era thought.

This rejection does not necessarily extend to capital punishment within lawful processes. "I didn't kill them for the sake of justice," Douglas weeps. "I killed them for revenge." The sin is not inherent in the act of execution, as the gang's actions qualify them for this end even in the religious leader's mind; the sin is in the motivation behind the act. On the horizon, though, there existed a new world situation, one that would appear during the cataclysmic 1960s. With that emergent sensibility would come an altered way of seeing. And, inevitably, changes in the Western, necessary to again reflect an ever-evolving vision of the way the world works so that the genre would once more speak to an audience at a particular moment in time.

Act of nature or will of God? Both the silent Old San Francisco *and sound-era* San Francisco *(shown here) insist that the wrath of Yahweh against America's Sodom caused the 1906 earthquake. Courtesy Metro-Goldwyn-Mayer.*

OLD TESTAMENT AND NEW
DAYS OF WRATH, ANGELS OF MERCY

Stop those Christian bells!
—CHRIS BUCKWELL IN *OLD SAN FRANCISCO*, 1927

Another means of organizing Westerns to more fully understand their implications (while risking the wrath of poststructuralists everywhere) is to divide
the genre into Old and New Testament oaters. The former are those oaters
that imply the presence of a wrathful Yahweh ready to rain down hellfire and
brimstone; the latter offer a gentle Jesus willing to forgive sins so long as the
perpetrators mend their ways. They might also be termed the "Hebraic" as
compared to the "Christian" Western. The former is on view in many Hollywood films about the Barbary Coast, reputed during the second half of the
nineteenth century to have become the American Sodom and Gomorrah.
Westerns set there often play the 1906 earthquake not as a natural occurrence
but as an act of God, equal in his wrath as anything in early Bible stories.

   In *Old San Francisco* (Alan Crosland, 1927), righteous Old Testament
Charlie (actor unknown), horrified by the decadence around him, screams
out on street corners that God's anger will soon be unleashed on those who
created "an underworld on top of the earth." Particularly offensive to Charlie's value system is Asian crime lord Chris Buckwell (Warner Oland), who

at one point attempts to corner and rape a Spanish noblewoman (Dolores Costello). Desperate, she calls on a "God of vengeance" to appear and rescue her. As ghosts of conquistadors mass to protect her purity, the earthquake appears as God's handiest means to preserve her virginity.

One of the most interesting elements here is that the Christian principle is represented by the Catholic Church, not the case in most early movies. If anything, those first flickers tended to assume the view that Protestantism was *the* American Christian religion, "our" ancestors those Anglicans who landed at Plymouth Rock. Times were changing; that long-standing prejudice had at least belatedly begun to decline. That may have to do with the many Italian and Irish immigrants who had, during the decades preceding this film's release, arrived at Ellis Island, as well as a new wave of Hispanic and mestizo immigrants coming across the Rio Grande in the Southwest. To take a generous approach toward Hollywood's growing sense of inclusion, at least of diverse Christians, we might want to believe the most liberal-minded and progressive among the filmmakers were eager to use their vast mass-communication apparatus to fight against existing prejudices. As Darryl F. Zanuck was the producer of this film, that may well be the case here. His later work as head of production at Twentieth Century-Fox reveals a strong desire to portray religious (Jews in *Gentleman's Agreement*, Elia Kazan, 1947) and ethnic (African Americans in *Pinky* (Kazan, Ford, 1949) among them, in the best light. There also remains the possibility that minorities were perceived as potential ticket-buyers and the tendency to dramatize them well had more to do with box-office concerns than with public consciousness. As is often the case with Hollywood, likely the reasoning involved a combination of the two factors.

However well the Catholic Hispanics come off in the film, *Old San Francisco*, like so many other movies of the time and practically all other aspects of popular culture from the early twentieth century, combines pro-Christian values with xenophobia and racism toward Asians: "In the awful light of an outraged, wrathful, Christian God, the heathen soul of the Mongol stood revealed," one of the final title cards to this silent epic declares. As their world explodes, director Crosland cuts back again to Old Testament Charlie, as if to remind us that this was no accident. As promised in scripture, here was the fire next time, American-style.

The Old Testament Western flourished during the silent era as Victorianism, despite that queen's death in 1901, proved slow to disappear. The so-

The priest and the politician. In San Francisco, *a driven religious leader (Spencer Tracy) and an amoral raw capitalist seeking political office (Clark Gable) are sharply divided until the earthquake brings them together. Courtesy Metro-Goldwyn-Mayer.*

called Roaring Twenties changed most everything. D. W. Griffith, whose old-fashioned epics had qualified him as the most popular filmmaker in the country and for that matter the world up until the advent of the Great War, found it ever more difficult to attract audiences to his traditionalist films. A new generation of young people now flocked to contemporary films starring Clara Bow and the young Joan Crawford. By 1930 Griffith's career was all but finished; he made only a single sound film, a quasi-Western (*Abraham Lincoln*, 1930), then retired when that epic failed at the box office. New moviemakers seized control of the industry. While they hardly abandoned the Bible, more often than not they embraced a more forgiving New Testament viewpoint.

Hollywood removed all traces of anti-Asian sentiment while retaining and even furthering the religious element in the earthquake story for *San Francisco* (W. S. Van Dyke II, 1936). The suitably named Blackie (Clark Gable) is a Rhett Butler-ish naughty-but-nice charmer. He's befriended by a devout priest, Father Mullin (Spencer Tracy), who, no matter how nefarious Blackie's activities may be, continues to insist that if only Blackie's ambition might be redirected toward community good rather than individual gain, he could yet become great man. "Trouble with you," the priest explains to Blackie, "is that you don't *believe* in anything." Actually, the priest is wrong there. Blackie is a humanist, decent in dealing with other people, far more likely to end up in this good Catholic man of the cloth's vision of purgatory than in hell. Blackie's problem is that, at this point, he doesn't believe in anything bigger or grander than the immediate here and now, failing to acknowledge something up above and out there that might endow the everyday world with a greater meaning.

Early on, Blackie breaks not only local laws but one of the Ten Commandments by sleeping with a married woman from the Nob Hill upper crust. The sequence roughly parallels the earlier one in Crosland's film that caused the earthquake to occur. Here, though, we encounter more of a New Testament interpretation of the event, suggesting that with honest repentance, a man's soul—and with it the city itself—may yet be saved by a forgiving God. Blackie loses interest in adultery after virginal good girl Mary Blake (Jeanette MacDonald) wanders into his saloon. A former librarian as well as a heartland preacher's daughter, she hopes to support herself with an honest job as a singer. Father Mullin marvels that she could remain so innocent in this, "the most Godless city in America." Casually dismissing theology, Blackie considers all such talk "hocus pocus." When he puts a sexy costume on Mary for her appearances, the priest rages that Blackie has at last gone too far: "You're not going to exploit this girl!" In the priest's mind, she should sing high opera.

After the earthquake, a forlorn Blackie searches the city's ruins, hoping Mary, whom he has come to truly love, survived. Ordinary people form a chorus and perform religious songs, including "Nearer My God to Thee," hoping faith will see them through. The priest and Blackie come face to face again on a devastated street. At once, the priest sees a change in the gambler's eyes, manner, temperament.

> BLACKIE: I want to thank God. What do I say?
> FATHER MULLIN: What's in your heart.

His hubris gone, Blackie falls down on his knees, for the first time experiencing humility. At that moment, Mary steps out of the shadows, safe. Her survival seems more fate than coincidence, a reward from on high for Blackie's belated acceptance of a higher power. His personal blessing is accompanied by a larger social one. "The fire's out," someone calls from the crowd. The

We want "a new deal!" Set in 1906, San Francisco is approached from a mid-1930s sensibility. An image of a united working class is derived from murals painted on public buildings by FDR's Works Progress Administration. Courtesy Metro-Goldwyn-Mayer.

citizens, women and men, march over a hill to initiate work on a new Frisco. All appear lifted from some Soviet propaganda picture by Sergei Eisenstein or V. I. Pudovkin about the community of workers, though with one significant difference: the song the San Franciscans sing is religious. Group action is distinguished for American audiences from the godless aspect of communism Russian-style that so frightened the U.S. public. Again, practicality can reconcile opposites: a God-ordained socialism, fused with old-time religion, could work in America even as godless communism had in Russia. The tableau recalls some small-town post-office wall on which WPA workers painted New Deal murals, inspired by FDR's faith in the working class.[1]

To the hammer and sickle, a cross can be added with no damage done on either side. In America, anything's possible.

Viewed back to back, *Old San Francisco* and *San Francisco* respectively offer Old and New Testament incarnations of a single momentous event. In the long run, the New Testament vision would dominate. Characters who spout moralistic rather than truly moral attitudes come off, in the practical geography of the screen West, as extremists who do more harm than good.

Typical of them is Walter Huston as "the sin-killer," the grandest Bible-thumper in all of Texas in *Duel in the Sun*. Visiting a ranch where the family

Hellfire and brimstone. In Duel in the Sun, *a self-righteous, self-appointed minister (Walter Huston) terrifies a young woman (Jennifer Jones), demanding that she remain pure of sexual desire to avoid damnation and in the process ruining her entire life. Courtesy The David O. Selznick Studio.*

has adopted a half-Indian girl (Jennifer Jones), he takes one look at her physical beauty and becomes nearly hysterical. "Under that blanket," he wails, "there's a woman sent from the *devil* to drive men *crazy*." An extreme Puritan, he is prejudiced against Pearl for her race, which he considers devilish. More than for her status as an Indian, this voice of radical Protestantism despises that Pearl is a half-breed, representing a mixing of the races—his own Anglo (in his mind, superior) blood watered down by combination with what he views as inferior people of color. He resembles Archdeacon Claude Frollo in Victor Hugo's *The Hunchback of Notre Dame* (1831) and his uncontrollable obsession for the lowly gypsy Esmeralda; like Frollo unable to admit his own lust, he blames the guiltless woman for being born beautiful.

Duel in the Sun's zealot forces the poor teenager down on her hands and knees and leans over her in an offensively patriarchal manner: "Pearl, you can be a woman of sin or a woman of God. Which is it going to be?" Vulnerable and ignorant, she begs him to help her find salvation. Most viewers, then and now, sympathize more with the well-meaning child-woman than with the intimidating male figure. Refusing to acknowledge a healthy middle ground, the preacher hastens Pearl's downfall by convincing the confused female that her attractiveness can only be considered evil incarnate. The work itself, though, is hardly antireligious. Lillian Gish, once D. W. Griffith's favorite symbol of pure Christianity, plays the elderly, kindly wife of the ranch owner (Lionel Barrymore). She finds Pearl charming and would like to see the girl marry her own gentle son (Joseph Cotten). That way, the wife feels, Pearl's ripe sexuality could be harnessed for the good within the acceptable context of a Christian marriage.

Often, extremist attitudes toward religion, notably of an Old Testament type, are expressed by the worst sort of white-trash criminal element, implying that the filmmakers reject this harsh brand while confirming the goodness of Christianity at its most forgiving. In *The Unforgiven* (John Huston, 1960), a lonely Confederate veteran (Joseph Wiseman) who haunts a Texas family for past sins, real or imagined, spouts scripture whenever he attempts to menace them. In *Will Penny* (Tom Gries, 1968), the aging head (Donald Pleasence) of a kill-crazy clan constantly refers to the Lord as his boys steal from honest locals. The historical Jesse James, played by Robert Duvall in *The Great Northfield Minnesota Raid* (Philip Kaufman, 1972), sounds much like a Pentecostal preacher, which is not unlikely, given that the second husband of the James boys' mother did hold such a position.[2] Jesse here appears obsessed with his name's similarity to Jesus. When Jesse plans the legendary bank robbery, he describes the coming event as Armageddon collapsed into the apocalypse, concluding his tirade with "Amen!" Frank (John Pearce) sighs proudly, "My brother's near to a saint." Other, less insane gang members rather view religion as a last resort. When Cole Younger (Cliff Robertson) is wounded, the outlaws ask an old gypsy woman to offer incantations in hopes of saving him. One of the boys grouses to a nearby preacher that if the gypsy can't pull it off, "maybe you and the Good Book will come in handy." Not necessarily, though.

More often than not, religion—if kept practical rather than impossibly idealistic—will save the day. This proves true especially in the medium-budget oaters produced at Republic under the guidance of studio boss Herbert J. Yates. In *Hellfire* (R. G. Springsteen, 1949), Bill Elliott plays Zeb Smith, an amoral gambler who mends his ways when a preacher dies after catching a bullet meant instead for Smith. Appropriately, this preacher was played by H. B. Warner, who had been Jesus in *The King of Kings* (Cecil B. DeMille,

1927). Inspired to complete the preacher's mission, one more of those half-finished churches still in frame form, Smith originally plans to turn in the beautiful lady bandit Doll Brown (Marie Windsor) for the reward money. Once he gets to know her, the reformed gunman realizes what a fine person she is and instead sets out to rehabilitate her so they can in time marry and carry on the Lord's work together. Achieving a noteworthy balance between film titles, Republic released *Brimstone* (Joseph Kane, 1949) hot on the heels of *Hellfire*, with Walter Brennan cast as the kind of hateful, nonreligious menace to incoming settlers, all good Christians, that he played in *My Darling Clementine*. Rod Cameron embodies a Lassiter-like figure who comes to the nesters' survival, though this time Mormons are nowhere to be seen.

In what may be the studio's most exemplary work, Republic would subsequently release a highly allegorical Western in which the argument is forwarded that Old Testament vengeance must give way to New Testament retribution and the Lord allowed the final judgment as to who will live and who should die. *The Showdown* (Dorrell McGownan and Stuart E. McGownan, 1950), shot in the postwar noir style, opens with an image of Shadrack Jones (Bill Elliott) in a cemetery recovering a buried body. This is the corpse of his brother; he demands to know the caliber of gun that killed the lad so as to track down the assassin. When the old-timer Cap McKellar (Walter Brennan) offers to read over the re-interred man, Shadrack demands to know if he's ordained. "You don't need to be a preacher to read the Book over a man's grave," Cap suggests. "All you need is a friendly feeling toward your fellow man." On the American frontier, religion has less to do with formalities and pedigrees than with attitude and emotion.

Still, there is a major irony to come. The two join a cattle drive, Shadrack certain one of the cowboys is the murderer. Upon discovering the guilty drover's identity, Shadrack will kill him. His religiosity established, sidekick Cap—who draws on the audience's memory of Brennan's character Groot in *Red River* two years earlier—serves as the moral conscience:

> I'm gonna ask you to forget about the man who killed your brother. There was a time when I felt that way also. Anybody did me, or my kind, wrong, I had to get even. But I learned something, son. I learned that what a man thinks either makes or destroys him. And there's nothing more harmful than thinking about revenge. It poisons your mind and rots your guts. It leaves a brand on you that never fades.

The sentiment is superb, the sort of thing Tom Dunson in *Red River* needed to hear as a potential offset to his desire for vengeance on Matthew Garth. In *The Showdown*, though, Cap adds a spiritual dimension to the equation: "There's a force or a power or whatever you want to call it out there" that "enacts retribution" with no need for man's interference. Abandon the old religious adage, the character and the film tell us, that God helps those who help themselves. When an old cross discovered on a dead cowboy is given to Shadrack he at last begins to take Cap's words to heart and agrees to abandon his dark quest. That, however, is not the end. In the final moments Shadrack learns that it was Cap who killed his brother. Fatally wounded (not by Shadrack) and in severe pain, Cap begs to be put out of his misery. Now, Shadrack cannot pull the trigger, perversely enjoying the suffering endured by the enemy he thought was his friend, freed from guilt because he vowed not to take the life of the guilty man. But Shadrack reveals that he has arced when he tells one of the cowboys to take the cross he now adores and give it to the dying Cap for comfort.

Cap's reply is a perfect line to conclude this odd, in some ways alarmingly religious Western: "God bless you!"

The age-old story of love and hate. Though set in the Depression-era Deep South, Night of the Hunter'*s sex-obsessed, Ripper-like, self-appointed preacher (Robert Mitchum) embodies earlier such characters in generic Westerns. Courtesy United Artists.*

We three. Until a strict religious and political structure is imposed on a California mining town by newcomers, a woman (*Jean Seberg*) and two men (*Lee Marvin, Clint Eastwood*) enjoy doing what comes naturally. The arrival of Christian civilization ruins everything in Paint Your Wagon. *Courtesy Paramount Pictures.*

THE CHURCH
AND THE SALOON
CATHOLIC VERSUS PROTESTANT WESTERNS

The solitude and freedom of the wilderness created
a perfect setting for either melancholy or exultation.
—RODERICK FRAZIER NASH, *WILDERNESS*
AND THE AMERICAN MIND, 1967

The distinction between Old and New Testament Westerns can be augmented by another dichotomization, this between Protestant and Catholic visions. These offer unique, even oppositional interpretations, presenting alternative Dream Wests, each with its own moral system at work in its unique narrative structure. Risking the charge of simplification, for our purposes the basic tenets of the Catholic reading of the Bible and later Protestant reaction against it might be boiled down to a pair of elemental phrases and the diametrical implications that can be drawn from them.

A Catholic conception of redemption as essential to the religion's practicality for adherents may be viewed as an insistence on the primacy of Jesus's words after saving the woman taken in adultery from death by stoning. First, Jesus challenges her would-be executioners: "Let he who is without sin among you throw the first stone." When this quiets the crowd as people sense their own guilt on at least one of the commandments at some point in their lives, Jesus does not appear to embrace this unnamed woman but, in John 8:11, sends her off with tacit disapproval of her actions and a warning: "Neither do I condemn you; go, and do not sin again."

We are not informed as to whether she follows Jesus's instructions. Should she, entirely on her own, mend her ways, apparently this nameless woman will be saved. If she does not, she has doomed herself. All that Jesus in this anecdote offers is an opportunity for redemption.

A second chance is the concept on which the American Dream would be founded. Having sinned does not condemn one to hell for eternity. Only a personal failure to resolve the situation favorably according to the Old Testament will do that. She, like all of us, is on her own, now with freedom of choice. If she should fail, even that does not necessarily doom her to hellfire and brimstone. For those who mean well, there exists the possibility of purgatory.

The Protestant Reformation might be considered to have evolved out of a rejection of the purgatorial compromise.[1] It is not for nothing that the most extreme among this alternative Christian denomination called themselves Puritans and perceived themselves as born into an elect, a small number of people who are essentially perfect and, as such, predestined for glorious immortality.[2] It is not enough, as in Catholicism, to control one's dark desires and "not sin again" by controlling bad thoughts and doing the right thing. To Catholics, that may be the ultimate victory, owing to the concept of original sin in which every person has a light and dark side and creates his or her own fate by adhering to or breaking God's rules.[3] For the Protestant in general and the Puritan specifically, that is not good enough. To even think black thoughts or feel wrong emotions is enough to doom a person.

Jesus states in Matthew 5:8, "Blessed are the pure in heart, for they shall see God." That means they and, for the Puritans, they alone. There is no such thing as purgatory because half-measures are worthless. It is not enough to repress forbidden acts and so keep the body pure. If a darkness exists in the heart, soul, or mind, that is enough to doom a person by eliminating him or her from the elect.

To fully appreciate the distinctions between what are essentially Catholic and Protestant Westerns, it is first helpful to glance again at an extreme example of the film that stands in opposition to conventional Christianity, embracing the pantheistic, romantic strain that dominates the genre. *Paint*

Your Wagon (Joshua Logan, 1969) starred two rugged actors associated with red-state sensibilities, Clint Eastwood and Lee Marvin. Yet it is necessary to note that in addition to being directed by a person more associated with liberal Broadway plays and their film versions (*Picnic*, 1955; *Mister Roberts*, 1955; *Bus Stop*, 1956), the script from the original stage musical (1951) was entirely excised, with some songs by Alan J. Lerner retained. The book was replaced with one written by Paddy Chayefsky, the New York intellectual playwright and TV screenwriter known for *Marty* (1955), *The Americanization of Emily* (1964), *The Hospital* (1971), and *Network* (1976). Chayefsky created his original treatment for *Paint Your Wagon* during the zenith of the 1960s youth movement that crystallized at the Woodstock music festival. Though the film's setting may be red-state mining camps of the frontier, the sensibility we encounter is blue-state progressive.

Mining partners Old Ben (Marvin) and Young Pardner (Eastwood) discover gold on the day they meet. They live in a primitive camp where, free of interference from political and religious dictates of any mainstream society, the two share a ménage à trois common-law arrangement with Elizabeth (Jean Seberg), a free-spirited beauty. Their innocent American Eden ends as new settlers bringing Puritan values move in alongside the rough-hewn miners. Prostitutes who had been welcome and even adored are driven out after a parson damns them. Most moralistic of all, though, are the respectable women who all but spit on such soiled doves. As to the romantic triangle, everything is altered. Elizabeth grows self-conscious about her out-of-the-ordinary relationships and decides one lover must leave. We are left with a sense that paradise has once more been lost now that Victorian morality has intruded on what was previously an agreeably amoral setting. As Nash, a student of the historical West put it, "The pastoral condition seemed closest to paradise and the life of ease and contentment."[4] Here is a neopagan vision that challenges not only Catholicism and Protestantism but all Judeo-Christian moral underpinnings. As to the film's heroes, though, it was now time to, as in the Bible, move east of Eden, where one dreams of recapturing the lost golden age.

If *Paint Your Wagon* posited an extreme example of organized religion destroying an organic lifestyle, other Westerns offer happier alternatives. *The Woman of the Town* (George Archainbaud, 1943) relates a yarn based on a true story about a prostitute named Dora Hand (Claire Trevor) who lived in Dodge City during its heyday. Bat Masterson (Albert Dekker) is amazed to

A realistic compromise. Rejecting the Puritanical notion of a perfect elect, a Catholic priest (H. B. Warner) tolerates his girl-child (Jeanette MacDonald) singing in a saloon so long as she shows up to perform in church on Sunday mornings, in Girl of the Golden West. *Courtesy Loew's/Metro-Goldwyn-Mayer.*

learn that the same woman who sings like an angel in church on Sundays also performs in the town's most popular bar, bringing the boys who can afford something extra up to her back room for more personal attention after the show. Bat's difficulty in accepting her dual identity forms the drama's crux. In the end, Bat falls deeply in love with Dora because of, rather than in spite of, her refusal to choose one way or the other.[5]

Similarly, the establishments of church and saloon, in opposition or in tandem, will play an essential role in defining any individual Western film's philosophy and helps us to discriminate between Catholic and Protestant oaters. Few films embody the Catholic vision as fully as *The Girl of the Golden West* (Robert Z. Leonard, 1938), adapted from a lavish David Belasco stage musical.[6] Early on we meet Father Sienna (H. B. Warner) of Monterey, California, whose adopted daughter (Jeannette MacDonald) owns the Poker, a saloon in a nearby mining town. She serves drinks to miners and cowboys. None of this bothers the good father so long as his ward continues to sing "Ave Maria" on the Sabbath in California's first cathedral. A balance is tolerated here between the worldly and the sacred. His benevolent attitude toward her profession (we are never certain whether he doesn't know, knows but doesn't care, or lives in denial that her saloon songs are provocative and that she provides other services for the fellows) stems from his belief that human beings aren't purely good or evil but a mix. Her name, Mary, adds to the paradox. Spiritually, she's as virginal as the mother of Jesus yet has no compunctions about acting in the manner of Magdalene. The sheriff (Walter Pidgeon) says to her about the existence of the saloon: "With you in it, the Poker's a church, so far as I'm concerned." By the very nature of her innate goodness—not to say purity—she makes the frontier if not heaven, then at least a high-style purgatory on earth.

The opposite approach holds that there is good and bad, right and wrong, and absolutely nothing in between. According to this position, a person is among the elect or the damned. This stringent Protestant view appears in *The Twinkle in God's Eye* (George Blair, 1955). While the earlier film's Father Sienna, obviously a Catholic, worried as much about the daily plight of his flock as their immortal souls, here Protestant pastor William Macklin II (Mickey Rooney) never aids or attempts to help a single suffering individual. His only interest is in building a church, in and of itself no great surprise for any genre aficionado who has seen *My Darling Clementine* and the significance of this building to the West in history and Hollywood movies. Less expected is his hard-line approach. This pastor insists the church be constructed next door to the saloon. The owner (Hugh O'Brian) tries to reason with him, offering the funds needed to build his church if only it will be relocated on the far side of town. Reverend Macklin will not budge. Locals must learn that they have to enter one building or the other. Only if the saloon is driven out of business will Macklin accomplish his goal; he scorns practical realism. This is idealism at its extreme. The townsfolk must live in absolute purity, or they are doomed. His stance becomes so arch that the piece moves beyond any mainstream Protestantism, expressing instead the stricter code of early Puritans.

Few Westerns are as absolute in their Protestant views as *The Twinkle in God's Eye*, and likewise not many are as overtly Catholic as the 1913 novel *Three Godfathers* by Peter B. Kyne (1880–1957) and the seemingly endless string of theatrical and TV films adapted from its conceit of Old West gunfighters as the Biblical wise men. Kyne's book presents an overtly hard-boiled example of pulp fiction that, in what many would consider true Irish fashion, reveals a deep sentimentality beneath the gruff surface. The sentiment helped make this and Kyne's other potboilers hugely popular among the Irish immigrants pouring into what was becoming an increasingly multicultural America.

Among those who stepped off the boat from the Emerald Isle were John Feeney of County Galway and Barbara Curran from the Aran Islands.[7] They married and gave the world a son, John Ford, who would retell Kyne's tale of the unlikely godfathers three times in film. The first film version, however, hailed from another director. *The Three Godfathers* (Edward Le Saint, 1916) starred Harry Carey (Sr.) in a bare-bones retelling. Carey returned to his role three years later in Ford's ambitious *Marked Men* (1919), the film that cemented a relationship between Hollywood's first great Western actor and the greatest director of Westerns.

More elaborate still was *Three Bad Men* (John Ford, 1926). Here, the title characters (Tom Santschi, J. Farrell MacDonald, Frank Campeau) discover a young woman (Lee Carlton) in need of mentoring. When a group of land-grabbers enters the area with plans to seize farms from the good settlers, a minister (Alec B. Francis) reminds the pilgrims that they constitute an incarnation of an ancient race: "And, as He led the children of Israel into the promised land, so will he lead us." John Ford builds on the book's allegorical elements to provide an early personal take on the Western.

Though not a Ford film, the first sound version further emphasized Catholic elements in this tale in the seeming paradox of its title: *Hell's Heroes* (William Wyler, 1930). During the robbery of New Jerusalem's bank, one outlaw commands the teller, "Start reaching for heaven, stranger, or you're headed for hell." Following their pre-Christmas escape into the desert, the man called Barbed Wire (Raymond Hatton) quotes the Bible, emphasizing the words of Jesus. Another notes when they reach a parched waterhole that it is likely to "stay dry from now until I get religion." Though he means this as a mock, he isn't all that far off from what will indeed soon transpire.

Any Protestant notion of pure, good heroes versus simple, black-hearted villains is absent. The title aside, the vast prairie appears an earthbound purgatory, the yarn itself offering a vision of sainthood that harkens back to the sinner Saul of Tarsus re-creating himself as Paul the true believer. A man whom these gunfighters kill was the husband of a dying woman they now discover in the desert, which makes their unconscious quest for redemption more personal. The men baptize her baby with sand, yet another example of the practicality with which religious tradition must be rethought on the frontier. When the final surviving man crawls back to town, the innocent child safely delivered there before the outlaw dies, church bells ring. It's Christmas morning, and to borrow from the British bard Robert Browning, God's in his heaven and all's right with the world, thanks to this good bad man who redeemed his life and saved his soul at the last possible moment.

Though a modest B picture, *Miracle in the Sand* (Richard Boleslawski, 1936), in many respects captures the true spirit of Kyne's book. Sometimes known as *Three Godfathers*, this version provides not a trio whose portraits are sketched in shades of gray but an evil triad, black-hearted enough to casually kill as they rob. When the gang hits New Jerusalem, the leader, Bob Sangster (Chester Morris), spots a nice young banker (Robert Livingston), engaged to the outlaw's former fiancée (Irene Hervey). The pleasant fellow is decked out as Kris Kringle. With a cruel smile, Sangster dispatches the unfortunate man, shrugging and sarcastically commenting, "There ain't no Santa Claus!" When his companions (Lewis Stone, Walter Brennan) vow to protect a dying woman's baby after they encounter these innocents on the desert, Sangster must be constrained from abandoning the child. Here, though, the most extreme—and extremely effective—moral arc occurs.

Alone, carrying the child for reasons he can't comprehend, Sangster comes upon a waterhole only to realize it's been poisoned. Employing the little girl as his mute priest, he launches into a lengthy confession of previous sins, vowing to do a single worthy act before expiring. Seized by what appears to be a heaven-sent solution, the man is inspired to drink his fill. This temporarily revives him so that, while dying, he's able to carry the child to town on Christmas morning, where she is more or less born again.

Ford's third and final version, *3 Godfathers* (1948), offers the most broadly appealing rendition of what film historian William K. Everson once tagged the genre's "most oft-told tale."[8] Here the title characters (John Wayne, Pedro Armendáriz, Harry Carey Jr.) are so lovable, even harmless, it's impossible not to like them from the outset. Still, they have a bad habit of relieving banks of money. When Robert Marmaduke Hightower (Wayne), the last survivor, drags himself and the child back to New Jerusalem, he only has to redeem a relatively minor crime. Allowed to live by the Lord, Ford, or both,

An alternative to My Darling Clementine. *In place of Ford's church as central to the community, revisionist filmmaker Robert Altman in* McCabe and Mrs. Miller *shows the people building its structure, then becoming rugged individualists and abandoning it. Courtesy Warner Brothers.*

he's feted by the sheriff (Ward Bond), the sheriff's wife (Mae Marsh), and other townsfolk before heading off to serve a brief prison term, then hurry back to their bosom. Hightower is allowed to leave by train in the context of Ford's signature shot.[9] A gorgeous young woman (Dorothy Ford) shows up at the station to see him off; it's from over her shoulder that we watch Hightower depart. Obviously, he couldn't qualify for membership in any rigid Puritan elect. But he'll feel right at home when he returns to what, apparently, must be a Catholic town. In John Ford's personal variation of our Dream West, no one is expected to be perfect. Or pure.

A notably different approach would be taken toward the concept of churches by modernist filmmakers. In *McCabe and Mrs. Miller* (Robert Altman, 1971), originally to have been titled *Presbyterian Church*, the story unfolds in a frontier community where pioneers upon arrival immediately set to work building the church, suggesting righteousness. Once that structure is completed they set up whorehouses and saloons that they frequent. From what we see, no one ever attends church; a post-1960s attitude casts a cynical view as they pay lip service to organized religion while living fully in a jaded world. The one time everyone hurries to the church is when it catches fire and burns down. In truth, though, the West and its religious enclaves did not exist in such a state. Churches were well attended; they were made practical for people then reinventing themselves through the characteristically American experience of turning savagery into civilization.

In this notion of the country as original and ever-evolving, drawing upon Old World attitudes while developing a new vision that encompasses but is not limited to them, an organic religiosity not restricted to Catholicism or Protestantism appears, seemingly on its own accord. An American religion drew from numerous sources tossed into the same melting pot that the people themselves came to see this new nation would become.

Practical religion on the first frontier. In Ford's Drums along the Mohawk, *the minister (Arthur Shields) blesses his community—and reminds the men that if they do not show up to fight Indians he'll personally execute them. Courtesy Twentieth Century-Fox.*

ONWARD, CHRISTIAN SOLDIERS

THE PISTOL AND THE PULPIT

I'm on a mission from God!
—SARA IN *TWO MULES FOR SISTER SARA*, 1970

However essential religion may be to the Western film, mixed messages from the genre would confuse religious issues as well as those of a political nature. In most liberal-progressive Westerns, the pistol and pulpit are posited as opposites. Exemplary is *The Little Shepherd of Kingdom Come* (Andrew McLaglen, 1961), based on a 1903 novel by John Fox Jr. In it, a Civil War veteran (Jimmy Rogers), radicalized by his wartime experiences, creates a ministry and tries to convince pioneers to abandon violence. Other films depict such a holy man in a less charitable light. In *High Noon*, Gary Cooper's lawman steps into the local church and asks for volunteers to help fight four menacing outlaws. The wishy-washy minister (Morgan Farley) shrugs and admits that "the choice between good and evil seems pretty clear here," only to quote scripture: "The Lord says thou shalt not kill." Moments later Will Kane walks out alone. For a viewer, there's little doubt Kane is the man we ought to respect, the town's minister a coward and/or fool.

A surprisingly large number of Westerns portray the gun and the cross as natural allies. In *Drums along the Mohawk*, shortly before the battle at

Oriskany Falls people hurry to the church. There the minister (Arthur Shields) turns his eyes heavenward, addressing "Jehovah, oh God of *battles!*" Later, during the siege of Fort Stanwix, Old Pete (Francis Ford) is caught by Indians who plan to burn him alive. It is the minister who seizes a gun and shoots his friend to spare him the agony of burning, saying, "Forgive me Lord for what I'm about to do." Only when the fighting is done does he fall into catatonia: "I *killed* a man!" The minister refers not to Indians who fell before his rifle; he is remorseful only for Pete, though convinced he did act rightly. A similar occurrence in *The Alamo* involves the parson (Hank Worden), who joins the other defenders on the wall for the battles. Indeed, all Alamo films by their very nature ally pistol and pulpit if for no other reason than that the building was both fort and mission.

This theme was not confined to adult Westerns. Gene Autry tells his juvenile sidekick (Dick Jones) in *Last of the Pony Riders* (George Auchainbaud, 1953) that the young man will need serious protection if he is to work for the express. Smiling, the boy replies that he's got it "here" (holding up a shotgun with one hand) and "here" (a Bible raised in the other). Two films shot back to back by the independent producer-director Albert C. Gannaway brought a near-fantasy element into play. In *The Badge of Marshal Brennan* (1957), Jim Davis plays an outlaw on the run who happens upon the tin star of a deceased lawman. Pinning it on to conceal his identity, the outlaw finds his body and soul taken over by the spirit of a man who deeply believed in law and order and in old-time religion. In *Man or Gun* (1958), MacDonald Carey enacts a wanderer with no commitments to secular or sacred values until he discovers a pistol that belonged to a deceased hero. Shortly, he does not so much fire that gun in the name of good as he allows the gun to itself shoot at those who threaten law and religion; he merely holds it while this agent of the Old Testament Yahweh performs its own bloody work. In each film, the man carries and uses God's gun.

On occasion, the preacher himself is comfortable with a brace of pistols. No film more effectively presents this than *Stars in My Crown* (Jacques Tourneur, 1950). The story opens as preacher Josiah Doziah Gray (Joel McCrea) marches into a saloon and calmly explains he's about to deliver his first sermon. When drunkards laugh out loud, Gray shoves aside his long, black waistcoat, draws the pistols from their holsters, points them at the men, and starts preaching. No one utters a word, much less argues. Afterward he "convinces" everyone in town to take part in the building of their church. Yet he, no hellfire and brimstone extremist, is happy to have the saloon open every day but the Sabbath, and shows tolerance for those of a pantheistic bent.

One of his best friends, Jed (Alan Hale), chooses not to attend church and worships in his own way on his land. He's Christian in spirit, though, the Good Samaritan willing to extend a hand. Gray accepts this even if a baptism will not prove forthcoming. When supposedly good Christians decked out in the robes of Klansmen burn down the farm of a black man (Juano Hernandez), Jed and his sons clean up the place. When night riders return, Jed's clan stands guard, ready to kill if necessary to defend the African American.

There's nothing narrow about this preacher's vision. He perceives a young doctor (James Mitchell) who settles in the community as an ally, not a competitor. Here science and religion are compatible, a far cry from today's conservative views. Religion has the last word when someone takes sick.

DOC: I did all I could.

FARMER/HUSBAND: I know it. Doc. Now we need *another* kind of help.

Such peaceful coexistence between seeming opposites, one more example of American practicality, underlines the film. Doc initially scoffs at religion yet experiences a turning point. When the young teacher (Ellen Drew) he loves takes sick and he can't help, Doc sends for the preacher.

In other films, the religious figure attempts to keep pulpit and pistol separate until pushed into violence by necessity. When Anglo outlaws raid a peaceful Indian village in *Rooster Cogburn* (Stuart Millar, 1975), a well-meaning missionary (Katharine Hepburn) recites the Lord's Prayer. When the words are done she summons up an earlier Biblical phrase to make clear that the land must be purged of bad men. "All those who take the sword must perish by the sword!" She herself takes up a gun, tempering a New Testament love of victimized Natives with an Old Testament eye-for-an-eye desire for, if not vengeance, then justice of a violent order. This dedicated church lady journeys with the title hero (John Wayne), a lawman, as an equal (for a helping of right-wing feminism) in the destruction of destroyers. In Wayne's initial reluctance to take her along, he shouts her protests down with a quote from Paul: "Let your women be silent in church." In the end, he could not get the job done without her and readily admits as much.

Far more frequent are the films in which a gun-toting male preacher assists a sheriff in carving civilization out of chaos, law and order and religion symbolically set side by side. Willie Nelson does this for R. G. Armstrong in *Red-Headed Stranger* (William Wittliff, 1986). Willie's parson carries a cross in one hand and a pistol or a shotgun in the other. Another film, also starring a country-music recording star, provided one of the most fully realized variations. In *Rio Diablo* (TVM, Ron Hardy, 1993), Kenny Rogers wears the white collar of a preacher. His character, Quentin Leech, stops by an outlaw camp for water and conversation. The moment their guard is down, he draws his guns. A bounty hunter, Leech wears the collar to disarm his targets; he is a fake soul-saver. But is he? Later he quotes scripture and fingers a small Bible. Apparently, he once was a religious man, and the death of his wife so embittered him he had to step away from the pulpit and pick up a pistol to rid the world of evil.

Rogers's role in this film, like Anthony Quinn's in the earlier *Guns for San Sebastian* (Henry Verneuil, 1968), marks an even more specific subdivision of the Western's holy subgenre. Quinn plays Leon Alastray, a Mexican outlaw during the period of Spain's domination. Escaping from pursuers, he rides into a church. There a kindly old priest (Sam Jaffe) offers him sanctuary. "Only God gives orders here," the priest tells the authorities. In gratitude, Alastray accompanies the priest on a long trek to a distant mission. Always, Alastray insists he's not religious. "You worry about your prayers," he tells the priest. "I'll worry about my stomach." When the priest dies, Quinn's character is inspired to wear the deceased man's robes and take his place. At first he does so to survive, but a growing sense of mission overcomes him. In time he takes the task set on his shoulders by coincidence or fate seriously. A warrior, he helps the peons wipe out a deadly gang. Though he never officially becomes a Catholic priest, this anti-hero based on a true story achieves a sort of secular sainthood.[1]

However controversial such a masquerade may sound, it appears not only in films from the culture-rocking 1960s but also some from Hollywood's golden age. A playful sequence in *The Mark of Zorro* (Rouben Mamoulian, 1940) allows for secular sensuality to unfold in the unlikely confines of a Catholic church. Zorro, the apparently harmless Don Diego de la Vega (Tyrone Power), disguises himself as a friar and takes confession from a lovely señorita (Linda Darnell) whom our hero loves, hardly in a platonic sense. Diego as friar offers sympathy to the confused girl, insisting he will

The miracle. The semihistorical Guns for San Sebastian *tells of a hardened outlaw (Anthony Quinn) who is mistaken by simple people of a remote area for a priest and, in time, rises to the occasion. Courtesy Metro-Goldwyn-Mayer.*

save her soul, and attempts to seduce her, at one point kissing her hand lovingly. If several interlopers had not happened by, we are left believing the pair would have made love under the towering cross and nearby statue of the Virgin. Before the film concludes, the hero becomes a secular savior to the people.

The transition from rogue to quasi-religious figure would be taken further in films made after the Hollywood production code of 1933–1966 gave way in 1967–1968. In *A Town Called Hell*, alternately titled *A Town Called Bastard* (Robert Parrish, 1971), Robert Shaw's unnamed priest character is actually an artisan who masquerades as a religious man to gain access to great paintings. By film's end, he converts to a populist priest and joins the peons when fascist authorities threaten both art and life. In *The Wrath of God* (Ralph Nelson, 1972) Father Oliver Van Horne (Robert Mitchum) wears a frock and gives absolution but also smokes, drinks, and associates with whores.

This Western charade subgenre allowed a feminist twist with *Two Mules*

Challenging the dichotomization of women. In Two Mules for Sister Sara, *the protagonist (Shirley MacLaine) constantly confounds Hogan (Clint Eastwood), who cannot comprehend whether she's a Madonna or a Magdalene and finally accepts that she's a bit of both. Not coincidentally, the 1970 film was written even as feminism reached its second wave. Courtesy Universal Pictures/Malpaso.*

for Sister Sara, in which the female lead (Shirley MacLaine) is the fake. When anti-hero Hogan (Clint Eastwood) saves her from bad guys, this exchange takes place:

SARA: It was a miracle that you found me when you did.
HOGAN: Just an accident.
SARA: You believe there are no miracles?

He does at the time, though Hogan will be converted. Later, he learns that she is actually a whore posing as a religious pilgrim. At first he's outraged. Then he shrugs and accepts this. The point of the piece is that it doesn't matter; she's good, even Christian, regarding her actions in relationship to other people. Any old ways of defining good and evil cannot survive in a jaded world.

The ongoing combination of pastor and *pistolero* would again be separated into its components for *Diamante Lobo* (Gianfranco Parolini, 1976), an Israeli-made Western also known as *God's Gun*. A nonviolent preacher (Lee Van Cleef) is shot dead by an outlaw (Jack Palance). Upon learning this, the preacher's twin brother (also Van Cleef) plans to avenge the murder. But he had promised his now deceased twin he would never again use his gun to kill. This oath leaves him in an awkward spot. Should he strap on his pistols or keep his word? In another display of that practicality associated with the genre and America itself, he vows to track down the men responsible, using every means to exact revenge and/or justice other than a pistol. After all, he didn't promise his late brother he would not employ a Bowie knife or . . .

Even in films that feature preachers unwilling to carry guns, pulpit and pistol often work together. In *The Parson and the Outlaw* (Oliver Drake, 1957) a preacher (Charles "Buddy" Rogers, who also produced the film) seeks out Billy the Kid (Anthony Dexter) only to learn that the notorious outlaw has vowed to retire. Lately, though, Jack Slade (Sunny Tufts) has terrorized the countryside. The reverend persuades Bonney to take up his guns again, though this time the Kid will fight "the *good* fight." Another low-budget film, *The Lawless Eighties* (Joseph Kane, 1957), relates the little-known though true tale of William Wesley Van Orsdel (John Smith), who attempted to bring the Good Book to a frontier community. Realizing the rednecks could not be subdued by prayer alone, he allows a gunfighter (Buster Crabbe) to reorient his once-mercenary pistols as God's guns. On occasion, a gun-toting preacher will turn out to be evil. In *5 Card Stud* (Henry Hathaway, 1968), Reverend Jonathan Rudd (Robert Mitchum) carries weapons to shoot down anyone he finds offensive. He has less in common with Joel McCrea's hero in *Stars in My Crown* than with Mitchum's own earlier demented false-prophet character Harry Powell in *The Night of the Hunter* (Charles Laughton, 1955). At the end of *5 Card Stud*, hero Van Morgan (Dean Martin) discovers that the self-styled savior is actually the serial killer he's been tracking.

The opposite possibility proves equally potent in many religious Westerns. In *The Quick and the Dead* (Sam Raimi, 1995) the town is none too subtly named Redemption. Here a petty tyrant, allegorically referred to as Herod (Gene Hackman), brings together the West's top gunfighters for a competition. But what good would the event be without a holy man to crucify? Cort (Russell Crowe) is dragged in and chained. Herod tempts the Jesus-like figure to take up the gun he swore never to use again and fight for his life. "The preacher has the Lord on his side," Herod snarls. "He will only need one bullet." Whipped and scorned, the preacher still tries to avoid violence; he eventually is forced to use a gun, doing so only for self-defense. Apparently this is acceptable, abetted by his refusal to win anything for himself other than survival so as to do good in the world. By the end, Cort and his guardian angel, Ellen (Sharon Stone), kill off Herod; the town can at last

An alternative to hellfire and brimstone. Preachers who keep their sermons short and sweet, then encourage parishioners to dance are shown as an evolving—and preferable—all-American answer to New England Puritan roots. In My Darling Clementine *the preacher (Russell Simpson) turns his service into a party. Courtesy Twentieth Century-Fox.*

live up to its name. From what we see, Cort appears ready to fill the functions of both lawman and preacher, bringing politics and religion together.

In many previous films the two-gun preacher also turns out to be a savior. The aptly titled *Heaven with a Gun* (Lee H. Katzin, 1969) features Glenn Ford as Pastor Jim, a former shootist now operating as a man of God while still wearing pistols. He finds himself torn between his affections for a Magdalene-ish prostitute (Carolyn Jones) and for a Virgin Mary–like woman (Barbara Hershey). However much he would like to follow the path of gentle Jesus, he realizes this is not practical. He can never win over a vicious cattle baron (John Anderson) who's been harassing a flock of sheepherders. Only by employing guns can the preacher get the job done. A similar allegorical element appeared two years earlier in *The Christmas Kid* (Sidney W. Pink, 1967). Jeff Hunter, who earlier played Jesus in *King of Kings* (Nicholas Ray, 1961), returned to that role as a sagebrush savior born in a humble stable. Three drifters happen upon the scene and deliver presents. In time, the boy becomes a gunman who puts down outlaws with his twin Colts. He's trans-

formed into a forgiving figure after surviving two moral challenges, temptation by the Magdalene figure Marie (Perla Cristal) and by a raw capitalist
(Louis Hayward), who, Satan-like, offers him riches in exchange for his soul.

In some cases, the savior figure is actually crucified, including Quinn's
character in *Guns for San Sebastian*. *Valdez Is Coming* (Edward Sherin, 1971)
suggests that a long-suffering Latino lawman (Burt Lancaster) becomes a
savior of the Southwest when evil Anglo villains crucify him. The hero in *The
Shooter*, also titled *Deadly Shooter* and *Desert Shooter* (Fred Olen Ray, 1997),
is crucified, then helped down by a woman, creating a visual Pieta. Though
a full-scale crucifixion doesn't take place in *Man of the East* (Enzo Barboni,
1972), Holy Joe (Harry Carey Jr.) is the leader of an outlaw trio that perhaps
surprisingly lives by religious values. Like many earlier pistol-and-parson
types, Holy Joe leads a congregation into church at the point of a gun, ready
to shoot down anyone who misbehaves. As to his intoxication, Joe invokes
God in offering a practical excuse: "I don't think he'd deny a sinner a good
shot of whiskey now and then." Carey is, of course, playing a variation on his
father's role in a version of *Three Godfathers*.

Hart of the West. William S. Hart established an unbending Puritanical attitude in his highly moralistic films. This outlook came to be associated with many other early examples of the genre. Courtesy the William S. Hart Estate.

HARTS OF THE WEST

THE GOSPEL ACCORDING TO CLINT

We all got it coming, kid.

—WILLIAM MUNNY IN *UNFORGIVEN*, 1992

The vengeance theme reached its apex in the violent, stylized, often surreal spaghetti Westerns of the 1960s and early 1970s. The very title *God Forgives, I Don't* (Giuseppe Colizzi, 1969) implies revenge drama at its most extreme in the context of a self-consciously religious oater. Likewise, in *Adios, Sabata* (Frank Kramer, Gianfranco Parolini, 1971) a small Mexican village is ravaged by outlaws. A bitter child prays for the legendary gunfighter Sabata (Yul Brynner) to arrive and kill the oppressors. A kindly priest, worried about the boy's soul and hoping to save him, approaches.

PRIEST: You must try to forgive, not sink into revenge.
CHILD (EYES GLARING): Sabata *is* God!

The priest attempts to remain New Testament in outlook; the boy believes in a God of vengeance worthy of Yahweh. In an ever darker world that emerged following political assassinations, the escalation of war in Southeast Asia, and in time the Watergate scandal, events suggested that this

Redefining "the good." For a politicized director like Sergio Leone, old simplistics were undermined and satirized. Clint Eastwood's man with no name in The Good, the Bad, and the Ugly *is good only in contrast to far more evil men within Leone's cinematic canvas of a West in which morality is relativistic. Courtesy United Artists.*

might not be the right time for gentle Jesus. To survive in what had come to appear to even the most mainstream of people as a meaningless cosmos, they must turn to Sabata, all in black, a terminating, avenging angel, rather than to a genial Shane.

A more recent variation appears in *The Legend of God's Gun* (Mike Bruce, 2007). The outlaw Diablo (Kirkpatrick Thomas) makes life hell on earth for decent citizens. He's challenged by an avenger whose biblical aspect is emphasized in the credits, where actor Robert Bones is billed as "Gunslinger/Preacher." This figure represents one more variation on a theme—the man with no name—that Sergio Leone, who did not invent but certainly perfected the spaghetti Western, had all but patented with rising genre star Clint Eastwood. It was not for nothing that in *The Good, the Bad, and the Ugly* (1966) Leone placed a halo effect over the head of the cold-blooded killer Eastwood portrayed. Presaging postmodernism, Leone depicted good and bad, much to the chagrin of old-timers like John Wayne, not as objective truths but as subjective observations and everything else in the postmodernist cosmos as relative.[1]

Eastwood's "good" character achieves this status only in contrast to Lee Van Cleef's "bad" one as the villain of the piece because he is so much worse than the hero. Right and wrong exist only in context and in comparison. No wonder, then, that when Eastwood, having established himself as a producer-director, contacted the Duke to ask if they might co-star in one of the auteur's upcoming films, Wayne replied with an angry missive. He expressed resentment for everything that Eastwood had done to, in Wayne's mind, destroy the classic Western, particularly with Eastwood's first Western as a director, *High Plains Drifter* (1973).[2]

Initially in Leone's spaghetti Westerns and eventually in films that he personally directed in America, Eastwood did in fact offer nouveau Westerns albeit in a classical mode. The problem for Wayne was that as a visionary artist, Eastwood did not reach back to Ford's films but to another, and clearly alternative, early example of what the Western could do and say within the virtually limitless expanse of the genre. Less than a year after D. W. Griffith proved with *The Birth of a Nation* that an epic feature-length film could more than make its money back, actor and director William S. Hart (1864–1946) brought the oater from its primitive flicker origins—in the nickelodeon-era venues where "Bronco Billy" Anderson had thrived—to a far more ambitious level in theme and narrative with his starring role in *Hell's Hinges* (Charles Swickard, 1916).

Puritanical (rather than Catholic as were all of Ford's Westerns) in concept, this tale involves a well-meaning young minister from the East, Bob Henley (Jack Study), who in the company of his appropriately named sister Faith (Clara Williams) travels to isolated Placer Gulch. The clerical examining board that sent the young minister there naïvely believed—romantics, whether they knew it or not—that the West would be God's good garden, a place where the minister would feel right at home and flourish. Instead, the frontier reveals itself as the opposite, nicknamed Hell's Hinges by a population that revels in drinking and whoring. What unfolds is Hart's "serious, almost preacherly commitment to moralizing in his art,"[3] through a style best described as "austere,"[4] considering the foreboding tone of what occurs.

The young minister and his sister meet, among other residents, Blaze Tracy (Hart). A swaggering cowboy, he distances himself from varied lowlifes by his considerable courage and a certain ironic detachment that allows him to appear to be with them but not of them. He alone is intrigued by the newly arrived visitors' dedication to the Bible. In time, he does the right thing for the wrong reason—physical attraction to the woman rather than any true commitment to God, at least so far. Blaze "learns to desire faith by experiencing desire for Faith."[5] His conversion to Christianity by this worldly route in no way runs counter to the work's Puritan sensibility.

Radical religion meets reactionary politics. In Hell's Hinges Blaze (William S. Hart), a born-again, self-righteous avenger, comes to believe that the vast majority of human beings ought to be wiped off the earth, and he happily sets out to perform that function. Courtesy Kay-Bee Pictures/ Triangle Film Corporation.

A strong physical bond between man and woman, especially when kept platonic except in desire until marriage, would not have been disparaged by the Protestantism of early Americans.[6]

Blaze casts a male gaze at the woman when not devouring her Good Book.[7] Shortly it becomes apparent to all that her brother's New Testament approach, to gentle the locals, won't work. When the town's church burns down at mid-movie and the minister dies, Blaze unofficially takes up the mantle as God's self-appointed agent, creating the fire and pestilence that burns down this American Sodom-Gomorrah. Old Testament retribution works where New Testament attempts at forgiveness and redemption have failed. Finally, Blaze and Faith ride away, wise enough not to, like Lot's wife, glance back.

Similarly, at the end of *Unforgiven* (1992), a nearly identical avenging angel, Will Munny (Eastwood), damns the town where his best friend, Ned Logan (Morgan Freeman), was murdered. Though this mythic figure does not burn the entire town to the ground, he does set fire to the saloon, portrayed as the black heart of an evil place. An element of religious allegory, apparent in Eastwood's early directorial efforts, takes form here. During the darkest of nights, thunder crashes and lightning flashes above to suggest that nature itself now openly rebels against the miscarriage of justice below. Munny shoots and kills one after another of the townsfolk he holds responsible. Those who quiver in shadows as he slowly steps toward his white horse (symbolically so, and Munny one more pale rider), they hear this purveyor not so much of mean-spirited vengeance but of righteous retribution call out: "Any of you take a shot at me, I'm gonna kill his wife. His friends. I'll burn his house down." He vows to come back and "kill every one of you sons of bitches" and most likely their children too, as the sins of the fathers are visited upon the sons. He'll kill and kill until there is no one left to kill and do so with God's full blessing. In a sense, he is God, or at least the deity's presence on earth. Gentle Jesus did not get the job done; perhaps it's time for what the poet Yeats calls a "rough beast" to arrive, his turn come around at last.

It's a nasty job. But, hey, someone's gotta do it! "A man's gotta do what a man's gotta do" is an underlying theme of all Westerns, from Hart and Ford through Eastwood and Leone to whoever will take on the mantle of genre master next. Those words are the Western distilled, implicit in every oater ever made—romantic or classic, Old Testament or New, liberal or conservative, traditional or nouveau, twentieth or twenty-first century, Protestant or Catholic, brilliant or bad. That is because the phrase—right or wrong, good or bad—is at the heart of the ideology of the American Western genre. And the Western, wherever one happens to be made, represents a crystallization of America at the movies.[8] What a man has to do may be progressive or traditionalist, depending on the man of the moment and the film in which he appears. No matter: he does it (whatever "it" happens to be) not because he wants to but because he has to. Gentle or harsh, Alan Ladd or Clint Eastwood, he is a man on a mission.

For Eastwood's own sense of not only Christian or even Protestant but absolutely Puritanical mission, he reaches back past Ford, who no doubt would not have approved (*Clementine* is about taming, not scourging a town), to Hart. Ford's town is, at the end of *Clementine*, born again. The towns we observe in *Hell's Hinges* and *Unforgiven* curl up and die like Sodom and Gomorrah. In its final sequences *Clementine* reveals that in Ford's view even the nastiest place can prove capable of redemption. For Hart, as for Eastwood, the message is "Burn, baby, burn!"

In *Tumbleweeds* (King Baggot, 1925) we meet a couple in search of a homestead. Desperate, they kneel and pray for heavenly help. Immediately they come across a trace of farmable land. Fittingly humble, they pray again, this time expressing thanks. When the outlaw element tries to steal their homestead they pray a third time. At that moment, a figure rides forward across the prairie headed toward them. He (Hart) will provide the answer to their sincere request, employing his gun as a tool of wrath. Six decades later, in 1985, director-star Eastwood began one of his most famous films, *Pale Rider*, with an identical image. Eastwood's own character is a preacher, though not one who believes in forgiveness of sins. A settler child, Megan (Sydney Penny), gazes down at the dirt where her beloved dog lies dead, killed by rawhiders. Heartbroken, she recites the Lord's Prayer and asks God to bless her with a miracle. Her aura dissolves into our first image of the title character, riding in on a white horse.

Deliberately, squinty eyes staring straight ahead, the rider stolidly heads in their direction as we hear thunder up on the mountain. He appears oddly reminiscent of Charlton Heston as Moses in *The Ten Commandments* (Cecil B. DeMille, 1956), self-righteous, full of moral fury, and utterly . . . unforgiving. In *Pale Rider*, this preacher, one more man with no name, will coldly, calculatingly, clinically kill all the transgressors, none worthy of redemption. The bad cowboys in their graves at last, the good settlers will finally get on with their lives, the town purified through hellfire and brimstone. Without a word, the preacher mounts and returns to the high Sinai from whence he came with nary a backward glance.

That also describes the conclusion of *Shane*. In that 1953 film, however, the all-too-human hero played by Alan Ladd likely dies as he dissolves into the thousand hills. In *Pale Rider* the preacher may actually be deceased before he even arrives. A zombie from God, his stoic figure encounters an arch-enemy (John Russell) who, confused, states: "The man I'm looking for is dead." A Wild West Lazarus, the ghostly pale rider has risen from a plot of ground he passes and acknowledges. An even more significant distinction between the golden age of *Shane* and the dark era of Eastwood can be drawn between their iconic heroes. It is important to note that although he drew heavily from *Shane* for his narrative, Eastwood has spoken dismissively of that classic.[9] *Pale Rider* might be read as an answer to and repudiation of Stevens's classic in terms of its religious connotations. Shane attempts to avoid violence and wants nothing more than to become one with the farmers.

He cannot; he buys their tranquility in the future through bloodshed in the present, in the process damning himself to self-exile. Though he kills, Shane does so with reluctance, as a last measure. No wonder he has been described as "a savior in the saddle."[10] Though Shane does what he must, he would have preferred to cast his pistol aside. Eastwood's anti-hero has no such trepidations. Like Caesar, Eastwood's pale rider came, saw, and conquered.

The first Western that Eastwood directed, *High Plains Drifter* (1973), offers his original homage not to Ford but to Hart. It features a minimalist's vision of a rural crossroads not in the rich details of a Ford film but as a stark rendering that all but insists on an allegorical reading. Eastwood takes this a giant step further: his hell on earth is guarded by a dwarf (Billy Barty). The on-screen result could be described as that bizarre comedy Western *The Terror of Tiny Town* (Sam Newfield, 1938) as Federico Fellini might have remade it.

DWARF: What did you say your name was?
DRIFTER: I didn't!

Possibly he's the previous town marshal, whipped and killed by the populace. That's left unclear by an ambiguous ending. No question, though, that he arrived for blood. Not surprisingly, this film's vision reveals a contempt for organized religion and for the notion of the church as the town's moral center. By implication, Eastwood rejects Ford's point of view as hopelessly outdated, helping us grasp Wayne's reaction to Eastwood's work. Despite the public misconception that Eastwood more or less took over where Ford and Wayne left off, theologically as well as in terms of its politics the Eastwood Western practically satirizes the guarded optimism of Ford-Wayne-Fonda films, standing at the far side of this genre's long stretch of possibilities.

In Ford's Tombstone the preacherlike leader of the good flock extends his hand to Fonda's character and is, with a sincere smile, accepted by the good man with a gun. In *Pale Rider* a local religious leader makes the mistake of taking a friendly approach to the rider by calling him "brother."

DRIFTER: I'm *not* your brother.
REVEREND: We're all brothers in the eyes of God.

The rider stares at the man as if he's a fool and turns away in disgust. The townsfolk meet in church to discuss their problems, reminiscent of a scene in *High Noon* (Fred Zinnemann, 1952). That film rejected Ford's progressive view of the church as the town's communal conscience as the Deacon (Russell Simpson) and his men offer to help Earp at the O.K. Corral. In *High*

"Thank God for Josey Wales!" Eastwood's most memorable character in a Western he directed has more in common with Old Testament avenging angels than gentle Jesus. The famed logo shot in which pistols form a cross hints at an allegorical element. Courtesy Warner Brothers/Malpaso.

Band of outsiders. France's Jean-Luc Godard, who made a film with this title, is thought of as a leftist, Eastwood a man of the right. Both are actually radicals, as Clint's title character reveals in The Outlaw Josey Wales *when he creates a loose confederacy of society's dregs. Courtesy Warner Brothers/Malpaso.*

Noon, when Hadleyville's townsfolk refuse to leave their sanctuary, director Zinnemann and writer Carl Foreman set the pace for Eastwood Westerns; it is not surprising, then, that Wayne hated *High Noon* as much as he did Eastwood's films.[11]

Eastwood's vision proposes both radical religion and reactionary politics, qualifying the piece as far from the more mainstream Republicanism-cum-spirituality offered by Ford and Wayne. A cruel character, Eastwood in most of his guises seeks not justice or law and order but hard, cold revenge. He is not like many previous Western heroes (other than Hart), who are destroyed by indulging in blood-letting. Nothing in *High Plains Drifter* suggests even a patina of criticism of his approach. The drifter takes red paint and scribbles "Hell" over the signpost leading into Largo, recalling *Hell's Hinges*. When the drifter gives a frightened man orders to paint the town red and the fellow asks if that includes the church, with fiery eyes Eastwood's character spits out, "*Especially* the church!" Humanity, in the gospel according to Clint, exists beyond hope. His anti-hero brings not the possibility of redemption but outright Armageddon.

"It's what people know about themselves inside that makes them afraid," he mutters in a line that might be taken as the movie's message: a condemnation of humanity. The only significant precedent in the sound era occurred in *No Name on the Bullet* (Jack Arnold, 1959), in which a hired killer (Audie Murphy) rides into a similar town, paid by his unknown sponsor to shoot its worst citizen. Everyone in the area immediately assumes himself to be the target because of some despicable act in his past. We can perhaps better understand, then, why Leone, impressed by that film, had hoped to talk Murphy into playing the man with no name in his trilogy. As in *Hell's Hinges*, here is a town that deserves what it gets. The rider burns Largo to the ground on his way out, moving beyond avenging angel to a terminating one worthy of Luis Bunuel's anti-Catholic contemporary films.

In time, Eastwood's vision would mellow at least slightly. His character in *The Outlaw Josey Wales* (Eastwood, 1976) becomes a savior to a small, makeshift community. After their varied enemies are destroyed, an elderly woman looks upward and cries out: "Thank *you* for Josey Wales!" Even here Wales helps his flock to survive and flourish through violence, not only out of necessity but from desire for it. Wales may be heaven-sent, but it is from an early incarnation of Yahweh, not a gentle Jesus. He is not, like Shane, some savior in the saddle but a cold-eyed horseman of the coming apocalypse.

Ever less country for old men. Two anachronistic, aging lawmen team up for a final mission in Ride the High Country. *One (Joel McCrea) remains steadfast to "the code" they lived by, while the other (Randolph Scott) is sorely tested by the lure of gold and contemporary amorality. Courtesy Metro-Goldwyn-Mayer.*

THEN CAME SAM!
FROM PAPPY TO PECKINPAH

The death of God must be followed by a long torment of nihilism.
—FRIEDRICH WILHELM NIETZSCHE, *THUS SPOKE ZARATHUSTRA*, 1884

If any American-made Westerns exceed those of Eastwood in projecting a postmodern sensibility, they are the ones made by Sam Peckinpah (1925–1984). Essentially, the films of "Old Sam," as he was sometimes fondly as well as unappreciatively known, presaged the new American cinema that would include dark visions, *Taxi Driver* (Martin Scorsese, 1976) and *Apocalypse, Now* (Francis Coppola, 1979) among them. Peckinpah cut his artistic teeth as writer-director on 1950s TV Westerns such as *The Rifleman* and *Gunsmoke*, followed by his own *The Westerner* (1960), the most honest depiction of an old-time cowboy to appear on television at the time it was made. He then made a transition to movies with *The Deadly Companions* (1961). His characteristic attitude toward religion—profoundly pessimistic, though sometimes merely cynical—first appeared in this B movie. In a town that has a saloon but no church, the bartender rolls down a curtain to cover a painting featuring a nude woman, while a parson (Strother Martin) prepares to hold services.

At this early point, Peckinpah drew on elements from the films of Ford, who by the early 1960s had begun to consider retirement. Most obvious among the connections is that both directors depict respectable women in a disparaging light. One, who might have been among that all-female-citizens committee of Puritans driving prostitute Dallas (Claire Trevor) out of town in *Stagecoach*, scorns prostitute Kit Tildon (Maureen O'Hara) and her bastard son. "If they're going to heaven," the sad child tells his mother, "let's you and me *not* go." While Ford only attacked self-righteous extremists, Peckinpah is considerably less sparing. Religion, even of the natural and organic type Ford admires in *Clementine*, comes under attack in Peckinpah's body of work.

Ride the High Country (1962) was released only a few months after *The Man Who Shot Liberty Valance*. Ford cast John Wayne and James Stewart in roles that recapitulated much of their earlier work in A Westerns, while Peckinpah brought together their B oater equivalents Joel McCrea and Randolph Scott. McCrea plays Steve Judd, an old-time lawman who remains true to his code even as the encroachment of the early twentieth century causes the old frontier to fade. His one-time partner Gil Westrum (Scott) has long since capitulated to an emergent amorality, though our focal hero does not yet realize this. They, accompanied by a punk kid (Ron Starr), accept the job of riding off to a distant mining town and returning with a payload of gold. En route, the small party happens upon a little spread. The farmer (R. G. Armstrong) at once reveals that he's a Christian in the narrowest sense: "Oh, Lord! Forgive them the mercenary devices that bring them here!"

This self-righteous figure's arch approach is also directed at his teenage daughter, Elsa (Mariette Hartley). Catching her in a relatively innocent flirtation with the kid, the father beats and abuses the girl, certain that her sensuality, which clearly threatens him in a way that it doesn't anyone else, represents a continuing evil on earth. There's a strong suggestion that his deceased wife may have cheated on him, adding to his bitterness and anger. He represents traditionalist Puritanical Christianity at its worst. But while Ford consistently contrasted and condemned extremist behavior with natural, practical Christianity of a pantheistic American order, Peckinpah damns that too.

The mining camp on high turns out not to be a pastoral Eden but a rural slum full of degenerate men and women. A marriage ritual between the naïve girl and her fiancé (James Drury) begins quietly but transforms into a maimed rite worthy of those in Shakespeare's corrupt Denmark. The participants become ever drunker; the legality of the judge (Edgar Buchanan) is

Maimed rites. An anti-Romantic, Peckinpah portrays a community in Ride the High Country *that proves more corrupt than the city below. A virgin (Mariette Hartley) is forced by a cynical miner (James Drury) into a less than legal marriage in a brothel. Courtesy Metro-Goldwyn-Mayer.*

questionable. "I'm not a man of the cloth," he admits. "This is *not* a religious ceremony." God does not reside here, not even in a Romantic sense, though all live close to nature. No splendor will be found in this grass, no glory in the wildflowers. The groom, caring nothing for his virginal bride's hesitation, plans to take her by force. Worse, his male family members, led by a self-righteous patriarch (John Anderson) derived from Walter Brennan as Old Man Clanton in *Clementine*, appear eager to enjoy her after he's finished.

Whether or not God is dead in this early Peckinpah film, he surely isn't present. Here is an absurd cosmos, hurtling toward an endgame. Morality has become separated from objectivity, and values are now subjective at best, a point not lost on Steve Judd:

ELSA: My father says there's only right and wrong. Good and evil! Nothing in between. It isn't that simple, is it?

JUDD: No. It isn't. It should be. But it isn't.

No wonder that in addition to refusing all roles in Eastwood films, John Wayne never worked for Peckinpah, either. Peckinpah offered an early on-screen rejection in the Western genre of the worldview Wayne staunchly asserted two years earlier in *The Alamo*: "There is right and there is wrong!" Still, a nobility does surround McCrea's character Steve Judd, who, despite his knowledge that what should be falls short of what is, continues to operate in a moral fashion. If morality turns out to be but subjective, a mental construct that humans impose on the world rather than perceive in it, he has lived with this too long to give up on that idea now. He does not know whether his minor good actions in a sea of bad ones will win him a place in heaven, if it exists. He does understand that he has always operated in this fashion.

Now, Judd helps to redeem his fallen partner when he realizes the necessity of doing the right thing despite his nagging doubts. If existential in outlook, he will not surrender to nihilism.

WESTRUM: (*distraught*) What do you know?
JUDD: (*shrugging*) You just *know!*

What precisely does Judd know? That by dying with values intact if tested he may "enter God's house justified." It's the closest a postmodernist can come to heaven, and all he requires. Under the shadow of a huge mountain, as Steve Judd passes from this world to the next, if there is one, his melancholy smile suggests he has accomplished that.

In 1973 an older, more jaundiced Peckinpah would portray his version of an oft-told tale in *Pat Garrett and Billy the Kid*. Once again William Bonney (Kris Kristofferson) shoots down Bob Ohlinger (R. G. Armstrong), a cruel deputy who had tormented the Kid. To bring the incident more in line with Peckinpah's own vision, Ohlinger is played now as a scripture-spouting hypocrite who taunts Billy: "Repent, you son of a bitch!" Ohlinger is played by the same actor who was cast as the girl's father in *High Country*; essentially Armstrong plays that character again, this time as a historical man with a specific name.

Armstrong would again play a religious figure in *Major Dundee* (Sam Peckinpah, 1965), though this one has a considerably more likable nature. The script by Harry Julian Fink concerns a Civil War–era raid into Mexico by Union troops accompanied by Confederate prisoners to rescue several children from Apaches. The title character (Charlton Heston) initially rejects an offer from Reverend Dahlstrom to join his party: "God has nothing to do with it; I intend to smite the wicked, not save the heathen." Dahlstrom does come along and soon proves his worth by standing up for a black cavalry-man (Brock Peters) who, insulted by a racist Southerner, is heartily beating the bigot. "Preacher, you sure kick up a lot of dust with your sermons," one admiring volunteer beams. Dahlstrom is the most admirable religious man in all of Peckinpah's work; he even leads the soldiers in a chorus of "Shall We Gather at the River?"—a hymn associated with John Ford and Howard Hawks Westerns—after one of their company is killed. For once, Peckinpah offers nothing sardonic in the tone of a scene of reverence.

Then the film darkens. The group arrives at its destination on Christmas Eve and falls into an ambush. "Merry Christmas!" the major snarls, his voice full of irony, for they now appear abandoned by God. Intriguingly, the reverend changes roles at this point. Instead of a spiritual guide, he sets his Bible aside to become a secular figure and serve as a doctor to wounded men. When one of the Rebs (Warren Oates) is shot for attempted desertion, there is no prayer ceremony at the burial, as the image fades to black.[1] During the river battle with which the film concludes, Reverend Dahlstrom is seen fighting alongside the other men, apparently having entirely given up his previously assigned role. When he is killed, there is the sense that God has died with him; Peckinpah's vision pushes toward nihilism.

In the opening of Peckinpah's most controversial (in its time) and most discussed (ever since) Western, *The Wild Bunch* (1969), he makes clear that his complex vision is at once radical and reactionary; he scorns the romantic liberal point of view as hopelessly naïve while satirizing all Christian conservatism as equally invalid. A dozen gunmen disguised in uniforms of General John Pershing's expeditionary force into Mexico circa 1916 ride into a sleepy little Texas border town. Nothing is as it seems; apparent forces of law and order have arrived to create chaos. Worse than the adults are the small children. Pike (William Holden), the outlaw leader, reins his horse by them, glancing down at their play. The Mexican boys and girls have captured a scorpion; they drop it onto an anthill while giggling. Immediately the foes struggle, the scorpion stronger though the ants outnumber it. The children's eyes fill with wicked joy at this mini-Armageddon. We catch a quick glimpse of Pike, horrified at the contrast between what he thought was innocent play and the cruelty the children enact instead. Soon Pike will set into motion a horrible act as well. Here is a film that takes the naturalism from Frank Norris's *McTeague* and Erich von Stroheim's *Greed* and reprises it for modern viewers.

Produced in 1968 and released a year later, *The Wild Bunch* offered a genre piece that paralleled in attitude the confused mindset of a rapidly altering America. JFK's liberal idealistic New Frontier seemed far more distant than even five years earlier. Shortly the violence of Vietnam would be carried to the United States with the Kent State University shootings; any belief that Americans were engaged in another crusade of the type fought against Hitler a quarter-century earlier was rendered nil once the public learned of the Mai Lai massacre, a slaughter of Southeast Asian civilians by members of the U.S. military.[2] When Pike steps into the bank he and his bunch plan to rob, the words he utters are the same as those of at least one officer in Vietnam to his American troops: "If they move, *kill* them!"

Irony overcomes Peckinpah's opening as outside on the streets, Puritanical townspeople gather around a wild-eyed preacher (Dub Taylor) who incites them to march down the streets. They hold hands and sing "Shall we gather at the river," though in context this seems less a happy reference to Ford's *Clementine* than a desire to undermine any sentimental worldview. These are not the tolerant pioneers of Ford's imagination but narrow-minded moralists. They do not want to save souls, only to shut down the saloons. "I solemnly promise, God help me, to abstain from all liquors!" one cries out, part of a growing temperance movement that was at once religious and political,[3] setting the scene for the fusion of these American elements in the early twenty-first century.

Then there are the armed men with badges, led by a railroad boss (Albert Dekker) who wants to wipe out the wild bunch not because what they do is wrong but because they cost his company money. He is a far cry from Henry Fonda as Wyatt Earp. At this man's insistence, townsfolk have not been warned as to what's about to happen; he would rather see the innocent die than allow word of his trap to possibly become known to Pike Bishop. The outlaws' raid on the bank is known to the marshals because a former gang member (Robert Ryan), now a toady for the railroad, informed on his one-time compatriots, but the populace has been kept ignorant owing to a fear of tipping off Pike. When the shooting starts, parading Christians are caught in the crossfire and mowed down by both sides. A sense of absurdity rather than old-fashioned action fills the screen with what would come to be called Peckinpah's "ballet of blood."[4]

As surviving gang members ride out, they pass the Mexican children who have now escalated their play by dropping matches down on both scorpion and ants as they desperately attempt to kill one another before all are consumed by the flames. The children laugh louder than ever, their reaction chilling to even the most jaded audience. When the holocaust is over, little

Anglo children rush out onto the streets to playfully reenact the shootout they have witnessed, giddy at the sight of all the dead bodies in grotesque positions worthy of the legendary painting *Guernica*. Here, though, the dead and dying are not portrayed as innocent victims, and there is no simple enemy to blame. Any moral dialectic still present during the pre–World War II era is gone. All is chaos, anarchy, and confusion, an amoral universe in which "good" and "bad" are reduced to outdated concepts.

Once again, the American frontier—however painstakingly authentic the details of costuming, guns, and gear—does not exist on screen for its own sake. Rather, it is a template onto which a filmmaker at any specific moment may impress a worldview. The auteur's filmcraft also reflects the way the frontier appears to the generation in the audience, through manipulation of genre conventions.

When we rejoin Pike and a few others out on the prairie, one man who is too wounded to keep up is shot dead by Pike. Some of the others suggest that a burial might be in order, but Pike's closest companion, Dutch (Ernest Borgnine), brings his cynical view of religious rituals into the conversation. Dutch sarcastically suggests they might also sing hymns over the dead man, then hold "a church supper" in his honor. Realizing they were wrong, the gang leaves the body to rot or be eaten by buzzards.

Incredibly, though, these figures of darkness who might have represented the bad in a Ford film are the best that this God-forsaken realm has to offer. Agents of chaos these men may be; still, there is something about them that makes them worthy of our attention, perhaps even admiration, in a way neither the Christians nor the Law and Order League can in this context elicit. In an absurd cosmos, the wild bunch represents the best of a terrible lot to which humanity has devolved. On some level, while spreading chaos they continue to live by values. Although the code of the underworld rather than the code of the West, it at least evokes loyalty:

PIKE: When you side with a man, you stay with him. And if you can't do that, you're like some . . . *animal*!

When a young Latino gang member, Angel (Jaime Hernandez), is captured and tortured by Mexican troops, Pike leads his remaining companions on a suicide mission that allows them to go out in style as he mutters,

"I wouldn't have it any other way." Here we encounter a universe in which religion is not only irrelevant but so absurd that the characters cannot even consider it as a viable alternative.

"It's all spoilt now," one mountain man sadly sighs toward the end of A. B. Guthrie's novel *The Big Sky* as he accepts that a golden age, real or imagined, has passed. Likewise, an old mentor to the wild bunch (Edmond O'Brien) observes, "It ain't the way it used to be, but it'll do." He speaks to Deke (Ryan), the man who betrayed the gang for a previous betrayal by Pike. Now these two put aside their differences and ride off together. Life goes on. It may no longer mean anything, but it does continue.

Peckinpah allows the image of the two men riding away to dissolve into an earlier scene, an over-the-shoulder shot looking back as the bunch leaves a Mexican village where they were once hailed as compadres, as heroes, even, to descend into oblivion or immortality. The poignant effect is enhanced by soft, sweet Latino music. We move into the image, are at one with it, totally awash in its seeming reality. But Peckinpah will not end the film on that note. Suddenly this widescreen shot transforms into a carefully confined rectangle that swiftly shrinks in size until it appears like some horizontal postage stamp on an enormous black screen. We are allowed to consider the scene in this form, clearly not reality now but a self-conscious creation by an artist, only for a moment. This diminished recall of those times before everything "got spoilt" disappears as the words "The End" appear over that spot on the screen.

Somehow, we sense these words refer not just to the movie we've been watching but the genre itself, at least in any traditional form. For this has been a transitional piece, evoking genre conventions only to destroy them once and for all. Even the phrase "The End" disappears, leaving us, finally, in total darkness. That, of course, is the essential theme to the piece we have just witnessed: postmodern nihilism by way of Sam Peckinpah.

"Are you listenin', God?" If The Wild Bunch *convinced many moviegoers that Peckinpah was both nihilist and atheist,* The Ballad of Cable Hogue *(with Jason Robards) suggested otherwise. Courtesy Warner Brothers.*

COUNT NO MAN LUCKY UNTIL HIS DEATH

THE WESTERN AS AMERICAN TRAGEDY

Tragedy is a human drama taking place under the constant eye of a deity.
—JOHN SIMON, *NATIONAL REVIEW*, OCTOBER 16, 1989

Though the bulk of Peckinpah's work during the 1960s would be of an increasingly violent nature, he did begin the following decade with a film that many critics considered a throwback to the kinder, gentler sort of elegiac Western he had presented in *Ride the High Country*. *The Ballad of Cable Hogue* (Peckinpah, 1970), following hard upon *The Wild Bunch*, served in Old Sam's canon much the same sort of a spot that the forgiving story of *The Outlaw Josey Wales* had in relationship to the harsh, embittered *Pale Rider*—*Ballad* offers at least a sign of hope in a dark world, of guarded optimism in spite of all the blackness circling around and above. Here Peckinpah spins what seems to be shaping up as a leisurely yarn about an old desert rat (Jason Robards) abandoned in the desert by his partners (L. Q. Jones, Strother Martin) when their water supply can only support two men. The area appears desolate, a barren badlands identified by the ugliest animals: a gila monster in the opening shot, a rattlesnake at mid-movie, a half-starved coyote in the final shot. Cable wanders the landscape and—by chance, destiny, perhaps a miracle worthy of those old-fashioned novels by people like Peter Kyne—happens on a spring. After reviving himself, Cable files a claim, builds a way station for wagon trains and stagecoaches, and in time becomes successful and even relatively wealthy. Always, though, he waits for the day when fate will deliver his one-time betrayers into his clutches, that theme of long-standing revenge underlining this atypical genre piece.

Like the overwhelming sense of nihilism that presses down cruelly and constantly on the self-doomed members of the wild bunch, if God has died no one thought to inform Cable. From the very beginning, while still searching for a drop to drink, Cable trustingly gazes heavenward:

> Ain't had no water since yesterday, Lord. Gettin' a little thirsty. Uh, just thought I'd ... mention it.

The silence prevails, temporarily at least, as it might in a mid-1960s Bergman film. That doesn't stop Cable from trying again, his throat now so parched he can hardly speak:

> Yesterday, I told you I was thirsty. And I thought you might send me some water. Now, if I'm a sinner, send me a drop or two, and I won't do it no more. (Pause.) I *mean* that, Lord!

Whether he spoke in seriousness, mockery, or some combination of the two, Cable Hogue has made a deal with his maker. The question is whether God will, if he exists and has not abandoned our little world out of disappointment in humankind, answer. Still, though, nothing. Finally, Cable grows arrogant, much like Moses, commanded to beg a rock for water, and instead, tongue-tied, striking it with his staff:

> Ah, four days without water. You don't think I put in my suffering, Lord, *you* try goin' dry fer a spell.

At last, he gives up any hope of surviving. This does not, however, turn him into a disbeliever. Like some Tevye of the Great Southwest, Cable continues the conversation:

> Lord, *you* call it. Amen!

At that moment, there's water, directly beside him. His prayers have been answered. There is a God! Here is tangible proof. After drinking his fill, though, Cable—like so many tragic figures in literature, particularly those in plays from the Greek Classical era[1]—quickly forgets the humility in the words he spoke that seemingly caused a higher power to save him. Only when Cable admitted his weakness, throwing himself on the mercy of this force, did he receive what he'd asked for. Like so many before him, Cable falls into the hubris that has brought down tragic figures in works from Sophocles through Shakespeare:

This is Cable Hogue. *I* found it. Me!

Yes, he will reap the rewards of the water, which, as a stage driver (Slim Pickens) tells him, is "worth more than gold." Here we are again in capitalist America; politics will shortly join religion as a central theme. But no matter how high Cable rises in the world of men—or more correctly, this microcosm of the world—and no matter that he conducts himself decently enough, Cable must as inexorably as Oedipus be brought down for the arrogance of excessive pride. There is no harm in conceiving himself smarter and stronger than other men. More than once he proves that to be the case. Cable's tragedy—the only source of a true tragedy in the ancient world, as here on America's wasteland, a frontier equivalent of that stretch between Thebes and Corinth, Sam Peckinpah's own Colonnus—comes when a hero loses sight of his place in the cosmos, far beyond an immediate here and now. Despite what he dared say, Cable did not find that water; God gave it to him. And, as the book insists, the Lord giveth and taketh away, whether Yahweh from kings of old Israel, Zeus from the princes of Attica, or God from an American who dares to believe the oldest and most dangerous falsehood: that he is the master of his own fate. Lest we forget, when Shakespeare wrote that line for Julius Caesar, he put it in the mouth not of the flawed but decent Brutus but the Machiavellian villain Cassius. As always, we must consider the source.

Shortly, a Greek chorus arrives on the scene in the guise of a stagecoach full of people. Among those inside is a well-heeled businessman (William Mims) and his overweight, pretentious wife (Kathleen Freeman). While commenting on Cable's lonely situation, the man resorts to Bible language: "the wrath of God" will be visited upon people of "disobedience" like

Beware of false prophets. Joshua (David Warner) presents himself as a speaker of the faith of no particular religion in The Ballad of Cable Hogue. *He is accepted into Cable's emergent American empire so long as he pays his own way. Courtesy Warner Brothers.*

Hogue. The man casts the curse because Cable, already becoming a raw capitalist, refuses to give people water unless they pay. Although Cable (and we) might forget those words, they will return to haunt him. Shortly after the stagecoach leaves, another religious voice appears, as Joshua (David Warner). His first words with Cable, who almost shoots the intruder, are significant:

JOSHUA: I'm a man of God!
CABLE: Well, you damn near joined him.

Joshua represents religion at its most ethically situational, trying to use his white collar to get some of the water other men must pay for, mixing Christianity with a low form of capitalism disguised as mercy.

JOSHUA: Cast thy bread upon the waters—
CABLE: Ten cents, you pious bastard. What church did you say you were with?
JOSHUA: The Church of the Wayfaring Stranger, a denomination of my own creation.

Enthusiastically, he shares with Cable photographs of the "sisters" he has met and "enlightened." All are nude or seminude images of fallen women. Joshua uses his fake religiosity to conquer as many females as possible; a penny-pincher, he would like to avoid payment if in any way possible. Cable shows no interest in extending any such Christian charity. Pay or die of thirst. Josh pays.

Cable may represent individualism, but there must also be a community for this American equation to be complete. He heads into the nearest polis. In town, religion turns out to be far more conventional and Puritanical than that expressed by Josh, precisely the sort of narrow-mindedness Ford condemned. As Cable spends some time with the blond hooker Hildy (Stella Stevens), his attempts to fully enjoy their sexual encounter are interrupted by one more of those oft-despised preachers of hellfire and brimstone (John Anderson) howling from the street below. "God's presence and material elements are being threatened by the devil!" he screeches. This extreme conservative sees any scientific or technological breakthrough, some of which have begun to pop up in the town, as signs of a coming apocalypse: "Inventions are the work of Satan!" His congregation sings "Shall We Gather at the River?" referencing the frequent use of that hymn in the now-nostalgic Ford films. As if to heap insult on injury, Peckinpah has their tent fall down on

"Shall We Gather at the River?" Though this traditional hymn appears in films by John Ford and Sam Peckinpah, the context is different. Ford treated his religious pilgrims with deep respect, while here in The Ballad of Cable Hogue *Peckinpah reduces them to the level of circus clowns. Courtesy Warner Brothers.*

the righteous people inside, causing them to stumble around in fast motion like so many Keystone Kops.

Earlier, to talk a banker into believing he really has found water, Cable mentions that Joshua has seen it and can verify its existence.

> CABLE: You wouldn't doubt a man of the Gospel, would you?
> BANKER: That's the *first* man I'd doubt.

Cable's eyes twinkle. He knows at once that he and the banker will become great friends. Organized religion, not the presence or worth of God, is attacked here. Not long afterward, Joshua likewise heads into town, announcing, "If I cannot rouse heaven, I will attempt to raise hell." He does so with a young married woman (Susan O'Connor) and attempts to use a telegram, obviously sad, that has just now reached the vulnerable woman as a means of seducing her. Josh is not above employing his collar as a means to win trust, and soon he is fondling her breasts. "I feel your pain . . . flowing out of your heart . . . and into my hand." The interruption of her husband (Gene Evans) entering the room causes Joshua to change tactics; he forces the fellow down on his knees and offers a blessing before making a run back to the sanctuary of Cable Springs.

If Joshua has any appropriate words, they have to do with Cable's burning desire to find and kill his one-time partners; he tries to talk his friend out of such violence.

> JOSHUA: "Vengeance is mine, sayeth the Lord."
> CABLE: That's OK with me, just so long as he don't take too long and I can watch.

Hildy, thrown out of town by the self-professed good women, a reference to Dallas's treatment in Ford's *Stagecoach*, joins the men at the spring. Her good common sense and truly (not pretentiously) Christian views serve as Cable's conscience. She agrees wholeheartedly with Joshua:

> It ain't worth it, Hogue. Revenge always turns sour.

It is Hildy the prostitute who represents religion most honestly and simply; she says grace before the three of them eat with sincerity and apprecia

Where spirituality and sexuality meet. Peckinpah's off-handed approach to the two sorts of passion, religious and romantic, brings them together in a scene in Cable Hogue *that has Joshua (David Warner) seducing a young bride (Susan O'Connor). Courtesy Warner Brothers.*

tion. Apparently, her warnings about vengeance and its corruptive potential have an impact. When destiny finally does bring the two former partners back into Cable's self-created microcosm, he shoots only the one (Jones) who is about to kill him and spares the other (Martin), who, however despicable, does not go for a gun. Fate in time also brings back Hildy, who had left their little American Eden for San Francisco. There she did finally fulfill her hope to become rich; she married a wealthy man who later, she assures us, died "happy." Now they are both successful. Cable turned his back on the corruptive element of revenge; Hildy sees no reason why she and Hogue can't enjoy life:

> We got nothin' but time, Hogue.
> Nothin' but time.

Time, though, is and always has been the essence of the tragic vision. In Peckinpah's cosmos, the Lord works in mysterious ways, as in allegorical narratives since the first human stood on two legs. For humans to put off what is important for too long is to pretend to be God, which can only lead to disaster. Cable may well have redeemed himself somewhat by setting vengeance aside. While that may save his soul, it is not enough to allow him to escape

Killed while attempting to hold back the twentieth century. The automobile serves as a harbinger of the shape of things to come; Hildy (Stella Stevens) realizes Cable (Robards) will die happy, not having to face a future in which old men are unwelcome. Courtesy Warner Brothers.

some sort of celestial punishment. His hubris in claiming personal reward for what the Lord provided may seem a minor mistake to a modern realist. To the metaphysic, it's the very sort of thing that cursed Oedipus some 2,500 years ago. God or the gods must be acknowledged; failure to do so proves the ultimate flaw. Ironically, just as the preacher in town predicted, an invention provides the deus ex machina by which Cable meets his end. Hildy's motorcar slips gears and rolls down the hill; Cable is run over by a symbol of the future. The film began with his attempt to strike a pact with God and ends with a funeral oration. Joshua does the speaking, relying on a biblical allusion:

He came stumbling out of the wilderness, like a prophet of old.

His attitude concerning Cable's worth comes far closer to Ford's Catholicism than William S. Hart's Protestantism:

He wasn't a good man. He wasn't a bad man. But, Lord, he was a man!

And, as such, the very template of the vision of man in relationship to God is offered from Genesis:

In some ways, he was your divine reflection, Lord. Heaven may be beyond hope; hell a distinct possibility. Hogue lived here in the desert. Hell will not prove too hot for him.

More likely than not, Cable will find himself in purgatory. As Joshua describes Cable, the deceased was the essence of the American spirit when it comes to religion, a true pantheist at heart:

He never went to church. He didn't need to. The whole desert was his cathedral.

In his mellowest film, then, Peckinpah appears notably and perhaps surprisingly similar to Ford in decrying the worst forms of organized religion through the drama that all takes place under the constant gaze of a deity who may sometimes seem far away but can always intervene. Only in dying can we be assured nothing on earth can ever again hurt us, physically or spiritually. The Greeks believed in death as a merciful release from the horrors of life. So, too, apparently, did the ultimate moviemaking maverick, Old Sam.

Happiness is a warm gun. The endurance of firearms in what critic John G. Cawelti has labeled "the six-gun mystique" must be dealt with by any serious student of the West or Westerns. Here, little boys and grown men stare adoringly at the "one in a thousand" prize rifle in Winchester '73. *Courtesy Universal Pictures.*

BORN AGAIN

OF COWBOYS, CHRISTIANITY, AND CONVERSION

No one can see the kingdom of God without being born again.
—JESUS TO NICODEMUS, JOHN 3:3.

Though neither politics nor religion is openly addressed in *The Naked Spur* (Anthony Mann, 1950), the film assumed a liberal approach to the ideology of raw capitalism while taking a traditional stance toward non-Puritanical Judeo-Christian values. James Stewart stars as Howard Kemp, an embittered man who has turned bounty hunter, bringing in outlaws not because it's the right thing to do but "strictly for the money." He captures the wicked Ben Vandergroot (Robert Ryan) accompanied by Lina Patch (Janet Leigh), who has become the villain's virtual slave. There is no moral put-down of her for this circumstance; she represents yet another flesh-and-blood angel of mercy, indicated by strains of "Beautiful Dreamer" on the soundtrack whenever she comes on screen. The gun as a way of life is accepted here as well, as it is in *Winchester '73* and Mann's other Westerns.

The killing of her despised master by the hero does not bother Lina at all. As one of the women in the musical *Chicago* might say, he had it comin'. At the end, though, the hero must make a moral choice: bury the body and ride away with the girl as his common-law wife or bring the body back for the reward and, in the process, lose her forever. Here arrives the protagonist's moment of truth. Mann cuts to a close-up of Leigh, more sensuous yet more ethereal than ever. With great difficulty, Kemp does the right thing. The final shot conveys a purity so convincingly rendered that even a postmodernist could approve of its artistry if not accept the philosophy: as celestial music plays, the two ride off toward a pantheistic heaven on earth. Simply put, Stewart's character has been born again.

This concept of conversion underlines many Westerns, *Shenandoah* (Andrew V. McLaglen, 1965) typical of them. Here Stewart plays a Southern patriarch who hopes his family can remain neutral during the Civil War. In the evenings he prays before supper since he gave his word to his late lamented wife that he would do so. But a tragic arrogance appears in his tone and words: "God, *we* cleared this land. Done it all by ourselves, but we thank *you* just the same." He merely goes through the motions, also the case on Sundays when they all attend church. When his youngest son is seized by Yankees, causing the patriarch and most of his offspring to head out in search of the boy, the situation appears divine punishment for past hubris. At the end, the patriarch returns to the farm, but most of his children have died in accidents.

Though the arrogance has been beaten out of his tone, the words remain the same at evening prayer: "We . . . uh . . . It would not be here . . . [if] we hadn't done it . . . ourselves." This time, though, he pauses; he simply cannot continue. Devastated, he visits his wife's grave as a last resort. "If only I knew what you thought . . . " His monologue halts as church bells ring in the distance. With a sad smile, he confides to Martha, "You never give up, do you?" The coincidence strikes him as meaningful; he packs up the surviving family members, and they go to the meeting. The look in this character's eyes suggests he wants more than anything to be born again, but he needs some sign.

He receives it. At that point, the missing son reappears, by fate or happenstance. The father takes this as a nod from on high. So does the pastor (Denver Pyle), who smiles and asks the congregation, "Shall we rise and sing?"

On the frontier, history's or Hollywood's, religion may not provide a man's first option but can offer his last resort. As pioneer John Doucette says in *Quincannon, Frontier Scout* (Lesley Selander, 1956), "Three things a man has to have handy in the West: a dry rifle, something to eat, and a prayer. Many times, a prayer's the only answer." The idea of being born again, closer in concept to Protestant regeneration than to Catholic redemption,[1] has

A sign from above. (a) James Stewart's farmer in Shenandoah *swears on his wife's grave that he'll bring their family to church as she wanted though he no longer believes. (b) When with the desperation of some Old Testament patriarch he begs for a sign, a long-lost son arrives during the ceremony. Courtesy Universal Pictures.*

been around for centuries, but the ideology of it solidified into a movement in the late 1950s and early 1960s in direct reaction to the perceived threats of communism abroad and nihilism at home. Films like *The Naked Spur* and adaptations of Kyne's *Three Godfathers* contain a germ of the idea in embryo, and *The Alamo* portrays the idea outright. Individual spiritual rebirth leading to salvation returned as a viable option in the frenzied late 1960s.

By 1970 the born-again movement had become organized, efficient, and widespread. While it has been associated with conservative politics, in recent years fused first with the Republican Party and then the tea-party movement, we must note that our first born-again president was Jimmy Carter, a liberal Democrat. Johnny Cash, a popular country singer and TV cowboy, combined his traditionalist beliefs with progressive politics. In the twenty-first century, the ideology has mostly solidified within more reactionary elements of our deeply divided red state/blue state dichotomy.

A predecessor to *The Alamo* in an emergent subgenre, *Gunfire* (William Berke, 1950) more or less offered an early example during the postwar era. McCarthyism at home, with its divisive impact on the nation, and the Korean conflict overseas led to the realization that there never would be a war to end all wars. Former sinner-outlaw Frank James (Don "Red" Barry) finds religion here. When asked, following brother Jesse's death, if he's going to head out after the Ford boys, the older James brother replies, "Vengeance is mine, sayeth the Lord," then goes back to farming. From this point on the film's incarnation of Frank James constantly reads and quotes from a Bible, far closer to the truth than the historical character's dramatic yet fanciful pursuit of the two fugitives in *The Return of Frank James* (Fritz Lang, 1940) with Henry Fonda.

In *Gunfire*, Frank is nothing if not consistent. When his son (Paul Jordan) lies to a lawman about his father's whereabouts, the boy expects to receive praise for helping dad. Instead, Frank takes out his belt and whips the boy for breaking God's commandment about lying. When he is at last pushed to the limit, Frank does ride out after Charlie Ford (Steve Pendleton). Bob (Roger Anderson) already is dead in this fictionalized version. Not wanting her husband to renege on his vows, Frank's wife (Kathleen Magginetti) calls after him, "At least take your Bible. And give him a chance!" Frank does as told, seeking justice rather than revenge.

The same narrative and thematic paradigm recurs more than a decade and a half later in a more ambitious film, *Nevada Smith* (Henry Hathaway, 1966). Drawn from the most compelling section of Harold Robbins's novel *The Carpetbaggers* (1961), this epic film relates a yarn about a quiet youth (Steve McQueen) incited to track down and kill each of the three men (Karl Malden, Arthur Kennedy, Martin Landau) who murdered the hero's Anglo father and raped his Indian mother. A reversal of audience expectations occurs when the boy is discovered alone on the prairie by neighbors (John Doucette, Josephine Hutchinson):

MR. McCANLES: Revenge isn't God's way.
MRS. McCANLES: You go get 'em, Max!

For once, it is the husband who warns against taking the vengeance trail, the wife who encourages the youth, Max Sand, to ride out for blood lust.

Cowboy crucifixion. Nevada Smith *rates as another anti-gun Western; the logo image of Steve McQueen suggests one more Christian allegory. Courtesy Paramount/Embassy Pictures.*

Perhaps her reasoning can be better appreciated when we consider the terrible fate of another woman, presumably her only female friend. Max goes through the process of what Joseph Campbell might have called the hero quest.[2] An older mentor, Jonas Cord Sr. (Brian Keith), teaches the boy Max to use a gun for his protection but tries to dissuade him from employing it for vengeance and thus destroying his soul. Cord teaches Max to read in hopes of civilizing—that is, Christianizing—him. Not too surprisingly, the book he reads is the Bible. If Max can't learn from the wisdom found there, Cord warns him, "you'll turn yourself into the same kind of *animal* you're trying to track down." This clearly is not a Romantic Western, as it implies that natural man is not the best man.

Various women Max meets and loves along the way—a Native American (Janet Margolin) he convinces to give up prostitution, a Cajun (Suzanne Pleshette) whose death he inadvertently causes—try to dissuade him from vengeance. "You're a dirty *animal*," the Cajun tells him with her final breath, "worse than the man you killed." Max's eyes reveal at the movie's midpoint that she is right. The central question: Having killed twice, can he find salvation in time?

The answer is yes. Toward the end, Max has shed the skin of the nice boy he once was and assumed the self-created identity Nevada Smith, a cold-blooded gunman. Yet in a chance meeting with a dedicated priest (Raf Vallone), Max recalls Cord's heartfelt warnings. "Stop while you can," the priest begs, handing Max another Bible. "Save yourself!" When Max confronts the final killer (Malden), he cannot pull the trigger. As in the later *Ballad of Cable Hogue*, the bad man mistakenly thinks our hero to be a coward. Rather he's become, as in the final line of dialogue in that Peckinpah film, "a man!" Not in the macho sense; actually, the opposite of that. A human being.

Only a fool would fail to grasp how much courage it takes *not* to murder his enemy. Here is Wild Bill Elliott from *The Showdown* revised for a mid-1960s audience. "You're just not worth killing," he says, leaving vengeance to the Lord. At that moment Nevada Smith disappears forever and Max Sand is born again.

A relatively recent addition to the religious Western developed during the early twenty-first century. Most of these films were produced by small indie companies in Western states. They appear to be created in reaction to Hollywood's desertion of old-fashioned, traditional Westerns and its embracing of the more nihilistic form of the genre. *No Country for Old Men* might be

A ray of hope. During the 1940s even the darkest of noir Westerns allowed for a hint of Christian values in a world on the brink. In The Ox-Bow Incident a spiritual African American (Leigh Whipper) embodies decency. Courtesy Twentieth Century-Fox.

thought of as a fair representation of the edgy consciousness that controls Hollywood today, while what once constituted mainstream mentality for movies has had to go underground, an idea associated during the 1960s with the radical left and now more likely with the religious right.

In *Jericho* (Merlin Miller, 2000), the angelic loner Joshua, apparently the Bible character reborn on the American frontier, is played by African American actor Leon Coffee. Josh finds an amnesiac Anglo (Mark Valley) and in caring for him calls the man Jericho. This Joshua fights his battle not with a sword of fire but a sweet savior's kindness, harming no one, helping the lost soul to regain his identity. Learning that his ward may possibly be a killer, Joshua spends seven years trying to save the man's soul, admitting he's doing "a little work for the Lord." This and other films combine what were once thought to be liberal-progressive attitudes toward race with what are still perceived as traditionalist views about faith.

One vivid example of this subgenre is *Miracle at Sage Creek* (James Intveld, 2005). Thadd Turner's script sets the concept of goodness in religious faith, cutting across any issues deemed insignificant. Most obvious among them is race. Billy (Carey Thompson), a black man who drives the stagecoach, is treated in a colorblind manner by all the town's good Anglos because of Billy's obvious adherence to Christian values. This hardly would have been the case in the actual West. Far closer to reality was the vision in *The Ox-Bow Incident* (William A. Wellman, 1943), based on a 1940 novel by Walter Van Tilburg Clark. The religious black man Sparks (Leigh Whipper), perhaps the only true Christian in following the ways of Jesus in a town composed of pompous Anglo Christians, is marginalized by other citizens. They do not speak to him as they do one another and never let him attend the whitewashed church. Yet when three innocent victims are lynched by those very people, now a mob, it is Sparks who prays and sings a hymn for their souls.

In Intveld's contemporary Christian Dream West, *Miracle at Sage Creek* concerns the testing of an Anglo family's faith. Though the drama is supposedly set on the frontier, each family member must pass through a moral crisis on the order of what many serious-minded Christians face today. The father, Seth (Daniel Quinn), senses immediately that something has gone awry and their family values are on the edge of collapsing as their life situation sours. One breakfast sequence with Grandpa and the children sets up the situation and their problems.

> SETH (TO CHILD): Forgot to say your prayers this morning? (*The child doesn't answer.*) Helped me a lot at your age.
> GRANDPA: Ike doesn't pray.
> SETH: Some people lose their way.

Ike (David Carradine) is this film's version of the menacing cattle baron from countless earlier oaters. Here, his hardness and cruelty specifically are assigned to this embittered man's lack of religious faith. In a variation on Charles Dickens's *A Christmas Carol* (1843), Ike proves to be such a Western Scrooge that he refuses to give his cowhands the holiday off. "Just another workday," he scoffs. As to Seth and his wife, Mary (Sarah Aldrich), whose long-standing faith also is tested by their increasingly difficult circumstances, the filmmakers go out of their way—perhaps surprisingly to some observers—to make clear that minister Seth and his beloved Mary enjoy a healthy sex life. This is not some Victorian-era vision of the Old West in which sexuality even for married couples is to be scorned. In this enlightened, modernized Christian vision, current values are projected onto the past. The evangelical auteur sees nothing wrong with a husband and wife enjoying each other's company sensually as well as spiritually, as we can clearly tell from their moments together when alone.

Still, they must overcome existential doubt. When the child Kit (Wyatt Turner) runs a high fever and appears about to die, Mary assaults her husband: "Where's your God now?" Even pagan religions are, perhaps surprisingly, in this context acknowledged as essentially good. While Seth prays to Jesus, an elderly Native medicine man stops by the cabin and adds his sincere request to Wakan-Tonka. Faith, in the end, is faith. The Tiny Tim figure recovers. True belief in a higher power conquers all, even Ike, who has hated Indians ever since several family members were killed in a raid. Now that a Native American has aided in bringing beloved Kit back from the brink, our Ebenezer is born again. "I hope we can live together as neighbors," he says to the previously estranged Anglos and also to the Indians, racism defeated by religion, "as neighbors . . . and *friends*." That's good enough for Mary, whose own renewed commitment is evident in what she tells her husband as they sit down for Christmas dinner: "Seth, will you say grace?"

As in *Jericho*, what was once considered a radical leftish insistence on racial and ethnic integration has now become American mainstream, even as what was once the Hollywood Western's mainstream point of view on faith now appears in alternative films too square for the hip Hollywood of today. Still, there is a market for these born-again Westerns as well as for their nihilistic opposites. Albeit marginal, a red-state Western—though one that has been expanded to encompass what were in the past considered blue-state values about race and ethnicity—has organically evolved out of America's altered political and religious terrain. The existence of each reaffirms the genre's broad scope and ability to express contrasting ideas from different artists for their varied constituencies. This has always been true of the cinematic canvas we call the Western.

A time for faith. Perhaps no single image so vividly captures the old men and their faith-based politics as John Wayne's direct address to God in The Alamo. *Such a sequence seems unlikely to ever appear again in today's postmodern and often nihilist Westerns from today's radicalized Hollywood. Courtesy Batjac Productions/United Artists.*

NO COUNTRY FOR BOLD MEN

THE WESTERN FILM IN THE
TWENTY-FIRST CENTURY

Oh, give me land, lots of land under starry skies above
Don't fence me in

—COLE PORTER, 1934

If the born-again Westerns of the early twenty-first century represent a pendulum swing away from the near-nihilistic films that preceded them during
the final days of the twentieth, then *No Country for Old Men* (Joel Coen
and Ethan Coen, 2007) might be read as the next, perhaps necessary stage
of a cinema-studies Marxist dialectic: the considerable force of movement in
one direction creates an even more powerful shift toward its opposite. In this
piece we encounter both politics and religion of a highly conventional order
that are challenged in the most outrageous manner.

In its opening sequences, this film, derived from a novel by Cormac
McCarthy and set in Texas during the 1970s, we meet a world-weary lawman
(Tommy Lee Jones) considering retirement. In the present tense, Ed Tom
drifts back over his career in the most melancholy of tones: "I was sheriff of
this county when I was twenty-five years old," he sighs. His entire life, Ed
wants us to understand, has been dedicated to enforcing law and order as
codified in the American legal system. Implied here is that the rules evolved

from the U.S. Constitution, as influenced by British common law whose moral ideology is traceable back to the Bible. Ed Tom has always revered law and order as it has developed in America, as well as the divine law he, like fellow traditional folk, believes to be handed down by Yahweh to Moses, from him to the people, then and now, once and forever. Amen!

Ed Tom—in many regards the last of the old-timers—has, however imperfectly, done the best he could to live by a value system some might tag the code of the West. That West is America itself, distilled from actual history into a dream of who Americans should and ideally could be as a people. That code, a twentieth-century conception in popular arts, narrative and visual, derived from Romantic notions of European chivalry. Imposed on nineteenth-century fictional and nonfictional characters and settings, the code was ingested into a mythology that for much of the citizenry no longer holds true during the twenty-first century. Often, as in *No Country for Old Men*, some expressions of popular culture appear to self-consciously attack the myths.

Ed's sense of deep personal pride, which never spills over into all-consuming or ultimately tragic hubris, is augmented by his heritage. He is possessed of an abiding belief in family values: "My grandfather was a lawman; my father, too." Adding to this continuum is an overlap Ed likewise wants us to know about: "Me and him was sheriffs at the same time; him up in Plano, and me out here. I think he was pretty proud of that." As is our narrator-hero. Then Ed's memory ripples out further, beyond his own forefathers to a long line stretching back to the great men of the West, those town-tamers who disarmed the wild but more often than not hapless cowboys. Such men—perhaps in real life, certainly in films and on television—fully lived out their belief that the only effective way to end violence was to forsake it: "Some of the old-time sheriffs never even wore a gun!" That was true of deputy marshal Wyatt Earp in life as in film. It's not for nothing that in *Tombstone*, when his brothers decide they must march to the O.K. Corral, an unarmed Wyatt runs to his hotel room to pick up a pistol, a long-ago gift from dime novelist Ned Buntline that Wyatt keeps boxed up in a drawer.

Why the terrible sadness, then, on Ed Tom's part? He relates a recent case that pushed him to leave a profession he adores even though he knows he has a few good years left in him. A youth murdered three people, without rhyme or reason. Though several lawyers tried to get the kid off on the grounds that he was insane at the time of the crime, the boy will have none of it; set him free, he boasts, and he'll do it again. And *soon*! Though a simple man like Ed Tom might never even have heard the term "nihilism," that's what he's now come face to face with. And the darkness horrifies, even demobilizes him. This is not morality versus immorality, which Ed could understand. Rather, a cloudy shade of gray has descended that depresses and demoralizes Ed as it did the Davy Crockett of John Wayne's creative imagination in *The Alamo* before his religious and political conversion at mid-movie.

Ours is an amoral age in which everything that Ed Tom, Davy, Wyatt, and all most fervently believe in has been shattered. This is a world that, as Nietzsche warned as early as 1886, has moved beyond good and evil. If Ed Tom is to continue to exist, then, even with his precious star set aside, this firm, fine man must go on believing that once upon a time in the West, things were different. There was good, as John Wayne put it, and there was bad. You went one way or the other. And you were defined forever by the direction you took.

Ed Tom draws any strength he can from this final shard of hope. He knows such an America existed. After all, he saw it in the movies. Seeing is believing. For him, this is the way it once was: our American actuality, not just some Dream West. As Pirandello would put it, right you are as you think you are. Reality exists in the mind. This may be no country for old men that Ed begrudgingly inhabits. All the same, he can draw on memories of the good old days the way Hollywood, if not history, says they once were. The way conservative-minded Americans believe they can be again, once we discover the magical means of turning past fantasy into future reality.

"I want my culture back!" the tea partiers scream. In his own way, so does a fellow lawman Ed Tom joins for a cup of coffee rail about kids with hair dyed green and his inability to comprehend where things are headed. And so, in a more tolerant way, does Ed Tom himself.

After all, thinking back to the supposed golden age, the Clantons did not take on the Earps without reason. The O.K. Corral duel was *about* something, gun control in particular, politics and religion in general. Those two factions represented opposing views, but their passionate beliefs in their own sides of complex issues were equally genuine. And their beliefs defined them. That bloody confrontation, however horrible, made sense. Here was a Socratic dialogue communicated with smoking six-guns.

As to those old-timers—Ed Tom's father and grandfather, Earp, Bat Masterson, James Butler Hickok—our tired hero can only wonder "how *they*

"The Second Coming." The poet Yeats predicted an anti-Christ "slouching toward Bethlehem to be born." The amoral, undying monster (Javier Bardem) personifies that brute force in the 2007 Western No Country for Old Men. *Courtesy Paramount Pictures/Miramax.*

would operate in our times." The question already had been raised by Larry McMurtry in the novel and subsequent TV miniseries *Streets of Laredo* in the character of an old-timer named Call, a role played by James Garner in that film and earlier by Jones in the classic *Lonesome Dove*. Call faced off with a figure like Anton Chigurh (Javier Bardem), the cold-blooded killing machine Ed attempts to not only capture but comprehend. In time Ed comes to realize that he can never grasp the existence of this Terminator in Texas, a realistically rendered version of the 1930s Universal Studios Frankenstein monster resurrected in sequel after sequel that at each film's end crawls off to rise from ashes and kill again.

Chigurh is the poet Yeats's "rough beast,"[1] his hour come 'round at last, a "motiveless malignancy,"[2] who kills less for monetary gain, despite the vast sum of drug money involved, or even out of some perverse pleasure taken from inflicting cruelty. Chigurh takes lives because he cannot conceive of doing anything else with his own existence: I kill, therefore I am.[3] A once-meaningful frontier where even bad men could be expected to operate on some level of logic—however much we, like Ed Tom, may want to believe in such a bygone though clearly better world—is part of American folklore immortalized in paintings by Russell and Remington, books by Wister and Roosevelt, films by Ford, Hawks, Hathaway, Walsh, and even to a degree Clint Eastwood and Sam Peckinpah than anything that ever actually existed.

Writing in a waning twentieth century, McMurtry seems way ahead of his time in depicting absurdist violence that has long existed. And he was not the first. In *The Twilight Zone* TV episode titled "Execution," which aired on CBS on April 1, 1960, Rod Serling presented a malevolent figure embodied by actor Albert Salmi in one of that series' many Western-oriented episodes. The reverse of *No Country's* meaning was expressed: the man of the past here appears a throwback, a Neanderthal, a beast, while the decent, dedicated scientist of our time (Russell Johnson) appears good and civilized. The distinction is in the philosophies of McMurtry and Serling, the Western merely an open form on which either or any literary or philosophic vision can be imposed in the twentieth or twenty-first century; since 1900 the ideals of Victorianism gradually gave way to modernism, then modernism to postmodernism.

More often than not, that traditional vision of the Old West was created by blue-state literary lights and cinematic geniuses who glorified or degraded the frontier experience in view of their own attitudes. King of the Cowboys Roy Rogers may have popularized the tune "Don't Fence Me In," but that beloved ode to freedom was written by the legendary Manhattan sophisticate Cole Porter.

In truth, then, it is less that there were good or bright days way back as compared to bleak or bad ones now than that the Western can express different, even oppositional views on the same subject in any period. Examples of the genre largely depend on who happens to hold their auteurial reins at the moment the works are created and on the societal situations out of which they derive and to which they must play on screen. Artists impose their distinct approaches to life onto the oblique canvas of far frontiers.

Hence, *The Treasure of the Sierra Madre* (John Huston, 1949), based on a novel by the elusive author B. Travern,[4] offers an invaluable example of the manner in which previous Westerns flirted with nihilism only to back away at the last moment. Three prospectors (Humphrey Bogart, Walter Huston, Tim Holt) search for and discover gold high up in the mountain range. But in one more warning against raw capitalism, Fred C. Dobbs (Bogart) goes insane with fear that his friends might try to steal his money, and he attempts to kill them. They survive; he does not. As the story reaches its conclusion, members of a savage, primitive gang searching for food or guns rip open the gold bags; they have no idea how valuable "yellow sand" is and allow a fortune to blow away with the wind. Our two surviving protagonists come across the paltry remains of their hard work. The older, Howard (Huston), urges the younger, "Laugh, Curtin my boy, *laugh*! It's a great joke played on us by God, or nature, or whatever you choose to call it. But the gold's gone back to the hills." He throws back his head, roaring at the absurdity; Curtin joins in, as do the Mexicans.

Gradually, this laughter grows louder, crazier, until it grows frightening. For a moment, they all appear to be surrendering to the encroaching darkness, accepting that we all are lost in the stars and that if there was a God who created this speck in the universe,[5] he has either died or tired of us and wandered away. Yet Howard's precise words are important: though in this early example of postwar noir cinema he does bring up the question of whether there is a higher power, Howard clearly asserts that there is indeed something out there. The implication is that, to borrow from George Lucas and *Star Wars* (originally to have been titled *Cowboys in Space*),[6] as well as Shakespeare himself speaking through the voice of Hamlet, there is providence in the fall of a sparrow; a force, rough-hewn though it may be, purposefully plays tricks on us.[7]

And, in the end, life is not what it makes of us but what we make of it.

More importantly, Huston's film does not end there. If it did, our final image of men howling madly would register as nihilistic. There is an epilogue: Curtin recalls a fourth partner (Bruce Bennett) who briefly joined them but was killed in a fight with Indians. That fellow, Curtin knows, had a wife. He will do the right thing—seek her out, using what little money he has salvaged to make certain she will survive. *Treasure* ends with him heading off to accomplish that. Even in a world that exists on the edge of insanity or absurdity it remains possible for at least one good man to still do one good deed, however small. The size of the act matters less than the sincerity of his humanistic gesture.

The same situation occurred a few years earlier in William Wellman's *The Ox-Bow Incident* (1943). In the penultimate scene we view the lynch mob, fully aware they have hanged the wrong men, drinking themselves into oblivion in the midday darkness of a desolate saloon. Our hero (Henry Fonda), who attempted to halt the hanging, then steps outside into the sunlight. He reminds his sidekick (Harry Morgan) that the youngest of the innocent victims (Dana Andrews) mentioned a wife. The film ends with them likewise riding out to see how they might be of help. Amid all the blackness there remains a ray of light. Even one, however slight, is enough.

Such a vision is not confined to the Western, or even America, and is expressed during the following years in nongeneric international cinema. In

Do the right thing. At the conclusions of The Treasure of the Sierra Madre *and* The Ox-Bow Incident *(shown here), the "old men" (Henry Fonda, Harry Morgan) do attempt to make an impact for the good of humanity. Their faith may have been sorely tested, but it is not lost, at least not yet. Courtesy Twentieth Century-Fox.*

Rashomon (Akira Kurosawa, 1950) the priest tells the woodcutter, "You have restored my faith," after that pathetic man attempts to do a minor decent action in hopes of making up for some of his previous failings in life. If not in God, then he at least restores the priest's faith in man. Likewise, the final shot of Ingmar Bergman's *The Seventh Seal* (1957) is not the iconic one of death leading off those who failed to survive the long ordeal but of a simple family unit—Joseph, Mary, and a messianic child—realizing that the storm has passed and riding off into the hopeful sunlight as a new (in every sense of the term) day dawns. In a universe that exists after Nietzsche, circa 1900, declared that God is dead, such secular humanism is perhaps the most and best we can even hope for. At least until *No Country for Old Men* informed us that even this final hope may no longer be viable.

But back to those Western noirs of the 1940s. Fonda and Morgan in *Ox-Bow* are the old men of whom Ed Tom spoke, encountered here when they were still young. The West was dark then too, the saving grace being those who wished to make things better and believed that doing so remained viable. To again draw on Yeats's poem "The Second Coming," the problem now is that the good lack "all conviction" while the bad remain full of "passionate intensity." Ed Tom is, after all, leaving public service behind to hide away from the world on a remote ranch. He is a Southwestern version of Axel Heist in Joseph Conrad's *Victory* (1915), accepting that the world cannot be gentled, crawling off (Conrad here under the clear influence of Schopenhauer's pessimism) to try and make a separate peace, frightened that the dark creatures he has seen and recoiled from may in time follow him even here, to this remote rural Eden where he and his wife quietly work and live and love.

Perhaps surprisingly, that earlier vision of guarded optimism remained true even at the end of Sam Peckinpah's darkest film, *The Wild Bunch* (1969), which moved further in the direction of outright nihilism than any Western to appear before it, excepting only Eric von Stroheim's *Greed* (1924). Most viewers recall *The Wild Bunch* concluding with the brutal gun battle between four remaining gang members and an entire company of Mexican soldiers. But there was one scene yet to come. A former gang member (Robert Ryan) who betrayed his old-men comrades meets up with the group's elder spokesman. Though he is played by Edmond O'Brien, it would appear Peckinpah and his actor of choice consciously modeled this character on Walter Huston in *Treasure* from two decades earlier. *The Wild Bunch* then concludes with a similar scene. The two laugh at the great joke played on them by . . .

In time, though, the laughter stops. However much fate or human personality has set them against one another, each grasps that the other is all he has left. They are, after all, the final remnants of a dying breed. Once young, now old men in a no-man's land for their sort, they are anachronisms searching a barren landscape for some hint of solace that may no longer come from anywhere.

They recall the code of their one-time leader Pike (William Holden): "When you ride with a man, you *stick* with him!" The movie concludes with the two heading off together, if not entirely friends, then at least no longer enemies; hoping to keep the memory of their bunch alive, this shot of them dissolves into an image of the final good days.

No Country for Old Men finds even such revisionist Westerns, seemingly so unglamorous and realistic in their time, dishonest. It initiates a new form of cowboy film in which the Dream West is not only reconsidered but, along with any still-extant genre elements, more or less demolished. By its end, a loner (Josh Brolin) and a modern bounty hunter (Woody Harrelson), flawed yet still decent characters, are dead, and the vicious creature who kills for reasons no rational human can grasp is still at large. It's not supposed to be that way, at least according to the old-timers—or the old movies. But this is a modern film, or, more correctly, a postmodern one.

Ed Tom, the last of the decent old men, can only throw down his tin star, even as Gary Cooper's Will Kane did at the end of *High Noon* (if here that scene takes place off screen) and steal away with his wife. The only possible hope of goodness in a world gone mad is the individual family unit, where values may still exist. All the same, the undying creature may, and likely will, return at some point in the future. In the present, he remains out of sight but not out of Ed Tom's mind. Someday, the thing will slouch their way.

To paraphrase Nietzsche, a joke is an epitaph on an emotion. If he was correct about that, then *No Country for Old Men* is a great, terribly dark joke about the death of those emotions and ideas once, long ago, revered as the code of the cowboy. The way of the West. The American value system reduced to essentials. And, again, the cowboy is not in this context that low-paid, blue-collar worker on a tired, undernourished nag. No, not that cowboy who once existed and still does. The *other* one. The man who rides tall, a Percival of the prairie, our savior in a saddle. The knight whose presumably white hat substitutes for ancient armor and whose gun is his sword, swinging with a deadly casualness by his side. The man with no name. Everyone knows this. Also, though, this cowboy is a man who never was, as few realize, the fictional rider of our celluloid sage, an American hero as ideal, inspirational, but impossible as Achilles or Arthur. Not as they were, if they ever actually were, but as poets and, in the twentieth century, filmmakers reinvented them.

So! The Dream West, with its codes and clichés? Now it exists not in contemporary cowboy films (compare the ending of the twenty-first-century *3:10 to Yuma* with that of the original!) but only in old movies—and memories of those movies.

In the Coen brothers' film's final moments, Ed Tom shares his memory of a recent dream with his wife. In it he was young again, riding with his father, an old man in every sense of the term, through a clean range of pristine mountains, the very terrain that Gene Autry waxed poetic about in so many singin' cowboy films. Ed Tom's mentor rode up ahead to fix a fire, cook dinner, make a camp the two would warmly share in the manner of, say,

Law and order, liberal-progressive style. The single most significant theme of traditional Westerns is dispelling chaos and creating a functioning community. Midway through My Darling Clementine, *Wyatt (Henry Fonda) takes a moment to relax and consider his now half-completed chore. Courtesy Twentieth Century-Fox.*

Randolph Scott's character and his young sidekick (Ron Starr) in *Ride the High Country*. A moment of purity in the West as it always should have been came to Ed Tom in a dream, perhaps the only place this fantasy frontier ever existed. One man's individual dream, our shared dreams as encountered in Hollywood movies.

But dreams, in due time, die. As Ed tells his wife (Tess Harper), "I woke up."

He woke up from the West that should have been to face the West that is and, however terrible to grasp, always had been. Once we find the courage to set glorious myths aside and instead inhabit that grossly inferior cosmos that, for want of a better term, we choose to call, in a word, reality.

Dream West. John Ford and others of his era offered a romanticized vision—the way we ought to have been if not necessarily the way we were—that strikes fans of twenty-first-century grim, realistic Westerns as quaint, curious, nostalgic, and as out of date as the bygone frontier itself. Courtesy Twentieth Century-Fox.

NOTES

INTRODUCTION

1. For an introduction to the basic ideology as it has evolved over the past century and a half, begin with Alex Johnston, *Cowboy Politics: The Western Stock Growers' Association and Its Predecessors* (Calgary, Canada: Western Stock Growers' Association, 1971), and/or Gene M. Gressley, *Bankers and Cattlemen: The Stocks-and-Bonds, Havana Cigar, Mahogany-and-Leather Side of the Cowboy Era* (Lincoln: University of Nebraska Press, 1971).

2. The similarities of farming in the South and ranching in the West, particularly as experienced by the man who would later be president, are chronicled in the first three chapters of Julian E. Zelizer, *Jimmy Carter*, American Presidents (New York: Times Books, Henry Holt, 2010); the same material is presented in a charming combination of bleak honesty and sentimental recollection in Jimmy Carter, *An Hour before Daylight: Memories of a Rural Boyhood* (New York: Simon and Schuster, 2001).

3. Perhaps the most objective analysis of Reagan's boyhood can be found in the first four chapters of Michael Schaller, *Ronald Reagan* (Oxford, England: Oxford University Press, 2010); the president's own, more sentimental retelling of the same events is shared in the first five chapters of Ronald Reagan, *An American Life: The Autobiography* (Simon and Schuster, 1990), also produced in audio.

4. Scott Rasmussen and Doug Schoen, *Mad as Hell: How the Tea Party Movement Is Fundamentally Remaking Our Two-Party System* (New York: HarperCollins, 2010).

5. Though certainly biased, no single work so well captures the distinct policies of leading twenty-first century Democrats than Ari Berman, *Herding Donkeys: The Fight to Rebuild the Democratic Party and Reshape American Politics* (New York: Farrar, Strauss, and Giroux, 2010).

6. Rush Limbaugh employed the term "extremist" among many others to describe President Obama on his influential radio show at least thirty-nine times as of this writing.

7. On April 12, 2006, then governor Romney signed into law the Massachusetts Health Care Insurance Reform Law, chapter 58 of the Articles of 2006 for that state.

8. Harlow Giles Ungar, *American Tempest: How the Boston Tea Party Sparked a Revolution* (Cambridge, MA: Da Capo Press, 2011).

9. Ibid., 27–39.

10. McComb is quoted in Evan Thomas, "Don't Mess with Texas," *Newsweek*, April 15, 2010, p. 30.

11. Kate Zernike, *Boiling Mad: Inside Tea Party America* (New York: Times Books, 2010).

12. Though there are endless books either about or touching on the subject of a supposed American golden age in the ongoing conservative worldview, few will prove as entertaining for liberals as well as traditionalists (and baseball fans of all political philosophies) as George F. Will, *One Man's America: The Pleasures and Provocations of Our Singular Nation* (New York: Three Rivers Press, 2009).

13. James P. Owen, *Cowboy Values: What America Once Stood For* (Guilford, CT: Lyons Press, 2008).

14. In Thomas, "Don't Mess with Texas."

15. A perfect book to initiate any study of the Western hero in popular culture, particularly as set against his less romantic reality, is William W. Save, *The Cowboy Hero: His Image in History and Culture* (Norman: University of Oklahoma Press, 1985).

16. Several books chronicle Autry's transformation from B-Western actor-singer to influential businessman and TV producer. Recommended are Holly George-Warren, *Public Cowboy No. 1: The Life and Times of Gene Autry* (New York: Oxford University Press, 2009), and Don Cusic, *Gene Autry, His Life and Career* (Jefferson, NC: McFarland, 2010).

17. Richard White, ed., *King Arthur in Legend and History* (New York: Routledge, 1998), with various essays, all valuable and several exceptional, on Arthur, Camelot, and the historical origins of the myths and legends of the Round Table.

18. For two all but oppositional yet remarkable readings of the Arthur myth and its political-religious connotations, as well as the imposition of later chivalric traditions onto this canvas from the past, see Emma Jung, *The Grail Legend* (Princeton, NJ: Princeton University Press, 1998), and Elizabeth Pochoda, *Arthurian Propaganda: Le Morte D'Arthur as an Historical Ideal of Life* (Chapel Hill: University of North Carolina Press, 2009).

19. Robert Warshow, *The Immediate Experience: Movies, Comics, Theatre, and Other Aspects of Popular Culture* (Cambridge, MA: Harvard University Press, 2002).

20. In Thomas, "Don't Mess with Texas," 30.

21. Jill Lepore, *The Whites of Their Eyes: The Tea Party's Revolution and the Battle over American History* (Princeton, NJ: Princeton University Press, 2010).

22. For a fair and balanced guide to the document and how the language, values, and standards of that time did affect its writing see John R. Vile, *A Companion to the United States Constitution and Its Amendments* (Santa Barbara, CA: Praeger, 2005). To fully comprehend the contemporary Right's "origination theory" check out Edwin Meese III, Matthew Spalding, and David F. Forte, *The Heritage Guide to the Constitution* (Washington, DC: Regnery, 2005).

23. Ron Paul, *The Revolution: A Manifesto* (New York: Grand Central, 2009). Also see his son's assessment of the movement, including Ron Paul's role in spreading it to a national level, in Rand Paul, *The Tea Party Goes to Washington* (New York: Center Street, 2011).

24. Karl Rove flatly stated that he believed Sarah Palin lacked the "gravitas" to be elected president; he said this during an interview on a Fox News broadcast that was repeated several times on October 27, 2010.

25. Perry speech, Austin, April 15, 2009.

26. "Spread the wealth around" was the perhaps unfortunate (at least in context) concept expressed by then candidate for the presidency Barack Obama while speaking to a man on the street, "Joe the Plumber" Wurzelbacher, in Toledo, Ohio, on October 13, 2008.

27. Perry interview, "The Perry Doctrine," *Newsweek*, April 15, 2010, p. 32.

28. Thomas, "Don't Mess with Texas," 29.

29. Ibid., 30.

30. "Fighting the Wimp Factor" was the *Newsweek* cover story in 1987 shortly after Vice President George H.W. Bush announced his candidacy for the upcoming presidential race. This, despite the fact that he was a decorated World War II hero, made clear that one's popular image as a result of television had little if anything to do with actual identity. His wife, Barbara, testily said, "The camera hates him; it scrunches George all up." Many observers of contemporary politics as filtered through popular culture believed that however fit he was for the office, Bush won in large part because he set out to consciously imitate the vocal mannerisms of John Wayne and then had the good fortune to run against Democrat Michael Dukakis, who appeared wimpier on TV than Bush.

31. A superbly satirical fictionalization of the Marlboro Man incident and the manner in which actor David Lean eventually turned against the industry that made him famous and wealthy but also incurably ill with cancer appears in Christopher Buckley, *Thank You for Smoking* (Colorado Springs, CO: Random House, 2006); there is also a film version in 2006.

32. John Wayne, press interviews in Washington, January 20, 1977.

33. For a succinct version of this complex situation and the process by which Jackson's specific version of populism took hold precisely when it did, see Sean Wilentz, *The Rise of American Democracy* (New York: W. W. Norton, 2005), specifically 168–175.

34. Wayne, press interviews, January 20, 1977.

35. Carter's complex role in this incident is vividly brought to life by Noel Mauer and Carlos Yu in the final quarter of *The Big Ditch: How America Took, Built, Ran, and Ultimately Gave Away the Panama Canal* (Princeton, NJ: Princeton University Press, 2010).

36. The manner in which this incident allowed Reagan to control the role playing during the 1980 election is essential to Adam Clymer, *Drawing the Line at the Big Ditch: The Panama Canal Treaties and the Rise of the Right* (Lexington: University Press of Kentucky, 2008).

37. John Wayne, open letter to the U.S. Senate, October 10, 1977, emphasis mine.

38. Ibid.

39. Jimmy Carter, eulogy for John Wayne, June 11, 1979.

40. The myth that good guys wore white hats, bad guys black, was first dispelled by William K. Everson in *A Pictorial History of the Western Film* (New York: Citadel Press, 1969). In his introduction and throughout this early analysis of the genre, Everson points out how many heroes, from Hopalong Cassidy to Zorro, wore black hats; the attire that identifies a villain is more likely to be a finely tailored suit.

CHAPTER ONE

1. For a first-rate starting place to cover this fascinating and complicated issue as it applies to the West and other aspects of U.S. history, see Robert Toplin, *History by Hollywood: The Use and Abuse of the American Past* (Champaign: University of Illinois Press, 1996).

2. Surprisingly few books cover such aspects of the Tombstone conflict. For one that attempts as broad a spectrum of possibilities as to that brief if important outburst of violence and does

achieve most of its considerable ambitions see Jeff Guinn, *The Last Gunfight: The Real Story of the Shootout at the O.K. Corral—and How It Changed the American West* (New York: Simon and Schuster, 2011).

3. For this element of the broad canvas, the best-regarded book is a recent one: Lynn R. Bailey, *"Too Tough to Die": The Rise, Fall, and Resurrection of a Silver Camp; 1878–1900* (Tucson: Westernlore Press, 2010).

4. Yet another Easterner who helped to create our Dream West, Stuart N. Lake (1889-1964) was born in a small, upstate New York town called Rome and in time visited the aging Wyatt Earp in California to "get the facts set down" before Earp and his era passed. Apparently it never occurred to Lake that much of what the old-timer told him might be fiction rather than fact; the once revered, now highly debatable, to say the least, even somewhat (in)famous 1931 book *Wyatt Earp, Frontier Marshal* was reprinted in paperback in 1994 for the publisher, Pocket Books (Parsippany, New Jersey), to cash in on the release of the Kevin Costner film the same year.

5. For an authentic description of daily duties for an actual town marshal on the frontier, see James D. Horan, *The Authentic Wild West: The Lawmen* (New York: Gramercy Books, 1996).

6. One of the most telling biographies of Wyatt Earp is Casey Tefertiller, *Wyatt Earp: The Life behind the Legend* (New York: Wiley and Sons, 1999).

7. Fabulous examples of the pulp-fiction writing style, plus a fine essay on the form, appear in Bill Brown, ed., *Readings on the West: An Anthology of Dime Westerns* (New York: Bedford Cultural Edition, St. Martin's Press, 1997).

8. The roots of this movement and reasons for its emergence are explained fully and clearly in Harold Bloom, *Agon: Towards a Theory of Revisionism* (New York: Oxford University Press, 1982).

9. Dennis Hopper, open quote to the press (this author included) in September 1969, looking forward to the national release of his film *Easy Rider*.

10. The actor-director tells his own version of the story, intriguingly if a bit too self-servingly, in Dennis Hopper, *Out of the Sixties* (Santa Fe, NM: Twelvetrees Press, 1986).

11. The relationship of Reagan to cowboy politics is the subject of the February–March 2008 issue of *American Cowboy* magazine, which looked to the coming election to analyze Reagan's lasting legacy.

12. For a full explanation of how and why Reagan and other contenders were passed over in favor of the unknown Parker, see Paul F. Anderson, *The Davy Crockett Craze: A Look at the 1950's Davy Crockett Phenomenon* (Granada Hills, CA: R&G Productions, 1996).

13. For a relatively conventional study of the (relatively) "quiet heroics" involved, see Richard B. Morris, *Witnesses at the Creation: Hamilton, Madison, Jay, and the Constitution* (New York: Holt, Rinehart, and Winston, 1985). For a controversial, revisionist approach to the same material, see Christopher Collier, *All Politics Is Local: Family, Friends, and Provincial Interests in the Creation of the Constitution* (Lebanon, NH: University Press of New England, 2003).

CHAPTER TWO

1. The shoot-out is most faithfully re-created from inception to aftermath on a virtually second-by-second account in Paula Mitchell Marks, *And Die in the West: The Story of the O.K. Corral Gunfight* (Norman: University of Oklahoma Press, 1996).

2. The remarkable number of wild shootings compared to the rarity of actual gun duels is best recounted in James Reasoner, *Draw: The Greatest Gunfights of the American West* (New York: Berkley Trade, 2003).

3. *Who Rides with Wyatt* presents the events of Earp's Tombstone years with considerable accuracy,

adding a dramatic through-line by focusing on a (fictional) friendship between Wyatt and John Ringo. Names of historical people are employed with the exception only of Nellie Cashman, reimagined as Earp's frigid or repressed love interest Evie Cushman.

4. The creation of this film and others by Edison and Porter as well as the entire experience of early East Coast filmmaking is recounted in Paul C. Speher, *The Movies Begin: Making Movies in New Jersey, 1897–1920* (Newark, NJ: Newark Museum Association, 1977).

5. Perhaps nowhere has the need to provide strong and highly visual motivations for film characters been so effectively and entertainingly chronicled as in William Goldman, *Adventures in the Screen Trade: A Personal View of Hollywood and Screenwriting* (New York: Grand Central, 1989).

6. See Michael F. Blake, *Hollywood and the O.K. Corral: Portrayals of the Gunfight and Wyatt Earp* (Jefferson, NC: McFarland, 2006).

7. A near-perfect rendering of the situation in Arizona during those pre-statehood years is found in Douglas D. Martin, *An Arizona Chronology: The Territorial Years 1846–1912* (Tucson: University of Arizona Press, 1963).

8. The onetime (honest) Indian agent, later newspaper editor and mayor in Tombstone tells the story of his relationship with Wyatt in John P. Clum, *It All Happened in Tombstone* (Outing, MN: Northland Press, 1965; originally published 1929).

9. Perhaps the most balanced biography so far is Gary L. Roberts, *Doc Holliday: The Life and Legend* (Hoboken, NJ: Wiley, 2007).

10. For an alternative view to the notion of Wyatt Earp as hero and peacemaker, see Steven Lubet, *Murder in Tombstone: The Forgotten Trial of Wyatt Earp* (New Haven, CT: Yale University Press, 2006).

11. The development of gun control, so often the source of hysterical propagandizing from either side, is calmly and intelligently recalled in Lee Kennett and James La Verne Anderson, *The Gun in America: The Origins of a National Dilemma* (Westport, CT: Greenwood Press, 1975).

12. The flying of this banner at Gonzales, Texas, during what may have been the initial skirmish of the conflict that devolved into the war for Texas independence is presented in Chester Newell, *History of the Revolution in Texas, Particularly of the War of 1835 and '36* (Charleston, SC: BiblioBazaar, 2009; originally published 1838).

13. The correct title is the (Christopher) Gadsden flag, the first actual banner carried into battle during the American Revolution, also the initial flag of the Continental Marines, though its implied message at that time had practically nothing to do with the kind of ideology tea partiers employ it for today. See Frederick Cocks Hicks, *The Flag of the United States* (Washington, DC: Government Printing Office, 1918), for a brief but accurate history of its construction and use.

CHAPTER THREE

1. Of the many and diverse (pro, con, and balanced) books about the man known as Old Hickory, few come close to one of the most recent in presenting his many sides and absolute genius as a hardcore populist: Jon Meacham, *American Lion: Andrew Jackson and the White House* (New York: Random House, 2009).

2. The roots of a populism that cuts across party loyalties in America are ably drawn and described in Lawrence Goodwyn, *The Populist Moment: A Short History of the Agrarian Revolt in America* (Oxford, England: Oxford University Press, 1978).

3. Leonard Maltin, *The Disney Films* (New York: Crown, 1973), 122–124.

4. The distinction between the pop-culture phenomenon Davy Crockett and the historical personage of David Crockett is smartly and entertainingly presented in Michael Wallis, *David Crockett:*

The Lion of the West (New York: W. W. Norton, 2011); for my review of the book see *True West* magazine, August 2011.

5. No better version of the event itself, as well as the incidents preceding and following, is available than Gloria Jahoda, *Trail of Tears* (San Antonio, TX: Wings, 1995).

6. The need for educated intellectuals like Henry Clay to bring a populist hero like Crockett into their party to achieve a sense of political verisimilitude is revealed in Michael F. Holt, *The Rise and Fall of the Whig Party: Jacksonian Politics and the Onset of the Civil War* (Oxford, England: Oxford University Press, 2003).

7. Frémont's similarities to and differences from other Western heroes, including his own scout Kit Carson and the earlier David Crockett, will be best appreciated by reading Tom Chaffin, *Pathfinder: John Charles Frémont and the Course of American Empire* (New York: Hill and Wang, 2003). There is also a fictionalized version of Frémont's story that now shares its title with this volume.

8. The disastrous attempt to imitate the ongoing Iroquois Confederacy in the United States' own earliest experiments at self-government and its utter impossibility and impracticality of functioning in a rapidly developing America is best understood by reading Mary E. Webster's analysis of *The Federalist Papers* (CreateSpace, 2008).

9. Texas's favorite son and author James Frank Dobie describes both the post–Civil War trail drives and the situation that awaited the cowboys following three months of dust, disease, and other assorted devilments, Native Americans the least threatening among them, in Dobie, *Up the Trail from Texas* (New York: Random House, 1955).

10. How a sickly Eastern boy reinvented himself by riding tall in the saddle is excellently retold in Roger L. Silvestro, *Theodore Roosevelt and the Badlands: A Young Politician's Quest for Recovery in the American West* (New York: Walker, 2011).

11. The remarkable changeover from one political philosophy to its precise opposite, necessarily simplified here in *Dream West* though related with accuracy, certainly, is developed in depth in Lewis Gould, *Grand Old Party: A History of the Republicans* (New York: Random House, 2003).

12. The influence of the Dixiecrats and their eventual sense of betrayal by what they perceived as the party of Jackson is well recalled in Kari Frederickson, *The Dixiecrat Revolt and the End of the Solid South* (Chapel Hill: University of North Carolina Press, 2000).

13. John A. Andrew, *Lyndon Johnson and the Great Society* (Lanham, MD: Ivan R. Dee, 1999).

14. Rick Perlstein, *Before the Storm: Barry Goldwater and the Unmaking of the American Consensus* (New York: Nation Books, 2009).

15. The manner in which a law-and-order approach to civil disobedience transformed into what legally came to be considered a "police riot" becomes vividly clear in the meticulously researched Frank Kusch, *Battleground Chicago: The Police and the 1968 Democratic Convention* (Chicago: University of Chicago Press, 2008).

16. An honest attempt to separate myth from reality can be found in Allen Barra, *Inventing Wyatt Earp: His Life and Many Legends* (Lincoln, NE: Castle Books, 2009).

17. The highly dubious version of the story that the woman known as Sadie set down on paper remains available and makes for fascinating reading just so long as one does not mistake her self-serving employment of poetic license in these "recollections" as anything remotely approaching objective historicity: Josephine Sara Marcus Earp, *I Married Wyatt Earp* (Tucson: University of Arizona Press, 1994).

CHAPTER FOUR

1. Even before Heston's over-the-top use of the phrase on May 20, 2000, and the National Rifle Association's embracing of it as a motto, a similar expression about the need to "pry" guns out of their grasp was popular among the Citizens Committee for the Right to Keep and Bear Arms, in Bellevue, Washington.

2. This and other events in the earliest days of the war are precisely chronicled in Bernon Arthur Tourtellot, *Lexington and Concord: The Beginning of the American Revolution* (New York: W. W. Norton, 2000).

3. This conclusion is based on conversations with the film's producers that I conducted within the months after its release for several newspaper stories.

4. For a sense of the full spectrum of theatrical films see either Phil Hardy, *Encyclopedia of Western Movies* (Minneapolis, MN: Woodbury Press, 1984), or Herb Fagen, *Encyclopedia of Westerns* (New York: Facts on File, 2003). For TV Westerns see Douglas Brode, *Shooting Stars of the Small Screen: An Encyclopedia of TV Western Actors* (Austin: University of Texas Press, 2009).

5. A fascinating variety of essays about Westerns with a strong emphasis on the adult variety of the 1950s and how they both reflected and helped to shape that decade can be found in Gregg Rickman and Jim Kitses, *The Western Reader* (Ann Arbor: Limelight Editions, University of Michigan Press, 2004).

6. The best biography of the man goes against the grain of most thought about this Texas shootist, as its title dares to suggest: Jack Burrows, *John Ringo: The Gunfighter Who Never Was* (Tucson: University of Arizona Press, 1996).

7. Myriad biographies of the boy born Henry McCarty in a New York City slum are of course available, but one that offers a fascinating slant from a Latino point of view is Miguel Antonio Otero, *The Real Billy the Kid* (Santa Fe, NM: Arte Público Press, 1998; originally published 1936).

8. The myth of a close friendship between the two was initiated in the book that the lawman who shot Billy not only wrote but, on orders from his editors and publishers, was encouraged to embellish for dramatic effect: Pat F. Garrett, *The Authentic Life of Billy the Kid* (New York: Skyhorse, 2011; originally published 1882). As to the book's title, "Ol' Patsy" Garrett was renowned for his acerbic sense of humor.

9. Charlton Heston, exclusive interview with this author, July 1979.

10. An independently published volume nails the actuality of the process of civilization in this area in a way that no other does: Michael R. Wilson, *Crime and Punishment in Early Arizona* (Linden, NJ: Stage Coach Books, 2004).

CHAPTER FIVE

1. For tracing the concepts of heroes dedicated to strict codes and the tradition of horseback riding, see Richard Barber, *The Knight and Chivalry* (Suffolk, England: Boydell Press, 2000).

2. The work about this goddess that most stresses her relationship to military strategy and the taming of horses is Lee Hall, *Athena: A Biography* (Cambridge, MA: Da Capo Press, 1997).

3. Though considered out of date by many contemporary historians, the finest book ever written about the daily life of the working cowboy remains Philip Ashton Rollins, *The Cowboy: His Characteristics, His Equipment, and His Part in Development of the West* (New York: Charles Scribner's Sons, 1922).

4. The daily lifestyle of a mountain man as well as his relationship to the greater fur industry in early

nineteenth-century America are the subject of Fred R. Gowans, *Rocky Mountain Rendezvous: A History of the Fur Trade 1825–1840* (Layton, UT: Gibbs Smith, 2005).

5. Joseph Campbell, *The Hero with a Thousand Faces* (Novato, CA: New World Library, 2000).

6. Perhaps the definitive collection of writings can be found in Jean Roy, ed., *Jean-Jacques Rousseau and the Revolution*, Proceedings of the Montreal Symposium May 25–28, 1989 (La Verne, CA: North American Society for the Study of Jean-Jacques Rousseau, 1991).

7. The evolution of the ideology is well documented in Isaiah Berlin and Henry Hardy, *The Roots of Revolution* (Princeton, NJ: Princeton University Press, 2001).

8. Owen Wister, *The Virginian: A Horseman of the Plains* (New York: Signet, 2010; originally published 1902), 7.

9. Jack Schaefer, *Shane* (New York: Bantam, 1983; originally published 1949), 4.

10. Turner's original thesis, developed in the early 1890s, and other key writings are found in Frederick Jackson Turner, *The Frontier in American History* (New York: Henry Holt, 1920), reprinted several times and now digitized and available online.

11. Michael Marsden, "Savior in the Saddle: The Sagebrush Testament," in *Shane: Critical Edition*, edited by James C. Work, 393–404 (Lincoln: University of Nebraska Press, 1984).

12. The relationship of firearms to the cult of masculinity is nowhere so well analyzed as in John G. Cawelti, *The Six-Gun Mystique Sequel* (Bowling Green, OH: Bowling Green State University Popular Press, 1999).

13. Richard Slotkin, *Gunfighter Nation: The Myth of the Frontier in Twentieth-Century America* (New York: Harper Perennial, 1992), 396.

14. Ibid., 398.

CHAPTER SIX

1. This ongoing trend was first discussed in some depth in Dan Kilen, *The Peter Pan Syndrome: Men Who Have Never Grown Up* (New York: Dodd, Mead, 1983).

CHAPTER SEVEN

1. A recent reprint with a delightful foreword by present-day humorist Dave Barry reveals the American Dream of success through dedication and hard work in its original, embryonic form: Benjamin Franklin, *Poor Richard's Almanack* (New York: Modern Library, 2000; originally published 1732–1758).

2. The Horatio Alger stories from their humblest beginnings during the early twentieth century and the vast impact these writings had on future discourse in industrial-era America is intelligently analyzed in Richard Weiss, *The American Myth of Success: From Horatio Alger to Norman Vincent Peale* (Chicago: Illini Books, University of Illinois Press, 1988).

3. For an objective look at the idea of cattle as capital and the manner in which this industry had to adjust to developing scientific technology in order to survive, see Sherm Ewing, *The Ranch: A Modern History of the North American Cattle Industry* (Aspen, CO: Mountain Press, 1995).

4. Business rather than high adventure is the subject of Eric Jay Dolin, *Fur, Fortune, and Empire: The Epic History of the Fur Trade in America* (New York: W. W. Norton, 2011).

5. Its title aside, for the most factual work on this elusive historical figure, see Richard Dillon, *The Legend of Grizzly Adams: California's Greatest Mountain Man* (Lincoln: University of Nebraska Press, 1993).

6. The uniqueness of this particular fur trapper as well as the personal qualities that allowed him to transcend problems (alcohol, gambling) that plagued others of his ilk and become a successful businessman in the fur industry are discussed throughout and evident even in the title of Barton H. Barbour, *Jedediah Smith: No Ordinary Mountain Man* (Norman: University of Oklahoma Press, 2011).

7. The manner in which this artist's initially liberal politics were (to be polite) tested by McCarthyism and the 1950s Red Scare and this transition's impact on his future work is the subject of the excellent Thomas H. Pauly, *American Odyssey: Elia Kazan and American Culture* (Philadelphia: Temple University Press, 1985).

8. Radisson's role as an "I came, I saw, I conquered" figure in American business history is the subject of Grace Lee Nute, *Caesars of the Wilderness* (St. Paul: Minnesota Historical Society Press, 1978).

9. The rise and fall of this brief-lived empire, as well as "the Radisson problem" and that man's impact on its decline, is simply and well told in Richard Worth, *Voices from Colonial America: New France 1534–1763* (Washington, DC: National Geographic, 2007).

10. Ellen Glasgow, *Vein of Iron* (New York: Harcourt Brace, 1935). Also, for a fine study of how Glasgow's conscious vision of the pioneer spirit passed on to each generation by the female could help Americans weather the changeover from the final frontier to the bold new world of the industrial twentieth century, see Susan Goodman, *Ellen Glasgow: A Biography* (Baltimore, MD: Johns Hopkins University Press, 2003).

CHAPTER EIGHT

1. A lively discussion of films from this era and the unique reasons for the dominance of B oaters during the Depression can be found in Howard Hughes, *Stagecoach to Tombstone: The Filmgoer's Guide to Great Westerns* (London: I. B. Taurus, 2008).

2. For a notably fair and balanced view of the man born James Butler Hickok, see Joseph G. Rosa, *The West of Wild Bill Hickok* (Norman: University of Oklahoma Press, 1994).

3. The original statement on Mormonism, emphasizing the unique relationship of politics to religion, remains: Lycurgus A. Wilson, *Outlines of Mormon Philosophy* (Salt Lake City: Desert News, 1905).

4. For an overview of the Red Scare, see John McCumber, *Time in the Ditch: American Philosophy and the McCarthy Era* (Evanston, IL: Northwestern University Press, 2001). For a more specific focus on the Hollywood blacklist, see Reynold Humphries, *Hollywood Blacklist: A Political and Cultural History* (Edinburgh, Scotland: Edinburgh University Press, 2010).

CHAPTER NINE

1. "Back in the Saddle Again" was co-written by Gene Autry and Ray Whitley in 1939; the song appeared in several Autry Westerns and was featured at the opening and closing of each episode of the popular 1950s *The Gene Autry Show* on television. Autry employed the song's title again as the title for his autobiography (New York: Doubleday, 1978).

2. For this aspect of Ford's life, his career, and the utter inseparability of the two, none of the mostly excellent biographies comes even close to Joseph McBride, *Searching for John Ford: A Life* (New York: St. Martin's Press, 2001).

3. The full and amazing impact of this single piece of legislation on life in America in general and the West in particular is covered in fine detail in Jason Porter Field, *The Homestead Act of 1862:*

A Primary Source of the Settlement of the American Heartland in the Late 19th Century (New York: Rosen, 2004).

4. A revisionist view of the man and his work that overturns much of what has been thought, said, and written about Spencer appears in Mark Francis, *Herbert Spencer and the Invention of Modern Life* (Ithaca, NY: Cornell University Press, 2007).

CHAPTER TEN

1. On his MSNBC-TV news and editorial show *Hardball*, Chris Matthews continuously attacks the Far Right for its anti-environmental positions. Among the specific days when his ire was raised particularly high were February 8, June 8, and November 20, 2010, and June 23, 2011.
2. Shortly after John McCain picked Sarah Palin as his running mate for the 2008 presidential election, the media presented the public with her notably anti-environmental record. She responded by attacking what she called "extreme green" types (August 29–30, 2008) and continued to do so (August 15, 2010).
3. No sooner had Romney attempted to take a middle-of-the-road position than Limbaugh attacked him with considerable vitriol, particularly on June 8 and 10, 2011.
4. For a vivid overview of Ms. Carson's life and letters see Linda Lear, *Rachel Carson: Witness for Nature* (New York: Mariner Books, 2009).
5. Rachel Carson, *Silent Spring* (New York: Houghton Mifflin, 1962), 3.
6. A lively if somewhat simplistic biography of the cowboy star and his wife can be found in Howard Kazanjian and Chris Enss, *Happy Trails: A Pictorial Celebration of the Life and Times of Roy Rogers and Dale Evans* (Gulford, MT: TwoDot, 2005).

CHAPTER ELEVEN

1. How fascinating that the Mussel Slough tragedy, which actually does rate as a significant moment in U.S. history, has rarely been written about, in comparison to the O.K. Corral incident, which had considerably less impact but has become immortal in our legends. Two books that present the facts behind the Mussel Slough shooting are Terry Beers, ed., *Gunfight at Mussel Slough: Evolution of a Western Myth* (Berkeley, CA: Heyday Books, 2004), and Wallace Smith, *Garden of the Sun: A History of San Joaquin Valley* (Fresno, CA: Linden, 2004).
2. The formation, settlement, rise, and fall of Dodge City is well documented in Stanley Vestal, *Dodge City: Queen of Cowtowns: "The Wickedest Little City in America"* (Lincoln: Bison Books, University of Nebraska Press, 1998; originally published 1952).

CHAPTER TWELVE

1. The best analysis of this era can be found in Peter Biskind, *Easy Riders, Raging Bulls: How the Sex-Drugs-and-Rock 'n' Roll Generation Saved Hollywood* (New York: Simon and Schuster, 1999).
2. Among several books analyzing Leone's unique treatment of style and substance, content and form, perhaps the most perceptive is Robert C. Cumbow, *Once Upon a Time: The Films of Sergio Leone* (Lanham, MD: Scarecrow Press, 1991).
3. Alain Dugrand and Stephen Romer, *Trotsky in Mexico, 1937–1940* (Oxford, England: Carcanet Press, 1992).
4. For the complete shooting script see S. M. Eisenstein, *Que Viva Mexico!* (New York: Arno Press,

1972). For a superbly researched study of what went wrong and how, see Masha Salazinka, *In Excess: Sergei Eisenstein's Mexico* (Chicago: University of Chicago Press, 2009).

CHAPTER THIRTEEN

1. Margarita De Orellana and Kevin Brownwell, *Filming Pancho Villa: How Hollywood Shaped the Mexican Revolution* (Brooklyn, NY: Verso, 2004; originally published 1991).
2. Hans Bertens, "The Postmodern Weltanschauung and Its Relation to Modernism: An Introductory Survey," in *A Postmodern Reader*, edited by Joseph Natoli and Linda Hutcheon, 25–70 (Albany: SUNY Press, 1993).
3. The manner in which the Hollywood studio system in general, Metro-Goldwyn-Mayer in particular, had no qualms in reshaping material to fit the existing persona of any one star is presented in Steve Bingen, Stephen X. Sylvester, and Michael Troyon, *MGM: Hollywood's Greatest Backlot* (Santa Monica, CA: Santa Monica Press, 2011). James Robert Parish and Gregory Mank, *The Best of M-G-M: The Golden Years, 1928–1959* (Westport, CT: Arlington House, 1981), contains a complete analysis of the ways existing materials were shaped for the starring members of MGM's legendary "stock company."
4. For a delicious recounting of how the country's best-loved dessert all but defined the nation's eating habits from its earliest days, read and enjoy Shannon Jackson Arnold, *Everybody Loves Ice Cream: The Whole Scoop on America's Favorite Treat* (Cincinnati, OH: Clerisy Press, 2004).
5. Zygmunt Bauman, "Postmodernity, or Living with Ambivalence," in *Postmodern Reader*, edited by Joseph Natoli and Linda Hutcheon, 9–24 (Albany: SUNY Press, 1993).

CHAPTER FOURTEEN

1. Author's conversations with Patrick Wayne about Westerns in general, his father in particular, 1987.
2. George W. Bush all but defined the early part of his first term with the phrase, employing it for the first time in public on January 22, 2001, two days after his inauguration.

CHAPTER FIFTEEN

1. Boleslaw Mastai and Marie-Louise D'Otrange Mastai, *The Stars and the Stripes: The American Flag as Art and as History from the Birth of the Republic to the Present* (Old Saybrook, CT: Konecky and Konecky, 2002).
2. Marc Leepson, *Flag: An American Biography* (New York: St. Martin's Griffin, 2006).
3. John Wayne, interview in *Playboy*, May 1971.

CHAPTER SIXTEEN

1. Michael Wallis's recent Crockett biography is among the best.
2. In its opening big-city engagements in fall 1960 the director's cut ran 203 minutes; for the general road-show release the film was trimmed to 192 minutes.
3. Frank T. Thompson, *Alamo Movies* (Plano, TX: Republic of Texas Press, 1994), 47–53.
4. F. T. Thompson, 56.
5. Philip French, *Westerns: Aspects of a Movie Genre* (New York: Viking, 1973), 12–48.
6. John Sturrock, *Structuralism* (Malden, MA: Blackwell, 2003), in particular 123–154.

7. Robert Sampson, *John L. O'Sullivan and His Times* (Kent, OH: Kent State University Press, 2003), 83–87.
8. Ernest Lee Tuverson, *Redeemer Nation: Idea of America's Millennial Role* (Chicago: University of Chicago Press, 1980).
9. For a study of long-existing prejudices among various dominations and the manner in which these pressures eased following World War II, see Robert Wuthnow, *The Restructuring of American Religion* (Princeton, NJ: Princeton University Press, 1990).
10. Francis J. Bremer, *The Puritan Experiment: New England Society from Bradford to Edwards* (Lebanon, NH: University Press of New England, 1995).
11. Reginald Horsman, *Race and Manifest Destiny: Origins of American Racial Anglo-Saxonism* (Cambridge, MA: Harvard University Press, 1981), 36–39.
12. Anders Stephanson, *Manifest Destiny: American Expansion and the Empire of Right* (New York: Hill and Wang, 1996).
13. Roderick Frazier Nash, *Wilderness and the American Mind* (New Haven, CT: Yale University Press, 1967), 16.
14. David Ross Williams, *Wilderness Lost: The Origins of the American Mind* (Selinsgrove, PA: Susquehanna University Press, Associated University Presses, 1987), 15.

CHAPTER SEVENTEEN

1. The paradigm illustrated in the film *Paint Your Wagon* is spelled out in historical terms in the excellent Laurie F. Maffly-Kipp, *Religion and Society in Frontier California* (New Haven, CT: Yale University Press, 1994).
2. While numerous biographies of the man exist, the most fascinating is still the earliest account, written by a fellow *pistolero* who knew and loathed him: W. B. "Bat" Masterson, *Famous Gunfighters of the Western Frontier: Wyatt Earp, Doc Holliday, Luke Short, and Others*, originally printed as a series of newspaper articles in 1907, recently collected and published by Dover (New York, 2009).
3. Slotkin, *Gunfighter Nation*, 310.
4. Though the precise derivation of that term remains shrouded in mystery, its popularization came about with the 1950 publication of *The Lonely Crowd: A Study of the Changing American Character*, by David Riesman with Nathan Glazer and Reuel Denney, reprinted several times and more recently abridged and revised (New Haven, CT: Yale University Press, 2001).
5. Slotkin, *Gunfighter Nation*, 379.

CHAPTER EIGHTEEN

1. John Podhoretz, "Avatarocious," *Weekly Standard*, December 28, 2009.
2. Ann Marlowe, "The Most Neo-Con Movie Ever Made," *Forbes*, December 23, 2009.
3. Mike Taibbi, MSNBC news, December 27, 2009, first live and then repeated throughout the day and the following day.
4. No work more captures the totality of George Armstrong Custer, the good as well as the bad and the ugly, as Evan S. Connell, *Son of the Morning Star: Custer and the Little Bighorn* (New York: North Point Press, 1997).
5. Podhoretz, "Avatarocious."
6. Vatican radio and *L'Osservatore Romano*, January 10, 2010; also see Associated Press writer Alessandra Rizzo, "Vatican Says 'Avatar' Is No Masterpiece," *The Guardian*, January 13, 2010.

7. Randall Balmer, *Protestantism in America* (New York: Columbia University Press, 2005).

8. Alan C. Leidner, *The Impatient Muse: Germany and the Sturm und Drang* (Chapel Hill: University of North Carolina Press, 1994). For further reading see David Hill, ed., *Literature of the Sturm und Drang*, vol. 6 (Rochester, NY: Camden House, 2002). Each of these critically acclaimed volumes references the relationship of this Germanic movement to the coming ideology and sensibility that would be called Romanticism.

9. Barry Cunliffe, *The Ancient Celts* (Penguin, 2000). For an overview, see Miranda J. Aldhouse-Green, *Celtic Goddesses: Warriors, Virgins, and Mothers* (New York: George Braziller, 1996). For a more specific approach, consult Lochlainn Seabrook, *The Book of Kelle: An Introduction to Goddess-Worship and the Great Celtic Mother-Goddess* (Franklin, TN: Sea Raven Press, 2010).

10. For an analysis of the way simple crafts of everyday living are transformed in time to artistic artifacts, today as in the past, see Julia S. Ardery, *The Temptation: Edgar Tolson and the Genesis of Twentieth-Century Folk Art* (Chapel Hill: University of North Carolina Press, 1998).

11. A succinct analysis of how the Romantic music of that era directly relates to other aspects of emergent life, specifically politics, is found in Arthur Ware Locke, *Music and the Romantic Movement in France* (Charleston, SC: Forgotten Books, 2012; originally published 1920).

12. Mircea Eliade, *The Sacred and the Profane: The Nature of Religion*, trans. Willard R. Trask (San Diego, CA: Harcourt, 1987).

13. Paul Harrison, *Elements of Pantheism: Religious Reverence of Nature and the Universe* (Coral Springs, FL: Llumina Press, 2004).

14. Ruth H. Bloch, *Gender and Morality in Anglo-American Culture* (Berkeley: University of California Press, 2003).

15. See Rousseau, *Discourse on the Sciences and Arts (First Discourse) and Polemics* (1992), in *The Collected Writings of Rousseau*, edited by Roger Masters and Christopher Kelly, 13 vols. (Hanover, NH: University Press of New England, Dartmouth College Press, 1990–2010). For an accessible overview of the man's life and work, see Leo Damrosch, *Jean-Jacques Rousseau: Restless Genius* (New York: Mariner Books, 2007).

16. This concept is explored in the works of Richard Slotkin, particularly *Regeneration through Violence: The Mythology of the American Frontier, 1600–1860* (Norman: University of Oklahoma Press, 2000).

17. Ross Douthat, "Heaven and Nature," op-ed, *New York Times*, December 20, 2009.

18. "Ode: Intimations on Immortality." For a full description of this particular line and its meaning to several modernist poets influenced by Wordsworth, see George Bornstein, *Transformations of Romanticism in Yeats, Eliot, and Stevens* (Chicago: University of Chicago Press, 1976).

19. For a satisfying and accurate chronology of the creation of this form of worship, see Lewis Spence, *History and Origins of Druidism* (New York: Rider, 1949). For some striking examples of how worship of the "woode" can appear in modern poetry of an ancient spiritual origin, see L. M. Browning, *Oak Wise: Poetry Exploring Ecological Faith* (New London, CT: Little Red Tree, 2010).

20. "Primal sympathy" is a term by which Wordsworth designated his essential and ongoing notion that "the child is father to the man." An excellent analysis of this concept appears in Leslie Tuck-Henry, "Dream Children: The Internal Quest," PhD diss., McMaster University, Canada, 1977.

21. Wordsworth, "Ode: Intimations on Immortality."

CHAPTER NINETEEN

1. "Lines" is included in its entirety in a special collection of the poet's work assembled for

modern readers: Mark Van Doren and David Bromwich, *Selected Poetry of William Wordsworth* (New York: Modern Library, 2002).

2. A fan of Kirk Douglas's Western movies, Ken Kesey wrote the novel with just such a figure as his model for the cowboylike McMurphy, which is how Douglas played the part on Broadway in 1963. By the time Michael Douglas coproduced the film version a dozen years later, Western motifs had fallen out of favor, and the decision was made to convert McMurphy into a more modern figure. Interviews by the author with both Douglases, father and son.

3. This controversial theory had considerable impact when it appeared, first in a 1965 magazine article, then elaborated in Alvin Toffler, *Future Shock* (New York: Random House, 1970).

4. Robert Bly, *Iron John: A Book about Men* (Cambridge, MA: Da Capo Press, 2004).

5. The most exhaustively researched yet thoroughly entertaining volumes on these people of the Plains is to be found in Margot Liberty, *Cheyenne Memories* (New Haven, CT: Yale University Press, 1998), and George Bird Grinnell, *The Cheyenne Indians: The History and Lifeways*, edited by Joseph A. Fitzgerald (Bloomington, IN: World Wisdom, 2008). Also excellent is John H. Moore, *The Cheyenne* (Malden, MA: Blackwell, 1999). They dispel the *Dances with Wolves* myth that the Cheyenne were a genial people except when attacked by other Plains Indian tribes.

CHAPTER TWENTY

1. For further information on the Feeney family heritage and Irish elements apparent in Ford's films, including those set in the American West, you can't do better than to consult Scott Eyman, *Print the Legend: The Life and Times of John Ford* (Baltimore, MD: Johns Hopkins University Press, 2001), and Peter Cowie, *John Ford and the American West* (New York: Harry N. Abrams, 2004).

2. Recommended sources: Kevin Collins, *The Cultural Conquest of Ireland* (Cork, Ireland: Mercier Press, 1991); and James Connolly, *The Re-Conquest of Ireland* (Sioux Falls, SD: Nu-Vision, 2007; originally published 1915).

3. Of the many books written on this subject, the ones that focus on the Protestant English attempts to eliminate pagan Irish dancing from the Emerald Isle are Deidre Mulrooney, *Irish Moves: An Illustrated History of Dance and Physical Theatre in Ireland* (Dublin: Liffey Press, 2006); Jonathan W. Zophy, *A Short History of Reformation Europe: Dances over Water* (New York: Prentice Hall, 1996); and Joanne Asala, *Whistling Jigs to the Moon: Tales of Irish and Scottish Jigs* (Iowa City, IA: Kalevala Books, 1993).

4. William Lamont, *Puritanism and Historical Controversy* (Montreal: McGill Queens University Press, 1999).

5. For a lighthearted study of the relationship of dance to pagan cultures, past and present, particularly among female members of Wiccan sects, see Dorothy Morrison and Kristin Madden, *Dancing the Goddess Incarnate: Living the Magic of Maiden, Mother, and Crone* (Woodbury, MN: Llewelyn, 2006).

6. John P. Cullinane, *Aspects of the History of Irish Dancing* (Westwood, MA: J. P. Cullinane Press, 1987).

7. An excellent analysis of the Baptist vision of Christianity, including attitudes toward such "natural" activity as dance, can be found in Bill J. Leonard, *Baptist Ways: A History* (King of Prussia, PA: Judson Press, 2003); also see J. L. Bray, *Is It Wrong to Dance?* (Lexington, KY: Ashland Avenue Baptist Press, 1960; originally published 1935).

8. Though considered a combination of folk myth and fact, the "real" town too tough to die, or at least as real as anyone will likely reclaim it in modern times, remains Walter Noble Burns,

Tombstone: An Iliad of the Southwest (Albuquerque: University of New Mexico Press, 1999; originally published 1927).

9. Of all the many biographies on Wayne, the ones that contain particularly useful and extended discussions of his involvement with Batjac Productions are Randy Roberts and James S. Olson, *John Wayne, American* (Lincoln, NE: Bison Books, 1977), and Ronald Davis, *Duke: Life and Image of John Wayne* (Norman: University of Oklahoma Press, 1998).

10. For a full view not only of the remarkable manner in which old-time religion gradually became inseparable from the Southern hill country's unconsciously close-to-nature value system, as well as the extension of the unique notion of hillbilly spirituality to all other aspects of that lifestyle, read William Claassen, *Another World: A Retreat in the Ozarks* (Franklin, MD: Sheed and Ward, 2007).

11. The connection between these musicals, emphasizing both their interrelationship and avenues of independence, is the subject of Linnell Gentry, *A History and Encyclopedia of Country, Western, and Gospel Music* (Nashville, TN: Clairmont Corp., 1969; originally published 1961).

12. James Gilbert, *A Cycle of Outrage: America's Reaction to the Juvenile Delinquent in the 1950s* (Norman: University of Oklahoma Press, 1988).

13. John Earl Haynes, *Red Scare or Red Menace? American Communism and Anti-Communism in the Cold War Era* (Lanham, MD: Ivan R. Dee, 1995).

14. Daniel Dreisbach, *Thomas Jefferson and the Wall of Separation between Church and State* (New York: New York University Press, 2003).

CHAPTER TWENTY-ONE

1. For a complete analysis of the author's life and its relationship to both his fiction and his philosophy as expressed therein, see Axel Nissen, *Bret Harte: Prince and Pauper* (Jackson: University of Mississippi Press, 2000).

2. The relationship of Mormons to Indians and the ways the terrain they inhabited influenced both groups as well as their relationship is covered in Jared Farmer, *On Zion's Mount: Mormons, Indians, and the American Landscape* (Cambridge, MA: Harvard University Press, 2010).

3. Various views on why the event occurred and how it forever altered the relationship of Mormons to "Gentiles" in America are presented in Davis Bitton, *The Martyrdom Remembered: A One-Hundred-Fifty-Year Perspective on the Assassination of Joseph Smith* (New York: Aspen Books, 1994).

4. Newell G. Bringhurst and Darren T. Smith, eds., *Black and Mormon* (Champaign: University of Illinois Press, 2006).

5. Quoted from Mormon history records in Salt Lake City, Mormon reactions to the Brigham Young 20th Century film project, 1940–1941.

6. Margaret Drabble and Jenny Stringer, eds., *The Concise Oxford Companion to English Literature* (Oxford, England: Oxford University Press, 2007).

7. Ibid.

8. Ibid.

9. Donnare MacCann, *White Supremacy in Children's Literature: Characterizations of African Americans, 1830–1900* (New York: Routledge, 2000).

10. Alain Locke, ed., *The New Negro: Voices of the Harlem Renaissance* (New York: Touchstone, 1999; originally published 1925).

CHAPTER TWENTY-TWO

1. For the most all-encompassing analysis of the horrific event, see Will Bangley, *Blood of the Prophets: Brigham Young and the Massacre at Mountain Meadows* (Norman: University of Oklahoma Press, 2004).

2. This aspect of the aftermath of the film's release is most fully documented in Melvin Stokes, *D. W. Griffith's* The Birth of a Nation: *A History of the Most Controversial Picture of All Time* (Oxford, England: Oxford University Press, 2008).

3. Siegfried Kracauer, *Theory of Film* (Princeton, NJ: Princeton University Press, 1997; originally published 1960).

4. Scott Higgins, *Arnheim for Film and Media Studies* (New York: Routledge, 2010).

5. The immediate aftermath of the initial screenings of *Birth of a Nation* in Northern cities as well as the generalized anger expressed in many parts of the country form the crux of Michael R. Hurwitz, *D. W. Griffith's* The Birth of a Nation: *The Film that Transformed America* (Rochester, NY: Express Press, 2006).

CHAPTER TWENTY-THREE

1. Robert Warshow (1917–1955), the influential critic of *Commentary* magazine during the later years of his life, was instrumental in the now widely accepted move to appreciate popular culture as a form that ought to be dealt with in the same manner of intellectual appreciation as "high" or "serious" culture, initiating the breakdown of any imagined wall between the two without which this book could not have been written.

2. Everson, *Pictorial History of Westerns*.

3. Of all the variations of this story, perhaps the most true to the record, or what there is of it, can be found in Don Chaput, *The Earp Papers: In a Brother's Image* (New York: Affiliated Writers of America, 1994).

4. The Stoic philosopher and playwright Seneca the Younger (4 BCE?–65 CE) created a genre in which brutal vengeance and political analysis were strangely but satisfyingly fused, most notably in *Thyestes*. For complex reasons, among them certain similarities in the political situations in Rome during that era and Elizabethan England, Seneca's work was revived and led to such English imitations as Kydd's *Spanish Tragedy* and Shakespeare's own derivative, unfocused *Titus Andronicus* (circa 1588–1589), the Bard then bringing the revenge-tragedy genre to the height of genius with his *Hamlet*.

5. General Oliver O. Howard (1830–1909) dedicated himself to the equality of people of color in America, helping to found Howard University in 1867.

6. Effectively detailed in Fuad Shaban, *For Zion's Sake: The Judeo-Christian Tradition in American Culture* (London: Pluto Press, 2005).

CHAPTER TWENTY-FOUR

1. For an analysis of not only the WPA's public images but all the varied artistic forms that were affected by the Great Depression and FDR's plans to pull America out of it, see Morris Dickstein, *Dancing in the Dark: A Cultural History of the New Deal Era* (New York: W. W. Norton, 2009).

2. Of the man's many biographies, aficionados prefer Marley Brant, *Jesse James: The Man and the Myth* (New York: Berkley Trade, 1998).

CHAPTER TWENTY-FIVE

1. A vivid analysis appears in Lewis William Spitz, *The Protestant Reformation* (St. Louis, MO: Concordia, 1997).
2. The concept of a Protestant elect is compared to the radically different visions of humans' relationship to God in other varied denominations, particularly as they are taught to the public, in John L. Elias, *A History of Christian Education: Protestant, Catholic, and Orthodox Perspectives* (Malabar, FL: Kreiger, 2002).
3. Rudolf Steiner and D. S. Osmond, *The Concepts of Original Sin and Grace* (London: Rudolf Steiner Press, 1973).
4. Nash, 78.
5. The development of the entire cowtown, with an emphasis on the red-light district inhabited by Dora Hand and other prostitutes of that era, is well documented in Vestal.
6. William Winter, *The Life of David Belasco* (New York: Moffatt, Yard, 1918).
7. Though all Ford bios cover his family life and genealogy to some degree, it is not surprising that the one penned by his grandson pays the most attention to such details: Dan Ford, *Pappy: The Life and Times of John Ford* (New York: Da Capo Press, 1998).
8. Everson, 89.
9. Particular attention to the concept of a signature shot is paid by Peter Bogdanovich, *John Ford*, revised and expanded (Berkeley: University of California Press, 1978).

CHAPTER TWENTY-SIX

1. The best collection of anecdotes from this period appears in Jorge I. Dominguez, *The Roman Catholic Church in Latin America* (New York: Routledge, 1994).

CHAPTER TWENTY-SEVEN

1. Relativism and relativity, in relationship to the postmodern vision of life and reality, is effectively pursued throughout Claudia Moscovi, *Double Dialectics: Between Universalism and Relativism in Enlightenment and Postmodern Thought* (Lanham, MD: Rowan and Littlefield, 2001).
2. Richard Schickel, *Clint Eastwood: A Biography* (New York: Vintage Books, 1997), 291–293.
3. Slotkin, *Gunfighter Nation*, 242.
4. Ibid., 245.
5. Ibid., 248.
6. Richard Godbeer, *Sexual Revolution in Early America* (Baltimore, MD: Johns Hopkins University Press, 2002).
7. The once highly influential, now largely rejected theory was described by Laura Mulvey in "The Male Gaze in Movies," *Screen* 16.3 (Autumn 1975): 6–19. Mulvey's ideas are further developed in her *Visual and Other Pleasures* (New York: Palgrave Macmillan, 2009). For an excellent and objective analysis of Mulvey's theories and influence, see Carolina Hein, "Laura Mulvey, Visual Pleasure and Narrative Cinema," seminar paper (Norderstedt: GRIN Verlag, 2006).
8. Many books cover this concept; none do so as lucidly as Robert Sklar, *Movie-Made America: A Cultural History of American Movies* (New York: Vintage, 1994).
9. Clint Eastwood, interview in *Playboy*, March 1997.
10. Michael Marsden, "Savior in the Saddle: The Sagebrush Testament," in *Shane: Critical Edition*, edited by James C. Work, 393–404 (Lincoln: University of Nebraska Press, 1984).

11. John Wayne, interview in *Playboy*, May 1971.

CHAPTER TWENTY-EIGHT

1. It is difficult to determine whether this was a conscious artistic decision on Peckinpah's part or simply a result of the merciless cutting that took place when the film was taken away from him. For details on the battle between the director and his producer over *Major Dundee*, see Marshall Fine, *Bloody Sam: The Life and Films of Sam Peckinpah* (Donald I. Fine, 1991), 83–101.
2. The incident of March 16, 1969, is effectively investigated in Michael Bilton and Kevin Sim, *Four Hours in My Lai* (New York: Penguin, 1993).
3. Joseph R. Gusfield, *Symbolic Crusade: Status Politics and the American Temperance Movement* (Chicago: University of Illinois Press, 1986).
4. Determining the precise initial use of the phrase is not feasible, as many critics employed it in their reviews; the expression appears numerous times in essays in Stephen Prince, ed., *Sam Peckinpah's* The Wild Bunch (Cambridge, England: Cambridge University Press, 1998).

CHAPTER TWENTY-NINE

1. Ian C. Storey and Arlene Allan, *A Guide to Ancient Greek Drama* (Malden, MA: Blackwell, 2005).

CHAPTER THIRTY

1. The redemption is essential to the interpretations in Aidan Nichols, *The Shape of Catholic Theology: An Introduction to Its Principles and History* (Collegeville, MN: Liturgical Press, 1991).
2. The hero quest theme runs throughout Joseph Campbell's work, but nowhere is it so prominently developed as in Joseph Campbell and David Kudler, *Pathways to Bliss: Mythology and Personal Transformation* (Novato, CA: New World Library, 2004).

CONCLUSION

1. William Butler Yeats, "The Second Coming," 1919.
2. A wonderful phrase, though erroneously coined by Samuel Taylor Coleridge to describe, in a romanticist's terms, the villain Iago in *Othello*. Coleridge's essays on the Bard and other Elizabethan playwrights, as filtered through the limited and limiting vision of the Lake School, are collected in *Shakespeare, Ben Jonson, Beaumont, and Fletcher: Notes and Lectures*, first published in 1874 and now digitized and available online.
3. "I think, therefore I am" is originally stated in Descartes' *Discourse on the Method*, 1636.
4. The J. D. Salinger of macho Mexican expatriate writers, B. Travern (the pen name for an unidentified German scribe) lived (1882?–1969?) and loved south of the border; all supposed photographs of him are highly questionable as to their authenticity.
5. Maxwell Anderson and Kurt Weill's song "Lost in the Stars," 1949.
6. Lucas's original concepts for what would become *Star Wars*, including the pitch phrase "Cowboys in Space," are chronicled in virtually all biographies of the filmmaker; most highly recommended is Michael Kaminski, *The Secret History of* Star Wars*: The Art of Storytelling and the Making of a Modern Epic*. Kingston, Ontario, Canada: Legacy Books Press, 2008).
7. William Shakespeare, *The Tragedy of Hamlet, Prince of Denmark* (1599–1600), act 5, scene 4.

BIBLIOGRAPHY

Aldhouse-Green, Miranda J. *Celtic Goddesses: Warriors, Virgins, and Mothers*. New York: George
Braziller, 1996.

Anderson, Paul F. *The Davy Crockett Craze: A Look at the 1950's Davy Crockett Phenomenon*. Granada
Hills, CA: R&G Productions, 1996.

Andrew, John A. *Lyndon Johnson and the Great Society*. Lanham, MD: Ivan R. Dee, 1999.

Ardery, Julia S. *The Temptation: Edgar Tolson and the Genesis of Twentieth-Century Folk Art*. Chapel
Hill: University of North Carolina Press, 1998.

Arnold, Shannon Jackson. *Everybody Loves Ice Cream: The Whole Scoop on America's Favorite Treat*.
Cincinnati: Clerisy Press, 2004.

Asala, Joanne. *Whistling Jigs to the Moon: Tales of Irish and Scottish Jigs*. Iowa City, IA: Kalevala
Books, 1993.

Autry, Gene. *Back in the Saddle Again*. New York: Doubleday, 1978.

Bailey, Lynn R. *"Too Tough to Die": The Rise, Fall, and Resurrection of a Silver Camp; 1878–1900*.
Tucson: Westernlore Press, 2010.

Balmer, Randall, *Protestantism in America*. New York: Columbia University Press, 2005.

Bangley, Will. *Blood of the Prophets: Brigham Young and the Massacre at Mountain Meadows*. Norman:
University of Oklahoma Press, 2004.

Barber, Richard. *The Knight and Chivalry*. Suffolk, England: Boydell Press, 2000.

Barbour, Barton H. *Jedediah Smith: No Ordinary Mountain Man*. Norman: University of Oklahoma
Press, 2011.

Barra, Allen. *Inventing Wyatt Earp: His Life and Many Legends*. Lincoln, NE: Castle Books, 2009.

Bauman, Zygmunt. "Postmodernity, or Living with Ambivalence." In *A Postmodern Reader*, edited by
Joseph Natoli and Linda Hutcheon, 9–24. Albany: SUNY Press, 1993.

17

Beers, Terry, ed. *Gunfight at Mussel Slough: Evolution of a Western Myth*. Berkeley, CA: Heyday Books, 2004.

Berlin, Isaiah, and Henry Hardy. *The Roots of Revolution*. Princeton, NJ: Princeton University Press, 2001.

Berman, Ari. *Herding Donkeys: The Fight to Rebuild the Democratic Party and Reshape American Politics*. New York: Farrar, Strauss, and Giroux, 2010.

Bertens, Hans. "The Postmodern Weltanschauung and Its Relation to Modernism: An Introductory Survey." In *A Postmodern Reader*, edited by Joseph Natoli and Linda Hutcheon, 25–70. Albany: SUNY Press, 1993.

Bilton, Michael, and Kevin Sim, *Four Hours in My Lai*. New York: Penguin, 1993.

Bingen, Steve, Stephen X. Sylvester, and Michael Troyon. *MGM: Hollywood's Greatest Backlot*. Santa Monica, CA: Santa Monica Press, 2011.

Biskind, Peter. *Easy Riders, Raging Bulls: How the Sex-Drugs-and-Rock 'n' Roll Generation Saved Hollywood*. New York: Simon and Schuster, 1999.

Bitton, Davis. *The Martyrdom Remembered: A One-Hundred-Fifty-Year Perspective on the Assassination of Joseph Smith*. New York: Aspen Books, 1994.

Blake, Michael F. *Hollywood and the O.K. Corral: Portrayals of the Gunfight and Wyatt Earp*. Jefferson, NC: McFarland, 2006.

Bloch, Ruth H. *Gender and Morality in Anglo-American Culture*. Berkeley: University of California Press, 2003.

Bloom, Harold. *Agon: Towards a Theory of Revisionism*. New York: Oxford University Press, 1982.

Bly, Robert. *Iron John: A Book about Men*. Cambridge, MA: Da Capo Press, 2004.

Bogdanovich, Peter. *John Ford*. Revised and expanded. Berkeley: University of California Press, 1978.

Bornstein, George. *Transformations of Romanticism in Yeats, Eliot, and Stevens*. Chicago: University of Chicago Press, 1971.

Brant, Marley. *Jesse James: The Man and the Myth*. New York: Berkley Books, 1998.

Bray, John L. *Is It Wrong to Dance?* Lexington, KY: Ashland Avenue Baptist Press, 1960. Originally published 1938.

Bremer, Francis J. *The Puritan Experiment: New England Society from Bradford to Edwards*. Lebanon, NH: University Press of New England, 1995.

Bringhurst, Newell G., and Darren T. Smith, eds. *Black and Mormon*. Champaign: University of Illinois Press, 2006.

Brode, Douglas. *Shooting Stars of the Small Screen: An Encyclopedia of TV Western Actors*. Austin: University of Texas Press, 2009.

Brown, Bill, ed. *Readings on the West: An Anthology of Dime Westerns*. New York: Bedford Cultural Edition, St. Martin's Press, 1997.

Browning, L. M. *Oak Wise: Poetry Exploring Ecological Faith*. New London, CT: Little Red Tree, 2010.

Buckley, Christopher. *Thank You for Smoking*. Colorado Springs, CO: Random House, 2006.

Burns, Walter Noble. *Tombstone: An Iliad of the Southwest*. Albuquerque: University of New Mexico Press, 1999. Originally published 1927.

Burrows, Jack. *John Ringo: The Gunfighter Who Never Was*. Tucson: University of Arizona Press, 1996.

Campbell, Joseph. *The Hero with a Thousand Faces*. Novato, CA: New World Library, 2000.

Campbell, Joseph, and David Kudler. *Pathways to Bliss: Mythology and Personal Transformation*. Novato, CA: New World Library, 2004.

Carson, Rachel. *Silent Spring*. New York: Houghton Mifflin, 1962.

Carter, Jimmy. *An Hour before Daylight: Memories of a Rural Boyhood.* New York: Simon and Schuster, 2001.

Cawelti, John G. *The Six-Gun Mystique Sequel.* Bowling Green, OH: Bowling Green State University Popular Press, 1999.

Chaffin, Tom. *Pathfinder: John Charles Frémont and the Course of American Empire.* New York: Hill and Wang, 2003.

Chaput, Don. *The Earp Papers: In a Brother's Image.* New York: Affiliated Writers of America, 1994.

Claassen, William. *Another World: A Retreat in the Ozarks.* Lanham, MD: Sheed and Ward, 2007.

Clum, John P. *It All Happened in Tombstone.* Outing, MN: Northland Press, 1965. Originally published 1929.

Clymer, Adam. *Drawing the Line at the Big Ditch: The Panama Canal Treaties and the Rise of the Right.* Lexington: University Press of Kentucky, 2008.

Collier, Christopher, *All Politics Is Local: Family, Friends, and Provincial Interests in the Creation of the Constitution.* Lebanon, NH: University Press of New England, 2003.

Collins, Kevin. *The Cultural Conquest of Ireland.* Dublin: Mercier Press, 1990.

Connell, Evan S. *Son of the Morning Star: Custer and the Little Bighorn.* New York: North Point Press, 1997.

Connolly, James. *The Re-Conquest of Ireland.* Sioux Falls, SD: NuVision, 2007. Originally published 1915.

Cowie, Peter. *John Ford and the American West.* New York: Harry N. Abrams, 2004.

Cumbow, Robert C. *Once Upon a Time: The Films of Sergio Leone.* Lanham, MD: Scarecrow Press, 1991.

Cullinane, John P. *Aspects of the History of Irish Dancing.* Cork City, Ireland: J. P. Cullinane, 1987.

Cunliffe, Barry. *The Ancient Celts.* New York: Penguin, 2000.

Cusic, Don. *Gene Autry, His Life and Career.* Jefferson, NC: McFarland, 2010.

Damrosch, Leo. *Jean-Jacques Rousseau: Restless Genius.* New York: Mariner Books, 2007.

Davis, Ronald. *Duke: Life and Image of John Wayne.* Norman: University of Oklahoma Press, 1998.

Dickstein, Morris. *Dancing in the Dark: A Cultural History of the New Deal Era.* New York: W. W. Norton, 2009.

Dillon, Richard. *The Legend of Grizzly Adams: California's Greatest Mountain Man.* Lincoln: University of Nebraska Press, 1999.

Dobie, James Frank. *Up the Trail from Texas.* New York: Random House, 1955.

Dolin, Eric Jay. *Fur, Fortune, and Empire: The Epic History of the Fur Trade in America.* New York: W. W. Norton, 2011.

Dominguez, Jorge I. *The Roman Catholic Church in Latin America.* New York: Routledge, 1994.

Douthat, Ross. "Heaven and Nature." *New York Times,* December 20, 2009.

Drabble, Margaret, and Jenny Stringer, eds. *The Concise Oxford Companion to English Literature.* Oxford, England: Oxford University Press, 2007.

Dreisbach, Daniel. *Thomas Jefferson and the Wall of Separation between Church and State.* New York: New York University Press, 2003.

Dugrand, Alain, and Stephen Romer. *Trotsky in Mexico, 1937–1940.* Oxford, England: Carcanet Press, 1992.

Earp, Josephine Sara Marcus. *I Married Wyatt Earp.* Tucson: University of Arizona Press, 1994.

Eisenstein, S. M. *Que Viva Mexico!.* New York: Arno Press, 1972.

Eliade, Mircea. *The Sacred and the Profane: The Nature of Religion.* Trans. Willard R. Trask. San Diego, CA: Harcourt, 1987.

Elias, John L. *A History of Christian Education: Protestant, Catholic, and Orthodox Perspectives.* Malabar, FL: Kreiger, 2002.

Everson, William K. *A Pictorial History of the Western Film.* New York: Citadel Press, 1969.

Ewing, Sherm. *The Ranch: A Modern History of the North American Cattle Industry.* Aspen, CO: Mountain Press, 1995.

Eyman, Scott. *Print the Legend: The Life and Times of John Ford.* Baltimore, MD: Johns Hopkins University Press, 2001.

Fagen, Herb. *Encyclopedia of Westerns.* New York: Facts on File, 2003.

Farmer, Jared. *On Zion's Mount: Mormons, Indians, and the American Landscape.* Cambridge, MA: Harvard University Press, 2010.

Field, Jason Porter. *The Homestead Act of 1862: A Primary Source of the Settlement of the American Heartland in the Late 19th Century.* New York: Rosen, 2004.

Fine, Marshall. *Bloody Sam: The Life and Films of Sam Peckinpah.* Donald I. Fine, 1991.

Ford, Dan. *Pappy: The Life of John Ford.* New York: Da Capo Press, 1998.

Francis, Mark. *Herbert Spencer and the Invention of Modern Life.* Ithaca, NY: Cornell University Press, 2007.

Franklin, Benjamin. *Poor Richard's Almanack.* Foreword by Dave Barry. New York: Modern Library, 2000. Originally published 1732-1758.

Frederickson, Kari. *The Dixiecrat Revolt and the End of the Solid South.* Chapel Hill: University of North Carolina Press, 2000.

French, Philip. *Westerns: Aspects of a Movie Genre.* New York: Viking, 1973.

Garrett, Pat F. *The Authentic Life of Billy the Kid.* New York: Skyhorse, 2011. Originally published 1882.

Gentry, Linnell. *A History and Encyclopedia of Country, Western, and Gospel Music.* St. Clair Shores, MI: Scholarly Press, 1972.

George-Warren, Holly. *Public Cowboy No. 1: The Life and Times of Gene Autry.* New York: Oxford University Press, 2009.

Gilbert, James. *A Cycle of Outrage: America's Reaction to the Juvenile Delinquent in the 1950s.* Norman: University of Oklahoma Press, 1988.

Glasgow, Ellen. *Vein of Iron.* New York: Harcourt Brace, 1935.

Godbeer, Richard. *Sexual Revolution in Early America.* Baltimore, MD: Johns Hopkins University Press, 2002.

Goldman, William. *Adventures in the Screen Trade: A Personal View of Hollywood and Screenwriting.* New York: Grand Central, 1989.

Goodman, Susan. *Ellen Glasgow: Biography.* Baltimore, MD: Johns Hopkins University Press, 2003.

Goodwyn, Lawrence. *The Populist Moment: A Short History of the Agrarian Revolt in America.* Oxford, England: Oxford University Press, 1978.

Gould, Lewis. *Grand Old Party: A History of the Republicans.* New York: Random House, 2003.

Gowans, Fred R. *Rocky Mountain Rendezvous: A History of the Fur Trade 1825–1840.* Layton, UT: Gibbs Smith, 2005.

Gressley, Gene M. *Bankers and Cattlemen: The Stocks-and-Bonds, Havana Cigar, Mahogany-and-Leather Side of the Cowboy Era.* Lincoln: University of Nebraska Press, 1971.

Grinnell, George Bird. *The Cheyenne Indians: The History and Lifeways.* Edited by Joseph A. Fitzgerald. Bloomington, IN: World Wisdom, 2008.

Guinn, Jeff. *The Last Gunfight: The Real Story of the Shootout at the O.K. Corral—and How It Changed the American West.* New York: Simon and Schuster, 2011.

Gulick, William. *Bend of the Snake.* New York: Bantam, 1950.

Gusfield, Joseph R. *Symbolic Crusade: Status Politics and the American Temperance Movement.* Chicago: University of Illinois Press, 1986.

Hall, Lee. *Athena: A Biography.* Cambridge, MA: Da Capo Press, 1997.

Hardy, Phil. *Encyclopedia of Western Movies.* Minneapolis, MN: Woodbury Press, 1984.

Harrison, Paul. *Elements of Pantheism: Religious Reverence of Nature and the Universe.* Coral Springs, FL: Llumina Press, 2004.

Haynes, John Earl. *Red Scare or Red Menace? American Communism and Anti-Communism in the Cold War Era.* Lanham, MD: Ivan R. Dee, 1995.

Hein, Carolina. "Laura Mulvey, Visual Pleasure and Narrative Cinema." Seminar paper. Norderstedt, Germany: GRIN Verlag, 2006.

Hicks, Frederick Cocks. *The Flag of the United States.* Washington, DC: Government Printing Office, 1918.

Higgins, Scott. *Arnheim for Film and Media Studies.* New York: Routledge, 2010.

Hill, David, ed. *Literature of the Sturm und Drang.* Vol. 6. Rochester, NY: Camden House, 2002.

Holt, Michael F. *The Rise and Fall of the Whig Party: Jacksonian Politics and the Onset of the Civil War.* Oxford, England: Oxford University Press, 2003.

Hopper, Dennis. *Out of the Sixties.* Santa Fe, NM: Twelvetree Press, 1986.

Horan, James D. *The Authentic Wild West: The Lawmen.* New York: Gramercy Books, 1996.

Horsman, Reginald. *Race and Manifest Destiny: Origins of American Racial Anglo-Saxonism.* Cambridge, MA: Harvard University Press, 1981.

Hughes, Howard. *Stagecoach to Tombstone: The Filmgoer's Guide to Great Westerns.* London: I. B. Taurus, 2008.

Humphries, Reynold. *Hollywood Blacklist: A Political and Cultural History.* Edinburgh, Scotland: Edinburgh University Press, 2010.

Hurwitz, Michael R. *D. W. Griffith's* The Birth of a Nation: *The Film That Transformed America.* Rochester, NY: Express Press, 2006.

Jahoda, Gloria. *Trail of Tears.* San Antonio, TX: Wings, 1995.

Johnston, Alex. *Cowboy Politics: The Western Stock Growers' Association and Its Predecessors.* Calgary, Canada: Western Stock Growers' Association, 1971.

Jung, Emma. *The Grail Legend.* Princeton, NJ: Princeton University Press, 1998.

Kaminski, Michael. *The Secret History of* Star Wars: *The Art of Storytelling and the Making of a Modern Epic.* Kingston, Ontario, Canada: Legacy Books Press, 2008.

Kazanjian, Howard, and Chris Enss. *Happy Trails: A Pictorial Celebration of the Life and Times of Roy Rogers and Dale Evans.* Gulford, MT: TwoDot, 2005.

Kennett, Lee, and James La Verne Anderson. *The Gun in America: The Origins of a National Dilemma.* Westport, CT: Greenwood Press, 1975.

Kilen, Dan. *The Peter Pan Syndrome: Men Who Have Never Grown Up.* New York: Dodd, Mead, 1983.

Kracauer, Siegfried. *Theory of Film.* Princeton, NJ: Princeton University Press, 1997. Originally published 1960.

Kusch, Frank. *Battleground Chicago: The Police and the 1968 Democratic Convention.* Chicago: University of Chicago Press, 2008.

Lake, Stuart N. *Wyatt Earp, Frontier Marshal.* Parsippany, NJ: Pocket Books, 1994. Originally published 1931.

Lamont, William. *Puritanism and Historical Controversy.* Montreal: McGill Queens University Press, 1999.

Leidner, Alan C. *The Impatient Muse: Germany and the Sturm und Drang.* Chapel Hill: University of North Carolina Press, 1994.

Lear, Linda. *Rachel Carson: Witness for Nature*. New York: Mariner Books, 2009.

Leepson, Marc. *Flag: An American Biography*. New York: St. Martin's Griffin, 2006.

Leonard, Bill J. *Baptist Ways: A History*. King of Prussia, PA: Judson Press, 2009.

Lepore, Jill. *The Whites of Their Eyes: The Tea Party's Revolution and the Battle over American History*. Princeton, NJ: Princeton University Press, 2010.

Liberty, Margot. *Cheyenne Memories*. New Haven, CT: Yale University Press, 1998.

Locke, Alain, ed. *The New Negro: Voices of the Harlem Renaissance*. New York: Touchstone, 1999. Originally published 1925.

Locke, Arthur Ware. *Music and the Romantic Movement in France*. Charleston, SC: Forgotten Books, 2012. Originally published 1920.

Lubet, Steven. *Murder in Tombstone: The Forgotten Trial of Wyatt Earp*. New Haven, CT: Yale University Press, 2006.

MacCann, Donnare. *White Supremacy in Children's Literature: Characterizations of African Americans, 1830–1900*. New York: Routledge, 2000.

Maffly-Kipp, Laurie F. *Religion and Society in Frontier California*. New Haven, CT: Yale University Press, 1994.

Maltin, Leonard. *The Disney Films*. New York: Crown, 1973.

Marks, Paula Mitchell. *And Die in the West: The Story of the O.K. Corral Gunfight*. Norman: University of Oklahoma Press, 1996.

Marsden, Michael. "Savior in the Saddle: The Sagebrush Testament." In *Shane: Critical Edition*, edited by James C. Work, 393–404. Lincoln: University of Nebraska Press, 1984.

Martin, Douglas D. *An Arizona Chronology: The Territorial Years 1846–1912*. Tucson: University of Arizona Press, 1963.

Mastai, Boleslaw, and Marie-Louise D'Otrange Mastai. *The Stars and the Stripes: The American Flag as Art and as History from the Birth of the Republic to the Present*. Old Saybrook, CT: Konecky and Konecky, 1978.

Masterson, W. B. *Famous Gunfighters of the Western Frontier: Wyatt Earp, Doc Holliday, Luke Short, and Others*. New York: Dover, 2009. Originally published as news articles beginning in 1902.

Mauer, Noel, and Carlos Yu. *The Big Ditch: How America Took, Built, Ran, and Ultimately Gave Away the Panama Canal*. Princeton, NJ: Princeton University Press, 2010.

McBride, Joseph. *Searching for John Ford: A Life*. New York: St. Martin's Press, 2001.

McCumber, John. *Time in the Ditch: American Philosophy and the McCarthy Era*. Evanston, IL: Northwestern University Press, 2001.

Meacham, Jon. *American Lion: Andrew Jackson and the White House*. New York: Random House, 2009.

Meese, Edwin III, Matthew Spalding, and David F. Forte. *The Heritage Guide to the Constitution*. Washington, DC: Regnery, 2005.

Moore, John H. *The Cheyenne*. Malden, MA: Blackwell, 1999.

Morris, Richard B. *Witnesses at the Creation: Hamilton, Madison, Jay, and the Constitution*. New York: Holt, Rinehart, and Winston, 1985.

Morrison, Dorothy, and Kristin Madden. *Dancing the Goddess Incarnate: Living the Magic of Maiden, Mother, and Crone*. Woodbury, MN: Llewelyn, 2006.

Moscovi, Claudia. *Double Dialectics: Between Universalism and Relativism in Enlightenment and Postmodern Thought*. Lanham, MD: Rowan and Littlefield, 2001.

Mulrooney, Deidre. *Irish Moves: An Illustrated History of Dance and Physical Theatre in Ireland*. Dublin: Liffey Press, 2006.

Mulvey, Laura. "The Male Gaze in Movies." *Screen* 16.3 (Autumn 1975): 6–19.

————. *Visual and Other Pleasures*. New York: Palgrave Macmillan, 2009.

Nash, Roderick Frazier. *Wilderness and the American Mind*. New Haven, CT: Yale University Press, 1967.

Newell, Chester. *History of the Revolution in Texas, Particularly of the War of 1835 and '36*. Charleston, SC: BiblioBazaar, 2009. Originally published 1838.

Nichols, Aidan. *The Shape of Catholic Theology: An Introduction to Its Principles and History*. Collegeville, MN: Liturgical Press, 1991.

Nissen, Axel. *Bret Harte: Prince and Pauper*. Jackson: University of Mississippi Press, 2000.

Norris, Frank. *McTeague*. New York: Penguin Signet Classics, 2011. Originally published 1899.

Nute, Grace Lee. *Caesars of the Wilderness*. St. Paul: Minnesota Historical Society Press, 1978.

Orellana, Margarita De, and Kevin Brownwell. *Filming Pancho Villa: How Hollywood Shaped the Mexican Revolution*. Brooklyn, NY: Verso, 2009.

O'Sullivan, Donal Joseph. *Irish Folk Music: Song and Dance*. Cork City, Ireland: Mercier Press, 1974.

Otero, Miguel Antonio. *The Real Billy the Kid*. Santa Fe, NM: Sunstone Press, 1998. Originally published 1936.

Owen, James P. *Cowboy Values: What America Once Stood For*. Guilford, CT: Lyons Press, 2008.

Parish, James Robert, and Gregory Mank. *The Best of M-G-M: The Golden Years, 1928–1959*. Westport, CT: Arlington House, 1981.

Paul, Rand. *The Tea Party Goes to Washington*. New York: Center Street, 2011.

Paul, Ron. *The Revolution: A Manifesto*. New York: Grand Central, 2009.

Pauly, Thomas H. *American Odyssey: Elia Kazan and American Culture*. Philadelphia: Temple University Press, 1985.

Perlstein, Rick. *Before the Storm: Barry Goldwater and the Unmaking of the American Consensus*. New York: Nation Books, 2009.

Pochoda, Elizabeth. *Arthurian Propaganda: Le Morte D'Arthur as an Historical Ideal of Life*. Chapel Hill: University of North Carolina Press, 2009.

Prince, Stephen, ed. *Sam Peckinpah's* The Wild Bunch. Cambridge, England: Cambridge University Press, 1998.

Rasmussen, Scott, and Doug Schoen. *Mad as Hell: How the Tea Party Movement Is Fundamentally Remaking Our Two-Party System*. New York: HarperCollins, 2010.

Reagan, Ronald. *An American Life: The Autobiography*. New York: Simon and Schuster, 1990.

Reasoner, James. *Draw: The Greatest Gunfights of the American West*. New York: Berkley Trade, 2003.

Rickman, Gregg, and Jim Kitses. *The Western Reader*. Ann Arbor: Limelight Editions, University of Michigan Press, 2004.

Riesman, David, with Nathan Glazer and Reuel Denney. *The Lonely Crowd: A Study of the Changing American Character*. Abridged and revised. New Haven, CT: Yale University Press, 2001. Originally published 1950.

Roberts, Gary L. *Doc Holliday: The Life and Legend*. Hoboken, NJ: Wiley, 2007.

Roberts, Randy, and James S. Olson. *John Wayne, American*. Lincoln, NE: Bison Books, 1977.

Rollins, Philip Ashton. *The Cowboy: His Characteristics, His Equipment, and His Part in Development of the West*. New York: Charles Scribner's Sons, 1922.

Rosa, Joseph G. *The West of Wild Bill Hickok*. Norman: University of Oklahoma Press, 1994.

Rousseau, Jean-Jacques. *The Collected Writings of Rousseau*. Edited by Roger Masters and Christopher Kelly. 13 vols. Hanover, NH: University Press of New England, Dartmouth College Press, 1990–2010.

Roy, Jean, ed. *Jean-Jacques Rousseau and the Revolution*. Proceedings of the Montreal Symposium May 25–28, 1989. La Verne, CA: North American Society for the Study of Jean-Jacques Rousseau, 1991.

Salazinka, Masha. *In Excess: Sergei Eisenstein's Mexico*. Chicago: University of Chicago Press, 2009.

Sampson, Robert. *John L. O'Sullivan and His Times*. Kent, OH: Kent State University Press, 2003.

Save, William W. *The Cowboy Hero: His Image in History and Culture*. Norman: University of Oklahoma Press, 1985.

Schickel, Richard. *Clint Eastwood: A Biography*. New York: Vintage Books, 1997.

Seabrook, Lochlainn. *The Book of Kelle: An Introduction to Goddess-Worship and the Great Celtic Mother-Goddess*. Franklin, TN: Sea Raven Press, 2010.

Shaban, Fuad. *For Zion's Sake: The Judeo-Christian Tradition in American Culture*. London: Pluto Press, 2005.

Schaefer, Jack. *Shane*. New York: Bantam, 1983. Originally published 1949.

Schaller, Michael. *Ronald Reagan*. Oxford, England: Oxford University Press, 2010.

Shlapentokh, Vladimir, Joshua Woods, and Eric Shiraev, eds. *America: Sovereign Defender or Cowboy Nation?* Aldershot, England: Ashgate, 2005.

Silvestro, Roger L. *Theodore Roosevelt and the Badlands: A Young Politician's Quest for Recovery in the American West*. New York: Walker, 2011.

Sklar, Robert. *Movie Made America: A Cultural History of American Movies*. New York: Vintage Books, 1994.

Slotkin, Richard. *Gunfighter Nation: The Myth of the Frontier in Twentieth-Century America*. New York: Harper Perennial, 1992.

———. *Regeneration through Violence: The Mythology of the American Frontier, 1600–1860*. Norman: University of Oklahoma Press, 2000.

Smith, Wallace. *Garden of the Sun: A History of San Joaquin Valley 1772–1939*. Fresno, CA: Linden, 2004.

Speher, Paul. *The Movies Begin: Making Movies in New Jersey, 1897–1920*. Newark, NJ: Newark Museum Association, 1977.

Spence, Lewis. *History and Origins of Druidism*. New York: Rider, 1949.

Spitz, Lewis William, ed. *The Protestant Reformation: Major Documents*. St. Louis, MO: Concordia, 1997.

Steiner, Rudolf, and D. S. Osmond. *The Concepts of Original Sin and Grace*. London: Rudolf Steiner Press, 1973.

Stephanson, Anders. *Manifest Destiny: American Expansion and the Empire of Right*. New York: Hill and Wang, 1996.

Stokes, Melvin. *D. W. Griffith's The Birth of a Nation: A History of the Most Controversial Picture of All Time*. Oxford, England: Oxford University Press, 2008.

Storey, Ian C., and Arlene Allan. *A Guide to Ancient Greek Drama*. Malden, MA: Blackwell, 2005.

Sturrock, John. *Structuralism*. Malden, MA: Blackwell, 2003.

Tefertiller, Casey. *Wyatt Earp: The Life behind the Legend*. New York: Wiley and Sons, 1999.

Thomas, Evan. "Don't Mess with Texas." *Newsweek*, April 15, 2010.

Thompson, Frank T. *Alamo Movies*. Plano, TX: Republic of Texas Press, 1994.

Toffler, Alvin. *Future Shock*. New York: Random House, 1970.

Toplin, Robert. *History by Hollywood: The Use and Abuse of the American Past*. Champaign: University of Illinois Press, 1996.

Tourtellot, Bernon Arthur. *Lexington and Concord: The Beginning of the American Revolution*. New York: W. W. Norton, 2000.

Tuck-Henry, Leslie. "Dream Children: The Internal Quest." PhD diss., McMaster University, Canada, 1977.

Turner, Frederick Jackson. *The Frontier in American History*. New York: Henry Holt, 1920.

Tuverson, Ernest Lee. *Redeemer Nation: Idea of America's Millennial Role*. Chicago: University of Chicago Press, 1980.

Ungar, Harlow Giles. *American Tempest: How the Boston Tea Party Sparked a Revolution*. Cambridge, MA: De Capo Press, 2011.

Van Doren, Mark, and David Bromwich. *Selected Poetry of William Wordsworth*. New York: Modern Library, 2002.

Vestal, Stanley. *Dodge City: Queen of Cowtowns: "The Wickedest Little City in America."* Lincoln: Bison Books, University of Nebraska Press, 1998. Originally published 1952.

Vile, John R. *A Companion to the Constitution and Its Amendments*. Santa Barbara, CA: Praeger, 2005.

Wallis, Michael. *David Crockett: The Lion of the West*. New York: W. W. Norton, 2011.

Warshow, Robert. *The Immediate Experience: Movies, Comics, Theatre, and Other Aspects of Our Culture*. Cambridge, MA: Harvard University Press, 2002.

Weiss, Richard. *The American Myth of Success: From Horatio Alger to Norman Vincent Peale*. Chicago: Illini Books, University of Illinois Press, 1988.

White, Richard, ed. *King Arthur in Legend and History*. New York: Routledge, 1998.

Wilentz, Sean. *The Rise of American Democracy from Jefferson to Lincoln*. New York: W. W. Norton, 2005.

Will, George F. *One Man's America: The Pleasures and Provocations of Our Singular Nation*. New York: Three Rivers Press, 2010.

Williams, David Ross. *Wilderness Lost: The Religious Origins of the American Mind*. Selinsgrove, PA: Susquehanna University Press, Associated University Presses, 1987.

Wilson, Lycurgus A. *Outlines of Mormon Philosophy*. Salt Lake City: Desert News, 1905.

Wilson, Michael R. *Crime and Punishment in Early Arizona*. Linden, NJ: Stage Coach Books, 2004.

Winter, William. *The Life of David Belasco*. New York: Moffat, Yard, 1918.

Wister, Owen. *The Virginian: A Horseman of the Plains*. New York: Signet, 2010. Originally published 1902.

Worth, Richard. *Voices from Colonial America: New France 1534–1763*. Washington, DC: National Geographic, 2007.

Wuthnow, Robert. *The Restructuring of American Religion*. Princeton, NJ: Princeton University Press, 1990.

Zelizer, Julian E. *Jimmy Carter*. The American Presidents. New York: Times Books, Henry Holt, 2010.

Zernike, Kate. *Boiling Mad: Inside Tea Party America*. New York: Times Books, 2010.

Zophy, Jonathan W. *A Short History of Reformation Europe: Dances over Water*. New York: Prentice Hall, 1996.

INDEX OF FILMS
AND SHOWS

Broncho Billy (1980), 22

Canadian Pacific (1949), 122
Cannon for Cordoba (1970), 135
Cattle Town (1952), 101, 108
Cheyenne Autumn (1964), 190
Chisum (1970), 53, 99, 101, 153, 154, 155
Christmas Kid, The (1967), 282–283
Code of the West (1947), 11
Code of the West, The (1921), 11
Code of the West, The (1925), 11
Code of the West, The (1929), 11
Comes a Horseman (1978), 100
Count Three and Pray (1955), 104, 226
Covered Wagon, The (1923), 85, 119, 120, 183
Cuando ¡Viva Villa! es la muerte (1960), 144

Dakota (1945), 122
Dances with Wolves (1990), 194, 197, 208, 209
Daniel Boone (TVS, 1964–1970), 204–205
Davy Crockett, King of the Wild Frontier (1954),
    21, 34, 35, 36
Deadly Companions, The (1961), 295
Deadly Shooter. See Shooter, The
Deadwood (TVS, 2004–2006), 13
Death Valley Days (TVS, 1952–1970), 22
Deliverance (1972), 207–208
Denver and the Rio Grande, The (1952), 122
Desert Shooter, The. See Shooter, The
Diamante Lobo. See God's Gun
Doc (1971), 19, 22, 32, 41–43
Dodge City (1939), 121, 122
Dr. Strangelove, or How I Learned to Stop Worry-
    ing and Love the Bomb (1964), 40, 41, 146
Drums along the Mohawk (1939), 158, 159–161,
    179, 180, 274, 275–276
Duck, You Sucker (1971), 130–131, 134
Duel in the Sun (1946), 4, 70, 71, 72, 94, 96, 103,
    259, 260, 261

East of Eden (1954), 78
Easy Rider (1969), 20

Far Horizons, The (1955), 178, 179, 181
5 Card Stud (1968), 281
Fort Apache (1948), ii, 215, 216–217
Forty Guns (1957), 92, 101

Four of the Apocalypse (1975), 225
Frontier Marshal (1939), 27

Girl of the Golden West (1938), 268, 269
Git along Little Dogies (1937), 108–109
God Forgives, I Don't (1969), 285
God's Gun (1976), 280–281
Gold Mine in the Sky (1938), 86
Good, The Bad, and the Ugly, The (1966), 131, 286
Grapes of Wrath, The (1940), 89
Great Northfield Minnesota Raid (1972), 261
Great Sioux Massacre, The (1965), 194
Great Train Robbery, The (1903), 27, 59
Greed (1926), 117–118, 120, 299, 332
Green Mansions (1959), 202, 205
Gunfight at the O.K. Corral (1957), 16, 18, 27, 37
Gunfighter, The (1950), 48, 49, 63
Gunfire (1950), 318
Guns and Guitars (1956), 100
Guns for San Sebastian (1968), 278, 279, 283
Gunsmoke (TVS; 1955–1975), 5, 13, 26, 295
Gunsmoke: To the Last Man (TVM, 1992), 100

Hang 'Em High (1968), 57
Heaven's Gate (1980), 58, 100
Hell's Heroes (1930), 270–271
Hell's Hinges (1916), 287, 288, 289, 293
Hellfire (1949), 261–262
High Noon (1952), 48, 131, 165, 166, 167–168, 176,
    246, 292–293, 333
High Plains Drifter (1973), 287, 291, 293
Hills of Utah (1951), 114
Hombre (1967), 167
Home from the Hill (1960), 66, 67, 68–69
Home on the Prairie (1939), 100
Hondo (1953), 163, 164
Horse Called Comanche, A (1958). See Tonka
Hour of the Gun (1967), 17, 19, 29, 43
How the West Was Won (1962), 5, 123, 183
Hud (1963), 76, 167
Hudson's Bay (1940), 78–79, 80
Hunting Party, The (1971), 100

In Old Oklahoma (1943), 39
Iron Horse, The (1924), 85, 120–121, 184

Jeremiah Johnson (1972), 77

GENERAL INDEX

Bergman, Ingmar, 331
Berke, William, 11, 318
Berlin, Irving, 221
Bertolucci, Bernardo, 124
Bettger, Lyle, 18
Biden, Joseph, 1, 2
Bierce, Ambrose, 135
Big Sky, The (novel, 1947), 58, 77, 302
Black Maria (film company), 27
Blake, Michael, 208
Blue State (sensibility), 35, 38
Boetticher, Budd, 246
Bogart, Humphrey, 329
Bonaparte, Louis-Napoleon [III], 141
Bond, Ward, 161, 200, 213, 228, 244, 272
Bonney, William H. (aka "Billy the Kid"; aka
    Henry McCarty), 51–53, 154, 185, 220, 281, 298
Boone, Richard, 81, 167
Boorman, John, 207
Booth, Adrian, 220
Borgnine, Ernest, 301
Boston Tea Party, 3
Bow, Clara, 257
Boyd, Stephen, 250
Braga, Sonia, 211
Brando, Marlon, 144, 145, 209
Brennan, Walter, 18, 72, 74, 116, 167, 262, 272,
    297
Bridger, Jim, 230
Bronson, Charles, 168
Brooks, Richard, 127
Brown, Jim, 133
Brown, Johnny Mack, 246
Browning, Robert, 271
Bruce, Mike, 286
Brynner, Yul, 49, 138, 145, 168, 285
Buchanan, Edgar, 296
Buchanan, James, 235–236
Buckley, William F., 165
Buffalo Bill's Great Wild West (show), 56
Bull Moose (political party), 39
Buntline, Ned, 326
Burnette, Smiley, 86, 91
Burr, Raymond, 104
Burroughs, Edgar Rice, 199
Bush, George Herbert Walker, 1, 7, 8, 41
Bush, George W., 1, 7, 8, 41, 46

Byron, George Gordon, Lord, 196

Cabanne, Christy, 225
Cagney, James, 69, 70
Cain, Christopher, 235–236
Calhoun, Rory, 133
Cameron, James, 193
Cameron, Rod, 262
Campbell, Joseph, 56, 245
Capra, Frank, 87, 89–90, 113
Captivity Myth, 211
Cardinale, Claudia, 72, 123
Carey, Harry, Jr., 71–72, 227, 228, 271, 283
Carey, Harry, Sr., 70, 96, 184, 220, 270
Carey, MacDonald, 276
Carpetbaggers, The (novel, 1961), 318
Carradine, David, 100, 322
Carradine, John, 97, 184, 230
Carson, Kit, 36
Carson, Rachel, 108, 110
Carter, Jimmy, 2, 7–11, 20, 40–41, 318
Cash, Johnny, 318
Catlin, George, 56
Chayefsky, Paddy, 267
Chicago (stage/film musical,), 35
Chisum, John, 101, 150, 153–155
Choctaw Indian War, 35
Christmas Carol, A (novella, 1843), 322
Church of Jesus Christ of Latter-Day Saints,
    227–233, 235–243
Cimino, Michael, 58, 100
Civil War, 2, 26, 37–38, 76, 80–81, 85, 101, 121,
    131–133, 134, 226, 236, 261, 298–299, 316
Clanton Family, 18, 25–26, 29, 228, 246, 327
Clark, George Rogers, 177–178
Clark, Walter Van Tilburg, 322
Clay, Henry, 177
Clift, Montgomery, 69
Clinton, Hillary R., 1, 2, 3
Clum, John (Mayor of Deadwood), 29, 42–43, 53
Cobb, Lee, J., 100
Coburn, James, 101, 130, 134, 168
Code of the West (term/concept), 11
Code of the West (novel, 1934), 11–12
Coen, Joel and Ethan, 325, 333
Colbert, Claudette, 72, 73, 159, 161, 180
Colizzi, Giuseppe, 285

Collins, Joan, 249
Columbus, Chris, 199
Connors, Chuck, 147
Conrad, Joseph, 66, 209, 332
Conway, Jack, 140
Cooper, Gary, 54, 55, 60, 87, 89, 131, 132, 166, 275
Cooper, James Fenimore, 56, 121, 197–198, 200, 204, 211
Coppola, Francis Ford, 209, 295
Corbett, Glenn, 154
Cosmatos, George Pan, 18
Costello, Dolores, 256
Costner, Kevin, 24, 194, 208, 246
Cotten, Joseph, 70, 261
Covered Wagon, The (novel, 1922), 179
"Cowboy politics," 1, 3–4, 7, 11, 22
Crabbe, Buster, 281
Crawford, Joan, 72, 92, 93, 123, 257
Crockett, David, 21–22, 34–36, 150, 173–175, 177, 327
Crosland, Alan, 255
Cruze, James, 119
Curtiz, Michael, 121
Custer, George Armstrong, 194, 217

Daley, Richard, 42, 53
Dame, William H., 235–236
Darnell, Linda, 186, 278
Daves, Delmer, 13, 209, 247
Davis, Gail, 114
Davis, Jim, 276
Day-Lewis, Daniel, 124, 198, 199
Deadwood Dick (dime novel series), 204
Dean, Eddie, 98
Deardon, Basil, 248
Dehner, John, 52
Dekker, Albert, 39, 267, 300
Deliverance (novel, 1970), 207–208
DeMille, Cecil B., 55, 86, 121, 261, 290
Democratic Party, 1–4, 9–10, 35–36, 38, 40, 53, 177
Devine, Andy, 185, 191
De Wilde, Brandon, 12, 61, 76
Dexter, Anthony, 281
Diaz, Porfirio, 140, 144
Dickens, Charles, 322
Dieterle, William, 141

Dillinger, John, 85
Disney, Walt, 22, 108, 114, 211
Donati, Sergio, 130
Donlevy, Brian, 91
"Don't Fence Me In" (song), 325, 329
Doucette, John, 316, 318
Douglas, Kirk, 77, 108, 205, 227
Douglas, Melvyn, 95
Downs, Cathy, 189, 190, 214, 215
Drew, Ellen, 277
Dru, Joanne, 70, 154, 227
Druidism, 201, 214
Drury, James, 296, 297
Duel, Geof(frey), 53, 154
Duggan, Andrew, 248, 249
Duvall, Robert, 100, 261
Dwan, Allan, 27

Earp, Morgan, 25–26, 29, 186–187, 213
Earp, Virgil, 25–26, 29, 45, 51, 186–187, 213
Earp, Wyatt Berry, 13, 18–20, 25–26, 29, 35, 37–38, 42, 45, 47, 160, 186, 187, 190, 212–214, 246, 300, 326–327
East of Eden (novel, 1952), 78
Eastwood, Clint, 22, 134, 155, 157, 184, 264, 267, 280, 286, 287, 288–293, 297, 328
Edison, Thomas A., 27
Eisenhower, Dwight D., 174
Eisenstein, Sergei, 119, 127, 131
Elliott, Sam, 29
Elliott, William "Wild Bill," 261, 320
Enemy of the People, An (play, 1882), 165
Evans, Dale, 114
Evans, Gene, 251, 310
Everson, William K., 246, 271

Farnum, Dustin, 55
Farnum, William, 241
Farr, Felicia, 248
Farrow, John, 163, 165
Feist, Felix, 226
Fellini, Federico, 291
Feminine Mystique, The (book, 1963), 128
Ferrer, Mel, 205
Fetchit, Stepin, 116
Fink, Harry Julian, 298
Fleischer, Richard, 133

Fleming, Victor, 55
Flippin, Jay, C., 116, 118
Flying A Productions, 5
Fonda, Henry, 18, 20, 27, 28, 42, 98, 123, 159, 161,
    180, 182, 186, 188–189, 213, 215, 216, 291, 300,
    318, 330, 331, 334
Fonda, Jane, 135
Fonda, Peter, 20
Ford, Charles "Charlie," 318
Ford, Francis, 276
Ford, Gerald, 8, 9, 20
Ford, Glenn, 282
Ford, John, 5, 10, 13, 42, 57, 62, 70, 85, 86, 89,
    97–98, 120–121, 132, 143, 159–161, 165, 182,
    184–191, 211, 214, 216–217, 219, 225, 226, 227–
    228, 229, 270, 287, 289, 291–293, 295–296, 299,
    300–301, 310, 312, 328
Foreman, Carl, 292
Foster, Lewis R., 194
Fox, John, Jr., 275
Fraker, William, 206
Francis, Anne, 147
Franklin, Benjamin, 75
Freeman, Morgan, 288
Fremont, John Charles, 36
Friedan, Betty, 128
Frontier Marshal, aka *Wyatt Earp, Frontier
    Marshal* (book, 1931), 13
Fuentes, Carlos, 136
Fulci, Lucio, 225
Fuller, Sam(uel), 93
Future Shock (concept), 206

Gable, Clark, 77, 257
Gannaway, Albert C., 276
Garner, James, 19, 29, 42, 211, 328
Garrett, Pat, 52–53
Geer, Will, 51
Geronimo, 185
Gibson, Hoot, 184
Gish, Lillian, 70, 71, 261
Glasgow, Ellen, 82
Godard, Jean-Luc, 65, 292
Goldwater, Barry, 7, 40–41, 176
Gordon, George. *See* Byron, George Gordon,
    Lord
Grant, James Edward, 99, 149–150, 163, 174, 219

Grapes of Wrath, The (novel, 1939), 78
Great Depression, 6, 85–87, 91, 108–110, 140,
    184, 186
Great Society (social program), 40
Green Mansions (novel, 1904), 205
Grey, Zane, 11–12, 13, 235, 239–243, 245–246,
    248
Gries, Tom, 68, 133, 261
Griffith, D. W., 238, 241, 257, 261, 287
Guernica (Picasso painting, 1937), 301
Guthrie, A. J., Jr., 58, 77, 302
Guthrie, Woody, 86, 139

Hackin, Dennis, 22
Hackman, Gene, 281
Haggard, Merle, 207
Haig, Charles, 243
Hale, Alan, 277
Hamill, Pete, 41–42
Hamilton, George, 66, 67
Hand, Dora, 267–268
Harmon, Mark, 20
Harris, Ed, 183, 243
Harris, Joel Chandler, 232
Harris, Richard, 209
Harte, Bret, 225–226
Hart, William S., 284, 287, 288, 289–291, 293, 312
Hartley, Mariette, 296, 297
Haskin, Byron, 122
Hathaway, Henry, 5, 91, 149, 229, 281, 318, 328
Hatton, Raymond, 270
Hawkeye (character). *See* Natty Bumppo
Hawks, Howard, 58, 69, 76, 77, 79, 81, 140, 165,
    167, 227, 299, 328
Hawthorne, Nathaniel, 197, 208
Heart of Darkness (novel, 1899), 209
Heaven with a Gun (1969), 282
Hecht, Ben, 140
Heflin, Van, 226
Henry, Will, 26
Hepburn, Audrey, 202, 205
Hepburn, Katharine, 102, 277
Hernandez, Jaime, 301
Hernandez, Juan, 277
Hershey, Barbara, 282
Hersholt, Jean, 17
Hervey, Irene, 271

Heston, Charlton, 44, 45–46, 53, 68, 157, 178, 210, 290, 298

Hiawatha (book, 1855), 204

Hickok, James Butler "Wild Bill," 38, 86, 327

Hingle, Pat, 100

Hitchcock, Sir Alfred, 5

Hoffman, Dustin, 206

Holden, William, 299, 332

Holliday, John "Doc," 25–26, 185, 186–187

Hollywood Production Code, 279

Holt, Tim, 213, 329

Homestead Act (1862), 98

Hooker, Henry, 45

Hopkinson, Francis, 161

Hopper, Dennis, 20, 22, 124

Horatio Alger Myth, 75, 77

Hough, Edward Emerson, 119, 179

Howard, Mary, 240

Howard, William K., 11

Hoyes, Rudolfo Jr., 145

Hudson, Rock, 133

Hudson, W. H., 205

Hugo, Victor, 260

Hunnicutt, Arthur, 150

Hunter, Jeff(rey), 70, 282

Huston, John, 165, 261, 320, 329

Huston, Walter, 54, 229, 259, 260

Hutchinson, John, 318

Ibsen, Henrik, 165

Idylls of the King, 12

Intveld, James, 321

Iron John (gender concept), 207

Jackson, Andrew, 8, 35–36, 177

Jaeckel, Richard, 48, 49

Jaffe, Sam, 278

Jagger, Dean, 91, 229, 230, 232

James, Frank, 261, 318

James, Jesse, 261, 318

Jarre, Kevin, 29

Jefferson, Thomas, 177–179

Joffe, Roland, 197

Johnson, Ben, 60, 154, 227

Johnson, Chubby, 116

Johnson, Dorothy, 98

Johnson, Lyndon B., 9, 40

Johnson, Van, 80

Johnson County War of 1892, 57–59

Jones, Carolyn, 282

Jones, Dick, 271, 276

Jones, Jennifer, 71

Jones, L. Q., 305, 311

Jones, Tommy Lee, 325, 328

Juarez, Benito, 131

Jungle, The (novel, 1906), 124

Jurado, Katy, 105, 209, 210

Juran, Nathan, 22

Kane, Joe/Joseph, 86, 100, 108, 109, 113, 122, 220, 262, 281

Kasdan, Lawrence, 18, 100

Katzin, Lee H., 282

Kaufman, Philip, 261

Kazan, Elia, 78, 89, 95, 144, 229

Keach, Stacy, 42

Keighley, William, 203

Keith, Brian, 39, 320

Kelly, Grace, 166

Kennedy, Arthur, 118, 318

Kennedy, Burt, 26

Kennedy, John F., 8, 22, 40, 168, 176, 299

Kesey, Ken, 205

Keystone Cops, 310

Kilmer, Joyce, 226

Kilmer, Val, 29–30, 31

King, Henry, 85, 245

King Arthur and the Round Table, 5, 55–56, 333

King Ranch, 76

Kracauer, Siegfried, 238

Kramer, Frank, 285

Kramer, Stanley, 165

Kristofferson, Kris, 298

Kruschen, Jack, 152, 153

Kubrick, Stanley, 40, 176

Ku Klux Klan, 238

Kurosawa, Akira, 331

Kydd, Thomas, 246

Kyne, Peter B., 203, 205, 269–270, 317

Ladd, Alan, 12, 60, 63, 289–290

Lake, Stuart N., 13, 18

Lake, Veronica, 101

L'Amour, Louis, 163

Lancaster, Burt, 18, 37, 42, 127, 131, 132
Landau, Martin, 318
Lang, Fritz, 318
Last of the Mohicans, The (novel, 1826), 57, 211
Laughton, Charles, 281
Lawrence, D. H., 199–200
Leaves of Grass (book, 1855), 201
Legend of the Lone Ranger (1981), 206–207
Leigh, Janet, 315–316
Lenin, Vladimir Ilyich, 127, 140
Leonard, Robert Z., 268
Leone, Sergio, 72, 123, 130–131, 286–287, 293
Lerner, Alan J., 267
Lewis, Meriwether, 177–179, 181
Light in the Forest, The (novel, 1950), 205–206
Limbaugh, Rush, 108
Lincoln, Abraham, 32, 35–36, 40, 98, 160
"Lines" (poem, 1789), 203
Little Big Man (novel, 1964), 206
Little Shepherd of Kingdom Come, The
   (novel, 1913), 275
Lloyd, Frank, 150, 241
Logan, Joshua, 267
London, Jack, 131
Lone Ranger (character), 204, 206–207
Lonesome Dove (novel, 1985), 57, 68
Lone Star (film company), 246
Longfellow, Henry Wadsworth, 200, 204
Lopez, Perry, 152, 153
L'Osservatore Romano (publication), 194
Louisiana Purchase (1803), 177, 178
Lucas, George, 330

MacArthur, James, 205
MacDonald, Jeanette, 258, 268
MacFadden, Hamilton, 243
MacLaine, Shirley, 134, 280
MacMurray, Fred, 178
Madero, Francisco, 140
Madigan, Amy, 243
Madsen, Michael, 24
Mai Lai Massacre, 300
Malden, Karl, 318, 320
Malle, Louis, 128–130
Malory, Sir Thomas, 5
Mamoulian, Rouben, 278

Manifest Destiny (social concept), 85, 119,
   172–173, 177–181
Mann, Anthony, 50, 100, 118, 246, 315–316
Mann, Michael, 198–199
Marcus, Josephine (Earp), 43
Margolin, Janet, 320
Marigold, James, 13
Marlboro Man, 4, 7
Marshall, George, 5, 123
Marshall, Herbert, 70
Martin, Dean, 167, 281
Martin, Strother, 295, 305, 311
Marvin, Lee, 63, 98, 126, 127, 264, 267
Massey, Raymond, 78
Masterson, William Bartley "Bat," 37–38, 47–48,
   51, 267–268, 327
Mate, Rudolph, 80, 100, 178
Matthews, Chris, 107
Mature, Victor, 29, 30, 186, 188–189
McCain, John, 1
McCarthy, Cormac, 325
McCarthy, Joseph, 92, 144, 165–166, 318
McCarty, Henry. *See* Bonney, William H.
McComb, David, 3–4, 5
McCrea, Joel, 46, 47, 55, 276, 294, 296
McGovern, George, 2
McGowan, J. P., 11
McLaglen, Andrew, 53, 58, 98–99, 101, 150, 183,
   275, 316
McLaury, Frank and Tom, 25
McLean, David, 7
McMurtry, Larry, 57, 68, 76, 211, 328–329
McQueen, Steve, 49, 168, 252, 318, 319
McTeague (novel, 1999), 117–119, 300
Means, Russell, 198
Metro-Goldwyn-Mayer (studio), 118
Mexican-American War, 177
Miles, Vera, 70
Millar, Stuart, 277
Miller, Eve, 224, 227
Miller, Merlin, 321
Minnelli, Vincente, 66
Mitchell, Thomas, 165, 166, 184
Mitchum, Robert, 26, 66, 67, 133, 134, 145, 263,
   279, 281
Mix, Tom, 242, 243
Montgomery, George, 240, 243

Power, Tyrone, 229, 278
Price, Vincent, 79, 91, 229
Producer's Releasing Corporation (PRC film company), 246
Puenzo, Luis, 135
Pullman, Bill, 55
Pyle, Denver, 316, 324

Quinn, Anthony, 278, 279

Radisson, Pierre-Esprit, 78–80
Raimi, Sam, 281
Rains, Claude, 141
Ray, Fred Olin, 283
Ray, Nicholas, 72, 93, 282
Reagan Democrats, 41
Reagan, Ronald, 2, 7, 8, 9, 10, 11, 20, 22, 38, 41, 46, 53
Redford, Robert, 100
Red State (sensibility), 7, 10, 35, 38, 108
Remington, Frederic, 328
Renoir, Jean, 81
Republic studio, 86, 113, 114, 261, 262
Republican Party, 1–4, 6, 9–10, 36–38, 42, 98, 160–162, 177, 293, 318
Rettig, Tommy, 164, 248
Revolutionary War, 36, 158–162
Richter, Conrad, 95, 205
Riders of the Purple Sage (novel, 1912), 235, 239–243, 245
Ringo (aka Ringgold), John(ny), 48, 185
Ritt, Martin, 68, 76, 167
Robards, Jason, Jr., 19, 100, 123, 304, 312
Robbins, Harold, 318
Robertson, Cliff, 261
Robinson, Edward G., 100
Rockefeller, Nelson A., 160
"Rockefeller Republicans," 160
Rodríguez (Ruelas), Ismael, 141–143
Rogers, Charles "Buddy," 281
Rogers, Jimmy, 275
Rogers, Kenny, 278
Rogers, Roy, 5, 113–114, 329
Roland, Gilbert, 133
Romanticism, 193–202, 206
Romero, Cesar, 27, 132
Romney, Mitt, 2, 6, 108

Rooney, Mickey, 269
Roosevelt, Franklin D., 6–7, 39–40, 84, 86, 90, 109, 259
Roosevelt, Theodore, 38–40, 56, 57, 98, 102, 328
Rose Marie (operetta), 204
Ross, Betsy, 161
Rosseau, Jean-Jacques, 57
Rove, Karl, 6
Ruggles, Wesley, 183
Russell, Charles "Charlie," 328
Russell, Gail, 220
Russell, John, 135, 290
Russell, Kurt, 29
Ryan, Robert, 29, 127, 300, 302, 315, 332

Saldana, Zoe, 205
Salkow, Sidney, 194
Salmi, Albert, 250, 329
Santschi, Tom, 270
Saturday Evening Post (magazine), 179
Savallas, Telly, 146
Schaefer, Jack, 11, 56, 58–59, 103, 245
Schildkraut, Joseph, 141
Schweig, Eric, 198
Scorsese, Martin, 295
Scott, George C., 147
Scott, Randolph, 27, 42, 294, 296
Sears, Fred, 122
Seberg, Jean, 264, 267
Second Amendment, 46
"Second Coming, The" (poem, 1919), 289, 328, 332
Seger, Pete, 86
Selander, Lesley, 316
Seneca the Younger, 247
Serling, Rod, 329
Shane (novel, 1949), 11, 56–60, 245
Shaw, Robert, 135, 279
Shelley, Percy Byshe, 196
Sherin, Edward, 283
Sherman, George, 88, 133, 226
Shields, Arthur, 274, 276
Sidney, George, 221
Siegel, Don, 155
Silent Spring (book, 1962), 108
Silva, Henry, 251
Silverstein, Elliot, 209

Simpson, Russell, 282, 292
Sinclair, Upton, 124
Sledge, Mildred, 11
Smith, Alexis, 101
Smith, Jedediah, 77
Smith, John, 281
Smith, Joseph, 91, 229
Smits, Jimmy, 135, 139
Social Darwinism, 102, 149, 165
Spencer, Herbert, 102, 149, 165
Springsteen, R. G., 261
Sputnik, 176
Stamp, Terence, 234, 236
Stanwyck, Barbara, 89, 92, 93, 101
Steele, Bob, 246
Steiger, Rod, 130
Steinbeck, John, 78
Stevens, George, 11, 58, 65, 103
Stevens, Stella, 309, 312
Stewart, James, 50, 51, 87, 98, 104, 118, 190, 192, 195, 209, 210, 296, 315, 316, 317
Stone, Lewis, 271
Stone, Sharon, 281
Stowe, Madeleine, 197
Streets of Laredo (novel, 1993), 211
Strode, Woody, 128, 133
Sturges, John, 17–18, 19, 49, 168
Sullivan, Barry, 95, 101
Sutton, John, 79, 80

Taft, William H., 39
Tarzan of the Apes (novel, 1912), 199
Taylor, Dub, 300
Tea Party (political movement), 2, 3–4, 5–6, 46, 318
Tennyson, Alfred, Lord, 5, 12
Thorpe, Jim, 228
Three Godfathers (novel, 1913), 269–270, 317
Thus Spoke Zarathustra (book, 1994), 295
Tilghman, William, 38
Tiomkin, Dimitri, 174
Toffler, Alvin, 206
Tonto (character), 204
Tourneur, Jacques, 46, 276
Towne, Robert, 145
Tracy, Spencer, 96, 102, 103, 257
Trail of Tears, 36

Travern, B., 329
Treasure of the Sierra Madre, The (novel, 1926), 329
Trevor, Claire, 184, 203, 227, 267, 296
Trotsky, Leon, 130, 141
Truman, Harry, 40
Tucker, Forrest, 154, 220
Tufts, Sonny, 281
Tunstall, John, 51–53, 155
Turner, Frederick Jackson, 59
Turner, Thad, 321
Turner Thesis (historical analysis), 59
Twain, Mark, 200, 204
Twentieth Century-Fox (studio), 229, 241, 243, 256

Uncle Remus (character), 232

Vallone, Raf, 135, 320
Van Cleef, Lee, 250, 280, 286
Van Dyke, W. S., 199, 257
Van Orsdel, William Wesley, 281
Verneuil, Henry, 278
Victory (novel, 1915), 332
Vidal, Gore, 52
Vidor, King, 70, 101
Vietnam War, 20, 40
Villa, Pancho, 131, 135, 138, 139–141, 142, 143–146
Virginian, The (novel, 1901), 11, 54–60, 63, 245–246
Vittes, Louis, 145
Voigt, Jon, 207
von Habsburg, Maximilian, 141
Von Stroheim, Eric, 117, 299, 332

Wagner, Robert, 105
Walker, Clint, 147
Walsh, Raoul, 85, 139–140, 328
Walthall, Henry B., 140
Warner Bros. (studio), 141
Warner, David, 308, 311
Warner, H. B., 261, 267
Warren, Charles Marquis, 209
Warshow, Robert, 5, 245
Washington, George, 160
Wasp magazine, 119
Watergate scandal, 20